Oracle & Open Source

Oracle & Open Source

Andy Duncan and Sean Hull

O'REILLY®

Beijing · Cambridge · Farnham · Köln · Sebastopol · Tokyo

Oracle & Open Source

by Andy Duncan and Sean Hull

Copyright © 2001 O'Reilly & Associates, Inc. All rights reserved.
Printed in the United States of America.

Published by O'Reilly & Associates, Inc., 101 Morris Street, Sebastopol, CA 95472.

Editor: Deborah Russell

Production Editor: Leanne Clarke Soylemez

Cover Designer: Ellie Volckhausen

Printing History:

> April 2001: First Edition.

ISBN: 978-0-596-00018-9

[LSI]   [2011-06-03]

Table of Contents

Preface

A few short years ago, nobody could have imagined that the day would come when Oracle Corporation would not only tolerate the idea of open source software, but even incorporate it into its own product lines. And yet today the Oracle8*i* database has been ported to the open source Linux operating system, the open source Apache JServ web server is a vital part of Oracle's Internet Application Server (*i*AS) product, and hundreds of exciting applications are underway, linking open source programs to Oracle databases and providing a new world of tools for database administrators and developers everywhere.

Both of the authors are Oracle developers who are keenly interested in the theory and practice of open source software. For quite a few years, we have been developing and maintaining our own open source applications for Oracle and following with great enthusiasm the adoption of open source tools by Oracle and other commercial organizations. For most DBAs and developers, though, information on how Oracle meets open source has been hard to find and hard to assess.

Our main goal for this book is to provide at least a snapshot of where we are today in the Oracle/open source arena. We'll introduce the major open source technologies of special relevance to Oracle—Perl, Tcl, Python, Apache, GNOME, GTK+, and even some areas of Java—and explain how they are being used to build Oracle applications and connect to Oracle databases today. We'll also describe the best of the Oracle applications that are available to Oracle DBAs and developers. For all these tools, we'll provide introductory material, rough outlines of installation and configuration procedures (though we recommend you check the online documentation for details), and examples of usage.

We have a second goal as well, and that is to motivate you to consider writing your own Oracle open source applications in the future. The world of Oracle and open source is wide open. Developers are building exciting and innovative applications, but there is plenty of room for more. As we explain different applications in this book, we'll mention ways you can get involved with helping to extend their capabilities. We'll also show you how various applications are implemented, to provide models for your own development.

Audience for This Book

This book is aimed mainly at Oracle database administrators and developers who do not already have a lot of experience using and developing open source software. Those two audiences have somewhat different information needs:

- If you are an Oracle DBA who is primarily interested in downloading and running existing Oracle open source applications, you will be most interested in the applications chapters—Chapter 4, *Building Oracle Applications with Perl/Tk and Tcl/Tk*, Chapter 6, *Building Web-Based Oracle Applications*, Chapter 8, *Building Oracle Applications with Java*, and Chapter 10, *Building Oracle Applications with GNOME and GTK+*. In addition, you should certainly read Chapter 1, *Oracle Meets Open Source*. You should also at least skim Chapter 2, *Connecting to Oracle*, so you will understand how the applications you will be using interface to your Oracle database.

- If you are a developer who is considering building your own Oracle open source application, you will want to read the full set of chapters to learn what technologies are being used as building blocks for Oracle applications, how they connect to Oracle, and how other open source developers have built applications that you might use as models for building your own.

Perhaps you are already knowledgeable about the various open source technologies described in this book and are looking specifically for information about how to connect your applications to Oracle. In this case, you may find the introductions to Perl, Tcl, the Web, Java, and so on too basic, but we hope you will find useful information about their Oracle interfaces in the following chapters.

About This Book

The world of open source software is an active and constantly changing one. Trying to include up-to-date information about the full range of open source projects, programs, and installation procedures in hardcopy form is like trying to capture time in a bottle. Even trying to select a manageable number of technologies, and representative applications from each technical area, is a difficult task. As we go to press, if we're confident of one thing, it is that there will be readers who flip through these pages and say, "How *could* you leave out Program X?" To all the developers and users of such programs, our apologies. We have tried our very best to describe at least the basics of a reasonably broad range of those technologies and applications that seemed to us most applicable to Oracle developers and DBAs. We hope that if you disagree, or if you simply want other Oracle readers to know about other tools, you will take the time to write to us (see "Comments and Questions" later in this preface). We'll do our best to respond and to share what you say with other readers by providing information on the book's web site.

In addition, because the world of open source development is one of constant activity, we hope you will consult the URLs we've provided throughout this book (summarized in Table 1-2) for more up-to-date information than we can hope to provide in this printed book (we'll also try to keep the URLs current at the O'Reilly web page for this book). Remember, too, that what we describe in this book is only the tip of the iceberg. We have tried to select the best Oracle-related open source software for inclusion in this book, but we hope that more and even better software will be available in the future (maybe even some developed by our faithful readers). You can keep up with Oracle open source development by checking the following sites frequently:

Oracle Technology Network (OTN)
> OTN is an Oracle Corporation web site for developers, filled with an expansive and diverse range of online documentation for just about every Oracle Corporation product. If you're not already registered on OTN, you may have to set up an OTN logon and password in order to read some of the documents there. This is a quick process and well worth doing.
>
> > *http://technet.oracle.com*

SourceForge
> SourceForge is a free service for open source developers that offers access to online development services, mailing lists, message boards, and everything required for full web-based administration of your open source projects.
>
> > *http://sourceforge.net*

Freshmeat
> Freshmeat maintains the Web's largest index of open source software and is the first port of call if you're looking for specific applications, reviews, or anything else open source–based. Think of SourceForge as the code factory and Freshmeat as the marketplace.
>
> > *http://freshmeat.net*

Structure of This Book

This book is divided into 10 chapters and 3 appendixes:

- Chapter 1, *Oracle Meets Open Source*, introduces open source software, describes a bit of its history and philosophy, and explains how open source developers are now building Oracle applications using open source tools such as Tcl, Perl, Python, various Apache modules, Java, GNOME, and GTK+.

- Chapter 2, *Connecting to Oracle*, describes the Oracle Call Interface (OCI), the software that provides the "glue" connecting open source applications to the Oracle database. It introduces ODBC (Open DataBase Connectivity) and JDBC (Java DataBase Connectivity). It also describes, as an extended example, how Perl programs interact with OCI using additional layers of software that are more convenient to use.

- Chapter 3, *Tcl, Perl, and Python*, describes the most common scripting languages in use today and how to install and configure these languages and their graphical toolkits (e.g., Tk) in order to build graphical user interfaces (GUIs) for Oracle applications.

- Chapter 4, *Building Oracle Applications with Perl/Tk and Tcl/Tk*, takes a detailed look at the use and implementation of Orac and Oddis, Oracle applications built using Perl/Tk and Tcl/Tk, respectively.

- Chapter 5, *Web Technologies*, describes the main technologies used to build web-based Oracle applications today. It explains how to install the open source Apache web server and how to use Perl, Java, and embedded scripting for Oracle applications.

- Chapter 6, *Building Web-Based Oracle Applications*, describes the use and implementation of a variety of web-based Oracle applications: Karma, Oracletool, OraSnap, DB_Browser, PhpMyAdmin/PhpOracleAdmin, WWWdb, and Big Brother.

- Chapter 7, *Java*, describes the basics of Java programming and the Java technologies used to build open source applications today. It focuses on Java GUI applications, Apache JServ and servlets, and the use of JDBC.

- Chapter 8, *Building Oracle Applications with Java*, describes the use and implementation of several open source Java applications that access the Oracle database: jDBA, ViennaSQL, DBInspector, and DB Prism (along with its use with Cocoon).

- Chapter 9, *GNOME and GTK+*, describes the fundamentals of the GNOME Project and its effort to build a Linux desktop environment, as well as the GTK+ graphical toolkit, which is now being used to build quite a few Oracle applications.

- Chapter 10, *Building Oracle Applications with GNOME and GTK+*, describes the use and implementation of a number of Oracle applications built on GTK+: the Orasoft applications suite, GNOME-DB, gASQL, GNOME Transcript, and Gaby.

- Appendix A, *Oracle8i And Linux*, provides an outline of the procedures and issues you'll want to know about if you are installing Oracle8*i* on the Linux operating system. For details on the installation process and the Linux system in general, refer to the references in Appendix C.

- Appendix B, *PL/SQL and Open Source*, takes a look at a few interesting, current projects whose purpose is to build both open source software and a development community based on Oracle's popular PL/SQL language.

- Appendix C, *For Further Reading*, is a list of books and other resources that we personally have found helpful. We touch on many very different pieces of software in this book. We can't hope to cover them in any detail here, but we hope to spark your interest so you'll seek out additional information. This appendix tells you where to go next.

About the Software

When we first talked about writing this book, we assumed that we would include a CD-ROM containing all the software mentioned here. When we started working on it, however, and began to appreciate the enormous scope of open source tools and Oracle applications that we wanted to describe, we soon realized that a CD wasn't necessary, for two reasons:

- Software distributed in accordance with the Open Source Definition (described in Chapter 1) is, by definition, almost always available for immediate download over the Internet, free of charge. Therefore, along with the description of each piece of open software covered in this book, we'll include the appropriate FTP or HTTP web reference for downloading this software.

- Successful open source software also tends to evolve constantly, and often in unpredictable bursts of activity (sometimes following periods of stasis). Trying to get the hundred or so different pieces of software covered in this book onto a single CD-ROM at a single point in time would be a lot like hitting a hundred randomly moving targets with a single silver bullet. We thought it would be far better for you to download the latest, up-to-the-minute version of each tool you're interested in, straight off the Internet, just when you need it. The beauty of open source is that it's always available to you, at the click of a download button.

Conventions Used in This Book

The following typographical conventions are used in this book:

Italic
Used for filenames, directory names, function names, and URLs. It is also used for emphasis and for the first use of a technical term.

Constant width
> Used for code examples.

Constant width bold
> Used occasionally in code examples to highlight statements being discussed.

 Indicates a tip, suggestion, or general note. For example, we'll tell you if a certain feature is version-specific.

 Indicates a warning or caution. For example, we'll tell you if a certain operation has some kind of negative impact on the system.

Comments and Questions

Please address comments and questions concerning this book to the publisher:

O'Reilly & Associates
101 Morris Street
Sebastopol, CA 95472
(800) 998-9938 (in the United States or Canada)
(707) 829-0515 (international or local)
(707) 829-0104 (fax)

We have a web page for this book, where we list errata, examples, links, and additional information. You can access this page at:

http://www.oreilly.com/catalog/oracleopen

To comment or ask technical questions about this book, send email to:

bookquestions@oreilly.com

For more information about our books, conferences, software, Resource Centers, and the O'Reilly Network, see our web site at:

http://www.oreilly.com

Acknowledgments

As you might expect with a book of this kind, a tremendous number of people from the open source community have helped us put this book together, including many of the creators of the actual tools discussed here. We cannot thank them enough (although we'll do our best). We also are very grateful to the whole O'Reilly editorial and production team, including Debby Russell, our editor; Leanne Soylemez, the production editor; Ellie Volckhausen, who designed the cover; Rob Romano, who created the figures; and Caroline Senay, who helped throughout the entire process.

From Andy

When the opportunity to write this book first arose (its original spark was an idea for writing just a single chapter in a book on Oracle design tools), I never expected that we would cover so many different areas. Originally, I thought we would cover Perl, perhaps Tcl, and then round it all off with Apache. But as we dug down into the histories and uses of each tool, we went off on all sorts of different tangents. We found ourselves digging into an enormous variety of application areas, including Python, PHP, GTK+, Java (to our surprise), and many more. It was like being in a neverending Aladdin's cave of software delights, where every box of jewels opened up into yet another gold-lit cave of Oracle treasure. It has therefore been both a pleasure and a privilege to explore and chart these caves for you. We've been especially grateful to get help along the way from so many of the original creators of these inspiring tools. We've also benefited tremendously from the knowledge and inspiration of other reviewers and coworkers from Oracle Corporation, Sun Microsystems, Intel, and Oriole Corporation (among others), who all gave freely of their own time and thoughts. I would like to thank everyone who has helped us, and I truly hope they feel that we've done justice both to their development work and to their review of this book.

I'm dreading the bar bill, but without the following people, my half of the book would just not have been possible: Bruce Albrecht, Kevin Brannen, Tim Bunce, Alan Burlison, Alligator Descartes, Stuart Duke, Robin Dunn, Dave Ensor, Stéphane Faroult, Steven Feuerstein, Andy Gillen, Russell Herbert, Kevin Kitts, Jonathan Leffler, Stephen Lidie, Thomas Lowery, David B. Moffett, Marcelo Ochoa, John Ousterhout, Ezra Pagel, Ian Pilgrim, Tom Poindexter, Bill Pribyl, Alan Ranger, Eric S. Raymond, Axel Schlüter, Steve Shaw, Alex Shnir, Milan Sorm, Richard M. Stallman, Jared Still, Richard Sutherland, Bernard Van Haecke, Guido van Rossum, Mike Wilson, and Charles Wolfe.

I would also like to thank our omniscient editor Debby Russell, who asked all of the questions I'd hoped nobody would spot, nailed all my covertly attempted 2 A.M. fudges, and generally sculpted my incoherent ramblings into something approaching semi-reasonable English. Debby basically made this book into one I would really love to buy myself (if I hadn't already cowritten it).

Finally, and most importantly, I would like to dedicate every single one of the words I have written in this book to my wife, Sue, and our children, Ross and Ellie. When normal fathers were out pushing their children on swings, attending birthday parties, and helping load the washing machine, this one could only be glimpsed surrounded by books and wires in a darkened room with the shutters down, tapping at a keyboard for God, Harry, England, and Saint George. I hope that I can repay the faith, time, and patience they have indulged me with over the last year and make it up to them all. I'm going to be spending a lot of time in Disneyland!

From Sean

I'd like to thank Stéphane Faroult, Mark Gallay, and Gunnar Hellekson for their meticulous attention to the technical review of the book. I would be remiss if I didn't also thank the authors of the various tools covered in my sections of the book, including Alvaro del Castillo, Matthew Chappee and the Orasoft team, Nick Gorham, Chris Hardie, Stephan Heinze, Michael Lausch, Sean MacGuire, Vivien Malerba, Stewart McGlaughlin, Rodrigo Moya, Matias Mutchinick, Frederic Peters, Tobias Ratschiller, Klaus Reger, Jose Miguel Ronquillo, Adam vonNieda, and Chris Wiegand. And, of course, thanks go to the open source community as a whole, without which we wouldn't be here.

I'd also like to thank Andy, whose idea got us started writing this book, and whose ongoing energy kept us motivated and moving, and Debby Russell (and others on the O'Reilly staff), for recognizing and accepting our idea and encouraging us to do our best. Finally, I'd like to thank my parents, Joan and Ray, for encouraging me in computers and for sending me to good schools. I wouldn't be where I am today without them.

1

Oracle Meets Open Source

The combination of Oracle Corporation and open source software may appear to be an unlikely pairing. What could Oracle, with its history of ruthless competition, intense marketing, and cutthroat corporate life, have to do with the collaborative, altruistic, and apparently anti-corporate world of open source?

The answer, surprisingly, is quite a lot. In recent years, the gospel of the open source movement has spread far and wide, reaching even the corporate corridors and product lines of organizations like Oracle Corporation. Consider the following recent developments:

- Oracle8*i* has been officially ported to the freely available Linux operating system.

- The open source Apache web server is now distributed as part of the Oracle Internet Application Server (*i*AS).

- The open source Perl, Tcl, and Python scripting languages all provide modules supporting connections to Oracle databases.

- The Oratcl application, an open source program built on the Tcl scripting language, is now distributed as part of the Oracle Enterprise Manager (OEM) product.

- Dozens of excellent applications written by open source developers—Orac, Oddis, Karma, Oracletool, OraSnap, Big Brother, jDBA, GNOME-db, and many more—give Oracle database administrators and developers new tools for managing their databases and building new applications. And if one of these tools doesn't do exactly what's needed in a specific environment, the source code can be modified without restriction.

In our opinion, this new synergy between the corporate world of Oracle and the freewheeling world of open source is a great thing—the blended products we're starting to see truly do represent the best of both worlds.

The purpose of this book is to share what we know about this blending of Oracle and open source. It's a new world, and one that hasn't been examined much to date. Although many books have been written about some of the base open source technologies we'll be exploring in this book (for example, Perl, Tcl, and Apache), there has been very little written about the way these technologies are used with Oracle databases, and even less about most of the Oracle open source applications available to DBAs and developers. Although we can't possibly describe every open source technology in depth within the confines of this single volume, we'll try to provide a foundation. Our overriding goal is to shed light on as many of the open source technologies and applications as possible and on how they communicate with Oracle databases. In trying to achieve this goal, we'll weave together three distinct threads:

- We'll explore the major open source technologies on the current computing landscape—Perl, Tcl, Python, Apache, GNOME, GTK+, and even some open source corners of Java—and explain how they are being used to build Oracle applications and connect to Oracle databases.

- We'll describe the best of the Oracle applications that are currently available for you to download, use, and, if you wish, modify. Some of these applications are tools for performing database administration tasks; others provide frameworks for application development of your own.

- We'll try to motivate you to consider writing your own Oracle open source applications in the future.

The world of open source software is a wide-ranging one. In this book, we'll focus on the open source technologies that are most often used by Oracle developers:

Scripting languages
We'll focus on Perl, Tcl, and Python, the most popular languages and the ones providing the most solid connections to Oracle databases. Chapter 2, *Connecting to Oracle*, and Chapter 3, *Tcl, Perl, and Python*, describe how to obtain and install the base languages, how to use their companion graphics toolkits, and how they communicate with Oracle. Chapter 4, *Building Oracle Applications with Perl/Tk and Tcl/Tk*, describes two excellent open source applications: Orac, built on Perl, and Oddis, built on Tcl. Both are good examples of how you can build Oracle-based graphical user interfaces (GUIs) with open source scripting languages and toolkits.

The Web
We'll next look at an alternative to GUI applications—Oracle applications that use the Web, rather than a GUI, as the user interface. We'll focus on the

Apache web server, CGI programming with Oracle, and the use of such embedded scripting tools as PHP and EmbPerl. Chapter 5, *Web Technologies*, describes these open source technologies and how they connect to Oracle databases. Chapter 6, *Building Web-Based Oracle Applications*, describes an assortment of excellent web-based applications that can be used for Oracle database administration: Karma, Oracletool, OraSnap, DB_Browser, PhpMyAdmin/PhpOracleAdmin, WWWdb, and Big Brother.

Java

You may be surprised to see any coverage of Java in this book. Java is, after all, still a proprietary language of Sun Microsystems. Many open source developers are now building Oracle-based applications in Java, however, and Oracle is providing extensive support for Java connectivity. Chapter 7, *Java*, describes the basics of Java DataBase Connectivity (JDBC), which is used to connect programs to Oracle databases. It also describes the open source JDOM servlet API and some other Oracle-related aspects of Java, including the Apache JServ web server, now distributed with Oracle's Internet Application Server, and how you can use it to build Oracle Enterprise Java servlets. Chapter 8, *Building Oracle Applications with Java*, describes several excellent Oracle open source applications based on Java: jDBA, ViennaSQL, and DBInspector. It also explains how you can obtain and install DB Prism, a servlet-based tool for use with Oracle's PL/SQL and XML code facilities.

GNOME and GTK+

GNOME is an ambitious project aimed at creating a complete, open source desktop environment for Linux. Now that Oracle8*i* has been ported to Linux, GNOME and its excellent GTK+ graphical toolkit are available to Oracle developers. Chapter 9, *GNOME and GTK+*, describes the basics of GNOME and GTK+ and how you can use them to build graphical applications for Oracle. Chapter 10, *Building Oracle Applications with GNOME and GTK+*, describes the excellent Orasoft applications suite, a full-functioned database administration toolkit for Oracle DBAs, as well as several other GNOME/GTK+ applications that communicate with Oracle databases: GNOME-DB, gASQL, Gnome Transcript, and Gaby.

Although the sequence of chapters is roughly chronological (Perl and the other scripting languages were available before the coming of the World Wide Web, which preceded the development of Java and GNOME/GTK+), all four basic areas are still vibrant and fertile areas of open source activity, and all are focal points for Oracle application development. To a large extent, the choice of which open source technologies to use for developing an open source application is simply personal preference. Do you want to write in Perl, C, or Java? Do you want your user interface to be GUI or web-based? Fortunately, regardless of your choice, there is excellent Oracle connectivity available with all of the technologies we describe in this book. In subsequent chapters, we'll focus on this connectivity. As interesting and wide-ranging as these core technologies are, we'll try to limit our discussion to what you need to know in order to use them with Oracle, in an effort to keep this book a manageable size.

We've mentioned a lot of open source programs already, and we'll describe even more in this book. Table 1-2, included near the end of this chapter, provides a full list of the programs described, along with URLs for further exploration. (We'll also try to keep the URLs current at the O'Reilly web page for this book—see the preface for details.)

Introduction to Open Source

Before we get into the details of how you can use and build Oracle open source software, let's take some time exploring what open source is and why you might want to use it.

What Is Open Source?

The quick and dirty definition of "open source" is that it is software that's freely available: you can acquire it freely (it's usually downloaded from the Internet at no cost), and you can modify it freely (the source code is provided, not just the executable files). However, it's important that we refine this quick use of the word "free." There are important semantic differences between what the Free Software Foundation (FSF) defines as "free" and what the newer Open Source Initiative defines as "free." We'll explore both movements and their respective definitions later in this chapter. For starters, we'll just note the functional definition of "open source" from the Open Source Initiative web site, at *http://www.opensource.org*:

> Open source promotes software reliability and quality by supporting independent peer review and rapid evolution of source code. To be OSI certified, the software must be distributed under a license that guarantees the right to read, redistribute, modify, and use the software freely.

The OSI web site continues with a description of why open source is of such high quality:

> The basic idea behind open source is very simple. When programmers on the Internet can read, redistribute, and modify the source for a piece of software, it evolves. People improve it, people adapt it, people fix bugs. And this can happen at a speed that, if one is used to the slow pace of conventional software development, seems astonishing. We in the open-source community have learned that this rapid evolutionary process produces better software than the traditional closed model, in which only a very few programmers can see source and everybody else must blindly use an opaque block of bits.

A little later in this section, we'll discuss the open source license and the details of what it means to be OSI certified. For now, let's ask a few more questions.

Many people, accustomed to the traditional world of commercial software, are puzzled by the whole notion of open source. Why would anyone give away something of obvious value? Because they don't understand the motivation, they tend to distrust the product. They ask:

- How can open source software be any good if its author doesn't value it enough to charge for it?

- How can it be trusted to perform if it doesn't have the weight of a business behind it?

- How can it be responsive to users' needs if users don't have any contractual claim on it?

By even asking these questions, though, people are ignoring the clearest success stories of open source: Apache, the world's dominant web server; Perl, the world's dominant scripting language; and Linux, the world's most rapidly growing operating system kernel. All of these pieces of software have already been enthusiastically accepted by the corporate world as stable, successful, and, if not the best solutions in their fields, then at least major challengers. Many people seem to have a blind spot; they assume that because this software has, in fact, received commercial acceptance, it therefore can't be open source. But Apache, Perl, Linux, and the many other excellent pieces of software described in this book are indeed open source, through and through.

In the next few sections we'll look briefly at what open source is all about and why you, as an Oracle DBA or developer, might find it useful.* Then we'll shift our focus to the main open source technologies available today, how they've been used to communicate with Oracle databases, and how you can use them to build your own Oracle-based applications.

Why Open Source?

Considering the enormous amount of software that's available to you from Oracle Corporation and various other software providers, why should you, as an Oracle DBA or developer, care about open source software?

Open source software is free in several senses of the word. It is typically free of cost, which means that you don't have to pay for it. It is also free of code

---

* Many words have been written about the concept and value of open source. We're making a quick journey through a landscape that others have explored more fully, so we aren't likely to do complete justice to the history and philosophy of open source. We'll do our best to be accurate within the limits of this short chapter, but we recommend that you learn the full and very interesting story by consulting the excellent references listed in Appendix C, *For Further Reading*.

restrictions, which means that the source code is provided, and you are free to modify it. Let's look at these two characteristics in turn and consider their relevance to your life with Oracle.

Oracle DBAs and developers typically work in corporate environments. The stereotypical user of open source software is the guy in the garage, with no salary, no budget, and no deep corporate pockets. The typical Oracle DBA isn't in that category; he often has a reasonably generous budget for software. What he might not have, however, is the flexibility to use that budget as he sees fit. If you need a piece of software right now, but you can't buy it without going through a lengthy approval process, then those corporate pockets won't seem so deep after all. You might as well be in the garage.

We're overstating the point, of course, but clearly the ability to simply download and try out many different possible tools before settling on one is enormously beneficial.

The second characteristic of open source, the ability to customize the source code to suit you, is often even more important. Most Oracle DBAs and developers are in a hurry. They are constantly fighting fires and trying their best to support the disparate needs of the users in their organizations.

The rapid advancement of technology, combined with the ever-increasing needs of an interconnected world, make the life of an Oracle DBA or developer more complex than ever. At one time, a DBA might have been able to do her job using a single, straightforward administration tool, combined with a small system of character-based entry forms. No more: the need for 24×7 availability, distributed processing, data warehousing, and ever faster response times has led to a bewildering array of products and responsibilities. Web connections, telecom billing, secure payments, and a host of other problems abound. It is the lucky Oracle DBA these days who is not weighed down with a GSM mobile, a pager, and a Palm Pilot filled with difficult assignments scheduled for particularly unsociable hours, or the lucky Oracle developer who has already mastered all the latest web development tools, Java servlets, and XML data parsers. Every site is different, and every user's problem is a new one. An enormous advantage of open source software is that if it doesn't do what you need, you can adapt it.

The Motivation Behind Open Source

Although "open source" is a relatively new term,* its origins date back to the early days of computer software. And the more general concept of gaining value by giving value is one that predates computers themselves.

---

* The term "open source" was coined at a meeting in February 1998 of the first participants in what would later become the Open Source Initiative.

Most monetary economies in the corporate world are driven by some type of *control mechanism* or *exchange mechanism* (or, to be less technical, by the carrot and the stick). Let's suppose that you are a dedicated programmer working for *largeCorporationWidgets.com*, and your boss tells you to code up an Oracle Forms program or set up a database. You generally do as you're told. Why? Because you have previously agreed to be under the control of the company in return for various company benefits. The "stick" side of the equation is that if you fail to carry out an assigned task, you won't be paid and you may lose your job. On the "carrot" side, you will receive a salary in payment for doing your job, and eventually you may earn a promotion.

Until recently, these complementary rationales were the only generally accepted methods for driving innovative software creation (and for motivating dedicated programmers, most of whom have the natural herding instincts of paranoid tigers). However, hiding behind this control and exchange mechanism are two implicit assumptions:

1. *largeCorporationWidgets.com* controls all access to computing power and the network. If they fire you, you will no longer be able to write programs or communicate with any of your programming friends around the world. If you're a dedicated hacker,* this may be important to you.

2. You need the money.

In contrast, let's look at an alternative, rather plausible universe in which these two assumptions don't necessarily hold true. Suppose you're a gifted hacker at MIT who is happy living upon a secure research grant; or you're a well-paid professor of computer science at Stanford who wants to attract the brightest undergraduates; or you're a dedicated nighttime hacker, who makes enough during the day (possibly supporting legacy systems for *largeCorporationWidgets.com*) to pay for the latest workstation and a 24-hour, high-speed Internet connection. In all of these cases, you find yourself with an abundance of computer-related material goods, networks, and processing power, plus enough money to eat and pay the rent. When it comes right down to it, you simply don't require any more in the way of material possessions (computer or otherwise). In none of these cases is there any outside force that can persuade you to work any harder.

Given that money isn't a sufficient motive in these cases, what then could motivate you to write those programs? There are a number of possible motives:

---

* In this book, we occasionally use the term "hacker." As used here, the term is more or less synonymous with "open source programmer." Although "hacker" is sometimes used in the popular press to identify a person who breaks into systems (more properly, that's a "cracker"), that's not what we mean here. For more on hackers, see the definition in "The New Hackers Dictionary" (*http://eps.mcgill.ca/jargon/*).

- The need to achieve the highest possible status among your peers

- Pure scientific curiosity and the need to write programs that are interesting and fun

- The need to solve problems that are hampering your ability to do your job (in the open source world, this is known as "scratching a developer's itch")

Let's look at these three motives in turn.

The gift culture

The *gift culture* is an anthropological term that Eric Raymond, a major force in the open source community (we'll discuss his role a bit later in this chapter), first used to describe the culture of open source. In the world of software, the idea of a gift culture is, basically, that if you give away cool programs that do useful things for other people, then your stock will rise among your colleagues. The degree of regard in which others hold you will depend exponentially upon the quality of your gifts. This last point is the prime engine that drives the open source movement. Raymond writes that, in a gift culture:

> Participants compete for prestige by giving time, energy, and creativity away . . .
> In gift cultures, social status is determined not by what you control but by what you give away.*

Thus, when Larry Wall gives Perl (essentially, the Mount Olympus of open source software) away to the hacker community, he rises to a transcendental plane occupied by only a few other deities.† This pantheon is an extremely exclusive club, and no amount of money will buy you a membership card. You have to earn membership another way—by giving away the virtual crown jewels of your programming creativity.

The whole notion of the gift culture may seem strange to you, but note that the concept is not specific to the world of computing. Raymond writes:

> Gift cultures are adaptations not to scarcity but to abundance. They arise in populations that do not have significant material-scarcity problems with survival goods. We can observe gift cultures in action among aboriginal cultures living in eco-zones with mild climates and abundant food. We can also observe them in certain strata of our own society, especially in show business and among the very wealthy.‡

---

* Eric S. Raymond, *The Cathdral and the Bazaar* (O'Reilly), pp. 63, 79.

† In our opinion, the pantheon also includes Linus Torvalds, John Ousterhout, and Guido van Rossum (the creators of Linux, Tcl, and Python, respectively), as well as Richard M. Stallman (as Zeus) and Eric Raymond (as Hermes); we'll discuss Stallman a bit later in this chapter.

‡ Raymond, p. 79.

The need for innovation

There is a human need for progress, innovation, and building things of value that is by no means unique to the world of computing. Most scientists tend to gravitate to areas that intrigue them, for whatever reason, and a surprising number choose to focus on these areas even if there is little chance of immediate financial reward.

Consider Albert Einstein. Einstein spent many years studying on his own a topic of great interest to him: a comparison of James Clerk Maxwell's idea (circa 1865) that light traveled at a single relative fixed speed to Max Planck's alternative ideas (circa 1900) on constant light energy quanta. Einstein had ample opportunity to perform lucrative pre-World War I physics research for any one of the warlike governments of Europe, but he chose to stay ensconced within the quiet of his Swiss Patent Office in Berne. With no particular promise of financial reward, he was determined to resolve the problem of what would happen if you could travel upon Maxwell's constant-speed lightbeam in Planck's quantized universe.*

In the world of computer software, we see a similar process. Although much innovation is directed by the promise of financial reward, a good deal of energy goes into developing software that is simply interesting to an individual developer. Some of that development leads to blind alleys, of course, but in the best cases, developers create wonderfully innovative programs that ultimately become virtual standards.

The developer's itch

There are a great many interesting technical problems to solve and a great deal of challenging software to be written. How do open source developers decide how to spend their time? Most often, they start out trying to solve a particular problem or speed up a process that is getting in the way of doing their work in the most efficient way.

As Eric Raymond puts it, "Every good work of software starts by scratching a developer's personal itch." An individual developer is unsatisfied with the capabilities of a particular piece of software, so he decides to extend the program to suit his own needs. Maybe it turns out that other developers can benefit from his work. Ultimately, that extension, or modification, gets added to the general community of programs, just as in traditional science, one scientist's new theory gets added to the canon of established science. The most functional and usable programs become the foundation stones for the next generation of software. Since so much open source software is built on what has come before, no self-respecting open source developer would even contemplate keeping his innovations secret or

---

* For some excellent links on Einstein's life, see *http://www.westegg.com/einstein/*.

making them too expensive for his peers to acquire. Most such developers see themselves as being only the temporary torch bearers in an unending chain of runners. To fail to pass on the baton would be to forfeit all respect.

In a similar way, all scientists build upon the great ideas of the past. However creative and revolutionary Einstein's work was, it relied in part on work that had gone before. Without Maxwell's mathematical equations, published in the public domain for all to see, Einstein would not have been able to build upon them, and physics could have languished for a much longer time under the older Newtonian "optics" model. And, continuing in the scientific tradition, Einstein's work built a foundation for others to work on and modify in the future.

Sir Isaac Newton put it well. He spurned accolades for his many achievements and credited those scientists who had gone before him, saying: "I have stood upon the shoulders of giants."

A good example of this progression in the computing world is the Linux operating system, which we'll look at in somewhat more detail later in this chapter. Linus Torvalds took the ideas contained within Andrew Tanenbaum's Minix operating system and used them to create his own kernel. Torvalds' original motivation was an "itch," the desire to read Usenet news groups without becoming reliant upon the binary-only operating systems that at that time were the only systems available on PCs. Torvalds published his early efforts in 1991, and the Linux project rapidly grew to become the poster child for open source. However, Linux success would never have evolved as it did without the availability of the source code for Tanenbaum's Minix. And the many creative developments built on Linux—for example, the GNOME/GTK+ technologies we'll look at in Chapters 9 and 10— would probably never have come into existence.

A Brief History of Open Source

It may be useful to take a look back in time to see how we got where we are today. The concept of open source didn't just arrive, without precedent, on the computing scene. In some ways, as we've seen with Einstein, the basic motivations are as old as science itself. However, you'll be relieved to know that we'll confine our journey to the world of computing. Obviously, in this short section we can only touch on many events that are more complex and interesting than we can possibly express here. We apologize for the necessary brevity and oversimplification.

The early days of artificial intelligence

To start our journey, let's go back all the way to Alan Turing in 1945. After helping break the German military codes (including the infamous Enigma) in World War II, Turing began working for the National Physical Laboratory (NPL) in Britain on a project known as the Automatic Computing Engine (ACE). Although ACE wasn't the success Turing had hoped for, his ideas on artificial intelligence (such as the famous Turing test) permeated the NPL. Turing had a strong influence on Donald Davies, whose 1966 "Proposal for a Digital Communication Network" would later play a crucial role in the development of the ARPAnet in the United States.

With some cross-fertilization between NPL and the Massachusetts Institute of Technology, Turing's ideas on AI finally took root in 1956 under the leadership of John McCarthy (the inventor of Lisp) and Marvin Minsky, and culminated in the founding of the MIT Artificial Intelligence Project in 1960. A decade later, in 1971, the AI Lab at MIT took on perhaps its most famous student to date, Richard M. Stallman, thereby setting in place a chain reaction of crucial events that culminated in the GNU/Linux operating system. Before we get there, however, we need to look back at a second historical thread.

The rise of the Internet

In 1958, the United States government created the Advanced Research Projects Agency (ARPA). ARPA gradually began to take on much of the "blue-skies" computer research for the Pentagon and the rest of the U.S. defense establishment. In 1962, J.C.R. Licklider arrived at ARPA from MIT and put in place the research processes for networking and time-sharing operating systems. By 1969, these systems had come together into the ARPAnet project, which was the direct lineal ancestor of today's Internet.

The key to the ARPAnet's revolutionary communications system was a distributed, fault-resilient network with multiply redundant nodes. The idea was that, even if many of these nodes were damaged, messages would still be able to get through via whatever path remained. This model, originally developed by Paul Baran, was initially rejected by AT&T (which at the time supplied many of the American government's communication requirements), because it did not match their more centralized analog systems. However, the NPL scientist Roger Scantlebury later rediscovered Baran's work and combined it with Donald Davies' research. The result was the basic notion of *packet switching*, a concept on which the entire Internet rests. The ARPAnet subsequently went from strength to strength, eventually evolving into today's Internet. Before we jump too far ahead, though, let's look at the third thread in the interwoven origins of open source.

The birth of Unix

AT&T originally resisted Baran's multiply redundant and distributed network. However, in 1969, at the Bell Labs province of the AT&T empire, Ken Thompson invented a new operating system called Unix (the name was allegedly a pun on the earlier MULTICS system). Together with Dennis Ritchie's new C language, Thompson went on to make the Unix operating system truly portable by adapting it for a wide range of machines and creating portable Unix-based programs via the C programming language. The fact that the source code for Unix was also openly distributed to a large number of universities and institutions (the University of California at Berkeley played a particularly important role) helped with the operating system's portability. This was especially significant at the time because AT&T had been blocked from entering the computer business by a U.S. government antitrust measure in 1956.

From 1974 on, staff at Berkeley and Bell Labs worked in close cooperation to improve the original AT&T System V Unix (mainly on the Digital Equipment Corporation PDP-11). The operating system quickly became a favorite of hackers because of its special approach: it started with simple robust tools, which fed into more complex ones via the Unix pipe concept. In 1977, Bill Joy (later of Sun Microsystems) put together the first so-called Berkeley Software Distribution of Unix (BSD), which he worked on until 1982, when he joined the fledgling Sun Microsystems.

As Unix became more widely used—due particularly to its portability—it became the standard operating system for the ARPAnet in the early 1980s (which is why web addresses now use a forward Unix slash rather than a backward one). The promised land of open standards and source code distribution was now almost in sight: the computing world was on the verge of having a networking system (ARPAnet), an operating system (Unix), and a programming language (C), all of them relatively free, and all of them working nicely together.

Unfortunately, defeat was snatched from the jaws of victory through a failure to overcome two unforeseen road hazards: the high price of Unix workstations at the time and the Ma Bell corporate breakup.

Obstacles

The first obstacle to early domination by the forces of free software was the price of Unix workstations. They were within the price range of universities and corporations, but they weren't cheap enough for individuals. Ultimately, failure to lower the price led to the rise of relatively inexpensive, non-networked personal computers. Over the next 20 years, PCs with their plethora of proprietary software came to dominate the computer industry, pushing aside the lower end of the more technically advanced Unix workstations.

The second blow to early domination by free software came in 1984 when AT&T reached an agreement with the U.S. government to divest itself of its Bell telephone operating companies, in return for having the government lift the anti-monopolistic constraints of its 1956 decree. This development meant that AT&T could enter the computer business for the first time. Now, instead of giving its System V Unix operating system away, AT&T was able to exploit it commerically.

System V Unix became a proprietary product just like any other one! Even the BSD-related flavors of Unix were suddenly available only via Unix vendors and the increasingly expensive AT&T source license.

Richard Stallman, GNU, and the Free Software Foundation

Hackers around the world were appalled at the fate of Unix—but none more than Richard M. Stallman. (Most people regard Stallman as the grandfather of the open source movement, though he clearly separates himself from it by his parallel involvement with the Free Software Foundation, as we'll see later in this chapter.) A brilliant and creative programmer who came to MIT as an undergraduate, Stallman started working at the MIT Artificial Intelligence Laboratory in 1971, and basically never left. Stallman was part of the early hacker culture at the AI Lab and a fierce advocate of free software. Although many of his colleagues left MIT over the years to pursue commercial ventures (many of them joining Symbolics), Stallman continued to rebuff the commercial world. With the 1984 commercialization of Unix, he dug in for a fight. He decided to build an operating system—essentially, a free Unix—from scratch, forming the GNU Project.*

Before the dragon-slaying against AT&T's Unix could begin, however, Stallman needed to create a new type of software license in order to protect his forthcoming work. In 1985, he created the Free Software Foundation (FSF) and, through the foundation, sold copies of his software. Many people find Stallman's term "free software" confusing, and they are surprised that such software can be used to produce revenue. Most assume that the word "free" describes the price of the software. Stallman himself has provided one of the best statements on this topic:

> Free software is a matter of liberty, not price. To understand the concept you should think of 'free speech' not 'free beer'.†

Stallman's GNU General Public License became the standard for free software at the time. You can view the current version of this license at:

http://www.gnu.org/copyleft/gpl.html

In addition, for a more detailed look at the rich and interesting story of the GNU Project and the Free Software Foundation, see:

http://www.gnu.org/philosophy/why-free.html

In summary, the "copyleft" concept of the GNU General Public License says that you are free to download a program protected with the license (termed a *GPL program*), receive source code, and change that code if you want to. However, from

---

* GNU stands recursively for "GNU's Not Unix."

† You can read the Free Software Definition at *http://www.gnu.org/philosophy/free-sw.html*.

this point on, whenever you distribute this program—whether you've modified it or not—you must give the recipients the same rights you had when you received the original. In other words, you cannot take GPL programs and then make them proprietary or binary-only, granting all of the subsequent rights to yourself. You must give away these rights, including rights to the entire source code—even if you embed only the tiniest piece of GPL code within your program code—and even if your program is a much larger, previously proprietary body of work you wrote entirely yourself. This notion turned out to be a very controversial one, and one that businesses were loath to accept. As we'll discuss later (see "Open Source and the Commercial World"), taking a somewhat different approach to modern-day open source licensing has made the notion of open source more palatable to corporations. (There is another GNU license, the LGPL, or lesser GPL, which is not quite so rigorous. We'll discuss this license, particularly in relation to the GNOME Project, in Chapter 9.)

A Detour into Physics

To understand the thinking behind the debate on freedom that has swirled around Richard Stallman and the Free Software Foundation, let's leave the world of computing for a bit and journey backwards in time again to the days of Albert Einstein.

Imagine a world in which Einstein had not shared his genius with the world but had instead exploited his intimate knowledge of the Swiss patent system and wrapped relativity within a core of intellectual property rights. By now, *quantumRelativityWidgets.com* would be the world's largest and most powerful corporation, owning and controlling most of the planet's astronomical observatories, satellite communications platforms, and nuclear weapons systems via its closed proprietary knowledge of quantum mechanics and nuclear physics.

With the full complement of space technology and travel also within this huge corporation's domain, the future of humanity would itself be entirely under the beneficent and omnipotent control of *quantumRelativityWidgets.com* and its majority stock shareholders. And all of this privilege would have been based upon the openly published work of scientists prior to Einstein.

Now transfer this somewhat far-fetched image across from physical science to the alternative sphere of computer science, and you may begin to see why the proprietary versus open source code debate stirs such fierce passion in people like Richard Stallman.

Stallman's first serious GNU development effort was the *gcc* code compiler (which subsequently became the computer world's "default" C compiler). To obtain *gcc* or learn more about it, check out:

> *http://www.gnu.org/software/gcc/gcc.html*

Stallman's GNU Emacs editor has also become the most popular editor on Unix systems.

With a dedicated GNU Project team around him, Stallman spent the rest of the 1980s at MIT, gradually building the large set of tools needed to craft a truly free operating system.* By 1990, the GNU system was almost complete, except for one final element—the kernel, the beating heart of any operating system. The GNU Hurd project had long attempted to build this kernel, but they were still several years from completing it.

Enter Linux

Fortunately for our story, the seventh cavalry, in the shape of Linus Torvalds, arrived from Finland to save the day. He bore his trusty Linux kernel in place of a squadron of Winchester rifles. Linux came from an open tradition of its own, so its kernel was readily adopted by the GNU Project as the final part of the new operating system. By 1992, the first version of what became known as the GNU/Linux operating system was in place.†

Perhaps one of the most important developments emerging from the GNU Project was the development model that Linus Torvalds adopted for Linux. In contrast to the typical corporate development project, Torvalds took a different approach to the standard technique of hand-picking a few colleagues to work on a project with rigidly designed goals. Instead he adopted a "release early, release often" approach, which involved hundreds (if not thousands) of developers helping out in many disparate ways. There was something for every volunteer to do—from documentation to bug-chasing to hardcore coding of the kernel itself. The fact that a release might contain bugs wasn't seen as a failure, but instead as a challenge for the many enthusiastic volunteers. This is now recorded in the memorable phrase, "With many eyes, all bugs are shallow."

Frequent releases of the Linux product, bugs and all, were facilitated by CVS (the Concurrent Versions System, *http://www.cvshome.org*), which allows multiple

---

* Stallman himself officially left MIT in 1984 in order to prevent MIT from copyrighting his GNU work, but he was allowed to continue using the MIT AI Lab facilities.

† Many elements of the new operating system also came from BSD-Unix and the work of people such as Marshall Kirk McKusick. In 1994, Berkeley Software Design Incorporated, or BSDI (see *http://www.bsdi. com*), won a court battle with the torch-bearers of proprietary Unix to allow them to release a form of BSD-Unix (one stripped of any AT&T components) for free redistribution (4.4BSD-Lite, Release 2).

module authoring and provides the enhanced debugging facilities required for mass-development projects like Linux. CVS is now the dominant development tool for open source projects. The CVS development model is mainly democratic, though most successful projects involve one benign dictator (such as Linus Torvalds) at the center of the controlled chaos, calling the most important shots and settling the inevitable arguments. As you might expect, the success of this development model has baffled corporations that are accustomed to the top-down style of authoritarian software development.

The best of open source

The late 1980s and early 1990s saw the emergence of a number of superb pieces of open source software that have had an enormous impact on the computing world. We've already touched on the Linux operating system, possibly the greatest open source achievement to date. Others we put in this "best of" category (especially taking into account their potential for use with Oracle) include the Perl, Tcl, and Python scripting languages and the Apache web server. (Of course, there is a lot of excellent software out there, and others may disagree with our choices.) We'll briefly discuss each of these in the later section, "The Open Source Crown Jewels." In this book, we'll focus on how each of these open source tools is used to build Oracle applications; their scope is much wider, however, and we encourage you to learn more by consulting the references we've collected in Appendix C.

Open source in the commercial world

Throughout most of the 1990s, the high quality of open source software like Perl, Tcl, and Linux became more and more apparent even to the corporate world. Inside every company that followed the typical corporate development model were increasing numbers of individuals who downloaded, experimented with, and raved about both open source tools and open source approaches to building software. But even companies that were convinced of the quality of this software were suspicious of the stronger GNU Public License and the libertarian stance of Stallman and others in the Free Software movement.

As the decade progressed, some open source enthusiasts struggled to find a way to reconcile the worlds of free and proprietary software. They believed that the open source and commercial worlds didn't have to be at war, and that free and proprietary software, by coexisting, could benefit both sides. They wanted to figure out how to remove the stumbling blocks of the past and give the corporate world a way to use and contribute to the growth of open source software. Through a combination of savvy public relations and a new licensing paradigm, the "new" open source movement has had notable success.

Eric Raymond and The Cathedral and the Bazaar

Chief among the new open source pragmatists was Eric S. Raymond. Raymond, who wrote *The New Hacker's Dictionary* back in 1990 and subsequently became something of an anthropologist of hacker culture, has been a major player in the present-day open source movement. In addition to writing software, Raymond had been writing for years about open source history and philosophy. His 1997 essay, "The Cathedral and the Bazaar," was very well received by the developer community and fueled wider interest in open source.[*] In that essay, Raymond compares the typical commercial development method of the cathedral (where many organized master masons gradually construct a pre-planned and religiously awesome monolith) to the bazaar of Linux (where many apparently unorganized bricklayers build a fluid market of ideas and sustainable growth, which gradually becomes an unstoppable force).

In January of 1998 came the open source equivalent of "the shot heard 'round the world." Netscape announced that it would release the source code for its client product line, and CEO Jim Barksdale credited Raymond with being the "fundamental inspiration" for the decision. In the wake of this event, and the additional media interest generated by the March 1998 O'Reilly Free Software Summit, which brought 20 open source leaders together, Raymond effectively became the media spokesman for the movement. Gregarious and media-savvy, Raymond was the personality the media sought out to explain what this open source stuff was all about.

Raymond and others in the open source community were pleased by Netscape's announcement and the media attention, but they wanted to be sure that they took full advantage of this moment in history. They wanted to see more corporations release source code and use open source programs within their own products. They felt that the future of open source programming would be in peril if the outside world continued to regard the open source movement as anticommercial.

The Open Source Definition

One obstacle to commercial coexistence with open source in the past was the type of licensing attached to open source software. Back in the 1980s, corporations that wanted to use GNU Emacs and other tools from the Free Software Foundation were stymied by the rigorous GNU Public License. That legal document was a major impediment to official corporate adoption of GNU software. The new open source movement (which was starting to coalesce into the Open Source Initiative, OSI) wanted to find a way to protect open source software, while giving the corporate world some incentive to use and add to the pool of open source software.

---

[*] This essay and others by Raymond were collected into a book, also called *The Cathedral and the Bazaar* (O'Reilly). See *http://www.oreilly.com/catalog/cb/* for information; for most of the essays in their original form, visit *http://www.tuxedo.org/~esr/writings/cathedral-bazaar/index.html.*

The emerging Open Source Initiative looked at a number of previous types of free software licenses, including the GNU Public License, the X Consortium License, and the Perl Artistic License. They wanted to pull together the best aspects of these licenses and create a "software bill of rights." The document they came up with drew heavily from the Debian Free Software Guidelines written by Bruce Perens and was first published in the summer of 1997. The idea was that an open source program that met the definition would be "OSI certified." The Open Source Definition provides the imperial standard for protecting and certifying the quality of that software. A computer user or software developer who downloads a particular piece of open source software can know exactly where he stands in relation to a defined legal yardstick. We've included the text of the Open Source Definition at the end of this chapter, along with some additional explanation where we thought it would be helpful.

You'll find the most up-to-date version of the text of the Open Source Definition at:

> *http://www.opensource.org/docs/definition_plain.html*

You can also read Bruce Perens's essay on the definition at:

> *http://www.oreilly.com/catalog/opensources/book/perens.html*

The Open Source Crown Jewels

Like another pentagon of stars in a bright circlet constellation, there are five prominent open technologies that have gained the most attention over the past decade. Table 1-1 lists those technologies and web sites where you can obtain more information about each.

Table 1-1. The Open Source Crown Jewels

Technology	URL
Perl	*http://www.perl.org/press/history.html* *http://history.perl.org/PerlTimeline.html*
Tcl	*http://dev.scriptics.com/doc/tclHistory.html*
Python	*http://www.python.org/doc/FAQ.html#1.15*
Apache	*http://www.apache.org/ABOUT_APACHE.html*
Linux	*http://www.linux.org/info/index.html*

We've discussed Linux a bit already. In the following sections we'll look briefly at each of the other technologies; you'll learn much more about them all in subsequent chapters.

Perl

Perl (Practical Extraction and Report Language) was developed back in 1987 by Larry Wall as a way of making things easier—originally, for performing his own system administration tasks, and ultimately for a whole generation of developers. Perl is an interpreted scripting language that combines the best capabilities of a variety of other languages, but the whole of Perl is far greater than the sum of its parts. Perl was designed especially to be:

- Extremely fast, in order to be truly useful when scanning through large files

- Especially good at text handling, because data comes in many different forms within system files and Perl had to handle them all

- Extensible, in order for Perl to expand users' horizons, not restrict them

Perhaps the most accurate summary of what Perl is best at can be found in the *README* file written by Wall for Perl Version 1.0:

> Perl is an interpreted language optimized for scanning arbitrary text files, extracting information from those text files, and printing reports based on that information. It's also a good language for many system management tasks. The language is intended to be practical (easy to use, efficient, complete) rather than beautiful (tiny, elegant, minimal). It combines (in the author's opinion, anyway) some of the best features of C, sed, awk, and sh, so people familiar with those languages should have little difficulty with it. (Language historians will also note some vestiges of csh, Pascal, and even BASIC | PLUS.) Expression syntax corresponds quite closely to C expression syntax. If you have a problem that would ordinarily use sed or awk or sh, but it exceeds their capabilities or must run a little faster, and you don't want to write the silly thing in C, then perl may be for you. There are also translators to turn your sed and awk scripts into perl scripts. OK, enough hype.

Since it was first released, the language has gone from strength to strength. Over the years, an enthusiastic and partisan army of Perl volunteers has extended the language in a myriad of ways.* CPAN (the Comprehensive Perl Archive Network), an online repository of Perl core files, documentation, and contributed modules, has become a model for an open source development community. Perl has grown to be the "glue" language of the Internet and is ideally suited as a language for developing web applications and system management tasks and for allowing diferent systems to work well together. Perl 4 brought the release of modules allowing Perl to interact with Oracle databases. The current version of Perl, Perl 5, contains long-sought object-oriented features.

---

* New Perl modules go through an evolutionary process that begins with an individual developer's code, which she posts to CPAN. As others learn about the new module and start downloading, testing, and relying on it, it becomes more and more acceptable. If it's good enough, and if enough people and products rely upon it, the Perl gods ultimately might decide to include the new module in the next general Perl distribution.

Because Perl is such a powerful and extensible language, you'll find a lot of discussion of Perl throughout this book. Chapter 2 describes how to install Perl and connect it to Oracle databases. Chapter 3 focuses on Perl's use as a scripting language, especially the use of the Perl/Tk GUI toolkit. Chapters 4 and 6 provide examples of some excellent Perl-based Oracle applications.

Tcl

John Ousterhout began developing Tcl (Tool Command Language) in 1987 with the goal of creating a generic language that his students could use for all of their projects. They had been spending too much time developing new control languages for each individual project and too little time on their actual research. Ousterhout had the following objectives for Tcl:

- Extensibility, so new Tcl applications could add their own features to the basic structure of the language

- Simplicity, so Tcl could work easily with different applications and not restrict them

- Good facilities for integration and the ability to easily blend in any future language extensions

As with Perl, Ousterhout future-proofed Tcl, making it possible for new modules to be added as required by other developers. One of the most popular of these modules has been Ousterhout's own GUI toolkit (Tk). Since 1988, Tcl/Tk has been hugely successful with hundreds of thousands of users worldwide, ranging from NASA to teenage bedroom hackers. Chapter 4 describes how to install Tcl/Tk and how to use the modules that provide an interface to Oracle databases.

Python

In late 1989, Guido van Rossum was working with the Amoeba distributed operating system, trying to create more useful tools for Amoeba system administration. He began work on a new language, which he called Python. By 1991, he had made the language publicly available, and Python has grown in popularity ever since. Python was designed from the start as an object-oriented language, which distinguishes it from scripting languages such as Perl and Tcl. Van Rossum's goals for Python were to make it:

- Portable, so it would be truly operating system–independent

- Easy to learn

- In possession of a powerful standard library

Like Perl and Tcl, Python has a huge set of features and is appropriate for just about any programming purpose you can think of.

In Chapter 3, we'll describe how to install Python and its Tkinter windowing system. We'll also describe how to use Python to connect to Oracle databases.

Apache

Apache doesn't have a single founding father, in the way that Linux, Perl, Tcl, and Python do. The HTTP daemon program (*httpd*), developed by Rob McCool at the National Center for Supercomputing Applications (NCSA), University of Illinois, Urbana-Champaign, was the root project that Brian Behlendorf, Cliff Skolnick, and a number of other programmers ultimately turned into an open source web server. Apache has become enormously successful, and it is the leading web server in use today. It is a stable, scalable, and highly efficient product. Even Oracle Corporation is now embedding Apache within its Internet Application Server (*i*AS).

We'll describe how to install Apache in Chapter 5. In Chapter 6, we'll touch on Apache's use as an underlying technology for Oracle-based web applications, and in Chapters 7 and 8, we'll describe its use with Java applications—in particular, the Apache JServ web server now used by Oracle.

Oracle and Open Source

For most of its history, Oracle has not been particularly welcoming to open source from a corporate point of view, though individual developers and DBAs have historically used open source tools, like Perl, and shared their scripts and expertise with their peers.

But in July of 1998, the company announced that the Oracle8*i* database would be ported to Linux, with detailed information available at the annual Oracle Open World conference (held in San Francisco that fall), to which Linus Torvalds was invited as a guest speaker. At this conference, Kevin Walsh, an Oracle vice president, revealed the change in Oracle's thinking by calling upon Sun to put Java into the open source community. He thought Java would develop faster if Sun loosened its control:

> Sun should still decide what goes into Sun-blessed Java, but if they open the process, all those freeware versions of Java would have a lot less momentum. Linux is in many ways a reaction to Java. Open source is a different development model than what Sun has been pursuing, but it still merits consideration.

The conference was also attended by representatives from Intel and Netscape, who were as determined as Oracle to make Linux a non-Microsoft success.

The Oracle port to Linux was a watershed event in the history of open source. It was, of course, a significant event in its own right—the porting of the world's leading database to an open source platform. But the timing was also critical. Oracle's embrace of open source—at least in a limited way—sent a signal that the corporate world was taking open source seriously and making product decisions accordingly. In his "Revenge of the Hackers" essay, Eric Raymond wrote about this event:

> To sustain the momentum, we needed commitments not from hungry second-stringers but from industry leaders. Thus, it was the mid-July announcements by Oracle and Informix that really closed out this vulnerable phase.*

The promised port of Oracle8*i* to Linux arrived in a blur of activity that also included IBM's port of DB2, Oracle's biggest database rival in the high-end sphere, to Linux. Other vendors fell into line, and soon Linux ports of major commercial software were almost a matter of routine.

For those of us in the old guard, the availability of Oracle on Linux merely underlined what we knew all along, but for many others, this event legitimized Linux as a solid and serious business player. What's more, there was now an effective server-space alternative to Oracle on Windows NT for small development shops. If you wanted to build your own Intel-based server but didn't need all the horsepower (and cost) of a Sun enterprise-class computer, you could now provide Oracle-based solutions without resorting to NT.

 Some of us Linux zealots actually had Oracle running on Linux before the fateful day of the official port. Back in the days of Oracle7, it was, in fact, possible to get the SCO-Unix version of Oracle up and running with an emulator called *iBCS2*. But this approach was really only for the diehards; it certainly wasn't supported, and there were quite a few limitations.

We won't spend a lot of time in this book describing Linux (though Appendix A, *Oracle8i And Linux*, does contain guidelines for installing Oracle8*i* on this platform). There are many books that describe this wonderful operating system. With the latest version of the Linux kernel now released with support for a journaling file system and non-buffered, raw I/O devices—and even loose talk of parallel server support—there seem to be no limits other than the amount of Jolt Cola that can be consumed by Alan Cox to keep the Linux bandwagon rolling.† Linux has become a huge open source success story.

If you are interested in learning more about how the Oracle/Linux alliance is working out, visit the following sites:

> *http://www.redhat.com/marketplace/oracle/*
> *http://platforms.oracle.com/linux/*

---

* Raymond, p. 179.

† If you'd like to read more about the heroic Alan Cox, the chief lieutenant of Linux development, you can catch his regular diary at *http://www.linux.org.uk/diary/*.

http://www.calderasystems.com/partners/industry/oracle.html
http://www.suse.com/us/solutions/partners/oracle/

Open Source Summary

Table 1-2 lists all of the open source and other programs mentioned in this book. We tried to include the most up-to-date information possible at the time of publication, but because most of these programs are continually being enhanced, make sure to check out the sites listed in the table for current information.

Table 1-2. Open Source Technologies and Related Areas

Tool or Application	Chapter	Description and Online Sites
ACS	5	Ars Digita Community System, dynamic web-based solutions *http://www.arsdigita.com/pages/toolkit/*
ActivePerl	2	Win32 Perl from ActiveState *http://www.activestate.com* *http://www.activestate.com/activeperl/* *http://www.activestate.com/Products/ActivePerl/Download.html* *http://www.microsoft.com/downloads/*
AIX	2	Unix freeware packages *http://ftp.univie.ac.at/aix/*
Ant	8	Java-based build tool *http://jakarta.apache.org/ant/index.html*
Apache	5	The Apache web server *http://www.apache.org/, http://www.apache.org/httpd.html* *http://www.refcards.com/, http://www.apache.org/dist/* *http://httpd.apache.org/docs/windows.html* *http://www.apache.org/ABOUT_APACHE.html* *http://httpd.apache.org/dist/binaries/win32/* *http://xml.apache.org*
Apache JServ	7	Apache Java servlet web server *http://java.apache.org/jserv/index.html* *http://java.apache.org/jserv/dist/*
Apache mod_java	5	Apache Java module *http://java.apache.org*
Apache mod_perl	5	Apache Perl module *http://perl.apache.org* *http://perl.apache.org/#docs*
Apache mod_php	5	Apache PHP module *http://www.php.net*
Apache mod_plsql	8	Apache PL/SQL module *http://www.total-knowledge.com/downloads/mod_plsql/*

Table 1-2. Open Source Technologies and Related Areas (continued)

Tool or Application	Chapter	Description and Online Sites
Apache mod_ssl	5	Apache Secure Sockets Layer *http://www.apache.org/related_projects.html#apachessl* *http://www.rsasecurity.com* *http://www.covalent.net/raven/ssl/* *http://www.c2.net/products/sh2/* *http://www.int.c2.net/products/sh2/*
Aquarium	5	Modular web development *http://aquarium.sourceforge.net*
Big Brother	6	Integrated system administration monitoring *http://bb4.com* *http://bb4.com/demo.html*
BLT	4	Graphical charts for Tcl/Tk *http://www.tcltk.com/blt/* *ftp://ftp.tcltk.com/pub/blt/* *ftp://tcltk.sourceforge.net/pub/tcltk/blt/* *http://tcltk.com/blt/*
BSD-Unix	1	The Berkeley Software Distribution *http://www.bsdi.com*
C++	7	Object-oriented extension to C programming *http://www.research.att.com/~bs/homepage.html*
Cocoon	8	XML web content management *http://xml.apache.org/cocoon/*
CORBA	7	Common Object Request Broker Architecture *http://www.omg.org* *http://www.corba.org*
CVS	1	Concurrent Versions System *http://www.cvshome.org*
DB Prism	8	Java servlet Oracle application *http://www.plenix.com/dbprism/doc/Home.html* *http://www.telecomrg.com/darylcollins/prism/*
DB_Browser	6	Perl CGI database management *http://www.summersault.com/software/db_browser/*
DBD-Chart	4	Perl DBI driver interface for rendering charts and graphs *http://home.earthlink.net/~darnold/dbdchart/*
DBInspector	8	Java SQL tool *http://dbinspector.com*
Dbitotcl	3	Perl DBI linkage to Tcl *http://www.xdobry.de/dbitotcl/*
dbMan	4	Perl/Tk database tool *http://dbman.linux.cz* *http://www.fi.muni.cz/~sorm/dbman/*
DCOracle	3	Oracle connectivity package for Python *http://www.zope.org/Products/DCOracle/* *http://www.python.org/topics/database/modules.html*

Table 1-2. Open Source Technologies and Related Areas (continued)

Tool or Application	Chapter	Description and Online Sites
DDL-Oracle	4	Perl package to reverse-engineer DDL from Oracle database components *http://www.perl.com/CPAN-local/modules/by-authors/id/R/ RV/RVSUTHERL/*
EmbPerl	5	Dynamic Perl embedded within HTML *http://perl.apache.org/embperl/*
Epingle	9	GTK+ interface builder *http://www.epita.fr/~theber_s/epingle/epingle.html*
Gaby	10	GTK+ notepad data-handling package *http://gaby.netpedia.net*
gASQL	10	GTK+ relational modeling tool *http://malerba.linuxave.net*
Ghostscript	4	Open source PostScript printing *http://www.cs.wisc.edu/~ghost/*
The GIMP	9	The GNU Image Manipulation Tool *http://www.gimp.org* *http://www.gimp.org/download.html* *http://manual.gimp.org/* *http://gimp-savvy.com/BOOK/index.html*
Glade	9	GTK+ Interface Builder *http://glade.pn.org*
GNOME	9	GNU Network Object Model Environment, the Linux-based desktop GUI environment *http://www.gnome.org* *http://www.helixcode.com/desktop/download.php3* *http://www.gnome.org/start/source.html*
Gnome Transcript	10	Generic database table management *http://gtranscript.sourceforge.net*
GNOME-DB	10	GNOME-related database framework *http://www.gnome.org/gnome-db/*
GNU gcc	1	The GNU C compiler *http://www.gnu.org/software/gcc/gcc.html* *http://gcc.gnu.org* *http://www.redhat.com/swr/i386/gcc-java-2.95.1-3.i386.html* *http://packages.debian.org/stable/devel/gcc.html* *http://sunfreeware.com* *http://ftp.univie.ac.at/aix/aix432/* *http://jazz.external.hp.com/src/gnu/download2_95_2.html*
GNU Project	1	Philosophy and aims of the GNU License *http://www.gnu.org/copyleft/gpl.html* *http://www.gnu.org/philosophy/why-free.html*
GRAD	9	GTK+ Rapid Application Development *http://www.penguin.cz/~grad/*
GTK- -	9	Object-oriented GTK+-based GUI wrapper *http://gtkmm.sourceforge.net*

Table 1-2. Open Source Technologies and Related Areas (continued)

Tool or Application	Chapter	Description and Online Sites
GTK+	9	The extension of the GIMP ToolKit for other Linux GUI programs *http://www.gtk.org* *http://www.gtk.org/tutorial/* *ftp://ftp.gtk.org/pub/gtk/* *http://gtkada.eu.org* *http://www.gtk.org/beos/* *http://www.be.com* *http://gwydiondylan.org/gui.phtml* *http://www.netlabs.net/hp/richieb/gtk_eiffel.html* *http://www.ping.de/sites/zagadka/guile-gtk/* *http://www.cse.unsw.edu.au/~chak/haskell/gtk/* *ftp://ftp.gtk.org/pub/gtk/objc-gtkkit/* *http://agnes.dida.physik.uni-essen.de/~gnu-pascal/* *http://www.rit.net/sporter/gtkplusperl/* *http://www.daa.com.au/~james/pygtk/* *http://user.sgic.fi/~tml/gimp/win32/*
HP-UX Unix	2	Freeware packages *http://jazz.external.hp.com/src/index.html*
*i*AS	7	Oracle Corporation Internet Application Server *http://www.oracle.com/ip/deploy/ias/index.html?web.html* *http://www.oracle.com/ip/deploy/ias/*
Jakarta	7	The central Apache collection of Java projects *http://jakarta.apache.org/ant/index.html* *http://jakarta.apache.org/avalon/index.html* *http://jakarta.apache.org/ecs/index.html* *http://jakarta.apache.org/james/index.html* *http://jakarta.apache.org/jetspeed/site/index.html* *http://jakarta.apache.org/jmeter/index.html* *http://jakarta.apache.org/log4j/docs/index.html* *http://jakarta.apache.org/oro/index.html* *http://jakarta.apache.org/regexp/index.html* *http://jakarta.apache.org/slide/index.html* *http://jakarta.apache.org/struts/index.html* *http://jakarta.apache.org/taglibs/index.html* *http://jakarta.apache.org/tomcat/index.html* *http://jakarta.apache.org/turbine/index.html* *http://jakarta.apache.org/velocity/index.html* *http://jakarta.apache.org/watchdog/index.html*
Java	7	Platform-independent, object-oriented programming from Sun *http://www.javasoft.com* *http://www.gamelan.com* *http://technet.oracle.com/tech/java/* *http://java.sun.com/docs/books/tutorial/index.html* *http://java.sun.com/jdc/* *http://java.sun.com/docs/books/jls/html/index.html* *http://java.sun.com/products/jdk/1.2/docs/guide/jar/jarGuide.html*

Table 1-2. Open Source Technologies and Related Areas (continued)

Tool or Application	Chapter	Description and Online Sites
Java Database Explorer	8	Java GUI SQL tool *http://www.geocities.com/RodeoDrive/1620/jexplorer.html*
Java packages	7	Java for specific Unix flavors *http://www.ibm.com/java/jdk/download/* *http://www.unixsolutions.hp.com/products/java/index.html* *http://www.blackdown.org/java-linux.html* *http://www.freebsd.org/java/*
Java's JDBC	7	Java DataBase Connectivity *http://java.sun.com/products/jdbc/driverdesc.html* *http://java.sun.com/j2se/1.3/docs/guide/jdbc/getstart/bridge. doc.html* *http://technet.oracle.com/software/utilities/software_index. htm* *http://technet.oracle.com/software/tech/java/sqlj_jdbc/ software_index.htm* *http://download.oracle.com/otn/utilities_drivers/jdbc/817/* *http://technet.oracle.com/docs/products/oracle8i/doc_ library/817_doc/java.817/* *http://download.oracle.com/otn/utilities_drivers/jdbc/817/* *http://technet.oracle.com/tech/java/* *http://technet.us.oracle.com/tech/java/sqlj_jdbc/htdocs/jdbc_ faq.htm* *http://technet.oracle.com/tech/java/jroadmap/jdbc/listing. htm#998321* *http://technet.oracle.com/tech/java/info/jdbc_doc.htm*
Java's JDK	7	Java Developers Kit, for producing applets, Swing GUIs, and more *http://java.sun.com/products/jdk/1.2/* *http://java.sun.com/j2se/*
Java's JSDK	7	Java Servlet Development Kit, for developing server-side Java web applications *http://java.sun.com/products/servlet/* *http://java.sun.com/products/jdk/1.2/download-windows. html* *http://java.sun.com/products/OV_jservProduct.html* *http://www.apl.jhu.edu/~hall/java/Servlet-Tutorial/* *http://www.jguru.com/jguru/faq/faqpage.jsp?name=Servlets* *http://java.sun.com/products/servlet/download.html* *http://www.servlets.com*
Java Swing	7	Java's supplement to AWT (Abstract Windowing Toolkit) for building GUIs *http://java.sun.com/products/jfc/tsc/index.html* *http://www.inprise.com/jbuilder/* *http://www.webgain.com/Products/VisualCafe_Overview. html* *http://www.sun.com/forte/* *http://www7.software.ibm.com/vad.nsf/data/document2590/* *http://www.netbeans.org*

Table 1-2. Open Source Technologies and Related Areas (continued)

Tool or Application	Chapter	Description and Online Sites
Java XML	7	Linkage between Java, Oracle, and XML *http://www.jdom.org* *http://www.openxml.org* *http://www.oasis-open.org/cover/sgml-xml.html* *http://technet.oracle.com/tech/xml*
JBoss	8	Open Source EJB Server *http://www.jboss.org*
jDBA	8	Java DataBase Administrator SQL tool *http://sourceforge.net/projects/jdba/* *http://www.jdba.org*
JSP	5	JavaServer Pages, embedded HTML content *http://www.sun.com/software/embeddedserver/index.html* *http://www.esperanto.org.nz/jsp/jspfaq.jsp* *http://java.sun.com/products/jsp/*
Karma	6	Perl CGI web-based remote database monitoring *http://www.iheavy.com/karma/*
KDE	9	Kool Desktop Environment *http://www.kde.org*
Kora	B	Linux client for PL/SQL *http://members.nbci.com/uwagner/kora/*
LGPL	9	Lesser GPL License *http://www.gnu.org/copyleft/lesser.html*
Linux and Oracle	1	Oracle FAQs, installation and tuning *http://www.redhat.com/marketplace/oracle/* *http://platforms.oracle.com/linux/* *http://www.calderasystems.com/partners/industry/oracle.html* *http://www.suse.com/us/solutions/partners/oracle/* *http://www.doag.de/mirror/frank/faqunix.htm* *http://jordan.fortwayne.com/oracle/* *http://www.intrex.net/miket/SetupConfig.txt* *http://linas.org/linux/raid.html* *http://www.tomshardware.com* *http://www.linux.org/info/index.html*
Linux development	1	Alan Cox's Linux diary *http://www.linux.org.uk/diary/*
Lonyx	B	Oracle information resource *http://www.lonyx.com*
Lynx	5	Text-based HTML browsing *http://lynx.browser.org*
MacPerl	4	An adaptation of Perl for the Macintosh *http://www.iis.ee.ethz.ch/~neeri/macintosh/perl.html* *http://www.macperl.com* *http://www.macinstruct.com/tutorials/macperl/index.shtml*
Mason	5	Embedded scripting language *http://www.masonhq.com*

Table 1-2. Open Source Technologies and Related Areas (continued)

Tool or Application	Chapter	Description and Online Sites
MinML	8	Java XML configuration file processor *http://www.wilson.co.uk/xml/minml.htm* *http://freshmeat.net/projects.minml/*
MySQL	6	Open source database *http://www.mysql.com*
Nexus	7	Freely available Java web server *http://www-uk.hpl.hp.com/people/ak/java/nexus/*
OCI	2	The Oracle Call Interface *http://technet.oracle.com/tech/oci/* *http://technet.oracle.com/doc/server.815/a67846/toc.htm*
Oddis	4	Tcl/Tk-based Oracle Data Dictionary tool *ftp://www-b.informatik.uni-hannover.de/ftp/software/oddis/* *oddis-2.11.html*
Open source in general	1	Key books, project definition, and other related information *http://www.oreilly.com/catalog/cb/* *http://www.tuxedo.org/~esr/writings/cathedral-bazaar/* *index.html* *http://www.opensource.org/docs/definition_plain.html* *http://www.opensource.org/docs/definition.html* *http://www.oreilly.com/catalog/opensources/book/perens.html* *http://www.opensource.org* *http://www.oreilly.com/catalog/opensources/book/toc.html*
Orac	4	Perl/Tk tool for DBAs *http://www.perl.com/CPAN-local/authors/id/A/AN/* *ANDYDUNC/* *http://www.perl.com/CPAN-local/modules/by-module/Tk/* *http://www.perl.com/CPAN-local/modules/by-module/DBI/* *http://www.perl.com/CPAN-local/modules/by-module/Shell/* *http://sourceforge.net/projects/perldbadmin/*
Oracletool	6	Perl CGI-based DBA tool for the Web *http://www.oracletool.com* *http://www.oracletool.com/download.html*
OraExplain	3	Perl/Tk SQL tuning tool available in DBD::Oracle download *http://www.perl.com/CPAN/modules/by-module/DBD*
Oraperl	2	Original Perl extension for Oracle usage *http://www.geocities.com/Heartland/Meadows/2990/oraperl.* *html*
OraSnap	6	Oracle performance monitoring *http://www.stewartmc.com/oracle/orasnap/*
Orasoft	10	Linux-based Oracle tools *http://www.orasoft.org* *http://www.advantio.com*

Table 1-2. Open Source Technologies and Related Areas (continued)

Tool or Application	Chapter	Description and Online Sites
Oratcl	3	Tcl's Oracle connectivity project *http://download.sourceforge.net/oratcl/* *http://sourceforge.net/projects/oratcl/* *http://oratcl.sourceforge.net* *http://oratcl.sourceforge.net/pub/oratcl30_man.html* *http://www.nyx.net/~tpoindex* *http://www.nyx.net/~tpoindex/tcl.html#Oratcl*
OTN	2	The Oracle Technology Network *http://technet.oracle.com* *http://otnxchange.oracle.com*
Perl	2	Major scripting language *http://www.perl.com* *http://www.perl.org* *http://www.perldoc.com* *http://www.perl.com/pub/v/faqs/* *http://www.perl.com/CPAN/* *http://www.perl.com/CPAN-local/src/* *http://www.perl.org/press/history.html* *http://history.perl.org/PerlTimeline.html* *http://www.perl.com/CPAN-local/authors/id/G/GB/GBARR/*
Perl DBD::Oracle	2	The Oracle driver for Perl DBI *http://dbi.symbolstone.org/cgi/moduledump?module=DBD:: Oracle* *http://velocity.activestate.com/docs/ActivePerl/site/lib/DBD/ Oracle.html* *http://www.perl.com/CPAN/modules/by-module/DBD/*
Perl DBI	2	The generic DataBase Interface for Perl *http://dbi.symbolstone.org* *http://dbi.symbolstone.org/doc/faq.html* *http://www.perl.com/reference/query.cgi?database* *http://velocity.activestate.com/docs/ActivePerl/site/lib/ DBI.html* *http://www.perl.com/CPAN/modules/by-module/DBI/* *http://velocity.activestate.com/docs/ActivePerl/faq/ActivePerl- faq2.html* *http://www.activestate.com/Products/ActivePerl/status.html*
Perlplus	3	The Perl/Tk Netscape plug-in *http://www.perl.com/CPAN-local/modules/by-authors/id/F/ FH/FHOLTRY/* *http://home.rmi.net/~fholtry/*

Table 1-2. Open Source Technologies and Related Areas (continued)

Tool or Application	Chapter	Description and Online Sites

Perl/Tk	3	The main GUI ToolKit for Perl
		http://www.xray.mpe.mpg.de/mailing-lists/ptk/
		http://www.cpan.org/doc/FAQs/tk/ptkTOC.html
		http://starbase.neosoft.com/~claird/comp.lang.perl.tk/
		  ptkFAQ.html
		http://www.pconline.com/~erc/perltk.htm
		http://mysite.directlink.net/gbarr/PerlTk/tk-modlist.html
		http://www.egroups.com/group/Perl-Tk/
		ftp://ftp.funet.fi/pub/languages/perl/CPAN/modules/
		  by-module/Tk/
		http://www.lehigh.edu/~sol0/ptk/ptk.html
		http://www.activestate.com/Products/ActivePerl/status.html

PHP	5	Major web scripting language *http://www.php.net* *http://www.php.net/manual/en/intro_history.php*
PHP and Oracle	5	Oracle connectivity for PHP *http://www.php.net/manual/ref.oracle.php*
Php-MyAdmin	6	PHP database administration tool *http://www.phpwizard.net/projects/phpMyAdmin/index.html*
Php-OracleAdmin	6	The Oracle port of PhpMyAdmin *http://www.phporacleadmin.org*
PLNet and PL/SQL	B	The open source PL/SQL project *http://plnet.org* *http://plnet.sourceforge.net* *http://www.gt.ed.net/keith/plsql/* *http://www.w3.org/TR/NOTE-OSD.html* *http://www.revealnet.com/Pipelines/PLSQL/index.htm* *http://www.revealnet.com*
Python	3	Major object-oriented scripting language *http://www.python.org* *http://www.python.org/topics/database/modules.html* *http://www.python.org/ftp/* *http://www.python.org/doc/FAQ.html#1.15* *http://www.python.org/ftp/python/2.0/* *http://www.activestate.com/Products/ActivePython/* *Download.html* *http://www.ActiveState.com/download/contrib/Microsoft/NT/* *http://www.ActiveState.com/download/contrib/Microsoft/9x/* *ftp://ftp.scriptics.com/pub/tcl/tcl8_3/*
QPL	9	The Qt licenses *http://www.trolltech.com/products/download/freelicense/* *license.html* *http://www.trolltech.com/products/purchase/pricing.html*
RPMs	3	Red Hat Package Manager for code distribution *http://rpm.redhat.com/RPM-HOWTO/index.html* *http://rpmfind.net* *http://www.python.org/2.0/*

Table 1-2. Open Source Technologies and Related Areas (continued)

Tool or Application	Chapter	Description and Online Sites
Solaris Unix	2	Freeware packages *http://sunfreeware.com* *http://sunfreeware.com/faq.html*
Squid	5	Web caching *http://www.squid-cache.org*
Tcl and Tcl/Tk	3	Major scripting language that innovated the original Tk GUI ToolKit *http://www.neosoft.com/tcl/* *http://www.tcltk.com* *http://sourceforge.net/foundry/tcl-foundry/* *ftp://ftp.neosoft.com/pub/tcl/* *http://dev.scriptics.com* *http://dev.scriptics.com/doc/tclHistory.html* *http://dev.scriptics.com/software/tcltk/downloadnow84.tml*
Tcl Expect	3	Automation extension for Tcl *http://expect.nist.gov*
Tcl GroupKit	3	Groupware development for Tcl *http://www.cpsc.ucalgary.ca/projects/grouplab/groupkit/*
Tcl *[incr Tcl]*	3	Object-oriented Tcl *http://tcltk.com/itcl/*
Tcl *[incr Tk]*	3	Object-oriented Tcl/Tk *http://tcltk.com/itk/*
Tcl *[incr Widgets]*	3	Mega-widget set for Tcl/Tk *http://tcltk.com/iwidgets/index.html*
Tcl Tix	3	The Tk Interface extension *http://tix.mne.com*
TclX	3	An important Tcl extension *http://www.neosoft.com/TclX/* *http://dev.scriptics.com/ftp/tclx/*
Tomcat	7	Java-based web serving *http://jakarta.apache.org/tomcat/index.html* *http://jakarta.apache.org/site/faqs.html* *http://jakarta.apache.org/tomcat/jakarta-tomcat/src/doc/index.html*
Turbine	5	A Java-based framework for web applications *http://java.apache.org/turbine/*
utPLSQL	B	The unit testing framework for PL/SQL *http://www.extremeprogramming.org* *http://oracle.oreilly.com/utplsql/* *http://www.egroups.com/group/utPLSQL/* *http://www.stevenfeuerstein.com*
VDK	9	The Visual Development Kit for GTK+ *http://www.guest.net/homepages/mmotta/VDKHome/vdkbuilder.html*

Table 1-2. Open Source Technologies and Related Areas (continued)

Tool or Application	Chapter	Description and Online Sites
VDKBuilder	9	Rapid Application Development for VDK *http://www.guest.net/homepages/mmotta/VDKHome/vdkbuilder.html*
ViennaSQL	8	The Java SQL GUI tool *http://sourceforge.net/projects/vienna/* *http://vienna.sourceforge.net* *http://developer.java.sun.com/developer/techDocs/hi/repository/*
World Wide Web	5	Information on the World Wide Web's founder *http://www.w3.org/People/Berners-Lee/*
WWWdb	6	Text-based searching within databases *http://wwwdb.org* *ftp://ftp.funet.fi/pub/languages/perl/CPAN/authors/id/G/GA/GAAS/* *ftp://ftp.funet.fi/pub/languages/perl/CPAN/authors/id/G/GB/GBARR/* *ftp://ftp.funet.fi/pub/languages/perl/CPAN/authors/id/G/GR/GRICHTER/* *ftp://ftp.funet.fi/pub/languages/perl/CPAN/authors/id/R/RB/RBOW/* *ftp://ftp.funet.fi/pub/languages/perl/CPAN/authors/id/M/MS/MSCHWERN/* *ftp://ftp.funet.fi/pub/languages/perl/CPAN/authors/id/N/NW/NWALSH/* *ftp://ftp.funet.fi/pub/languages/perl/CPAN/authors/id/S/ST/STBEY/* *http://linux.twc.de/wwwdb/*
wxPython	3	wxWindows for Python *http://wxPython.org* *ftp://ftp.gtk.org/pub/gtk/python/*
wxWindows	3	The C++ GUI framework for all operating systems *http://wxperl.sourceforge.net* *http://www.roebling.de* *http://www.wxwindows.org/*
X Windows System	9	The GUI windowing system originally for Unix *http://www.x.org* *http://www.gnu.ai.mit.edu/directory/X.html*
Zend	5	The PHP scripting engine *http://www.zend.com*

The Open Source Definition

This section contains the full text of the Open Source Definition we described earlier in this chapter. You will find the text, with any updates, at:

> *http://www.opensource.org/docs/definition_plain.html*

On the Web, you may encounter other examples of "open source" licenses, particularly in situations where corporations are distributing the source code for their applications (while still retaining strict proprietary control over it). You will generally recognize these situations because at some point you'll be asked to accept some kind of disclaimer before they allow you to continue a download. Just remember that the definition found at *http://www.opensource.org/osd.html* is the one "true" definition with which any other license provisions must comply. Accept no substitute—especially if you're thinking of helping to develop an open source project of your own.

Here is the text of the Open Source Definition, in italics, with an explanation following each section:

1. Free Redistribution

   The license may not restrict any party from selling or giving away the software as a component of an aggregate software distribution containing programs from several different sources. The license may not require a royalty or other fee for such sale.

   You can make as many copies of a program as you like to keep, sell, or give away. You don't have to pay anyone for this privilege.

2. Source Code

   The program must include source code, and must allow distribution in source code as well as compiled form. Where some form of a product is not distributed with source code, there must be a well-publicized means of obtaining the source code for no more than a reasonable reproduction cost—preferably, downloading via the Internet without charge. The source code must be the preferred form in which a programmer would modify the program. Deliberately obfuscated source code is not allowed. Intermediate forms such as the output of a preprocessor or translator are not allowed.

   The source code must be available for you to to test, fix, and explore program code. This is the fundamental tenet of open source, the open source equivalent of "thou shalt not kill." Clever tricks, such as deliberately making the source code unreadable or providing intermediate forms of code (such as the C code output from original Pro*C programs) violate this provision.

3. Derived Works

   The license must allow modifications and derived works, and must allow them to be distributed under the same terms as the license of the original software.

   You are allowed to change the original program in any way you wish (for example, in order to fix bugs or, in your opinion, improve the program). If you wish, you can then redistribute it under the same license as the original; alternatively, you may be allowed to choose another licensing type for derived works.

4. Integrity of the Author's Source Code

The license may restrict source-code from being distributed in modified form only if the license allows the distribution of "patch files" with the source code for the purpose of modifying the program at build time. The license must explicitly permit distribution of software built from modified source code. The license may require derived works to carry a different name or version number from the original software.

In order to protect the original program authors, an open source license may restrict the distribution of modified source code if it also allows you to distribute patch files to modify it indirectly. Consider an example from the everyday world. You may receive a book written by a friend, but you aren't allowed to scribble in it before handing it on to a third acquaintance; however, you are allowed to make copious notes and, instead, distribute them in a separate notebook, clearly indicating that you are the second author. The original author also has the right to keep the original name. If you create derived works, you may have to rename your product. Similarly, you cannot change the cover title of your friend's book, but under this model, you can copy the entire book word for word, add a few chapters (which you presumably think improves the book), and then republish it under another name.

5. No Discrimination Against Persons or Groups

The license must not discriminate against any person or group of persons.

The license cannot stipulate who can and cannot download the program. For instance, the license cannot say, "Everyone can download this program except Englishmen with Scottish-sounding names, or Americans with Irish-sounding ones." Fortunately for those of us suffering from such a condition, open source plays no favorites.

6. No Discrimination Against Field of Endeavor

The license must not restrict anyone from making use of the program in a specific field of endeavor. For example, it may not restrict the program from being used in a business, or from being used for genetic research.

This clause builds on the previous clause by stating that the license may not stipulate what you can or cannot do with the downloaded program—for example, "My program cannot be used to promote Anglo-American authorship collaboration." (This point has raised much debate within the open source community, but it has been concluded that potentially difficult political arguments should be left to courts and legislatures.)

7. Distribution of License

The rights attached to the program must apply to all to whom the program is redistributed without the need for execution of an additional license by those parties.

The license must come fully and automatically into force when the program is downloaded, and must not require that any secondary licenses be obtained. For example, the license cannot state, "Now that you've downloaded this program, you must apply to *andy_j_duncan@yahoo.com* for enhanced and specific permission to modify the program."

8. License Must Not Be Specific to a Product

The rights attached to the program must not depend on the program's being part of a particular software distribution. If the program is extracted from that distribution and used or distributed within the terms of the program's license, all parties to whom the program is redistributed should have the same rights as those that are granted in conjunction with the original software distribution.

The license cannot restrict your rights if you acquire it from other than the usual source. Therefore a license cannot say something like the following: "You only acquire full rights with this program if you download it within the software bundle designed by *sean.hull@pobox.com.*"

9. License Must Not Contaminate Other Software

The license must not place restrictions on other software that is distributed along with the licensed software. For example, the license must not insist that all other programs distributed on the same medium must be open-source software.

The license may not say something like, "You are only allowed full rights to this program if you use it on a Linux platform." You should be able to use the downloaded program with any other program combinations or on any platform you like, without losing any of the original rights.

For a shorter official description of the Open Source Definition, with a step-by-step rationale for each of the nine conditions, see:

   http://www.opensource.org/docs/definition.html

Conformance

The earliest versions of the Open Source Definition contained a tenth commandment, detailing the various acceptable license types (such as the Perl Artistic License). Like the black riders in *The Lord of the Rings*, however, the first nine steps of the definition were judged to be the important ones. The older conformance commentary was replaced by an objective certification program of marked and approved license types. For the latest details on this, check the following page:

   http://www.opensource.org/docs/certification_mark.html

2

Connecting to Oracle

The Oracle Call Interface (OCI) is the Oracle software that allows the outside world access to the hidden core of the Oracle database. An open source application—or any other type of non-Oracle program—can use OCI to connect directly to Oracle via its internal SQL engine. OCI is a complex product, and this short chapter can't do justice to all of its capabilities. We'll cover only the fundamentals here, examining the basic Application Programming Interface (API) of OCI and how it is typically used with open source software. We'll introduce OCI and its main functions, and we'll explain how it relates to Open DataBase Connectivity (ODBC) and Java DataBase Connectivity (JDBC).

Although you can access OCI directly, most developers prefer a simpler and more convenient interface. As an example of how open source applications use such interfaces to communicate with OCI, we'll take a close look at how Perl applications use the Perl Database Interface (DBI) module (and its Oracle-specific driver, DBD::Oracle) to connect to Oracle databases. We've chosen Perl here because it was one of the first open source languages to communicate directly with Oracle; the interface dates from 1990, with Kevin Stock's original work on Oraperl. We'll describe other interfaces in their respective chapters (for example, Tcl with its Oratcl interface, and Python with its DBOracle interface, in Chapter 3, *Tcl, Perl, and Python*). Throughout this book, we'll mention, as appropriate, how various open source tools make use of OCI.

The Oracle Call Interface API

The Oracle Call Interface is the comprehensive API that is used to connect internally to the Oracle database server. OCI is based on C and provides all the requirements you might need to support your Oracle-based applications, including the following:

- High performance

- Security features, including user authentication

- Scalability

- Full and dynamic access to Oracle8*i* objects

- User session handles, dynamic connections, and session management

- Multi-threaded capabilities

- Support for accessing special Oracle8 datatypes, such as large objects (LOB), BFILE, and LONG

- Transactions

- Full character set support

At the most basic level, virtually all outside programs, from web applications to standalone GUI applications, interact with Oracle through this program layer. (The one major exception is the JDBC client-side driver, which we'll discuss shortly.)

Fortunately, the OCI libraries are automatically available in every Oracle database installation; there is no special installation process. You'll generally discover the appropriate files under the *$ORACLE_HOME/lib* and *$ORACLE_HOME/include* directories. Most open source applications have therefore accepted Oracle's open invitation to the database, and they use OCI to gain their front-door entry into the world of Oracle programming.

As Figure 2-1 indicates, OCI acts as the primary port of destination for every connection to and from the server. To simplify OCI's sometimes complex operations, other database APIs can also be wrapped around the OCI. Examples of such wrap-around APIs include the popular ODBC, the Java-based JDBC (at least partially, as we'll explain), and the Perl DBI. These three APIs are described in the following sections.

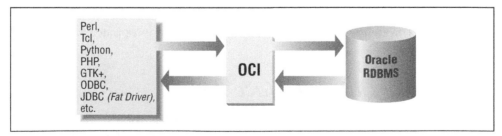

Figure 2-1. OCI links Oracle to the outside world

ODBC: Open DataBase Connectivity

Open DataBase Connectivity (ODBC) is an API designed to ease the task of communicating with different database types from within the same outside application program. ODBC, which was championed originally by Microsoft and the client/server architectures, following initial work by the SQL Access Group on their CLI standard,* provides all the functionality of the standardized SQL language. If a database supports the SQL/92 standard, then once you place the ODBC bridge between your programs and the Oracle server, you need only talk to the ODBC API; you don't need to worry about any specific Oracle or OCI code requirements.

If OCI is complicated and ODBC is simple, then why not just use ODBC, especially since you can use ODBC identically with other databases? There are several reasons why open source systems have generally tended towards using the home-grown OCI, rather than going through ODBC:

ODBC's extra layer reduces performance
> Because ODBC merely hides OCI from you rather than bypassing it, it becomes just another wraparound layer you have to wade through in order to get your data in and out of the database. If you can use OCI directly, you can cut out the middleman, increasing performance in the process.

ODBC provides a "one-size-fits-all" service
> Because ODBC is limited to the basic SQL standard (in order to work across every database type), using it means that you won't have access to some of the special features of Oracle—for example, the various types of LOBs (large objects). If you want to make use of these features, even occasionally, you can't use ODBC. With ODBC, you must remain entirely, and at all times, within the confines of its restricted set of universal functionality.

OCI is optimized for Oracle
> OCI is specifically designed to reduce Oracle memory usage and data round-trips, optimize the multi-threaded server (MTS), and generally work as efficiently as possible with its native Oracle database type. If you use ODBC's more generalized API, you won't reap the benefits of this specialization.

JDBC: Java DataBase Connectivity

Java DataBase Connectivity (JDBC) is very similar to ODBC in that it provides a "generic" database API for manipulating data across a wide range of database types. Also, you must use it with Java programs that employ the industry-standard *java.sql* packages. Oracle provides access to a number of different JDBC drivers

---

* The SQL Access Group was a consortium of vendors formed in the early 1990s. Their CLI (Call Level Interface) was an API attempt to support SQL across disparate systems.

that connect to the Oracle database. We'll discuss all of these in Chapter 7, *Java*. For now, though, we'll focus on the two driver types most often used for Oracle/ Java programming:

- The Thin JDBC Client-Side TCP/IP-Based Driver ("Type IV")

- The Fat JDBC/OCI JDBC Driver ("Type II")

As Figure 2-2 shows, the Fat JDBC/OCI Driver is similar to ODBC in that it uses OCI directly in order to access Oracle, whereas the Thin JDBC Driver does not. If your client-side Java programs use the Thin Driver (across a TCP/IP bridge), they can access their target Oracle databases directly without troubling OCI. This is achieved by building an OCI-like set of functions into the Thin Driver, thereby making it quite a portable solution.

In most systems, such as Perl, your Oracle access drivers must reside on the same machine as the database to enable you to pick up its OCI libraries. However, the Thin JDBC Driver is always much slower than the Fat Driver, because it has to carry around the baggage of this complex OCI-like burden. If you find that performance becomes a more pressing need than portability, you may therefore become tempted to employ the Fat Driver instead. We'll describe these tradeoffs in some detail in Chapter 7.

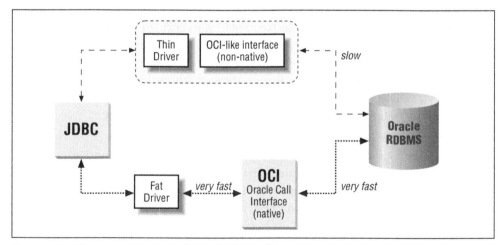

Figure 2-2. The two main types of Oracle drivers for JDBC

OCI Functions

There are hundreds of OCI functions, so we won't try to present a complete summary here. Table 2-1 lists the OCI functions most often used in the kinds of applications discussed in this book.

Table 2-1. OCI Function Summary

OCI Function	Description
OCIAttrSet()	Sets a handle attribute
OCIAttrGet()	Gets a handle attribute
OCIBindByName()	Binds a variable with a SQL placeholder by name
OCIBindByPos()	Binds a program variable and a SQL placeholder by position
OCIDefineByPos()	Defines a selected item by position for the output data buffer
OCIDescribeAny()	Describes an existing schema object
OCIEnvInit()	Initializes an environment handle
OCIErrorGet()	Returns an Oracle error message
OCIHandleAlloc()	Returns an already allocated handle
OCIHandleFree()	Deallocates a handl
OCIInitialize()	Initializes the OCI environment
OCILobRead()	Reads part of a LOB into a buffer stream
OCILobWrite()	Writes a buffer stream into a LOB
OCILogoff()	Logs off an Oracle database connection
OCILogon()	Creates an Oracle logon connection
OCIStmtExecute()	Executes a prepared SQL statement
OCIStmtFetch()	Fetches rows of data
OCIStmtPrepare()	Prepares a SQL statement
OCITransCommit()	Commits a transaction
OCITransRollback()	Rolls back a transaction
OCITransStart()	Starts a transaction
OCIServerAttach()	Establishes an access path to a data source
OCIServerDetach()	Deletes access to a data source
OCISessionBegin()	Creates a user session on the server

You'll find complete documentation on all of the OCI calls and other important programming information on the following web pages:

http://technet.oracle.com/tech/oci/
> The main home page for all things OCI on the Oracle Technology Network (OTN).

http://technet.oracle.com/doc/server.815/a67846/toc.htm
> The comprehensive *Oracle Call Interface Programmer's Guide* for Oracle8*i* (Version 8.1.5) which includes full descriptions for the literally hundreds of OCI functions available.

Our focus in this chapter is on accessing OCI from Perl's excellent connectivity tools. What if you want to go head to head with OCI without an intermediary? In addition to looking at the documentation listed above, you will learn a lot by examining existing code wherever possible, and by taking liberal advantage of the samples you'll find in the *$ORACLE_HOME/rdbms/demo* directory.

For more serious, full-blown examples of OCI programming, you might want to check out the code for some of the Oracle applications and tools we'll describe in later chapters of this book. Virtually all of them use OCI if you dig deep enough within the source code.

 If you're working with Oracle 8.1.5 on Linux, be sure to have the latest Version 8.1.5 patched up to 8.1.5.0.2, and note that some OCI samples have trouble compiling unless you're using at least Red Hat 5.2. Unfortunately, there were a lot of changes in *glibc* between some versions of Red Hat, necessitating a number of compatibility libraries (which basically map old *glibc* calls to new ones). There is a *glibc* patch from Oracle to cover this; the easiest way to find the latest version of this patch is to check on the *http://technet.oracle.com* web site. Just carry out a search on "glibc".

Perl

Perl is perhaps the most popular of all open source tools, and the earliest to appear of the major open scripting languages. It is also used frequently to write database applications. We'll explore the language in more depth in Chapter 3, where we also discuss other scripting languages. For now, we'll focus on how Perl is used to connect to Oracle databases via its Perl Database Interface (DBI) module. (Perl DBI provides a generic interface to a variety of databases, including Oracle.)

Perl has become an important tool for Oracle DBAs and developers because it is operating system–independent, powerful, flexible, remarkably quick to code, and extremely fast in execution. These capabilities are especially important if you are working in a rapidly changing environment where one day you might be populating a data warehouse from a difficult data source, and the next day generating a dynamic web application. Today's distributed corporate databases, so vital for the success of any business, have become almost too complex for their own survival, and many DBAs and developers have found that Perl is one of the best ways to tackle this complexity. With a script here and a script there, Perl can turn a potential data implosion into a real-world information explosion. Perl's magical ability is all the more magical because it's also freely available.

In the following sections we'll describe how you can obtain and install Perl on Unix, Linux, and Win32 systems. We'll also describe how the Perl DBI and DBD:: Oracle modules let Perl programs access the Oracle database, and we'll look at some examples of simple Perl programs that interact with Oracle.

These are the main web sites for Perl:

http://www.perl.com
http://www.perl.org
> The main Perl portals

http://www.activestate.com
> The ActiveState Win32 Perl portal site

A tutorial for basic Perl is outside the scope of this book. Fortunately, there are many excellent web sites and books containing the information you need to get going. We've collected references to what we consider to be the best Perl books in Appendix C, *For Further Reading*.

Later in this chapter we'll describe why Perl has become such an integral part of database programming, particularly on the Web, and how it connects so cleanly to Oracle databases. First, though, we'll describe how to install Perl on various platforms.

Installing Perl on Unix and Linux

There are three basic ways to get started with Perl on Unix and Linux systems, the third of which is best for reasons we'll explain shortly:

1. Find Perl already installed on your system.
2. Download a binary executable which will build Perl for you out of the box.
3. Configure and build Perl yourself from the source code.

Finding Perl already installed on your system

The first way to get started with Perl is obviously the easiest, though certainly the least fun. If Perl exists somewhere on your system, you can usually find it using the following command:

```
$ perl -v
```

This command should work similarly for most operating systems (assuming that *perl* is in your PATH environment variable, for locating system executables). Alternative commands you can use to find Perl under Unix include the following:

```
$ type perl
$ which perl
$ whence perl
$ locate perl
$ find / -name "perl*" -print
```

The large downside of finding Perl already on your system is that it may already be controlled by someone else, or it may be an old version. For example, you might find Perl 4, but you'll need Perl 5 for DBI. If you start with the fresh slate of

Perl 5 (such as 5.6), you'll also have the latest and greatest version of Perl and therefore be able to experiment a lot more.

Building Perl from a prebuilt package

This leads us to option 2, building Perl from a prebuilt executable binary. Even if this option is available to you, it has several disadvantages in comparison to building Perl from source, mainly because a prebuilt binary may not match the configuration of your local system:

- It may point to libraries that do not exist.

- It may have been compiled originally with C compiler switches and options that your system does not fully support.

- It may assume default paths that do not currently exist.

We therefore recommend that you always employ the build-from-source method (assuming that you are given that option). If you do need to go down the prepackaged route, be aware that most proprietary flavors of Unix do have some great freeware sites. Some of the best we've found are:

http://sunfreeware.com
http://sunfreeware.com/faq.html
>   For Solaris

http://ftp.univie.ac.at/aix/
>   For AIX

http://jazz.external.hp.com/src/index.html
>   For HP-UX

You'll find the appropriate installation instructions at each site. Here we'll run through the typical steps for Solaris. These are only guidelines; be sure that you obtain and read carefully the most up-to-date installation information for your own platform:

1. Download the latest Perl package, for your version of Solaris, from the web site.

2. Unzip the download (using either *gunzip* or *gzip –d*) as the root user.

3. Use *pkgadd –d* to add the package to your system.

For example, the following commands, issued as the *root* user, would install the standard Perl package:

```
$ gzip -d perl-5.005_03-sol7-sparc-local.gz
$ pkgadd -d perl-5.005_03-sol7-sparc-local
```

These kinds of steps (as specified on the appropriate site FAQ or within any accompanying *README* files) will build a fully functioning Perl system for you, adding the Perl executable to somewhere like */usr/local/bin/perl*. You'll follow similar steps for most of the other flavors of Unix.

 With some download browser screens, the prebuilt packages occasionally download without the **.gz* suffix. This confuses the *gunzip* program. If this problem occurs, you can solve it by simply renaming the downloaded file with the additional **.gz* suffixed extension.

Perl and Linux

Fortunately, virtually all of the latest distributions of Linux usually come with a fairly up-to-date version of Perl already on board. You may wish to upgrade this version at some point, however, and some vendors make this easy for you with various package-adding management facilities similar to those described above for Solaris.

For any of the Unix-like systems, including Linux, there is a third installation option; you may also want to install directly from source, as we describe in the following sections.

Building Perl from source: Phase 1

We think installing Perl from source is by far the best method for Unix, especially because it is now such a heavily automated process. It is rare now for Perl *not* to build successfully out of the box. For the latest information on building Perl from source, the best web site is CPAN, the Comprehensive Perl Archive Network. Check out:

> *http://www.perl.com/CPAN/*

The *README.html* file there will probably direct you to download the most recent stable version of Perl (which is usually several bug-fixed versions behind the latest "bleeding edge" development version). This can usually be found at:

> *http://www.perl.com/CPAN-local/src/stable.tar.gz*

If you want to download Perl from another site, check out the many well-signposted mirror FTP sites listed on the CPAN site. Once you locate the appropriate download site, follow these basic steps:

1. Download the tar file.

2. Unpack it.

3. Follow the instructions contained in the appropriate *README* and *INSTALL* files. These can vary widely from one operating system to another, but generally consist of running an intelligent and friendly configuration program,

which interrogates you and your machine for essential compilation information. In each new release, this configuration program becomes ever simpler.

4. Once the *configure* program has built up the required *make* files, you are just about ready to compile Perl.

If you don't have a C compiler . . .

Did we mention that you need a C compiler before you can complete your Perl installation? Not having a C compiler can become a bit of a Catch-22 situation, as compiling something like *gcc* from source can get a bit tricky (as you need at least some kind of basic C compiler to bootstrap *gcc*).* This process is perhaps beyond the realms of this book, though help is at hand. One of the best things to do in this situation is to get hold of one of the *gcc* packages from the freeware sites:

ftp://ftp.sunfreeware.com/pub/freeware/sparc/7/gcc-2.95.2-sol7-sparc-local.gz
   For Solaris

http://ftp.univie.ac.at/aix/aix432/gnu.gcc-2.95.2.1.exe
   For AIX

http://jazz.external.hp.com/src/gnu/download2_95_2.html
   For HP-UX

Fortunately, Linux systems almost always come with a pretty advanced version of the *gcc* C compiler already on board. If you want to get hold of the latest package, however, your Linux retailer will often provide you with a download site for the latest package—for example:

   http://www.redhat.com/swr/i386/gcc-java-2.95.1-3.i386.html
   http://packages.debian.org/stable/devel/gcc.html

However if you really want to win your open source spurs and compile *gcc* itself purely from source then you'll want to follow the relevant instructions at this site:

   http://gcc.gnu.org

When you've succeeded in compiling *gcc* itself, you acquire "total hero" status and can hold your head high in cyber cafes.

Once you've got a compiler on board, the Perl installation process will be looking for a generic *cc* C compiler (unless you alter this behavior by following the appropriate *INSTALL* file instructions). Make sure that your system can locate a *cc* program (even if it's only a symbolic link created by something like the *ln –s cc /usr/ bin/gcc* command). You may also want to make sure this is really a disguised *gcc*

---

* Most Unix systems come with some sort of C compiler. If yours doesn't, you'll almost certainly find a freeware site somewhere (e.g., *SunFreeware.com*) for that particular flavor of Unix, and you're likely to find a *gcc* C compiler package there. (Users of that system wouldn't have it any other way!)

program, because that's what Perl prefers. For instance, try to reach a situation similar to the following:

```
$ type cc
cc is /usr/bin/cc
$ ls -la /usr/bin/cc
lrwxrwxrwx  1 root root  3 Mar 18  2000 /usr/bin/cc -> gcc
$ type gcc
gcc is /usr/bin/gcc
```

Building Perl from source: Phase 2

Once you have your downloaded package and relevant C compiler in place, you can actually run the full Perl installation process as the *root* user. Follow these steps:

1. Unpack the latest stable Perl download:

   ```
   $ ls *.gz
   stable.tar.gz
   $ gzip -d stable.tar.gz
   $ ls *.tar
   stable.tar
   $ tar xvf stable.tar
   ```

2. Once this is unpacked, move into the appropriate directory and check out the *README* and *INSTALL* files:

   ```
   $ ls
   perl-5.6.0
   $ cd perl-5.6.0
   $ vi README INSTALL
   ```

3. Unless you want to change any of the defaults to match your system, the *INSTALL* file will ask you to carry out something like the following:

   ```
   $ rm -f config.sh Policy.sh
   $ sh Configure -de
   $ make
   $ make test
   $ make install
   ```

4. Though unlikely, you may get some errors on the way when running this set of instructions. If you do (and it has been known to happen), you must sort each step out before continuing with the next one. Once you think you've made it cleanly through each of these five steps (which should take just a few minutes), the magic phrase to check for is:

   ```
   Installation complete
   ```

5. Type in *perl –v* to confirm your success (as in Figure 2-3) and then slap a well-deserved camel badge on the side of your machine. Welcome to the clan.

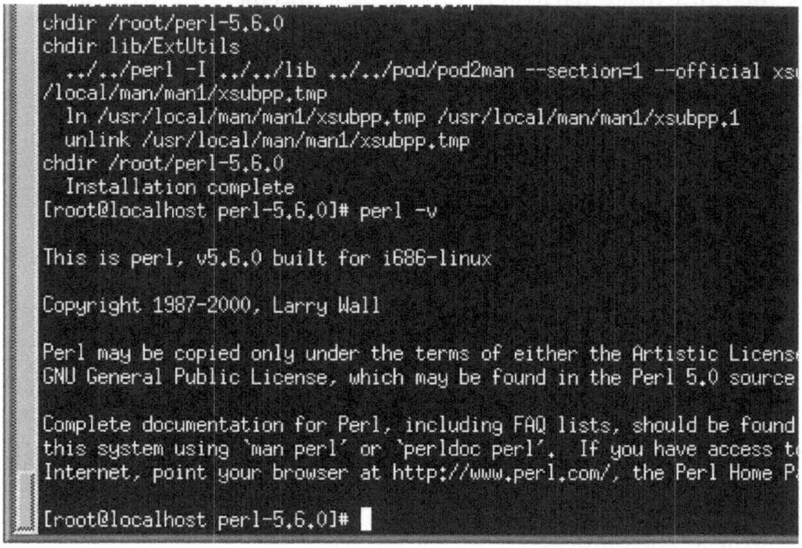

```
chdir /root/perl-5.6.0
chdir lib/ExtUtils
   ../../perl -I ../../lib ../../pod/pod2man --section=1 --official xs
/local/man/man1/xsubpp.tmp
   ln /usr/local/man/man1/xsubpp.tmp /usr/local/man/man1/xsubpp.1
   unlink /usr/local/man/man1/xsubpp.tmp
chdir /root/perl-5.6.0
   Installation complete
[root@localhost perl-5.6.0]# perl -v

This is perl, v5.6.0 built for i686-linux

Copyright 1987-2000, Larry Wall

Perl may be copied only under the terms of either the Artistic License
GNU General Public License, which may be found in the Perl 5.0 source

Complete documentation for Perl, including FAQ lists, should be found
this system using `man perl' or `perldoc perl'. If you have access t
Internet, point your browser at http://www.perl.com/, the Perl Home P

[root@localhost perl-5.6.0]# ▊
```

Figure 2-3. The final stages of installing Perl from source

Installing Perl on Windows

For Win32, downloading and installing ActiveState's ActivePerl is almost too easy in comparison to Unix. It makes wizened old Unix hackers suspicious that there must be more to it. If you follow these steps, though, you should have Perl up and running on your own particular Win32 system in just a few minutes:

1. Download the latest binary executable build of ActivePerl from the ActiveState site:

   http://www.activestate.com/activeperl/
       Home page

   http://www.activestate.com/Products/ActivePerl/Download.html
       Download*

2. This file will be called something like the following (downloading this could be longest step in this process, because the file below was over 7 MB):

       ActivePerl-5.6.0.623-MSWin32-x86.msi

3. If you haven't done so already, get hold of the appropriate Microsoft Windows program installer, MSI (which comes automatically with Windows 2000):

       http://www.microsoft.com/downloads/

---

* This download site also refers to every other possible download you may require to get your ActivePerl system going on your own particular Win32 platform (for example, you'll find DCOM downloads, etc.).

The ActivePerl pages should direct you to the exact address of the latest installer product that you will need.

4. Install the Windows installer itself, if it's not already on your system, by double-clicking on it (this installation may be almost instantaneous).

5. Once this is installed, double-click on the actual ActivePerl download, as in Figure 2-4.

6. After you answer some questions about where you want Perl to be installed, Win32 Perl should then be automatically installed directly onto your system, in the standard Win32 way. You can then test this with the *perl –v* test (as also shown in Figure 2-4).

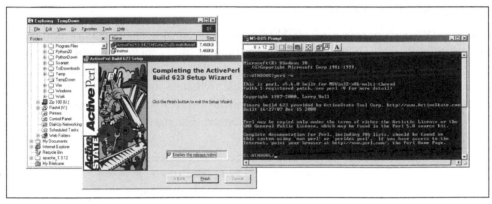

Figure 2-4. Installing and then testing ActivePerl

Perl DBI

If you're going to write Perl programs that communicate with your Oracle database, you need to install the Perl DBI module in addition to the standard Perl distribution. Perl DBI is a Perl 5 module used to connect Perl to Oracle (and other) databases.

Oraperl

An ancestral database connection program called Oraperl was available in Perl 4. After initial work in 1990, this program was created and consolidated by Oracle DBA Kevin Stock, in 1991, as a way to avoid using SQL*Plus for writing reports. Although Oraperl has been superseded by Perl's DBD::Oracle module, there is still a home page for it at:

http://www.geocities.com/Heartland/Meadows/2990/oraperl.html

With Oraperl, Kevin used OCI to bridge directly into the Oracle database, while using Perl to avoid having to get too low down into the OCI code. Over time, other similar Perl 4 programs appeared, such as Michael Peppler's Sybperl, designed for communication with the Sybase database.

ODBC and Perl DBI

In a parallel development, a Perl-based group had been working since September of 1992 on a specification for DBPerl, a database-independent specification for Perl 4. After 18 months, or so, they were ready to start implementing DBPerl. However, at this point, Larry Wall was just starting to release the alpha version of object-oriented Perl 5. Taking advantage of Perl 5 and the earlier CLI work from the SQL Access Group, the DBPerl group laid the foundations of Perl DBI within an object-oriented framework and created the new architecture in a similar form to that employed by ODBC (shown in Figure 2-5).

With the DBI architecture, you could transparently employ just one Perl module to bridge towards every other database type. Behind the scenes, Perl DBI required a database-dependent driver to provide the bridge to the specific database. In Oracle's case, this is Tim Bunce's DBD::Oracle, which is, in essence, another wrapper for OCI. Tim also wrote the Perl 5 emulation layer for Oraperl, enabling the gradual switchover to Perl DBI and DBD::Oracle, basing this upon Version 2.4 of Kevin Stock's original Oraperl.

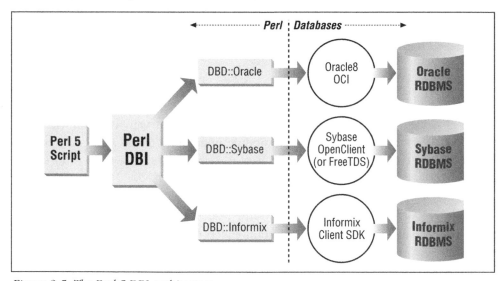

Figure 2-5. The Perl 5 DBI architecture

With Perl DBI, all the hard work of dealing with the OCI libraries has already been done for you. You need to concentrate only on including the appropriate Perl DBI API calls in your scripts. We won't try to describe all of the capabilities of the Perl DBI here, but Table 2-2 provides a summary of the main calls (DBI class methods).

Table 2-2. Perl DBI Summary

DBI Function	Description
available_drivers()	Returns a list of all available DBD drivers
data_sources()	Lists all databases available to a named DBD driver
connect()	Establishes a database connection
disconnect()	Disconnects a session from the database
err()	Returns the database engine error code
errstr()	Provides the database error message
prepare()	Prepares a single SQL statement for later execution
execute()	Executes a single prepared SQL statement
do()	Prepares and executes a single SQL statement
bind_param()	Binds a value within a prepared SQL statement
commit()	Commits a transaction
rollback()	Rolls back a transaction
table_info()	Fetches back information about a table
fetchrow_arrayref()	Fetches a row of data into a referenced array
fetchrow_array()	Fetches a row of data into an array
selectrow_array()	*prepare()*, *execute()*, and *fetchrow_array()* in one call
func()	Used to call database-specific functionality

There are two important code switches for use when establishing the initial database connection:

RaiseError
Used to force applications to raise fatal errors

AutoCommit
Switches explicit transactions on or off

The following are the main web sites for Perl DBI and DBD::Oracle:

http://dbi.symbolstone.org
The main Perl DBI home page

http://dbi.symbolstone.org/cgi/moduledump?module=DBD::Oracle
The main DBD::Oracle page

http://dbi.symbolstone.org/doc/faq.html
The main Perl DBI FAQ

http://www.perl.com/reference/query.cgi?database
The main Perl.com database page

http://velocity.activestate.com/docs/ActivePerl/site/lib/DBI.html
ActiveState's DBI page

http://velocity.activestate.com/docs/ActivePerl/site/lib/DBD/Oracle.html
    ActiveState's DBD::Oracle page

In addition to the main Perl DBI web site, which always carries the latest information, the ActivePerl DBI and DBD::Oracle pages are also excellent places for examining all of the DBI and DBD::Oracle code documentation online for the current versions ActivePerl itself is using.

The definitive book on the subject of Perl DBI is *Programming the Perl DBI* (also known as the "Cheetah Book"), by Alligator Descartes and Tim Bunce; see Appendix C for details.

Private DBD::Oracle database handle functions

There are several related DBD::Oracle functions called through the *func()* method, related to Oracle PL/SQL, which we'll demonstrate later in two examples. These are summarized in Table 2-3.

Table 2-3. DBD::Oracle Private Methods

DBD::Oracle Function	Description
plsql_errstr	Returns potential error text from the USER_ERRORS table
dbms_output_enable	Enables the DBMS_OUTPUT package for use with Perl
dbms_output_get	Gets a single line, or all available lines, using the DBMS_OUTPUT.GET_LINE call
dbms_output_put	Puts messages using the DBMS_OUTPUT.PUT_LINE call

---

The Future of DBD::Oracle

The combination of Perl DBI with DBD::Oracle is a very powerful one; we can't think of anything offered by another technology that it can't do. And if its author, Tim Bunce, should ever hear of such a thing, we're sure he'll be quick to release another version of DBD::Oracle onto CPAN. He is also developing another new Perl module, OCI::Oracle, which will make Perl's access to Oracle even faster and more wide-ranging.

Installing Perl DBI and DBD::Oracle

Once you have Perl installed, you'll need to install the Perl DBI module and its associated Oracle driver, the DBD::Oracle module, over Perl. We'll cover the two main installation paths in this section: one for Unix and Linux systems and the other for Windows systems.

Installing Perl DBI on Unix and Linux

Installing DBI and DBD::Oracle on Unix systems is almost always done from the source code. These are the central locations for the source:

http://www.perl.com/CPAN/modules/by-module/DBI/
http://www.perl.com/CPAN/modules/by-module/DBD/

Perl DBI installation is very similar to the installation of Perl we showed earlier in this chapter:

1. Download the latest stable Perl DBI compressed file.

2. Unpack the downloaded file.

3. Follow the onboard installation instructions (which may change over time).

4. Following in tandem, download the DBD::Oracle driver package and then go through the same installation sequence. You should also be sure you have the ORACLE_HOME, ORACLE_SID, and other environment variables set to enable the Oracle driver to pick up the correct OCI code living under ORACLE_HOME.

5. When you run *make test*, the Oracle driver will try to connect to your database. You can use the DBI environment variables DBI_USER, DBI_PASS, and DBI_DSN to ensure that DBI can connect to your already running Oracle database, or you can use the ORACLE_USERID environment variable. If you set this variable, set it to something like *scott/tiger@orcl*.

Tempting as it may to skip reading the documentation, we want you to avoid Homer Simpson–like "Doh!" situations. Believe us, it's well worth reading through every word of the *README* and *INSTALL* files distributed with the related DBI and DBD modules. If you do hit any problems, you'll almost certainly find the relevant explanatory note tucked deep inside the installation notes.

We'll now run through a full Unix DBI installation here, to complete the Perl 5.6 load we showed earlier:

1. For the first step, as the *root* user, make sure the Perl version you installed earlier is set up correctly:

   ```
   $ type perl
   perl is hashed (/usr/bin/perl)
   $ perl -v
   This is perl, v5.6.0 built for i686-linuxafter........
   ```

2. If you're happy with this output, carry on with the Perl DBI installation:

   ```
   $ gzip -d DBI-1.14.tar.gz
   $ tar xvf DBI-1.14.tar
   ```

```
$ cd DBI-1.14
$ vi README
```

3. Follow the standard Perl *README* instructions:

```
$ perl Makefile.PL
$ make
$ make test
$ make install
```

Perl DBI is now successfully installed, but to make use of it we have to get DBD::Oracle going as well:

1. At this point, make sure your test-target Oracle database is running, with the appropriate listener up. Also ensure that as *root*, you have the correct Oracle environment variables set up (including the special ORACLE_USERID mentioned earlier). You may choose to use TWO_TASK instead of ORACLE_SID:

```
$ ORACLE_HOME=/u01/app/oracle/product/8.1.5
$ export ORACLE_HOME
$ ORACLE_SID=orcl
$ export ORACLE_SID
$ ORACLE_USERID=scott/tiger@orcl
$ export ORACLE_USERID
```

2. As a final environment gotcha, you may also need to have your LD_LIBRARY_PATH environment variable pointing to all the right places to ensure that DBD::Oracle can pick up the OCI libraries:

```
$ LD_LIBRARY_PATH=$LD_LIBRARY_PATH:$ORACLE_HOME/lib
$ export LD_LIBRARY_PATH
```

3. We're now ready to unpack DBD::Oracle:

```
$ gzip -d DBD-Oracle-1.06.tar.gz
$ tar xvf DBD-Oracle-1.06.tar
$ cd DBD-Oracle-1.06
$ vi README
```

4. Again, you'll probably be asked to carry out the following steps:

```
$ perl Makefile.PL
$ make
$ make test
$ make install
```

You may find you'll have the most chance of encountering the odd "challenge" on the crucial *make test* step. Before you look at anything else, make sure that you have ORACLE_USERID and LD_LIBRARY_PATH set correctly, confirm your Oracle database is up (with plenty of memory available in the shared pool) and the Oracle listener is responding correctly to something like a remote SQL*Plus session (these few steps should get rid of 80% of the gremlins). Don't run *make install* until any problems you do have are sorted out, because we guarantee they'll come back to bite you.

Once you have successfully completed the *make install* step, lots of Perl DBI documentation will have been automatically installed while you weren't looking. To check this out, run the following pair of commands:

```
$ perldoc DBD::Oracle
$ perldoc DBI
```

Running *perldoc DBI* is particularly useful, because you will gain instant access to a full description of the entire API, with numerous worked-out examples. Moving onwards, now that DBI is fully installed, you may be itching to run your first script. We'll get to that shortly; for now, though, we must cover Windows.

Installing Perl DBI on Windows

As with the basic Perl install, ActiveState has created a virtually pain-free Perl 5.6 package installation process for Win32 systems. You can install Perl DBI fairly rapidly by following the instructions in this section. Before you do so, however, check out the following FAQ site, where you will find an expanded version of these instructions:

> *http://velocity.activestate.com/docs/ActivePerl/faq/ActivePerl-faq2.html*

1. Make sure you're connected to the Internet[*] and then visit the following page:

    > *http://www.activestate.com/Products/ActivePerl/status.html*

2. Choose the Perl packages you want to install; in this case, we are installing the following versions of Perl DBI and DBD::Oracle:

    > *DBI.ppd*
    > *DBD-Oracle8.ppd*

3. At the MS-DOS command line, back on your home machine, type in:

    ```
    ppm
    ```

4. This should bring up the PPM program prompt (remember that PPM was automatically installed earlier when you loaded the ActivePerl 5.6 version). Now type:

    ```
    install DBI
    ```

5. When this completes, type:

    ```
    install DBD-Oracle8
    ```

6. Quit out of the PPM program and the installation process is complete.

Yes, that's really all there is to it.

---

[*] You may need to set an environment variable, HTTP_proxy, to the name of your proxy server, if you're connected to the Internet through either a firewall or a proxy server. You will find information on further restrictions on using this at the FAQ site mentioned earlier.

Perl DBI and OCI

As we described earlier, Perl DBI actually uses OCI behind the scenes to make the connection to the Oracle database. This section will show how the two work together. We'll start with an example of a standard kind of Perl DBI script.

Basic Perl DBI example

Our first Perl DBI script (in Example 2-1) will simply connect to Oracle, run a straightforward SQL SELECT statement, print out the results, and finally log off from the database. We've highlighted certain key statements that we'll explain at the end of the example.

 Before you run this script, once again make sure that you have set the ORACLE_HOME and LD_LIBRARY_PATH environment variables correctly, as described earlier for the DBD::Oracle installation *make test* step.

Example 2-1. Basic DBI with HelloMiller.pl

```perl
use strict;
use DBI;

# Connect to Oracle database, making sure AutoCommit is
# turned off and potential errors are raised.

my $dbh =
    DBI->connect( 'dbi:Oracle:orcl',
                  'scott',
                  'tiger',
                  { RaiseError => 1,
                    AutoCommit => 0
                  }
                );

# Create the SQL.

my $sql = qq{ SELECT ENAME, JOB, SAL, DEPTNO FROM EMP };

# Prepare the SQL and execute.

my $sth = $dbh->prepare( $sql );
$sth->execute();

# Fetch output rows into array, plus prepare a
# print formatter for the results.

while ( my($ename, $job, $sal, $deptno) = $sth->fetchrow_array) {
```

Example 2-1. Basic DBI with HelloMiller.pl (continued)

```
    # Print out the formatted results.

    printf("%-10s %-9s %7.2d %2d", $ename, $job, $sal, $deptno);

    # If you find MILLER, say Hello! :-)

    if ($ename =~ /MILLER/){
       # Miller's Crossing...
       print ", Hello Miller!";
    }
    print "\n";
}

# Disconnect.
$dbh->disconnect();
```

What is going on in this example? First, the *HelloMiller.pl* program loads the *DBI.pm* Perl package with the following line:

```
    use DBI;
```

Note that you don't have to explicitly mention the DBD::Oracle module here. Perl DBI will work this out for you from the first parameter in the *DBI->connect()* function call.) Once we have a valid database connection, we can then prepare and execute the SQL, format the output, and then check for the appearance of MILLER, a favorite employee of ours. This is done using a basic example of Perl's regular expression capabilities. Once the SQL cursor loop is complete, we disconnect before the program exits. You can see the various output results in Figure 2-6; that figure shows the same script being run in two different operating system environments.

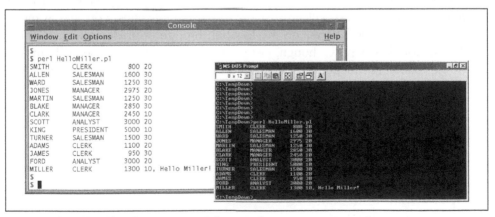

Figure 2-6. HelloMiller.pl running on Solaris and Win32

Understanding how Perl DBI works with OCI

Now that we've seen the magic in action, let's demonstrate the actual linkage between Perl DBI and Oracle OCI. To track down this mysterious smoke trail, we'll work through just one of the DBI calls in *HelloMiller.pl*, our vital attempt to connect to the target Oracle database.

The *DBI->connect()* function's first port of call is within the *DBI-1.14/DBI.pm* Perl file and, unsurprisingly enough, the enclosed *connect()* subroutine. Two of the more interesting calls within this method are:

```
my $drh = $class->install_driver($driver);
$dbh = $drh->$connect_meth($dsn, $user, $pass, $attr);
```

As mentioned earlier, Perl DBI works out which driver you want to use via the first parameter supplied to *DBI->connect()*. It then calls the relevant connection method for this driver in order to return the required database handle (which is ultimately stored in *$dbh*, the conventional name for this variable).

Now that we have obtained the driver, our traced call can route through to the *DBD-Oracle-1.06/Oracle.pm* Perl file, where it calls the corresponding *connect()* method that is specific to this database type. The crucial lines in the *Oracle.pm* Perl file are:

```
# Call Oracle OCI logon func in Oracle.xs file
# and populate internal handle data.
DBD::Oracle::db::_login($dbh, $dbname, $user, $auth, $attr)
   or return undef;
```

By using Perl's linkage to backend C via a technique called XS, this call is routed through to a compiled C file, *DBD-Oracle-1.06/dbimp.c*, that contains the vital *dbd_db_login6()* function. This is the actual place where the attempt at a login finally occurs. So that you will understand all the complexities, you may want to examine this file in detail later on, by looking through your downloaded DBD:: Oracle directories. For now, though, just be aware that *dbimp.c* essentially makes use of the following functions, to attempt to return a database session handle (or not, as the case may be):

OCIAttrSet_log_stat()
OCIEnvInit_log_stat()
OCIHandleAlloc_ok()
OCIHandleFree_log_stat()
OCIInitialize_log_stat()
OCIServerAttach_log_stat()
OCIServerDetach_log_stat()
OCISessionBegin_log_stat()

These functions may look somewhat familiar, but not quite like the OCI calls we looked at earlier; what is going on? To finally link these calls back to the "real" OCI functions in Table 2-1, we need to look at the C include file, *ocitrace.h*, which ultimately redefines our original "real" OCI calls to something more meaningful for use within the *dbimp.c* source file. For instance, the following lines get us right back to the OCI call for *OCIAttrSet()*:

```
#define OCIAttrSet_log_stat(th,ht,ah,s,a,eh,stat)              \
    stat=OCIAttrSet(th,ht,ah,s,a,eh);                          \
    (DBD_OCI_TRACEON) ? fprintf(DBD_OCI_TRACEFP,               \
    "%sAttrSet(%p,%u,%p,%lu,%lu,%p)=%s\n",                     \
    OciTp, (void*)th,(ht),(void*)(ah),ul_t(s),ul_t(a),(void*)eh, \
    oci_status_name(stat)),stat : stat
```

Thus, the OCI calls ultimately employed by Perl DBI to make an Oracle database connection are the following:

OCIAttrSet()
OCIEnvInit()
OCIHandleAlloc()
OCIHandleFree()
OCIInitialize()
OCIServerAttach()
OCIServerDetach()
OCISessionBegin()

Perl DBI and PL/SQL

Standard DBI can also be used to run PL/SQL statements. We'll run through such functionality in Example 2-2, using the *GET_VAL()* function supplied by default within the standard SCOTT/TIGER schema. We'll describe the highlighted statements at the end of the example.

Example 2-2. FindMillersSal.pl, Extending DBI Towards PL/SQL

```
use strict;
use DBI;

my $dbh = DBI->connect(
    'dbi:Oracle:orcl',
    'scott',
    'tiger',
    {
        RaiseError => 1,
        AutoCommit => 0
    }
) || die "Database connection not made: $DBI::errstr";

# Set up a return value to hold MILLER's salary, later.
my $millerSal;
```

Example 2-2. FindMillersSal.pl, Extending DBI Towards PL/SQL (continued)

```perl
# Evaluate the following code.
eval {

    # Prepare the function with lots of placeholding values.

    my $func = $dbh->prepare(q{
        BEGIN
            :sal := GET_SAL( :nameIn );
        END;
    });

    # Bind the input and output values.  Remember to tell Oracle
    # how many bytes to return for the answer, in this case 10.

    $func->bind_param(":nameIn", 'MILLER');
    $func->bind_param_inout(":sal", \$millerSal, 10);
    $func->execute;

    print 'MILLER\'s salary is: $ ';
    printf ("%7.2f", $millerSal);
    print "\n";
};

# If the evaluation fails, make use of DBI's error
# message string to provide a warning.

if ( $@ ){
    warn "Execution of GET_SAL() failed:\n$DBI::errstr\n";
}
$dbh->disconnect; # Tidy up and disconnect.
```

After you run the above example, you should see something like the following output to your command line:

```
MILLER's salary is: $ 1300.00
```

In addition to calculating MILLER's salary, this program is doing a few other things of interest:

1. It binds "in and out" values. We'll use these to run the PL/SQL function.

2. It executes the function within Perl's special *eval()* context braces. With this construct, we can run sections of code (including on-the-fly code snippets) that we know may occasionally fail. For example, in the above case, the code will fail if MILLER is no longer available in the database. However, even if the code fails within the *eval()* braces, the program itself won't fail. We merely check the special Perl *$@* variable afterwards.

3. If that variable gets set, the program runs special cleanup code—in this case, a simple warning making use of the *$DBI::errstr* value.

To test out this error functionality, we'll deliberately enter a flaw into the original program by commenting out the following line with the # character:

```
# $func->bind_param(":nameIn", 'MILLER');
```

When you run the program again, the evaluation warning should now return something like the following:

```
Execution of GET_SAL() failed:
ORA-01008: not all variables bound (DBD: oexec error)
```

DBD::Oracle private methods

In Example 2-3, we'll make use of DBD::Oracle's ability to give specialized Oracle functionality via the *func()* method to check on PL/SQL compilation errors within the USER_ERRORS table. An explanation follows this code.

Example 2-3. Making Use of the plsql_errstr Method in plsql.pl

```
use strict;
use DBI;

# Connect to Oracle database, making sure AutoCommit is
# turned off and potential errors are raised.

my $dbh =
    DBI->connect( 'dbi:Oracle:orcl',
                  'scott',
                  'tiger',
                  { RaiseError => 0,
                    AutoCommit => 0
                  }
                );

# Making use of plsql_errstr

# Step 1 - This should compile without error

if ( $dbh->do (q{
    CREATE OR REPLACE PROCEDURE plsql_errstr_test
    AS
    v_testnumber NUMBER;
    BEGIN
        v_testnumber := 666;
    END;
                }
            )
    ) {
    print "Statement 1 succeeded\n";
} else {
    print "Statement 1 failed\n";
}
my $err_msg = $dbh->func('plsql_errstr');
print "Message 1 : >", $err_msg, "<\n";
```

Example 2-3. Making Use of the plsql_errstr Method in plsql.pl (continued)

```
# Step 2 - This should fail because of the deliberate
# error of using "=" rather than ":="

if ( $dbh->do (q{
   CREATE OR REPLACE PROCEDURE plsql_errstr_test
   AS
   v_testnumber NUMBER;
   BEGIN
      v_testnumber = 666;
   END;
               }
             )
   ) {
   print "Statement 2 succeeded\n";

} else {
   print "Statement 2 failed\n";
}
my $err_msg = $dbh->func('plsql_errstr');
print "Message 2 : >", $err_msg, "<\n";

# Disconnect.
$dbh->disconnect();
```

There are two parts to this program (before running it, make sure your USER_
ERRORS table has no current entries):

1. In the first half of Example 2-3, we attempt to compile a piece of PL/SQL that
   should produce no errors. Message 1 should therefore be blank.

2. In the second half of the program, we compile a similar piece of PL/SQL with
   the same name. This is identical except that it contains a deliberate error.
   We've failed to use the standard := PL/SQL notation for setting the left-hand
   variable value. Message 2 should therefore report an error. Let's run it and find
   out:

   ```
   $ perl plsql.pl
   ```

   This should produce something similar to the following output:

   ```
   Statement 1 succeeded
   Message 1 : ><
   Statement 2 succeeded
   Message 2 : >Errors for PROCEDURE PLSQL_ERRSTR_TEST:
   5.20: PLS-00103: Encountered the symbol "=" when expecting one of the
   following:

      := . ( @ % ;
   The symbol ":= was inserted before "=" to continue.
   <
   ```

Our final piece of code in Example 2-4 demonstrates the use of *dbms_output_enable* and *dbms_output_get*, often used together to run anonymous PL/SQL from within Perl scripts to interrogate the database. (This technique is especially useful for Perl database administration programs such as Orac, described in Chapter 4, *Building Oracle Applications with Perl/Tk and Tcl/Tk*.)

Example 2-4. Making Use of dbms_get.pl

```
use strict;
use DBI;

# Connect to Oracle database, making sure AutoCommit is
# turned off and potential errors are raised.

my $dbh =
   DBI->connect( 'dbi:Oracle:orcl',
                 'scott',
                 'tiger',
                 { RaiseError => 1,
                   AutoCommit => 0
                 }
               );

# Step 1 - Enable the later collection of PL/SQL output

$dbh->func( 1000000, 'dbms_output_enable' );

# Step 2 - Prepare and execute our anonymous PL/SQL
# to find the database system date

my $sth = $dbh->prepare(q{
   DECLARE tmp VARCHAR2(50);
   oracle_system_date VARCHAR2(50);
   BEGIN
      SELECT TO_CHAR(SYSDATE) INTO oracle_system_date FROM DUAL;
      dbms_output.put_line('Oracle System Date: '||oracle_system_date);
   END;
                         }
                        );
$sth->execute;

# Step 3 - Retrieve the DBMS_OUTPUT string from the database
# and print out

my $ora_sysdate = $dbh->func( 'dbms_output_get' );

print ("dbms_get retrieved >", $ora_sysdate, "<\n");

# Disconnect.
$dbh->disconnect();
```

The Perl script in Example 2-4 does the following:

1. Step 1 enables the later collection of DBMS_OUTPUT information.

2. Step 2 prepares and executes the anonymous PL/SQL to collect the current Oracle database system date.

3. Step 3 picks up the required output. To test the script, run the following command:

    ```
    $ perl dbms_get.pl
    ```

    The output should look something like this:

    ```
    dbms_get retrieved >Oracle System Date: 11-FEB-01<
    ```

3

Tcl, Perl, and Python

In the first two chapters of this book, we set the scene for using and developing Oracle open source applications. In the remaining chapters, we'll look at the open source technologies that are best suited for developing the kinds of applications needed by Oracle database administrators and developers. The first port of call in our journey through the software cosmos of Oracle and open source is the world of scripted GUI solutions. In this chapter, we'll examine the three major open source scripting languages: Tcl, Perl, and Python. All three languages have been around for more than a decade, tracing their command-line origins back to the late 1980s. All three provide excellent functionality, are relatively easy to learn, run efficiently, have enthusiastic and active developer communities, and offer solid interfaces to the Oracle database. We'll describe the languages very briefly, discuss how to obtain and install them, and explore ports and interfaces available to Oracle with these languages:

Tcl/Tk

Tcl is an excellent and highly extensible scripted language developed by John Ousterhout back in 1987. In 1988, Ousterhout also started working on a GUI toolkit for Tcl that he called Tk. Over the years, Tcl/Tk has become the favorite of many engineers, software architects, and academics. Tcl/Tk provides an excellent approach to developing applications, including those based on Oracle. Tcl allows developers to create applications that run advanced control systems and C backend libraries with minimal amounts of scripted code, while controlling these applications via GUI applications (rapidly prototyped using Tk) on the frontend. Tcl/Tk becomes even more powerful when these GUI frontends are attached to Oracle backends, as we'll see later in the chapter. We'll also explain how to obtain and install Tcl and Tk, and we'll look at the following programs for Tcl:

— Wish, the windowing shell that is used to control Tcl/Tk GUI applications

— TclX, an extended implementation of Tcl; many applications built on Oratcl (e.g., WishX) take advantage of TclX capabilities

— Oratcl, Tcl's interface to the Oracle database

We'll also take a look at two Oracle GUI applications that are associated with the Tcl distribution:

— Wosql (Windowing Oracle SQL), a Tcl/Tk Oracle GUI application that offers SQL*Plus-like capabilities with menu-driven options

— IUD Maker (Insert, Update, Delete), an Oracle GUI application that is especially helpful for quickly building table maintenance programs

Perl/Tk

Perl has been an immensely popular scripting language since Larry Wall first developed it in 1987. Perl is an extremely fast, interpreted scripting language that combines some of the best features of a variety of other languages, including C, Pascal, and Unix's sed and awk. Perl is especially good at expression handling, scanning and manipulating text, and performing system management tasks. As time went on, it became clear that Perl needed a GUI toolkit, and, instead of building an entirely new one, Nick Ing-Simmons ported Tk to Perl. Later in this chapter, we'll describe how to obtain and install Perl/Tk and how to build Oracle applications by combining Perl/Tk with the Perl DBI and DBD::Oracle modules (described in Chapter 2, *Connecting to Oracle*). We will also describe the following:

— OraExplain, a Perl/Tk program accompanying the main DBD::Oracle distribution that may be used to examine SQL execution and tuning plans within an Oracle database

— The Perlplus plug-in, a Netscape plug-in that allows Perl/Tk applications to be run over the Web

Python

Python was developed in 1989 by Guido van Rossum with the goal of being an object-oriented language that was portable and easy to learn, had a powerful, standard library, and had the capacity for extension and operating system independence. When used with its database access library extension, Python (combined with its Tkinter windowing system) provides another excellent scripted solution for working with Oracle. In addition to describing how to obtain and install Python, we'll look briefly at the following:

— ActivePython, a Win32 version of Python similar in concept to ActivePerl

— DCOracle, a database extension to Python that provides an interface to the Oracle database

— WxPython, an alternative windowing system for Python that is based on wxWindows rather than Tcl/Tk

Why Scripted GUIs?

Before we plunge into the details of how Tcl/Tk, Perl/Tk, and Python/Tkinter connect to the Oracle database, let's take a step back and examine why we might choose a scripted GUI solution in the first place, as opposed to choosing the web, Java, and Linux solutions we'll cover in later chapters.

Anyone who's struggled to write even a simple interactive, forms-based program using the C curses libraries or the Hungarian notation of the Windows 3.1 API knows that even the most basic table maintenance program can require thousands of lines of frustrating code. Once you've written a few such programs, however, you quickly realize you're doing much the same thing on each occasion, painting virtually identical command buttons and text panels onto standardized program frames, with the programs themselves often driven by predictably structured menu loops. To take advantage of this repetition, standardized libraries of reusable GUI code (widgets or controls) have evolved in order to make such GUI programs far easier to code.

VHLS Languages

In what the evolutionist Stephen J. Gould would call an example of preadaptation, scripted languages became virtually ideal vehicles for creating GUIs out of these widget code libraries. Each line of a VHLS (Very High Level Script) language can represent many hundreds of lines of C widget code. Therefore, the potential is there to turn a thousand-line C program into a functionally identical scripted program of just ten lines (or even less, if you're a fan of obfuscation). By decreasing code length in this way, you'll save, by orders of magnitude, both time and the need to support lengthy programs.

There is a downside to VHLS languages, especially when they are used with interpretation rather than compilation, and that is their lack of speed. However, with GUIs operating in the colored world of human time and space, rather than the black-and-white nanosecond existence of a batch processor program, speed issues become pretty much irrelevant. Even hundreds of commands can be attached to a single button or movement on a VHLS application, and the high CPU power of modern workstations will smooth away its hidden wrinkles.*

Many such VHLS toolkits have been created to manage GUI screen widgets, but most of these are commercial products developed for a single windowing system. For a hard-pressed Oracle developer who's on a budget and working with heterogeneous systems, this may be unacceptable. What we need is something that will operate across different OS windowing systems, contain rich Oracle and widget

---

* It's a bit like the original Star Trek episode, "Wink of Time," where Mr. Spock becomes accelerated in time and space and fixes all of the Enterprise's usual many end-of-episode problems in a millisecond.

functionality, keep developers happy, offer quick prototyping, and satisfy our end users with looks, performance, and stability. If our chosen preference also offers full object orientation, high quality documentation, and a seamless linkup to other technologies, so much the better.

Comparing Tcl, Perl, and Python

Fortunately, all three of the open source scripted languages described in this chapter fit the bill. Tcl, Perl, and Python all share the benefits we're looking for in scripted GUI solutions. In the following sections, we'll see how each language stacks up in a number of different areas.

Object orientation

The holy grail of code reusability greatly aids in both creating large systems and saving development time. Code reusability is dramatically enhanced by the adoption of object orientation. Therefore, object orientation is a "must-have" requirement for any language we choose to help generate our Oracle database client applications.

Tcl

> Michael McLennan's *[incr Tcl]* extension to Tcl (the extension may be pronounced either "inker tickle" or "increment tickle") adds extra commands to the basic Tcl language to provide full support for object orientation and manipulation. The extension is named *[incr Tcl]* on the theory that if C++ is the object-oriented language progression from C, then *[incr Tcl]* is the Tcl way of saying Tcl++.

Perl

> The major difference between Perl 4 and Perl 5 versions is the adoption of full object orientation via data referencing and the magic of the *bless()* command, which helps create properly referenced objects.

Python

> Python has been fully object-oriented since its inception. This characteristic is one of the main reasons why so many members of the Python community love the language.

Linkage to C libraries

If we're going to be able to realize the goal of code reusability, as well as gain access to many important APIs (such as OCI), the scripting language we choose must be able to link itself into C code libraries.

Tcl

> The ability to link into C libraries was perhaps the main guiding principle behind the foundation of Tcl. Therefore, as you'd expect, extending Tcl to such libraries is not only possible in Tcl, but intrinsic to its core.

Perl

Similarly, cementing Perl and C together is the primary activity of many of the Perl package writers found on CPAN. Two main techniques are used to connect Perl and C: SWIG (the Simplified Wrapper and Interface Generator), created by Dave Beazley, and XS (for eXternal Subroutine), driven by the *h2xs* and *xsubpp* program tools. Both of these techniques create glue code in two files, one a Perl module bridge and the other a C wrapper file. As we saw in Chapter 2, Tim Bunce used XS with DBD::Oracle to link it to OCI.

Python

There are two APIs linking Python with C. The first is the *extending interface*, for calling C extensions from Python. The second is the *embedding interface*, for calling embedded Python code from C (either C or Python can be the controlling top layer). Tkinter itself is a good example of how well Python can be hooked up to C. It is composed of a C extension module and a Python module. The module works by wrapping the C-extended Tkinter module into Pythonesque classes.

Speed

As we mentioned earlier, it is not always essential that a language possess high speed for GUI usage. However, you will occasionally want to run system commands from inside your GUI, and these can require high speed. An example of such an operation is searching through a large target file for a particularly complex string.

Tcl

Tcl has often been perceived as being "slower" than Perl, but with the advent of Tcl 8.0 in 1997, the new bytecode-compiled model of Tcl shattered this illusion. It became far quicker than previous Tcl incarnations, and the "speed gap" with Perl essentially vanished.

Perl

The C code at the heart of Perl was originally handcrafted by Larry Wall to run as rapidly as possible. This need-for-speed has never left the Perl project. With dynamic memory management, efficient variable storage, and the heavy use of referencing, Perl is still an incredibly quick language, which is one of the main reasons why it remains so popular for CGI programming on the Internet.

Python

Because of its heavy use of objects, Python has never claimed the speed of batch-processed C programs. However, the easy extensibility to C modules, when required, always leaves plenty of room for maneuvering, should any kind of heavy batch processing become strictly necessary.

Rapid Application Development (RAD)

Rapid development is the primary benefit of programming with a scripted language. Programs written in such languages may not execute as rapidly as native-compiled C programs, but they are far quicker to create and turn around. This is a particular advantage if you're in a business where rapid program modifications are always taking place as a result of constantly changing customer requirements. Even in cases where you really do need a C or Java solution because of strict performance requirements, it can make sense to use scripted languages for the prototyping of your programs.

Tcl

Tcl is very well suited for prototyping C programs.

Perl

Perl is also well suited for prototyping C programs.

Python

Python, on the other hand, is extremely good at modeling Java programs. Because Python and Java have similar object-oriented roots, Python is particularly close to Java in style. If you are currently a Java/SQLJ programmer who needs to decide upon a scripted language to prototype with, you would do well to choose Python.

Regular expression handling

The regular expression handling available in scripted languages is often far superior to that of standard C, so this is a real strength of such languages. Tcl, Perl, and Python all have excellent and ever-improving regular expression engines.[*]

Tcl

The 8.1 version release of Tcl contained considerable advances in its handling of regular expressions.

Perl

Since its inception, Perl has always been known for its regular expression capabilities, again making it a highly useful tool for the creation of dynamic web content.

Python

Python integrates regular expressions into its core with the use of two modules. The *regex* module is coded in C, while its partner, the *regsub* module (which imports *regex*), is written in Python and is used for regular expression substitution.

---

[*] Whichever language you favor, one of the best books around for crafting your regular expressions is Jeffrey Friedl's *Mastering Regular Expressions* (O'Reilly).

Connecting to Oracle

Only you can decide which of the three scripted solutions is best for your particular application, platform, and personal preference in programming. You can be assured that all three of them will provide you with an attractive GUI toolkit. What's also crucial for this book is that they also provide an excellent interface to the Oracle database, as we describe next.

Tcl/Tk and Oratcl

This is the best established and most widely known scripting combination for use with Oracle. Tcl currently has one big nontechnical advantage as a scripting solution for Oracle applications, and that is its corporate acceptance. John Ousterhout's Tcl development work with Sun Microsystems between 1994 and 1998,[*] in combination with Oracle Corporation's adoption of the Oratcl interface program in its own Oracle Enterprise Manager product, gives Tcl a certain blue-chip respectability. Tcl has also won acceptance in the commercial world because of the presence of its Tcl/Tk web plug-ins that are ready to run out of the box, as well as a number of other useful add-ons.

Perl/Tk, Perl DBI, and DBD::Oracle

Perl/Tk, in conjunction with its database interface module, Perl DBI, provides you with everything you need to create effective GUI solutions for Oracle-based applications. Perl DBI cleanly wraps up OCI via its DBD::Oracle driver module, and Perl/Tk wraps up the Tk GUI widgets. Some major advantages for Perl as a scripting solution for Oracle applications are the rapidly expanding number of Perl/Tk widgets available for download (they're easily created because of Perl 5's object orientation) and the growing army of Perl DBI programmers out there. These battalions of enthusiasts are continually pushing back the functionality frontiers, particularly Perl CGI programmers using Apache Perl modules who need DBI to be right up on the instantiated jagged edge!

Python, Tkinter, and DCOracle

Python is a clean, modern, elegant language and an excellent choice for your first open source language, especially if you don't yet know C. In conjunction with its DCOracle module (which is undergoing constant enhancement), Python provides a specialized Oracle API needed to interface to the Oracle database, and Tkinter supplies the GUI side of the equation. One major advantage of Python is that complete object orientation was built into the language from day one. Thus, Python enables you to quickly deploy intensely useful programs with lots of functionality. This is particularly true within Java/ C++ environments.

---

[*] In 1998, the Sun FTP site was downloading 10,000 Tcl system requests a week.

The introductions are complete. Let's get down to business and look at each language in turn. Please note that in this relatively short chapter, we can hardly do justice to the capabilities of these wonderful languages. See Appendix C, *For Further Reading*, for references for further reading.

Tcl/Tk

We'll start our journey through the major scripting languages with Tcl (Tool Command Language, pronounced "tickle") and its companion graphics toolkit, Tk (prounounced "tee-kay"). Tcl/Tk grew from a sense of frustration. Back in 1987, Dr. John Ousterhout and his students at the University of California Berkeley were spending way too much time writing specific and widely differing command tools for their projects, rather than focusing their time directly on the goals of these projects. Ousterhout realized that a lot of this precious time could be saved if a robust, general-purpose, extensible scripted language could be implemented as a C library. That library could then be reused for all of the team's subsequent projects. Tcl was thus conceived; Ousterhout mostly wrote the new language in his spare time, and the first version was born in the spring of 1988. By 1989 Tcl was being released to early adopters, and after a USENIX conference in January 1990, the source code was placed on Berkeley's public FTP site and Tcl was quickly adopted by many engineers, software architects, and academics.

Tk: The GUI Toolkit for Tcl

When Apple released their superb GUI HyperCard system with great fanfare in 1987, Ousterhout realized that such a massive and monolithic development effort could not be matched by his students. However, he didn't want them locked out of the future of interactive software. Instead (in what was a forerunner to Eric Raymond's "bazaar" methodology), Ousterhout decided to gradually build reusable components that could plug directly into the rapidly evolving X11 Windows toolkit, which was itself a major innovation for Unix systems. He started work on Tk in late 1988 and framed it within the highly adaptable Tcl script control language. Within two years, Tk possessed enough functionality to be truly useful. Ousterhout had created a masterpiece in Tcl/Tk.

When Tk itself was released and made freely available via FTP, an explosion of development ensued. Many talented people created their own modules, which linked into Tcl/Tk to extend its basic core set of functionality.

What made Tcl/Tk so popular? There were two main reasons:

Speed of development
> On Unix, the only other real alternative for creating GUI applications at the time was Motif. Applications could be developed using Tcl/Tk 5 to 10 times more quickly than with Motif. The Tk advantage was clear.

Extensibility

> Because Tcl was so easily extensible, virtually everything developers wanted Tcl to do was a real possibility.*

Cross-fertilization followed the initial Tcl/Tk public FTP releases. New plug-in modules, such as Oratcl, which allowed Tcl/Tk applications to connect to Oracle, were soon developed and added to the core software. We'll get to Oratcl shortly after we've prepared the ground.

We've found the following Tcl/Tk web sites particularly useful:

http://www.neosoft.com/tcl/

> A major Tcl development page.

http://www.tcltk.com

> A central portal containing many useful Tcl/Tk links.

http://sourceforge.net/foundry/tcl-foundry

> A SourceForge Tcl repository.

The Tcl/Tk project now includes hundreds of thousands of developers world-wide. Its applications cover the entire range of computer applications, from multi-media applications to NASA spaceship control and engineering tools, and back to university research, its original home.

There are now many different extensions to Tcl/Tk. Here are some of the most popular:

http://tcltk.com/itcl/

> *[incr Tcl]*, Michael McLennan's object-oriented programming extension.

http://tcltk.com/itk/

> *[incr Tk]* is an *[incr Tcl]*-related download concerned with a mega-widget framework for Tk. (Mega-widgets are composite graphical widgets made up of simpler components, in the same way that, in building construction, brick "widgets" make up office building "mega-widgets.")

http://tcltk.com/iwidgets/index.html

> *[incr Widgets]* is another object-oriented mega-widget set.

http://tix.mne.com

> Tix, the Tk Interface Extension, is another useful collection of mega-widgets.

http://tcltk.com/blt/

> BLT is George Howlett's truly amazing graph and chart-making facility for Tcl/Tk. BLT is much loved by many a Wall Street statistical analysis programmer

---

* Tcl/Tk is so adaptable in fact, that there is even an attempt underway to link Perl DBI into Tcl; you can check it out at *http://www.xdobry.de/dbitotcl.*

and is described in Chapter 4, *Building Oracle Applications with Perl/Tk and Tcl/Tk.*

http://www.cpsc.ucalgary.ca/projects/grouplab/groupkit/
GroupKit is a Tcl extension to simplify groupware development between distance-separated teams and other multiuser environments.

http://expect.nist.gov
Expect is a Tcl extension used to automate the use of other programs, such as *telnet, rlogin,* and *ftp.*

http://download.sourceforge.net/oratcl/
Oratcl is a Tcl extension used to connect to Oracle databases.

Oratcl, the module that lets us access the Oracle database from within Tcl/Tk scripted programs, is the extension of most interest to us. Figure 3-1 shows graphically how the Oratcl package provides access to the Oracle database. Its approach is similar to the approach taken by the Oraperl module provided in Perl 4 (and replaced by the current Perl 5 Perl DBI and DBD::Oracle combination, as we'll describe later in this chapter). Oratcl directly employs OCI, the Oracle Call Interface described in Chapter 2, to drill through to an Oracle database without requiring the use of a generic database API.

We'll describe how to install and use Oratcl very soon. First, though, we have to explain how to install Tcl/Tk itself.

Installing Tcl/Tk

Tcl and Tk still come as two separate components with different version numbers, though each release of Tk is designed to run with a particular version of Tcl. The following is the master FTP site for downloading Tcl-related software (this site is also mirrored worldwide):

> *ftp://ftp.neosoft.com/pub/tcl/*

Installing Tcl/Tk under Unix

To install Tcl/Tk under Unix, perform the following steps:

1. Download the latest source code from one of the Tcl sites. The file will have a name representing the latest version (e.g., *tcl8.4.tar.Z*); save the file into a local installation directory (typically, something like */usr/local/src/tcl/tcl8.4.tar.Z* under Unix).

2. Read through the accompanying installation instructions, looking out for any changes from those included below. Usually, the installation is quite straightforward and very similar to the Unix Perl installation we described in Chapter 2.

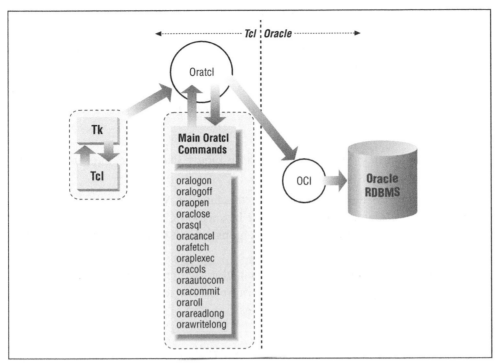

Figure 3-1. Requesting Oracle RDBMS information via Oratcl

3. You may wish to modify the default Unix installation directory from */usr/local*. To do this, follow the latest instructions in the *Makefile* within the unpacked *tcl8.4* example directory. Assuming you're happy with this default, work through the following steps:

```
$ zcat tcl8.4.tar.Z | tar xf -
$ cd tcl8.4
$ ./configure
$ make
$ make install
```

4. The installation should now be complete. However, if any of the steps above go wrong, you must sort the problem out completely before moving on.

Installing Tcl/Tk under Windows

Although Tcl/Tk is grounded thoroughly in Unix and X Windows, Tcl/Tk has also been successfully ported to Win32 systems by Ousterhout's development team at Sun Microsystems. The best starting point from which to download the Win32 self-extracting binary port is this:

http://dev.scriptics.com

As with ActivePerl (described in Chapter 2), this installation process uses typical Win32 self-extraction techniques and is usually entirely painless. Follow these general instructions, but be sure to check the online documentation for more detailed and up-to-date instructions. We downloaded Tcl/Tk 8.4a2 for Windows from the following site:

http://dev.scriptics.com/software/tcltk/downloadnow84.tml

Use the following instructions:

1. Download the *tcl84a2.exe* self-extracting binary executable into an appropriate temporary directory.

2. Double-click on this file to start up the familiar Win32 installation process. We've demonstrated this in Figure 3-2 by including the first installation screen you'll see (along with the "widget demonstration" you'll be able to run once the full installation is complete).

3. Once you've run through the full installation (which shouldn't take more than a couple of minutes), simply reboot your machine to get Tcl/Tk registered and installed in all of the right Win32 places.

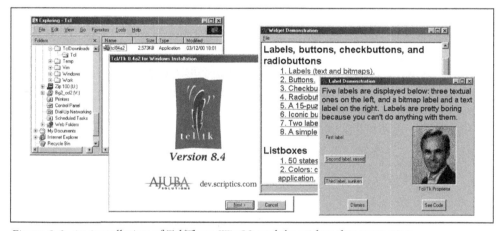

Figure 3-2. An installation of Tcl/Tk on Win32 and the widget demonstration

On Win32 systems, after the reboot is complete, you can go to Start → Programs → Tcl and start up the widget demonstration. By running this program, you'll be able to see most, if not all, of the widgets available under Tcl/Tk, including the simple label widgets shown in Figure 3-2. (We've chosen this example because you also get to see what Tcl/Tk proprietor John Ousterhout looks like.)

In addition to displaying widgets, the widget demonstration also allows us to see the actual code that generates the widgets. Just press the *See Code* button.

Wish: The Windowing Shell

Once you have Tcl/Tk installed under either Unix/Linux or Win32, you'll find that the main program used to control Tcl/Tk GUI applications is called Wish (the WIndowing SHell), which is automatically installed along with Tk in the following locations:

/usr/bin/wish
> On Unix systems

C:\Program Files\Tcl\bin\wish84.exe
> On Win32 systems

The Unix widget tour

Under Unix, there are several ways of running the Tk widget tour either explicitly or implicitly via the Wish interpreter (in contrast, with Windows you can start up the widget tour directly from a menu choice):

1. Switch to this directory:

   ```
   $ cd ../tk8.4a1/library/demos
   ```

2. You can run the widget demonstration directly, via the Wish interpreter:

   ```
   $ type wish
   wish is /usr/bin/wish
   $ wish widget
   ```

3. One alternative to running the widget demonstration directly is to make the widget file executable and let the *#!/bin/sh* "shebang" directive call up Wish via an *exec* command. You'll find an example in the first few lines:

   ```
   $ chmod +x widget
   $ ./widget
   ```

4. A second alternative is to run the program the "Unix" way, and change the top three lines of the widget file to call the Wish interpreter directly via the shebang directive, without the need for the *exec* call (which can be commented out):

   ```
   #!/usr/bin/wish
   # the next line restarts using wish \
   # exec wish "$0" "$@"
   ```

5. The same steps as our first alternative will then run the GUI program:

   ```
   $ chmod +x widget
   $ ./widget
   ```

The *../demos/README* file will point you to a number of other sample applications making use of the Wish interpreter.

A Wish example

Let's demonstrate the power of Wish in Example 3-1, a short program we wrote
for controlling fuel mixtures on a 23rd century interstellar starship. We'll describe
the highlighted statements at the end of the example.

Example 3-1. The starship.tcl Tcl/Tk Program

```tcl
# the next line restarts using wish \
exec wish "$0" "$@"

label .top -text "Starship Fuel Mixer"
pack .top
button .panic -text "It's worse than that Jim"
pack .panic

# Step 1

scale .dilith -label Dilithium -from 0 -to 99 -length 10c \
   -orient horizontal -command fuelBlendCheck
scale .antim -label AntiMatter -from 0 -to 99 -length 10c \
   -orient horizontal -command fuelBlendCheck
scale .warpc -label WarpCore -from 0 -to 99 -length 10c \
   -orient horizontal -command fuelBlendCheck
pack .dilith .antim .warpc -side top

proc watch_status status {
   label .alerts -textvariable $status
   pack .alerts -side bottom -pady 2m
}
watch_status alert_status

proc fuelBlendCheck value {
   global alert_status normal_status
   set threshold [expr [.dilith get] + [.antim get] + [.warpc get]]
   set color "Green"
   set button_state "disabled"

   # Steps 2 & 3

   if { $threshold > 199 } {
      set color "Red"
      set button_state "normal"
   } elseif { $threshold > 99 } {
      set color "Yellow"
   }

   set alert_status "Total: $threshold, Status $color"
   .alerts configure -background $color
   .panic configure -state $button_state
}
```

We won't dwell here upon the technical details of the Tcl language. That's a much larger subject than we can do justice to in this book (see the references in Appendix C, or visit the main Tcl sites listed earlier for online documentation).

To run this example:

- Under Win32, make sure that the filename suffix is *.tcl*. You'll then be able to double-click the file directly to bring up the program.

- Under Unix, make sure your DISPLAY is set and the file is executable before you run it:

```
$ DISPLAY=:0.0
$ export DISPLAY
$ chmod +x starship.tcl
$ ./starship.tcl
```

Let's walk through this example code and compare it to the accompanying Figure 3-3. Note the following:

1. You'll see that three scales are created to control the different mixtures of fuel on your starship.

2. In the *fuelBlendCheck* process, to which each of the slider scales is attached, if the total figure only goes over 100, as in our Win32 screen in Figure 3-3, you'll get a yellow alert.

3. If it goes over 200, as in our Linux screen in Figure 3-3, you'll be in red alert territory. Fortunately, when this occurs, a panic button becomes enabled. It doesn't do anything just yet, but we hope it will make you feel better if you press it in an emergency.

So, in just a few lines, you've got everything the Chief Engineering Officer on your starship might desire without having to dig deeply into the actual C and C++ libraries (and their thousands of lines of code) that drive the Tcl/Tk Wish program.

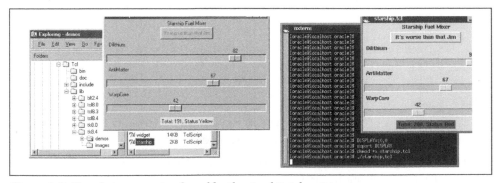

Figure 3-3. The alert screens produced by the starship.tcl script

TclX: Extended Tcl

TclX is an extension to basic Tcl that is required by some of the Oracle applications using Oratcl that we'll describe later in this chapter and in Chapter 4. TclX was created by Karl Lehenbauer and Mark Deikhans and was designed particularly to make Tcl a general-purpose programming language for the Unix environment. It provides system programming tasks such as file access and date and time manipulation. For example, TclX does the following:

- Enhances standard system calls (such as *fork*)
- Extends file handling capabilities
- Manages code library changes
- Provides the WishX GUI script for extending Tcl/Tk's standard Wish program

These are the main web sites for TclX:

http://www.neosoft.com/TclX/
> The TclX home page

http://dev.scriptics.com/ftp/tclx/
> The most up-to-date download site

Installing TclX on Unix

Follow these steps to install TclX on Unix systems:

1. Download the TclX source code from *http://dev.scriptics.com/ftp/tclx/*.

2. Unpack the TclX tar file and move into its resulting Unix directory:

    ```
    $ gzip -d tclx8.3.tar.gz
    $ tar tclx8.3.tar
    $ cd tclx8.3/unix
    ```

3. Read through the *INSTALL* file for detailed instructions. We'll show the basic steps here:

    ```
    $ make clean
    $ ./configure --with-tcl=$TCL_DIR/tcl8.4a1 --with-tk=$TK_DIR/tk8.4a1
    $ make
    $ make test
    $ make tktest
    $ make install
    ```

    The environment variable $TCL_DIR is the path up to the Tcl 8.4 source directory, and $TK_DIR points to the Tk 8.4 source directory.

4. The TclX installation should now be complete. We're now prepared to run the Oratcl GUI applications under Unix (see "IUD Maker: Oratcl's Table Maintenance Program" later in this chapter, and the section on Oddis in Chapter 4) that make use of TclX's WishX extension of the standard Tcl/Tk Wish program.

Installing TclX on Windows

For Win32 installation, the *../win/INSTALL.txt* file contains complete and lengthy instructions. Unfortunately, these require a full development environment, including either a Borland C++ 5.01 compiler (or above) or a Visual C++ 4.0 compiler. A self-installing Windows port is in progress, however, and you may prefer to wait a short while until this port appears, rather than perform the compilation yourself.

Oratcl

The main point of getting Tcl/Tk (and TclX) installed onto our database server machines is to interact with Oracle databases. The best way to do this is through Tcl's Oratcl module, a major gladiatorial champion within the Oracle scripted world. Oratcl was developed by Tom Poindexter, in conjunction with his work on Sybtcl; his crucial Oratcl Version 2.5 came in 1997. Todd Helfter has recently taken the helm from Version 3.0 and May 2000 onwards.

Oratcl is such a good tool that Oracle Corporation has chosen to embed it within several of their own Intelligent Agent products to assist the Oracle Enterprise Manager (OEM) suite of products. They're using Tcl/Tk to compensate for several intrinsic weaknesses within generic database software, in particular the following:

Getting around the "no database, no action" situation
> When the database instance is down, job scheduling with DBMS_JOB and other related packages comes to a dead stop.

Reversing control
> The Oracle database server exists within a self-contained bubble, usually under the imperial mastery of the operating system. However, we sometimes need to be able to overcome this limitation and reverse the direction of control, and Oratcl gives us this ability.

Getting outside the loop
> In the past, it has never been very quick or very easy to get Oracle to talk to programs living in the outside world. Many sword-wielding PL/SQL programmers, including ourselves, have wrestled bloodily in that arena with the DBMS_PIPE lion.* Oratcl can help us gain the necessary access to the outside world without all of this unnecessary aggravation.

The main web site for Oratcl is:

> *http://download.sourceforge.net/oratcl/*

---

* If you get in a tight spot and can't escape tackling this particular beast and its ravenous friends, you'll find a particularly helpful shield in the form of the *Oracle Built-in Packages* book mentioned in Appendix C.

All of the latest news on Oratcl can generally be found at the SourceForge project
and home pages:

> *http://sourceforge.net/projects/oratcl/*
> *http://oratcl.sourceforge.net/*
> *http://oratcl.sourceforge.net/pub/oratcl30_man.html*

You can also view valuable information on Oratcl at Tom Poindexter's home site:

> *http://www.nyx.net/~tpoindex*
> *http://www.nyx.net/~tpoindex/tcl.html#Oratcl*

Oratcl functions and oramsg global message array

Oratcl provides a large number of functions (which, ultimately, issue calls to OCI)
to enable you to invoke a variety of SQL, PL/SQL, and administrative operations.
The following tables summarize the various categories of Oratcl functions, as well
as the *oramsg* global message array used by the program. Table 3-1 contains the
SQL and PL/SQL functions. Its functions follow a similar path to those in Perl; for
instance, if you trace through the *oratcl.c* file you get with the download, you'll
find the following for the *oralogon* function:

oralogon

> This routes through to the *Oratcl_Logon* call.

Oratcl_Logon

> This makes use of the following direct OCI calls, all of which you may remem-
> ber from *DBI->Connect()* in Chapter 2:

> > *OCIInitialize()*
> > *OCIEnvInit()*
> > *OCIHandleAlloc()*
> > *OCIServerAttach()*
> > *OCIServerDetach()*
> > *OCIAttrSet()*
> > *OCISessionBegin()*

Table 3-1. Oratcl SQL and PL/SQL Functions

Function	Description
oralogon	Connects to the Oracle database.
oralogoff	Logs off from the Oracle database.
oraopen	Opens the SQL cursor.
oraclose	Closes the SQL cursor.
orasql	Delivers an Oracle SQL statement to the database server.

Table 3-1. Oratcl SQL and PL/SQL Functions (continued)

Function	Description
oracancel	Cancels any pending results from a prior *orasql* function.
orafetch	Gets the next row from the SQL executed by *orasql*.
oraplexec	Executes anonymous PL/SQL blocks (and bind values).
oracols	Gets the column names from the last *orasql* or *orafetch*, or with *oraplexec*, the bound variable names.
oraautocom	Similar to *AutoCommit* in Perl DBI; enables or disables the automatic commitment of executed SQL statements.
oracommit	Commits pending transactions.
oraroll	Rolls back pending transactions.
orareadlong	Reads the contents of a LONG or LONG RAW column into a file.
orawritelong	Writes a file to a LONG or LONG RAW column.

Table 3-2 contains the administrative functions for the Oracle database.

Table 3-2. Oratcl Administrative Functions

Function	Description
orastart	Starts up an Oracle database instance.
orastop	Shuts down an Oracle database instance.

Table 3-3 contains functions that let you access SNMP (Simple Network Management Protocol) functionality.

Table 3-3. Oratcl SNMP Functions

Function	Description
oradbsnmp	Gets SNMP MIB (Management Information Base) values.
orasnmp	Does either an SNMP *get* or *getnext* operation on the specified object.

Table 3-4 contains functions that let you communicate with the Oracle Intelligent Agent.

Table 3-4. Oratcl Intelligent Agent Functions

Function	Description
orafail	Shuts down and exits the Tcl script (for whatever reason).
orainfo	Used by Oracle jobs to pick up configuration information.
orajobstat	Sends current job statuses to the client.

Table 3-5 contains the Oratcl general-purpose utility functions.

Table 3-5. Oratcl Utility Functions

Function	Description
convertin	Converts parameter string from the client character set to the destination character set.
convertout	Converts parameter string from the destination character set to the client character set.
msgtxt	Returns the full message text for the given product name, message type, and number (e.g., "ORA-900: Invalid SQL statement").
msgtxt1	Returns only the message text for the given product name, message type, and number (e.g., "Invalid SQL statement").
orasleep	Pauses the Tcl script for a specified number of seconds.
oratime	Gets the current date and time.

Table 3-6 summarizes the contents of the Tcl *oramsg* message array. This crucial array allows you to access feedback from ongoing Oracle server messages. This array is shared by all of the open Oratcl database handles.

Table 3-6. oramsg Array Elements

Element	Description
oramsg (agent_characterset)	Returns the Intelligent Agent's current character set (e.g., US7ASCII).
oramsg (db_characterset)	Returns the database's character set.
oramsg (collengths)	Lists the column lengths returned by *oracols*.
oramsg (colprecs)	Lists the numeric column precisions found by *oracols*.
oramsg (colscales)	Lists the numeric column scales found by *oracols*.
oramsg (coltypes)	A list of column types returned by *oracols* (including CHAR, VARCHAR2, NUMBER, LONG, ROWID, DATE, RAW, LONG_RAW, MLSLABEL, RAW_MLSLABEL, and UNKNOWN).
oramsg (rc)	Finds the numeric "return code" of the last *orasql*, *orafetch*, or *oraplexec* call.
oramsg (errortxt)	The message text associated with *oramsg(rc)*. Several such messages can be returned by *oraplexec*.
oramsg (handle)	Indicates the memory handle of the last Oratcl function.
oramsg (jobid)	For job scripts only; returns the current job ID.
oramsg (language)	Returns the NLS language of the client (e.g., AMERICAN_AMERICA.US7ASCII).
oramsg (maxlong)	Limits the amount of LONG (or LONG RAW) data returned by *orafetch*.
oramsg (nullvalue)	Sets the default value returned for null columns.
oramsg (ocifunc)	Returns the numeric OCI code of the last OCI function used.
oramsg (oraobject)	For event scripts only; gets the object upon which the current script is acting.

Table 3-6. oramsg Array Elements (continued)

Element	Description
oramsg (orahome)	Returns the ORACLE_HOME value.
oramsg (oraindex)	Lists the SNMP index values from *snmp.ora.*
oramsg (orainput)	Lists, for job scripts only, all the input file names.

Jobs, events, and the Intelligent Agent

As you can see from the tables, Oratcl contains an impressive body of OCI-based functionality. By plugging Oratcl into Intelligent Agents, which work autonomously on database server machines, you can help tailor OEM to manage your own unique requirements remotely. OEM's Intelligent Agents make particular use of Oratcl in two related areas:

Jobs

Tcl jobs scripts are scheduled to run once or many times and are typically used to control backups. Typical jobs are long-lasting and may interact with pre-written SQL scripts.

Events

Tcl events scripts are much shorter-lasting and get fired off by monitor programs when certain (usually unwanted) events occur in the database. They report their findings to the Intelligent Agent, which may then take further action. These scripts do not generally interact directly with SQL scripts.

Oratcl helps Intelligent Agents do the following:

- Call operating system-dependent processes

- Accept or cancel jobs and events from the central OEM

- Collate, queue, and monitor various OEM information requests

- Deal with SNMP requests

These are only a few of the capabilities provided by Oratcl for the benefit of OEM. For much more detailed information, consult the *http://technet.oracle.com* web site, which will also supply you with any integration information you may need to blend Oratcl into Oracle's own products. To "roll your own" under Unix and Win32, follow our installation instructions in the next section.

 For Tcl/Tk open source developers, there is a hidden benefit of Oracle's decision to ship Tcl by default with their products. End users are sometimes more likely to accept Oracle-based control applications written in Oratcl because it is directly endorsed by Oracle Corporation.

Installing Oratcl

This section contains basic instructions for installing Oratcl, but check the *INSTALL* file and other online documentation for detailed and up-to-date information.

Installing Oratcl on Unix

Follow these steps to install Oratcl on Unix systems:

1. Download the source code from *http://download.sourceforge.net/oratcl/*. The file name will be based on the Oratcl version (e.g., *oratcl31.tar.gz*).

2. Unpack the downloaded file to produce all the necessary files and libraries.

3. You should then be able to compile Oratcl on most systems, as long as the right Tcl modules and required Oracle OCI libraries are also available on your machine (see the accompanying *README* file for further instructions).

4. Set the ORACLE_HOME and LD_LIBRARY_PATH environment variables:

   ```
   $ ORACLE_HOME=/u01/app/oracle/product/8.1.5
   $ export ORACLE_HOME
   $ LD_LIBRARY_PATH=$LD_LIBRARY_PATH:/usr/local/lib:$ORACLE_HOME/lib
   $ export LD_LIBRARY_PATH
   ```

5. Now you can configure and install. To do this, type the following commands:

   ```
   $ ./configure --prefix=/same/prefix/path/as/with/tcl/configure  \
   --exec-prefix=/same/exec-prefix/path/as/with/tcl/configure
   $ make
   $ make install
   ```

Installing Oratcl on Windows

Unfortunately, there is not yet a self-executing installation package for installing Oratcl on Windows. However, Windows installation is now much easier than it was with Oratcl 3.1. In the downloaded *tar.gz* file's *../win* directory, you'll find instructions within the *README.win* file on how to install a prebuilt version of Oratcl over your already installed Tcl/Tk 8.4a version for Windows. This directory contains two prebuilt files (with two more Tcl ones in the *../library* directory). The following are the steps we followed in order to install Oratcl onto our Windows box.

 Oracle must be properly set up on your machine, and Oratcl must ultimately have access to the *ociw32.dll* file under ORACLE_HOME to get hold of OCI.

---

1. Download the source code from *http://download.sourceforge.net/oratcl/*.

2. Create a download directory in which to store the *oratcl31.tar.gz* download:

   ```
   mkdir C:\WindowsOratcl
   ```

3. Unpack the *tar.gz* file into this directory.

4. Change to the following directory:

   ```
   cd C:\WindowsOratcl\oratcl-3-1-branch\win
   ```

5. Here you'll find the *README.win* file, which contains the necessary install instructions, which you may want to check for yourself:

   ```
   C:\WindowsOratcl\oratcl-3-1-branch\win> vi README.win
   ```

6. Now go to the following directory and create a new subdirectory (note that *progra~1* is the "Program Files" directory):

   ```
   cd C:\progra~1\Tcl\lib
   mkdir oractl3.1
   ```

7. Go back to the Oratcl directory and copy the following files to their target destinations (as per the instructions supplied by the *README.win* file):

   ```
   cd C:\WindowsOratcl\oratcl-3-1-branch\win
   copy oratcl31.dll c:\progra~1\tcl\bin\oratcl31.dll
   copy pkgIndex.tcl c:\progra~1\tcl\lib\oratcl3.1\pkgIndex.tcl
   ```

8. Now switch directories to locate the other two important Tcl files, and then copy them to their target destination, too:

   ```
   cd C:\WindowsOratcl\oratcl-3-1-branch\library
   copy oralob.tcl c:\program files\tcl\lib\oratcl3.1\oralob.tcl
   copy oralong.tcl c:\program files\tcl\lib\oratcl3.1\oralong.tcl
   ```

9. Your installation should now be complete. To test it out, try something like the following command sequence (making sure your Oracle database and listeners are running beforehand):

   ```
   C:\>tclsh84
   % package require Oratcl
   3.1
   % set handle [oralogon scott/tiger@orcl]
   oratcl0
   % set cursor [oraopen $handle]
   oratcl0.0
   % orasql $cursor "select ename,hiredate from emp where ename like 'M%'"
   0
   % orafetch $cursor
   MARTIN 28-SEP-81
   % orafetch $cursor
   MILLER 23-JAN-82
   % oraclose $cursor
   % oralogoff $handle
   0
   % exit
   C:\>
   ```

10. The appearance of MILLER was all we needed to confirm that our installation was successful.

Wosql: Oratcl's Wish SQL Processor

An excellent example of how Tcl/Tk and Oratcl can be combined is Tom Poindexter's Wosql (Wish Oracle SQL processor) program. Wosql behaves somewhat like Oracle's own SQL*Plus, but it also offers lots of useful menu-driven add-ons. In addition, the program provides a good example of an application on which developers can base their own Oracle Tcl applications.

The Wosql application comes as a standard part of older Oratcl distributions. Although it doesn't appear to be supplied in standard Oratcl 3.1 distributions, you can still pick up the 2.7 distribution from this site:

http://download.sourceforge.net/oratcl/

We hope that as Oratcl 3.1 moves towards 4.0, sample applications like Wosql will again be included in the standard distribution.

In this section, we'll take a look inside the Wosql code. First, let's see how Wosql's login screen works. If you look at Figure 3-4, you'll see the *Sign on* button, which you can press as soon as you've entered the correct login information. The code generating that button is shown here:

```
button $win.s.b.ok  -text "Sign on" \
-command "tryConnect \[$win.s.i.uid get\]
                     \[$win.s.p.pw get\] \[$win.s.s.ser get\]"
```

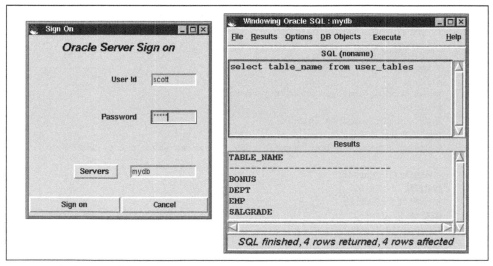

Figure 3-4. The Wosql database logon and main interactive screens

You'll notice that the command tied to the button is the *tryConnect* function, which you can examine in Example 3-2. In this part of the code, note the use of the *oralogon, oralogoff,* and *oraopen* commands (summarized in Table 3-1) to

establish and then test the important database handle. Note also the use of the
oramsg variable; as we mentioned earlier, *oramsg* is the global array widely used
in Oratcl programs to store Oracle server messages (see Table 3-6).

Example 3-2. The Connection Function in Wosql

```
proc tryConnect {id pw ser} {
  global env
  global oramsg
  global lda
  global cur
  global server

  if {"$lda" != ""} {
    set reconnect 1
  } else {
    set reconnect 0
  }

  # check for remote db spec
  if {[string first @ $ser] == 0} {
    set server $ser
  } else {
    set server $ser
    set env(ORACLE_SID) $ser
    set ser ""
  }

  set retcode [catch {set lda_tmp [oralogon ${id}/${pw}${ser}]}]

  if {$reconnect} {
    set win .r
  } else {
    set win ""
  }
  if {$retcode==0} {
    if {$reconnect} {
      oralogoff $lda
    }
    set lda $lda_tmp
    set cur [oraopen $lda]
    if {$reconnect} {
      destroy $win
      wm title    . "Windowing Oracle SQL : $server"
    } else {
      destroy .s
      createMain
    }
  } else {
    $win.s.err configure -text $oramsg(errortxt)
    focus $win.s.p.pw
  }
}
```

Once you've established a valid connection, the Wosql program displays an interactive screen (also displayed in Figure 3-4) and many helpful pop-ups via a long list of menu options, which you can invoke to interrogate your target databases. Besides giving you many different menu options, the screen on the right in Figure 3-4 also allows you to enter dynamic SQL (via the top frame of the screen) and execute it directly. The program begins setting up this functionality early in its life cycle by setting a particular global variable:

```
global execCmd
```

It then links this variable into the *doSql()* function:

```
# set what the Execute button should first do
set execCmd doSql
```

Once this is done, the following code snippet within the *createMain()* function finishes up setting the SQL execution functionality, as well as creating the rest of the screen. The mousetrap is then set:

```
# global variable execCmd is set by doSql in order to allow cancel
button .m.mb.exec  -text "Execute" -command {eval $execCmd}
                        -relief flat
```

Now, as soon as you've entered your required SQL code into the top frame, the stage is set for the *doSql()* function to do its good work, as shown in Example 3-3. We've annotated this code with step numbers (1 through 6). At the end of the code we'll explain what these steps do.

Example 3-3. The doSql() Code in the Wosql Program

```
proc doSql {} {
  global cur
  global oramsg                                             # Step 1
  global contFlag
  global stopFlag
  global appendclear

  set contFlag 1
  set stopFlag 1
  global execCmd
  set execCmd "set contFlag 0; set stopFlag 0"
  .m.mb.exec configure  -text "Cancel"  -state active        # Step 2

  set NO_MORE_ROWS 1403

  # first make a dash line, 256 chars long
  set d [repl_str "----------------" 16]

  set txtindx ""
  set txtcols ""
  set txtdata ""
  set txtlens ""
```

Example 3-3. The doSql( ) Code in the Wosql Program (continued)

```
set row ""
set cnt 0
set sql_str [.m.s.sql get 1.0 end]
set sql_filt ""
set rpc_rows 0

if $appendclear clearoutput

# filter out lines beginning with "#" or ";"              # Step 3
foreach f [split $sql_str \n] {
  # filter out comments
  set  ex1 [regexp -nocase "^#.*$|^ *#.*$" $f]
  # filter out "go"s
  set  ex2 [regexp -nocase "^;.*$|^ *;.*$" $f]
  if !$ex1$ex2 {
    append sql_filt "$f\n"
  } else {
    append sql_filt "\n"
  }
}
if {[string length $sql_filt] == 0} {
  setMsg "No SQL to execute"
  set execCmd doSql
  .m.mb.exec configure  -text "Execute" -state normal
  return
}

insSql
setMsg "Running SQL"
catch {.m.s.sql tag delete peo}
set dbret [catch {orasql $cur $sql_filt}]              # Step 4

if {$dbret==1} {
    .m.s.sql tag add peo "1.0 + $oramsg(peo)
chars" "1.0 + $oramsg(peo) chars wordend"
    .m.s.sql tag configure peo -foreground red -background white
    setMsg "Error: $oramsg(rc) : $oramsg(errortxt)"
  set execCmd doSql
  .m.mb.exec configure  -text "Execute" -state active
  return
} else {
  set rpc_rows $oramsg(rows)
  setMsg "SQL finished, getting results"
  chkMsg
}

set fmt ""
if {$oramsg(rc) != $NO_MORE_ROWS} {
  set row [orafetch $cur]
  chkMsg
}
set lastnext $oramsg(rc)
```

Example 3-3. The doSql() Code in the Wosql Program (continued)

```
  if {[string length $row] == 0} {
    set contFlag 0
  }

  while {$oramsg(rc) == 0 && $contFlag}  {                          # Step 5

    set rpc_rows $oramsg(rows)
    if {[string length $fmt] == 0} {
      set col_names [oracols $cur]
      chkMsg
      # extract long columns into separate areas
      set i [lsearch $oramsg(coltypes) long]
      while {$i >= 0} {
    lappend txtindx $i
    lappend txtcols [lvarpop col_names $i]
    lappend txtlens [lvarpop oramsg(collengths) $i]
    lvarpop oramsg(coltypes) $i
        set i [lsearch $oramsg(coltypes) long]
      }
      set fmt [formatCols $col_names $oramsg(coltypes)
$oramsg(collengths)]
      .m.o.out insert end [eval format \"$fmt\" $col_names]
      set dash $col_names
      for {set i 0} {$i < [llength $dash]} {incr i} {
    set dash [lreplace $dash $i $i $d]
      }
      .m.o.out insert end [eval format \"$fmt\" $dash]
    }

    if {[string length $row] == 0} {
      set fmt ""
    } else {
      set txtdata ""
      foreach i $txtindx {
        lappend txtdata [lvarpop row $i]
      }
      .m.o.out insert end [eval format \"$fmt\" $row]
      incr cnt
      if {[llength $txtindx] > 0} {
    set i 0
    foreach t $txtcols {
      .m.o.out insert end "" [lindex $txtcols $i]
      .m.o.out insert end [string range $d 0 30]
      eval .m.o.out insert end [split [lindex $txtdata $i] \n]
      .m.o.out insert end ""
    }
      }
    }

    if {$cnt % 20 == 0} {
      setMsg "$cnt rows so far...."
      update
    }
```

Example 3-3. The doSql() Code in the Wosql Program (continued)

```
    set row [orafetch $cur]
    chkMsg
 }

 if $stopFlag {
   setMsg "SQL finished, $cnt rows returned, $rpc_rows rows affected "
 } else {
   setMsg "SQL interrupted, $cnt rows returned "
 }

 set execCmd doSql
 .m.mb.exec configure  -text "Execute" -state normal       # Step 6
}
```

Here's what's going on in Example 3-3:

1. Notice, throughout the example, the heavy usage of the Oratcl variables and commands, such as *oramsg* and *orafetch*.

2. Early in the program, Oratcl changes the *Execute* button to display *Cancel*. This gives you an opportunity to break out of the selection statement while it's running.

3. The program then filters out any comments you may have embedded within your SQL. This ensures that the parser isn't confused later on. The program checks that you've actually inserted some valid SQL.

4. If these checks are satisfied, the *orasql* function is then called to execute the SQL via a global cursor.

5. The program then formats the results, prints them out with the associated metadata (such as *col_names)*, and prints out a helpful message telling you what it's just done—in our case, "SQL finished, 4 rows returned, 4 rows affected."

6. Finally, the *doSql()* function resets the *Execute* button to display its original message on the main screen, and the program gets ready to go again.

If you download the Wosql program inside the Oratcl 2.7 tarball from Source-Forge and take a look at the *createMain()* function, you'll find it also sets up a number of very useful menu options.

IUD Maker: Oratcl's Table Maintenance Program

Another excellent Oracle application available within the Oratcl 2.7 distribution from SourceForge installation is IUD Maker (Insert, Update, Delete). IUD Maker was developed by Tom Poindexter, author of Oratcl, and it requires use of TclX's WishX interpreter.

IUD Maker logs you on to the database and asks you to specify the name of the table you want to maintain. It then interrogates you for any required fields (such as the primary key fields) that you may wish to query on later, as well as any other columns you may wish to manipulate. Once you're happy with the setup, it automatically builds a GUI application (including its own login screen) with which you can later maintain your table.

IUD Maker can save you a great deal of work. Instead of spending two weeks cutting, pasting, and debugging thousands of lines from your old "C curses" table maintenance program to make another very similar one, you can have the whole thing done in about five minutes with IUD Maker! Figure 3-5 shows a sample IUD screen.

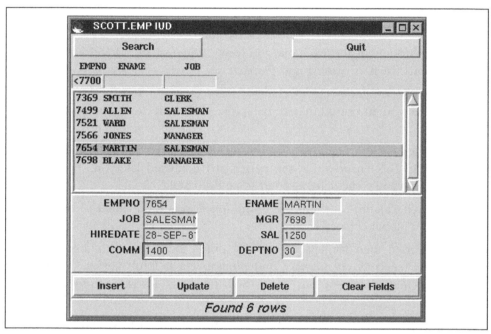

Figure 3-5. Example of a labor-saving GUI created by IUD Maker

Perl/Tk

As we discussed in Chapter 2, Perl was created by Larry Wall back in 1987. It is an extremely fast, interpreted scripting language that combines some of the best features of a variety of other languages, Perl is especially good at expression handling, scanning and manipulating text, and performing system management tasks.

Although some programmers prefer Perl and some prefer Tcl, everyone loves Tk. As we mentioned earlier, Tk was originally available only for Tcl, but in 1995, Nick Ing-Simmons (following up from Malcolm Beattie's initial work at Oxford University) removed Tk's original intrinsic need for Tcl and produced a much more portable set of code. He made this code directly acessible to many more languages, and it became known as pTk (portable Tk). As an encore, he wrapped this ported code in Perl, creating the *Tk.pm* Perl module. Thus, another open source star—Perl/Tk—was born.

Perl/Tk is an excellent scripted alternative to Tcl/Tk. If you've decided that the Perl DBI application interface is a good bet for quickly prototyping useful Oracle database tools and applications, then you'll find that one of the best ways of wrapping them up is within a Perl/Tk GUI program. Aided and abetted by a growing army of evangelists (including the indefatigable Stephen Lidie), Perl/Tk has flowered into an amazing collection of widgets, fulfilling virtually every widget collector's desire. Ing-Simmons' development of the Tk800 port (encompassing Win32's look-and-feel), combined with the robust growth of ActivePerl, means that Perl/Tk is now available on Solaris, Linux, and virtually every other flavor of Unix and Windows. Of course, the major benefit is that we can now use all of our Perl DBI/DBD::Oracle functionality within a superb GUI toolkit across a wide range of platforms.

These are the main web sites for Perl itself:

http://www.perl.com
http://www.perl.org
> The main Perl portals

http://www.activestate.com
> The ActiveState Win32 Perl portal site

The following are the main web sites for Perl/Tk:

> *http://www.xray.mpe.mpg.de/mailing-lists/ptk/*
> *http://www.cpan.org/doc/FAQs/tk/ptkTOC.html*
> *http://starbase.neosoft.com/~claird/comp.lang.perl.tk/ptkFAQ.html*
> *http://www.pconline.com/~erc/perltk.htm*
> *http://mysite.directlink.net/gbarr/PerlTk/tk-modlist.html*
> *http://www.egroups.com/group/Perl-Tk/*

Unix and Win32 Perl

Perl's origins were in the Unix world. However, Perl became very popular after Larry Wall released Version 1.0, and the tool soon outgrew its Unix roots. Windows developers started clamoring for access to Perl, which was fast becoming the "glue" language of the Internet. In 1995, in response to the market demand for Perl, Dick Hardt's team at Hip Communications (the company that eventually morphed into ActiveState) created the first Win32 port of Perl. This port, with its many specific Win32:: Perl modules, gave most Windows NT administrators their first taste of Perl. As time went on, more and more modules were added, and Perl was well on its way to becoming the de facto scripting language of choice on Windows platforms. Win32 Perl became so successful, in fact, that there was a substantial risk that it would evolve away from the original mother tongue of Unix Perl. But Perl's creator wasn't about to let that happen. Fortunately for the rest of us, Larry stepped in at the decisive moment, drew Excalibur from the stone, and wielded it above the masses. He forced the two development communities to cooperate, and the kingdom thus became one again.

Those not familiar with Perl may wonder why it matters. What difference would it make if the Unix and Win32 Perls were different? In fact, it is this hard-won unity that gives Perl its power. You can write a single script on one operating system, and as long as you don't use native methods, you can run it unchanged on every other kind of machine, from Linux to Windows NT through to Solaris and back again. That is a powerful advantage. Perl/Tk itself is an expression of this advantage. Because of Perl's universality, Nick Ing-Simmons was able to create the Tk800 releases embodying a Win32 look-and-feel. Therefore, you can now run identical Perl GUI programs on virtually every type of operating system (we'll say more about this later on).

Installing Perl/Tk over Perl 5

Chapter 2 explained how to install Perl and Perl DBI. Now we need to install Perl/Tk so we can start using this GUI toolkit to use and build Oracle applications.

Installing Perl/Tk on Unix

The following procedure should work with virtually all flavors of Unix:

1. Download the latest Tk module available at the CPAN master site (or related mirror). This module will have a name in the form *Tk800.xyz.tar.gz*:

   ftp://ftp.funet.fi/pub/languages/perl/CPAN/modules/by-module/Tk/

2. Unpack the tar file onto your machine.

3. Change to the relevant directory and check through the *README* files to see if there's anything specific to your operating system you need to know about.

4. In most cases, you should be able to follow the usual Perl installation steps:

   ```
   $ perl Makefile.PL
   $ make
   $ make test
   $ make install
   ```

The Perl/Tk install is perhaps one of the largest Perl modules you can build (aside from the main Perl distribution), and this procedure may take a few minutes to run. However, for those Perl enthusiasts who haven't seen Perl/Tk before, the testing stage can be a memorable moment, as you'll witness Perl GUIs popping onto the screen for the first time.

5. When the installation is complete, look for the *widget* program in the *../demos* subdirectory, and run this to see what you now have available in the form of GUI Perl-driven widgets:

```
$ perl widget
```

Installing Perl/Tk on Windows

The process of installing Perl/Tk on Win32 systems is similar to installing the Perl DBI and DBD::Oracle ActiveState packages, as described in Chapter 2.

1. Go to the following web site:

    http://www.activestate.com/Products/ActivePerl/status.html

2. At around the 1050 mark, you'll see the main Tk module, followed by many other extra Tk extensions. For now we'll just pick up the main Tk module. If you want to experiment, you may want to pick up the rest later.

3. Start up an MS-DOS control box and enter the PPM program:

```
ppm
```

4. Now install Tk at the PPM prompt:

```
install Tk
```

5. Enter "yes" to agree to the installation. Note that this is a large download and may take some time. Once this stage completes, however, with a burst of activity at the end, Perl/Tk is installed and you can quit out of PPM.

6. Now that the setup is completed, you should be able to find and run the *widget* (or *widget.bat*) program under Windows, as shown in Figure 3-6 (notice that Ousterhout gets in the frame again because his original work was intrinsic to Perl/Tk, as well as to Tcl/Tk).

```
cd C:\Perl\bin
perl widget
```

Installing Perl/Tk on Mac OS X

Rumors regularly scamper around the Perl/Tk mailing lists, suggesting that the port of Perl/Tk will be coming very soon to the new BSD Unix–related Macintosh operating system, Mac OS X. We're betting that Stephen Lidie is sure to be involved when it does emerge; therefore, one of the best sites for keeping up with this kind of news is his own site:

http://www.lehigh.edu/~sol0/ptk/ptk.html

See also the other Perl/Tk sites listed earlier.

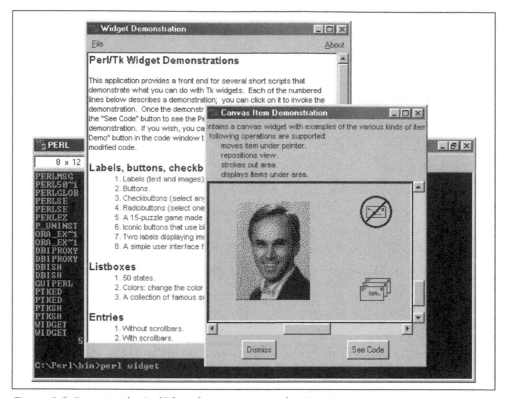

Figure 3-6. Running the Perl/Tk widget program under Win32

Program Structure in Perl/Tk

As with Tcl/Tk, the central reason why so many programmers like Perl/Tk is its speed of development. Whereas Java makes you write awkward mouse listeners and other modules that are prone to initial coding errors because of the volume and complexity of the code, Perl/Tk hides most of this nasty business of low-level control away from the script writer, letting you concentrate on the design.

A typical Perl/Tk program has three main steps (the last step, the simplest to code, also hides the most low-level programmatic difficulty):

1. Create the main window.

   All of the widgets in a typical program are owned in a hierarchical tree, with the main window (conventionally called *$mw* or *$top*) created at the head of the tree.

2. Build the required set of widgets.

   The widgets are configured, arranged, and packed as required by the application. These include menus, entry boxes, text widgets, sliding scales, canvases, buttons, labels, and many more. Where necessary, they are also tied to specific subroutines that are later called when the widget is manipulated in the appropriate manner (for example, when a button widget is pressed).

3. Start the event loop.

   This is a fairly simple continuous loop that wakes up every few milliseconds to check if anyone has pressed a button or moved a scale along. It then responds accordingly, running any subroutine commands that have been tied to widgets in Step 2. In human time and on modern machines, it is unusual to notice any action delay.

Figure 3-7 demonstrates the typical structure and information flow within a Perl/Tk script. The crucial process is the attachment of the program EXIT step to a particular widget. As it's looping every few milliseconds, the *MainLoop()* function accepts calls from the user's mouse clicks or command line to run various subroutines. When the appropriate widget is eventually selected, the EXIT routine is called. The event loop then drops out, shutting down the program in the process. Most windowing systems will generally allow you to shut down a window at the operating system level, usually by clicking an "X" symbol at the top right of the main window, but in full-featured applications, you'll often want to tie a button to this task as well, just to make things more straightforward for the user.

Connecting Perl/Tk to Oracle

Now that we've explained at least the basics of Perl/Tk, let's turn to Perl DBI and get down to some real honest Oracle connectivity. Like Perl DBI, the Tk module itself is "just another" Perl module, and it is treated as such. Getting back to our starship, we already have a program in Engineering controlling our "Crystallofusion" warp drive and supplying the necessary power. What we need now is a similar startup program for the baggy-suited, V-necked technician in the Transporter Room to slide up and down to get us to the planet below. Let's try to write one in Perl/Tk, shown in Example 3-4, as a precursor to our look at OraExplain (an excellent Oracle application based on Perl/Tk that we'll examine later in this chapter).

Example 3-4. A Simple Perl/Tk Example

```
#!/usr/local/bin/perl -w

# transporter.pl

# Step 1: Get Tk and create the main window.

use Tk;

my $mw = MainWindow->new(-title=>'Transporter');

# Step 2: Build up our collection of widgets and
```

Example 3-4. A Simple Perl/Tk Example (continued)

```
# pack them onto the screen.

$mw->Button(-text=>"Control Sliders")->pack(-side=>'top');

$mw->Scale(-label=>"Fuzz")->pack(-side=>'left');
$mw->Scale(-label=>"Spark")->pack(-side=>'left');
$mw->Scale(-label=>"Pop")->pack(-side=>'left');

# Step 3: Set the main loop action listener running.

MainLoop();
```

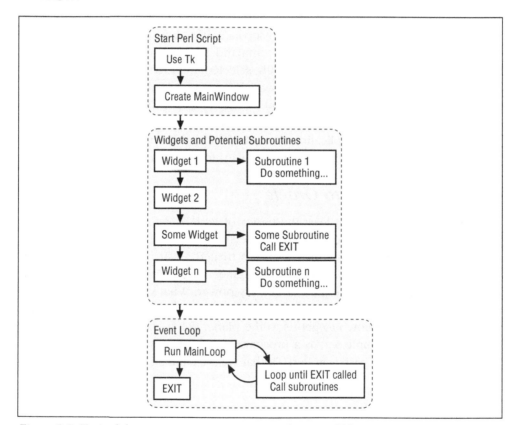

Figure 3-7. Typical three-part program structure within a Perl/Tk script

Once again, this is a pretty straightforward example, consisting of one button and three sliding scales. The resulting screen is displayed in Figure 3-8 (which also demonstrates the Win32 look-and-feel port of Tk). The main difference between this script and the related Tcl script we showed earlier is the use of Perl 5's intrinsic object orientation (hinted at with the use of the "->" arrow notation). Notice also that the top-level widget and main window screen, *$mw*, is heading a hierarchy of subservient widgets that drop off it like spiders from a web.

This hierarchical control and heavy use of object orientation give Perl/Tk an enormous amount of power within small amounts of code, as witnessed in the pretty spartan Example 3-4. Once the required widgets are packed and configured, the *MainLoop()* function takes over all the mouse listening and action running commitments.

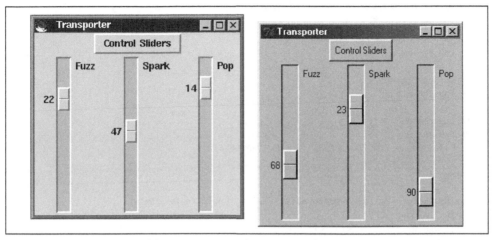

Figure 3-8. The GUI created by transporter.pl for Linux and Win32

There is a lot more to the Perl/Tk module, but rather than take you on a general widget tour, we'll get straight into one of the first Perl/Tk Oracle applications.

OraExplain

As we mentioned previously, when you download DBD::Oracle, you'll find the OraExplain program within the download. This program, developed by Alan Burlison, was one of the first widely available programs to use both Perl DBI and Perl/Tk together. OraExplain lets you examine your SQL cache and operate Oracle's EXPLAIN PLAN facilities. You can drill down into the detail of any SQL you wish to investigate, including that in the cache, and your investigations may help you tune your queries.

Although ActivePerl Win32 users don't normally need the full DBD::Oracle download (since their DBI needs are supplied by binary packages available via PPM), if they want OraExplain, they need to visit the relevant CPAN DBD page and download the full DBD::Oracle tarball, as described in Chapter 2. Once it has been downloaded and unzipped with a program such as WinZip, you'll see the OraExplain program within the tar file. OraExplain can then be copied out to the normal operating system.

Perl/Tk and Perl DBI combined

The OraExplain code in Example 3-5 is used to create the login dialog screen (we've added step numbers as comments, for later reference). You can see the resulting login dialog at the top left side of Figure 3-9.

Example 3-5. Login Dialog Code from OraExplain

```perl
sub login_dialog($)
{
my ($parent) = @_;

# Create the dialog
if (! $LoginDialog)
   {
   my $username = "/";
   my $password = "";
   my $database = $ENV{TWO_TASK} || $ENV{ORACLE_SID};

   # Step 1

   $LoginDialog = $parent->Toplevel(-title => "Login to Oracle");
   $LoginDialog->withdraw();
   $LoginDialog->resizable(0, 0);
   my $box;

   # Create the entry labels & fields
   $box = $LoginDialog->Frame(-borderwidth => 1, -relief => "raised");
   $box->Label(-text => "Username")
      ->grid(-column => 0, -row => 0, -sticky => "w");
   $box->Entry(-textvariable => \$username, -width => 30)
      ->grid(-column => 1, -row => 0, -sticky => "w");
   $box->Label(-text => "Password")
      ->grid(-column => 0, -row => 1, -sticky => "w");
   $box->Entry(-textvariable => \$password, -width => 30, -show => "*")
      ->grid(-column => 1, -row => 1, -sticky => "w");
   $box->Label(-text => "Database")
      ->grid(-column => 0, -row => 2, -sticky => "w");
   $box->Entry(-textvariable => \$database, -width => 30)
      ->grid(-column => 1, -row => 2, -sticky => "w");
   $box->pack(-expand => 1, -fill => "both", -ipadx => 6, -ipady => 6);

   # Step 2

   # Create the buttons & callbacks
   $box = $LoginDialog->Frame(-borderwidth => 1, -relief => "raised");
   my $cb = sub
      {

      # Step 4 - Note this is called by Step 3 below.

      if (! eval { login($database, $username, $password); })
         {
         error($parent, $@);
```

Example 3-5. Login Dialog Code from OraExplain (continued)

```
        $LoginDialog->raise($parent);
        }
    else
        {
        update_title();
        $LoginDialog->withdraw();
        }
    };

    # Step 3 - Note the command $cb, mentioned above in Step 4.

    $box->Button(-text => "Login", -default => "active",-command => $cb)
        ->pack(-side => "left", -expand => 1, -pady => 6);
    $box->Button(-text => "Cancel",
                -command => sub { $LoginDialog->withdraw() })
        ->pack(-side => "right", -expand => 1, -pady => 6);
    $box->pack(-expand => 1, -fill => "both");

    # Step 5

    $LoginDialog->bind("<KeyPress-Return>", $cb);
    }
# Activate the dialog
$LoginDialog->Popup();
}
```

Here's what's happening in Example 3-5:

1. A top-level widget screen *$LoginDialog* is formed, and then a short entry form is packed into the first frame for you to enter a username, password, and database connection string. These are stored in backslash-referenced text variables that have corresponding names.

2. The bottom half of the dialog screen is then formed within a second frame, as well as a callback subroutine, *$cb*, which is predefined for later use. This callback is set to call a further *login()* function (not detailed here), which will set up the actual database connection handle.

3. Two action buttons, *Login* and *Cancel*, are then packed into this second frame, with the *Login* button tied via *-command* to the callback function *$cb*. (Although this sounds so far like a soap opera plot, don't despair—we're nearly there.)

4. When you press the *Login* button, the *login()* function within *$cb* is evaluated with Perl's very handy *eval* function, ideal for trapping errors. On success, the Login Dialog will withdraw to the shadows, to return later when required. You now get access to the main screen—and away you go.

5. You may also notice the *<KeyPress-Return>* notation, which, when you press the Return key at any time, will attempt to connect you via the callback function to the desired database.

Once you've successfully logged in, *ora_explain.pl* lets you examine your SQL cache, use Oracle's EXPLAIN PLAN facilities, and perform a variety of other useful Oracle functions. Drill down into the various menu options and see for yourself.

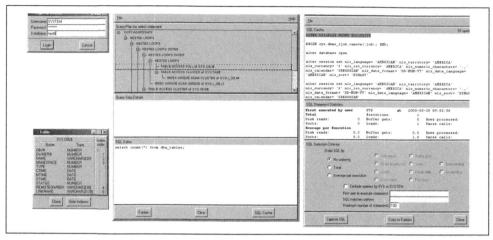

Figure 3-9. The login dialog and other main screens of OraExplain

We're great fans of OraExplain. It's an excellent Oracle analysis and tuning tool, and it also provides a solid example of an Oracle Perl/Tk open source application on which developers can base their own Perl/Tk applications. We'll examine another Perl/Tk DBI Oracle application in detail in Chapter 4.

Before we leave Perl/Tk and head on into Python territory, however, we'll just mention an exciting tool that could soon bring Perl/Tk to an Internet site near you.

Perlplus Plug-in

The Java Virtual Machine (JVM) is built into most current browsers, but it's not the only solution for running applications over the Web. If you're prepared to do a little extra work ahead of time, you can now also get Perl/Tk applications running over the Internet using the Perlplus Netscape plug-in, a Perl solution developed by Frank Holtry (with the help of Stephen Lidie and based upon original work by Stan Melax). Perlplus is similar in concept to some of the commercially available Tcl/Tk web plug-ins.* With heavy security built into it, Perlplus now runs under Solaris, Linux, and Windows, plus a host of other Unix variants. While still largely experimental (it's in the 0.95 version stage), Perlplus is developing rapidly towards the magical 1.0 release and already gives you a flavor of what will be possible soon.

---

* We're hoping that the Perlplus plug-in will perhaps come prebuilt with Perl/Tk at some near-future point (as the PVM—Perl Virtual Machine?).

The following are the main web sites for Perlplus:

http://www.perl.com/CPAN-local/modules/by-authors/id/F/FH/FHOLTRY/
   The main download site for the Perlplus plug-in

http://home.rmi.net/~fholtry/
   Frank Holtry's home page, where you can check out the latest on Perlplus and
   await the first out-of-the-box configurable releases for Unix and Windows

Installing Perlplus on Linux

The Perlplus program is as close to the leading edge as we come in this book, so
there is not yet a Perl-style configuration program. It's bare knuckle time if you
want to try installing Perlplus. The gzipped package from CPAN will contain the
latest instructions; we'll summarize the steps here:

1. Download the Perlplus plug-in source code.

2. Configure Perlplus by following the detailed instructions in the *INSTALL* file. In
   particular, see the discussion of compiler directives and environment variables. The most important of these is SECURE_CGI, which directs the plug-in
   to a specific CGI script later authorizing the security of any future Perl script
   run by Perlplus. (Extra notes are supplied, in the *README.Win32* file in the
   installation package, for compiling Perlplus with commercial Visual C++ compilers on Win32.) We employed the following configuration (which also
   assumed our local web server was running on port 8000):

   ```
   DEBUG=0
   PERL5005=1
   PERL_ROOT=/usr
   PERL_EXE=${PERL_ROOT}/bin/perl
   OPTIMIZER=-O
   MY_CFLAGS=${OPTIMIZER}
   MIME="application/x-perlplus:.ppl:Perl"
   CGI_TYPE="Content-type: application/x-secure-cgi\nContent-length:"
   SECURE_CGI="http://127.0.0.1:8000/cgi-bin/perlplus-secure.cgi"
   INCLUDES=/usr/include
   RM=/bin/rm
   ```

3. Next, clean up any old compilations (if you have any), compile afresh, and
   install the plug-in with a statement that depends on your operating system
   (such as Linux, Irix, or Solaris). The plug-in itself will be automatically transferred to your *$HOME/.netscape/plugins* directory:

   ```
   $ make clean
   $ make linux
   $ make install
   ```

4. Configure the Apache web server (Apache is covered in Chapter 5, *Web Technologies*) to accept the MIME-type *application/x-perlplus* and **.ppl* files types.
   We added this line to the *mime.types* file in the Apache *../conf* directory:

   ```
   application/x-perlplus    ppl
   ```

5. Now update the Netscape browser (choose Edit → Preferences from the menu, then Navigator → Applications in the left pane of the Preferences dialog) to link the *application/x-perlplus* MIME-type plug-in with the usual Perlplus script extension, **.ppl.* (Full instructions for doing this, along with everything else here, are also contained within the Perlplus *INSTALL* file.)

6. Use a CGI script *perlplus-secure.cgi* to verify the security of the called scripts. In this example on 127.0.0.1, we employed a simplified version:

```
#!/bin/sh
# perlplus-secure.cgi
echo  "Content-type: application/x-perlplus:.ppl:Perl\n"
sec_level=1
echo  "$sec_level"
```

7. Move this CGI script to your Apache web server's CGI bin, along with one of Frank Holtry's sample applications, which you'll also find in the Perlplus download. (We chose *ptk_test.ppl* because it was the first one we ever saw, and mighty impressive it was at the time, too.)

8. From the Apache web server home page, call up this Perlplus example program, as we've done in Figure 3-10.

We'll say more about Perlplus again in the next chapter, when we show how to connect the Orac application (built with Perl/Tk and Perl/DBI) to the Internet.

Python

Just when you thought it was safe to put this book down, download Perl or Tcl, and get going writing Tk applications for Oracle, there's yet another open source GUI scripted language you have to consider—Python. When used with the DCOracle database access library extension, Python (combined with its Tkinter windowing system) provides another excellent scripted solution for working with Oracle.

Python grew out of Guido van Rossum's work with the Amoeba distributed operating system and his need to create a more useful tool for Amoeba system administration. He first began working on Python in late 1989 and by 1991 was ready to post it to the Internet. Python grew out of the earlier ABC language and a blend of other design ideas—notably, those based around Modula-3. Van Rossum wanted to create a language that was portable and easy to learn and had a powerful, standard library and the capacity for extension and operating system independence.

People often assume that the Python language is named after the famous snake; however, it is in fact named after one of England's finest exports, "Monty Python's Flying Circus." Python now has a large and independent clan of enthusiastic supporters, and it is Eric Raymond's choice as the best first language for budding hackers. Python is similar in programming scope to both Perl and Tcl (that is to say, it is without bounds). Python is a fully object-oriented language, which offers

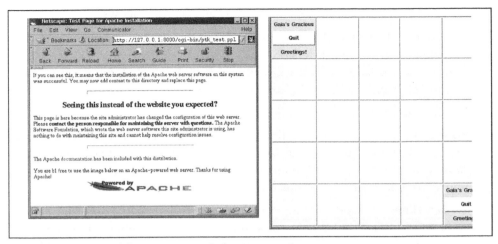

Figure 3-10. The Perlplus Netscape Perl plug-in at work

as many facilities and modules as are available for Perl and Tcl. The language can be used for whatever programming purpose you can think of (GUIs, XML, email, you name it). Python has now been successfully ported to most other operating systems, including virtually all flavors of Unix, Linux, Win32, and Macintosh.

The following are the main web sites for Python:

http://www.python.org
     The central portal for all things Python

http://www.python.org/topics/database/modules.html
     General coverage of various Python database modules

http://www.zope.org/Products/DCOracle/
     The main interface package between Python and Oracle

Installing Python

On commercial Unix systems, you will usually need to build Python from source. However, many binaries are now appearing for popular vanilla Unix types such as Solaris. There are also several alternatives for Windows installation.

Installing Python on Unix/Linux

Most Linux distributions already contain at least Python 1.5.2; however, Version 2.0 is expected to quickly become the new standard. If you'd like a later version than you have, you can download some Linux RPMs* from *http://www.python.org/2.0/*.

---

* The Red Hat Package Manager (RPM) is a popular mechanism used across most Linux distributions to install code packages such as Perl. You can find out much more about RPMs at *http://rpm.redhat.com/ RPM-HOWTO/index.html*; see also Chapter 9, *GNOME and GTK+*, and Chapter 10, *Building Oracle Applications with GNOME and GTK+*.

If you want to install Python from source, you can do so as follows:

1. To install Python (including the links to Tkinter, which itself relies upon Tcl/Tk), download the latest version from *http://www.python.org/2.0/#download*. In our case, the latest version was Python 2.0. (Note the helpful messages built into the file name: *BeOpen-Python-2.0.tar.gz.)*

2. Unpack this file to its *Python-2.0* home directory.

3. To get the Tkinter GUI side of things going, make sure that you've previously set up Tcl/Tk (as described earlier in this chapter) and you know which versions you've installed. We'll assume Tk version 8.4 for the rest of our installation steps, which we've performed under Linux.

4. To get Tkinter to work, before you do anything else, make sure the Python compiler will later be able to pick up the *libtk8.4.so* library file (here we assume it's lurking in the */usr/local/lib* directory from the Tcl/Tk build earlier). You do this by ensuring that the LD_LIBRARY_PATH environment variable is correctly set:

   ```
   $ LD_LIBRARY_PATH=/usr/local/lib:$LD_LIBRARY_PATH
   $ export LD_LIBRARY_PATH
   ```

5. Before actually configuring Python, you'll also need to go to the *Python-2.0/Modules* directory and edit the *Setup* file that you'll find there. In this file you'll find various instructions for compiling in the crucial *_tkinter* extensions. You'll find that these have been commented out by default (in case you haven't already set up Tcl/Tk and don't want Tkinter).

6. Since in this case we need the Tkinter extension to get our DCOracle GUI example to work later on, we must alter our *Setup* file to include everything necessary for *_tkinter* (on Linux):

   ```
   # The _tkinter module.
   # The TKPATH variable is always enabled, to save you the effort.

   TKPATH=:lib-tk
     _tkinter _tkinter.c tkappinit.c -DWITH_APPINIT \
         -I/usr/local/include \
         -I/usr/X11R6/include \
         -L/usr/local/lib \
         -ltk8.4 -ltcl8.4 \
         -L/usr/X11R6/lib \
         -lX11
   ```

7. You'll find many useful comments surrounding each line—for example, telling you what the X Windows library alternatives are. The really crucial line is the one detailing which versions of Tk and Tcl you'll be pointing Python's Tkinter at (in our case, 8.4 for both). Python 2.0 is preconfigured to work with Tcl/Tk versions 8 and over, so this is OK.

8. Now we can configure Python, make it, test it, and install it with all of its requisite libraries (for now, we'll accept the default final destination for the Python interpreter, which is */usr/local/bin/python*. See the *README* file for configuring in alternatives to this). Here is an outline of the steps:

```
$ cd Python-2.0
$ ./configure
$ make
$ make test
$ make install
```

9. The previous steps will also generate literally hundreds of compilation messages and test lines, which are excellent for debugging purposes should anything misbehave. If any of these steps goes wrong, be sure to sort it out before moving on. The ones to look out for are those involving the correct setting of LD_LIBRARY_PATH to get the right Tcl/Tk libraries, and those ensuring that the *../Python-2.0/Modules/Setup* file is set correctly for *_tkinter* usage on your particular flavor of operating system.

10. Assuming complete success, we should now be ready to get going with Tkinter. After running through the steps above, you may also want to confirm that your Python is slithering correctly with Tkinter before moving on. To do this, run one of the many thoughtfully provided demo programs. Make sure that you pick up your newly created Python by making */usr/local/bin* dominant within your PATH variable, and if you get display problems, set DISPLAY to your local terminal:

```
$ cd ../Python-2.0/Demo/tkinter/matt
$ PATH=/usr/local/bin:$PATH
$ export PATH
$ DISPLAY=:0.0
$ export DISPLAY
$ python slider-demo-1.py
```

You can see the results in Figure 3-11.

Installing Python on Windows

There are two main Win32 binary download alternatives for Python. The first set of binaries is available from the main Python portal's FTP area:

http://www.python.org/ftp/

For example, one can be found at the following URL:

http://www.python.org/ftp/python/2.0/BeOpen-Python-2.0.exe

These self-installing executables run smoothly under the usual Win32 Install Shield setup system. They also contain all the Tcl/Tk code necessary to run Tkinter for Python GUIs, should you choose to install it, without having to download this separately afterwards. There are other GUI techniques available to Python, such as

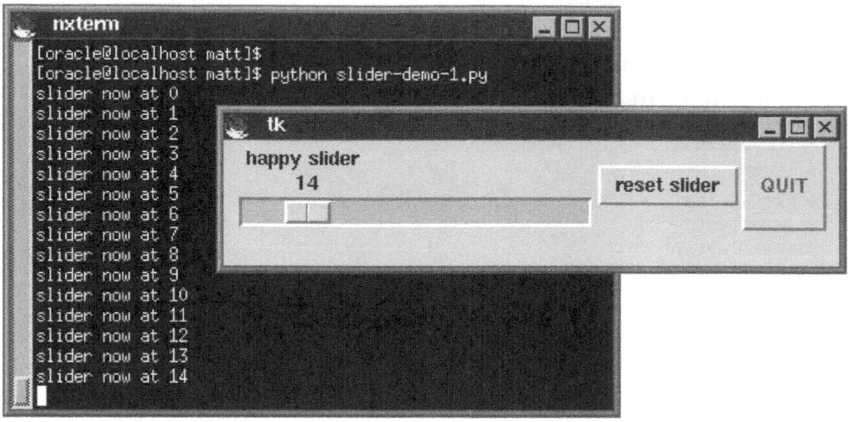

Figure 3-11. Running the slider-demo-1.py demonstration program

wxWindows covered later in this chapter; however, we think Tkinter is a good one to get started with, especially for shorter programs and particularly since it's so well documented.

ActivePython

There is also a Win32 version of Python available from ActiveState, similar in concept to ActivePerl (which we discussed in Chapter 2). You can download Active-Python (also based on Python 2.0) from this site:

> *http://www.activestate.com/Products/ActivePython/Download.html*

ActivePython also comes in Linux and Solaris flavors, and ActiveState promises that the following features will be available in the near future:

- Database support
- Further GUI toolkits
- Further specialized packages as required

The database support sounds particularly interesting. If ActivePython eventually comes with DCOracle built in (saving us having to install from source ourselves), it could become an attractive Python platform. Installing Win32 ActivePython will require the Microsoft Windows installer (MSI), as we mentioned earlier for ActivePerl, which you can find here for either Windows NT or Windows 98 (further versions available will be listed on the download page):

> *http://www.ActiveState.com/download/contrib/Microsoft/NT/InstMsi.exe*
> *http://www.ActiveState.com/download/contrib/Microsoft/9x/InstMsi.exe*

Once you've installed MSI, you can download the ActivePython MSI file and double-click on it, as shown in Figure 3-12, to install ActivePython directly on your PC.

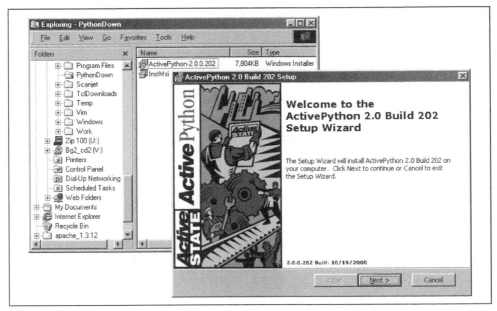

Figure 3-12. Installing ActivePython under Windows

For Tkinter to work, Build 202 of ActivePython requires a separate installation of a specific binary version of Tcl, *tcl832.exe*, immediately afterwards. This Tcl binary installer can be found at:

ftp://ftp.scriptics.com/pub/tcl/tcl8_3/

Using Tkinter with a GUI Example

Now that we've set up our basic Python environment, let's look at a simple Python GUI just to show you what's possible. As we mentioned earlier, one of the most popular ways to rapidly prototype GUIs in Python is Tcl's Tkinter interface.

In our continuing starship example, we currently have the power from Engineering and the Transporter Room has the requisite controls. The next thing we want to do is build a tricorder control for our trusty planet-bound starship medic. We're about to beam down with him to the surface of "Planet Salaris." Our doctor needs to try to locate all of those shape-shifting aliens that may be after the salt in our bodies. Our new Python GUI program will help in this life-and-death quest. Before we pick up the two doomed Redshirts from Security, the good doctor quickly programs his tricorder with the script shown in Example 3-6 to get it ready for the trip.

Example 3-6. The salaris.py File for Creating a Simple Tricorder Program

```
from Tkinter import *

win = Frame()
```

Example 3-6. The salaris.py File for Creating a Simple Tricorder Program (continued)

```
win.pack()

Label(win, text='Tricorder').pack(side=TOP)
Button(win, text='Beam Me Up').pack(side=TOP)

saltLevel = Scale(win, label="SaltLevel")
saltLevel.pack(side=LEFT)

alienLife = Scale(win, label="AlienLife")
alienLife.pack(side=LEFT)

glowingRocks = Scale(win, label="GlowingRocks")
glowingRocks.pack(side=LEFT)

win.mainloop()
```

The most important entry in Example 3-6 is the import of the Tkinter extension on the first line. This gets us everything we need on the GUI front. Comparing this Python script with earlier ones written in Tcl and Perl, you may agree that the creation of our three sliding scale widgets within this short Python program appears somewhat cleaner than with our previous shipboard programs. This less cluttered Python approach may appear even more lucid when compared to the accompanying screen output in Figure 3-13 (started under Win32 by double-clicking it under Explorer). Python's clarity can make its programs particularly easy to maintain. This characteristic is a real godsend in a multi-thousand-line system (or even in a twenty-line system!). Note how the highlighted code lines in Example 3-6 are faithfully reflected in the final GUI.

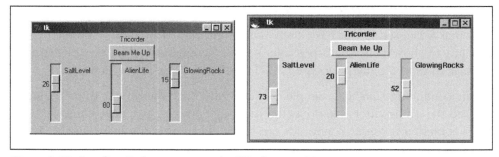

Figure 3-13. Our first Python screen under Windows and Linux

DCOracle

To allow Python applications to connect to Oracle databases, Digital Creations has created DCOracle, an open source extension that facilitates Oracle access from Python via the Oracle Call Interface (OCI), described in Chapter 2. Later on, we'll combine DCOracle with Tkinter inside a simple GUI program, but for now we'll just get it installed.

The main web site for DCOracle is:

http://www.zope.org/Products/DCOracle/

This Oracle database extension also follows the Python database API, which is covered at the following web page:

http://www.python.org/topics/database/modules.html

DCOracle is mostly written in Python, except for its *Buffer* and *oci_* low-level extension C modules. These particular DCOracle extensions contain a comprehensive range of OCI-based calls to provide the foundation for the functions listed in Tables 3-7, 3-8, 3-9, and 3-10.

Table 3-7. DCOracle Functions

Function	Description
Connect	Connects to the database via a string (*user/password@system*)
close	Closes the database connection down
commit	Commits pending transactions
rollback	Rolls back pending transactions
cursor	Creates a new cursor handle
prepare	Prepares supplied SQL for later execution
callproc	Calls a named body of PL/SQL with bound parameters as required
getSource	Brings back source code for the given PL/SQL object name
objects	Returns basic information on user objects

Table 3-8. DCOracle Cursor Object Functions

Function	Description
close	Closes the cursor
execute	Executes the supplied SQL operation
fetchone	Fetches the next row of cursor information
fetchmany	Fetches the next set of rows
fetchall	Fetches all remaining rows of a query

Table 3-9. DCOracle Handle and DBI Helper Object Functions

Function	Description
execute	Executes a database operation that has already been prepared
dbiDate	Constructs a date in the Python database API format
dbiRaw	Holds a raw binary value

Table 3-10. DCOracle Extensions to the Python Database API

Function	Description
procedures	Allows the manipulation of PL/SQL
length	Returns a Large Object (LOB) length
read	Reads data from a LOB
write	Writes data to a LOB

At present there are no compilation instructions with the download for Win32, though we're sure these will soon follow.

Installing DCOracle on Unix

To compile DCOracle under Unix and attach it to Python proper, follow these steps:

1. Download the source code for DCOracle from *http://www.zope.org/Products/DCOracle/*.

2. Unpack the latest stable download. If you need more information, see the extensive instructions accompanying the download (in our case, the latest download was 1.3.2).

3. Next, you'll need to compile the DCOracle extensions. (Unfortunately, we have not yet found any binaries for the DCOracle database package, though we're confident these will appear for Windows at some point. See the latest *README* files for up-to-date information.) First, though, move to where you'll later compile the DCOracle extensions:

   ```
   $ cd DCOracle-1.3.2/src
   ```

   Here you'll find various setup files, such as these:

   Setup-7.3.2
   Setup-8.0.4
   Setup-8.0.4-solaris-intel
   Setup-8.0.5-linux-intel
   Setup-8.1.5

   Pick whichever of these is most appropriate for your machine's version of Oracle (in our case, for Oracle 8.1.5, *Setup-8.1.5*) and copy it to a new *Setup* file, which the configuration process is expecting to find when you run it later:

   ```
   $ cp Setup-8.1.5 Setup
   ```

4. Now you need to prepare a *Makefile*. With the download, you'll receive a number of preinstallation *Makefiles*. Choose whichever one of these you want,

based upon your version of Python. Because we were using Python 2.0, we chose the latest pre-installation *Makefile*, which in our case turned out to be *Makefile.pre.in-1.5*. Perform these two steps to create the necessary *Makefile*:

```
$ cp Makefile.pre.in-1.5 Makefile.pre.in
$ make -f Makefile.pre.in boot PYTHON=python
```

Notice *PYTHON=python* in the second line. This is simply an instruction to let the later compilation process know that our Python executable (available under */usr/local/bin*) is actually called "python", as opposed to something like "python20".

5. We're virtually there now, but as with other Oracle-accessing programs (like DBD::Oracle for Perl), DCOracle relies entirely on presupplied Oracle OCI code. You therefore need to make sure it knows where the Oracle OCI libraries are living:

```
$ ORACLE_HOME=/u01/app/oracle/product/8.1.5
$ export ORACLE_HOME
$ LD_LIBRARY_PATH=$LD_LIBRARY_PATH:/usr/local/lib:$ORACLE_HOME/lib
$ export LD_LIBRARY_PATH
```

6. Now you can safely compile DCOracle with one simple build step:

```
$ make
```

Once you're through the compilation, start up the target Oracle database and its listener, and you should receive the same output you received from the presupplied Python test program:

```
$ python DCOracle_test.py scott/tiger@orcl
Import succeeded
Connect succeeded
```

This means you can continue.

7. To complete the installation process, make sure that your DCOracle extension is visible from the main */usr/local/bin/python* program (this is not done with a *make install* command). To achieve this, go to the main *DCOracle-1.3.2* directory and copy the two recently compiled extension files from the source compilation directory to the main *DCOracle* package directory:

```
$ cd DCOracle-1.3.2
$ cp src/Buffer.so DCOracle
$ cp src/oci_.so DCOracle
```

8. Now alter the previously unmentioned PYTHONPATH environment variable to ensure that Python can now find this new package directory under its *DCOracle-1.3.2* parental home:

```
$ PYTHONPATH=/myUnpackDir/DCOracle-1.3.2:$PYTHONPATH
$ export PYTHONPATH
```

Python can now "see" the DCOracle package when it is referenced within a program.

Using DCOracle

We'll build a very simple Python Tkinter GUI program (see Example 3-7) to demonstrate what's possible with DCOracle. You might like to extend this example once you've examined the DCOracle functions listed earlier (which are all well-documented within the download files).

Example 3-7. The sql.py DCOracle and Tkinter Demo Program

```python
from Tkinter import *
from DCOracle import *

class SQLTest(Frame):
    def printit(self):
        print "Employees"

    def createWidgets(self):

        self.employee = StringVar()
        self.employee.set("MILLER")

        self.radioframe = Frame(self)
        self.radioframe.pack()

        dbc = Connect('scott/tiger')
        c=dbc.cursor()
        c.execute('select ename from emp')
        for row in c:
            print row[0]

            self.radioframe.choc = Radiobutton( self.radioframe,
                                                text=row[0],
                                                variable=self.employee,
                                                value=row[0],
                                                anchor=W )
            self.radioframe.choc.pack(fill=X)

        dbc.close()

        self.entry = Entry(self, textvariable=self.employee)
        self.entry.pack(fill=X)
        self.QUIT = Button( self, text='QUIT', foreground='blue',
                        command=self.quit )
        self.QUIT.pack(side=BOTTOM, fill=BOTH)

    def __init__(self, master=None):
        Frame.__init__(self, master)
        Pack.config(self)
        self.createWidgets()

sqlExample = SQLTest()
sqlExample.mainloop()
```

The important part of this program is where we set up the *dbc* database connection before running into a Python cursor loop to generate all the necessary radio buttons, one per employee, via the *myCursor* variable. You can see the resulting output in Figure 3-14—a visual feast, we think you'll agree.

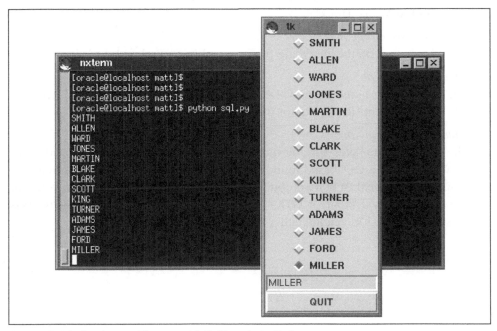

Figure 3-14. Combining Tkinter with DCOracle in Python

As we said earlier, we're hoping those folks at ActiveState get to work quickly on ActivePython and add self-loading packages for Tkinter and DCOracle (on Linux, Solaris, and Windows) in a way that's similar to what they've done to add Tk, Perl DBI, and DBD::Oracle for ActivePerl. If they do, Python may become simply irresistible.

wxPython

Tk is an immense achievement, but your fairy godmother still has one sparkling wish left up her sleeve—wxPython. The wxPython project, led by Robin Dunn, may ultimately overtake Tkinter as the main windowing tool of choice among developers in the Python community. The wxPython system encapsulates the free wxWindows C++ framework. It has also been ported to both Linux and Unix via the GTK/Motif environment. Its main advantage for Python users is its freedom from a reliance on Tcl/Tk and its use of C++ GUI libraries fitting neatly into the object-oriented Python framework. For more on wxPython and wxWindows, check out the following web sites:

http://wxPython.org

   The main web site for wxPython, which includes binary downloads for Windows and RPMs for Linux.

http://wxperl.sourceforge.net

   For information on this emerging project combining Perl with wxWindows.

http://www.roebling.de

   The wxDesigner home page; wxDesigner is a dialog editor and Rapid Application Development (RAD) tool for use with the wxWindows libraries.

http://www.wxwindows.org

   The wxWindows site, for information on everything else connected with wxWindows (the C++-based foundation for creating GUI applications across a range of platforms). When you build wxPython from source on Unix, you will first need either a Motif or GTK+ wxWindows environment; full instructions exist on this site for creating either of these alternatives.

In this chapter:
- *Orac*
- *Oddis*
- *Building Applications with Oratcl and BLT*

4

Building Oracle Applications with Perl/Tk and Tcl/Tk

The previous chapter introduced the use of the most popular open source scripting languages—Tcl, Perl, and Python, along with their GUI toolkits—and the Oracle interfaces built upon them. In this chapter, we'll take a detailed look at two particular Oracle applications, one from the Perl camp and the other from the Tcl camp:

Orac

A Perl/Tk GUI tool designed mainly for database and system administrators; it performs database management and performance tuning and also makes use of the Perlplus Netscape plug-in.

Oddis

A Tcl/Tk GUI tool conceptually similar to Orac and designed for both DBAs and developers; it performs database management and performance tuning, with a special focus on SQL tuning.

As yet, no major Python Tkinter Oracle application making use of DCOracle is generally available. We're hoping one of our faithful readers will remedy this situation in the near future.

In addition to describing what Orac and Oddis do (and briefly mentioning a few related tools, such as dbMan), we'll also spend some time looking at the implementations of these two Oracle applications. We're hoping that looking at these implementations might give you some good ideas for how to approach building your own applications. Although these relatively large applications were developed entirely independently from each other, it's interesting to see how their functionality overlaps.

In the second part of this chapter, we've also provided a small but fully worked-out example designed to show you the way that existing tools can be extended.

We'll take two existing base tools and then blend them together in a hundred or so lines of code to provide a new example application called TableSpacer. The purpose of TableSpacer is to graphically display Oracle table space usage. It is based on the following tools:

Oratcl

Tcl's Oracle module, introduced in Chapter 3, *Tcl, Perl, and Python*, which allows Tcl applications to interact directly with the Oracle database via OCI.

BLT

An extension to Tcl/Tk that adds plotting graphs and barcharts to Tk canvases. When combined with Oratcl, BLT has a lot of potential. Many engineers, NASA scientists, and astronomers have been using BLT as their bacon, lettuce, and tomato Tcl package for quite some time. Check it out—you could find yourself in stellar company.

Orac

Orac is a tool developed by one of your authors, Andy Duncan. It is built upon the base of Perl/Tk and its many widgets, and it employs Perl DBI to connect to the Oracle database. In this section, we'll describe how the Orac program makes use of many of the Perl/Tk widgets.

The Orac program was originally developed to provide a way of keeping a useful collection of Oracle DBA scripts wrapped up together in one central place. It is basically a GUI wrapper containing a large repository of prepared, configurable SQL scripts for interrogating and managing databases. Using Orac, users can rapidly apply these scripts to any target databases without having to copy them from one machine to another via complicated directory structure installs and environment variable setups. If these scripts are no longer up-to-date because of changes to the Oracle data dictionary, they can be modified or changed directly within the repository.

Orac first came about because Andy was working on a two-man team looking after 25 or so revenue-critical production databases and about 15 development databases at a large corporate data center. Although not particularly massive, the databases were constantly being upgraded by large teams of developers and being hit by as many as 500 sales representatives at a time. Something was required to ease the constant workflow generated by this activity. Orac became that something, starting out as a Perl/Tk GUI-wrapped script to kill spinning processes and gradually growing into a complete DBA toolbox with some system administration aids thrown in for good measure. Although Orac was originally aimed directly at DBAs (and partially at system administrators), as the program developed, it also acquired a number of Oracle development aids.

Orac's central SQL driving scripts were based largely upon those developed by others. Many of these ubiquitous scripts have floated around for years, and we can't easily attribute them. Some, though, are based on Brian Lomasky's superb collection (packaged up in his book, *Oracle Scripts*); he graciously gave permission for adaptation and use within the Orac program. As the program grew, Guy Harrison, author of the excellent *Oracle SQL: High Performance Tuning*, also allowed his very fine tuning scripts to be adapted for use within Orac. (See Appendix C, *For Further Reading*, for references to both books.)

Since Orac was first released on CPAN, many users have sent in additional scripts which have been used to enhance the program. Over time, the Orac program has evolved into a wide-ranging tool. It gives typical Oracle DBAs most of the basic answers they need when they interrogate a database for the background information necessary to perform database administration, tuning, or problem resolution. As most Oracle DBAs' lives are not typical, however, Orac also has enough flexibility deliberately built in to it to allow it to quickly adapt to differing situations. The program can easily be modified to ask many new questions as new needs arise.

Orac is so flexible that it has been ported for use under both Informix and Sybase. These ports employ the same GUI interface combined with a different set of menu configuration and SQL files. Indeed, if you should wish to, you can even switch databases mid-stream while using the program. But since this is an Oracle book, let's get down to Oracle business.

Installing Orac

You can download the Orac program from several locations on CPAN (the Comprehensive Perl Archive Network):

> *http://www.perl.com/CPAN-local/authors/id/A/AN/ANDYDUNC/*

This is linked to the following Perl module sites:

> *http://www.perl.com/CPAN-local/modules/by-module/Tk/*
> *http://www.perl.com/CPAN-local/modules/by-module/DBI/*
> *http://www.perl.com/CPAN-local/modules/by-module/Shell/*

Look for the latest tarball when you get to the FTP download sites—for example, *Orac-1.2.0.tgz* or later. Because the Orac program is a collection of relatively short Perl scripts, modules, and text and SQL files, rather than large C libraries, the download should be relatively quick.

Before you install Orac, you will need to preinstall the following on your system (the first three are covered in Chapter 2, *Connecting to Oracle*, the fourth in Chapter 3):

- Perl 5
- Perl DBI
- DBD::Oracle (which requires access to Oracle's OCI libraries)
- Perl/Tk

Perl's operating system independence transfers itself automatically to the Orac program, and the program is easily portable for Oracle DBAs and developers across many different platforms. Developed originally for Oracle 8.0.4 under Solaris, the program works just as well under Linux, Windows, and virtually all other environments where Perl can operate successfully. (Figure 4-1 shows the main Orac login screen under three different operating systems.)

The single major exception to this OS-independence rule is the Macintosh, as Perl/Tk has not yet been ported to the MacPerl system, although rumors are often floating about that this is being attempted. If the port occurs, it won't be to the "classic" Macintosh OS, but instead to the BSD Unix–based Mac OS X.

For current MacPerl usage, see:

> *http://www.tis.ee.ethz.ch/~neeri/macintosh/perl.html*
> *http://www.macperl.com*
> *http://www.macinstruct.com/tutorials/macperl/index.shtml*

We've included instructions in the following sections for installing Orac under the main three operating systems. (We're hoping that once Linux or any other Perl-friendly OS dominates the palm-held market, all of Perl will swiftly follow and enable Perl/Tk usage on third generation mobile phones et al via web plug-ins.)

Installing Orac on Unix

Once you have the correct Perl installation set up with the required Perl/Tk and Perl DBI modules, the Orac installation should be fairly straightforward under most flavors of Unix. Here we're using Solaris. The Perl environment was previously set up via a Perl package available from *http://www.sunfreeware.com*, which is an excellent site for all manner of GNU-related tools. Follow these steps:

1. Download Orac from one of the CPAN sites listed earlier. Then unpack it:

```
$ gzip –d Orac-1.2.0.tgz
$ tar xvf Orac-1.2.0.tar
$ cd Orac-1.2.0
```

```
$ ORACLE_HOME=/u01/oracle/8.1.5
$ export ORACLE_HOME
```

2. Run *orac_dba.pl*, first making sure that the top line of the file has the right
   Perl string address (e.g., *#!/usr/local/bin/perl*):

```
$ ./orac_dba.pl
```

Alternatively, run it with the Perl program directly:

```
$ perl orac_dba.pl
```

That's about it. Full instructions are also included in the *README* file.

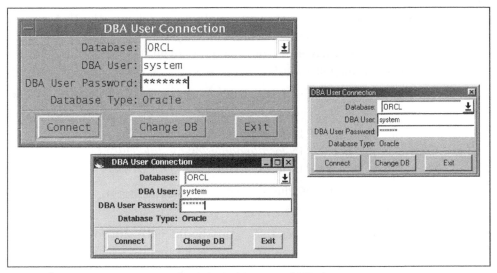

Figure 4-1. Orac connecting under Solaris, Linux, and Windows

Example 4-1 shows a typical helper script for running Orac. The example assumes
that you've installed it into a */usr/local/orac* directory and that you're running
Oracle 8.1.5.

Example 4-1. orac.sh (Script Itself Is Installed in /usr/local/bin)

```
#!/bin/sh
ORACLE_HOME=/u01/oracle/8.1.5 ; export ORACLE_HOME # For Perl DBI
ORAC_HOME=$HOME/.orac # Provides customisation for all users
export ORAC_HOME
cd /usr/local/orac/Orac-1.2.0 # Localises logging
perl orac_dba.pl & # Run in background
```

This is run with:

```
$ PATH=/usr/local/bin:$PATH ; export PATH
$ orac.sh
```

In general, all other Unix installations should follow a similar pattern. However,
we've provided a few additional notes specifically for Linux users. These might be

required when an older Perl version has already been prebuilt for you on your Linux distribution (it's not something you tend to find on Solaris boxes). Note also the setting of the ORAC_HOME environment variable in Example 4-1. We'll discuss this shortly, following the installation.

Installing Orac on Linux

These notes are adapted from those originally provided by Kevin Kitts, an Oracle DBA from Washington, DC, for Orac users using Red Hat 5.2. They supplement those already provided above for the standard Unix installation:

1. Get the latest source RPM for Perl and rebuild it beforehand. The Perl version supplied with an older distribution of Linux may not be adequate. The man pages for *rpm* on your flavor of Linux should explain how to do this, and the rebuild should be straightforward.

2. Get the latest Perl/Tk and Perl DBI/DBD modules from CPAN and compile them:

   http://www.perl.com/CPAN-local/modules/by-module/Tk
   http://www.perl.com/CPAN-local/modules/by-module/DBI
   http://www.perl.com/CPAN-local/modules/by-module/DBD

3. Make sure you can get SQL*Plus to work first. If that works, make sure the DBI/DBD *make test* step passes.

If you complete these steps successfully, you should have no problem running Orac under Linux.

Installing Orac on Windows

Back in the dark ages of ActivePerl 519, another prominent Washington, DC, Oracle DBA, Charles Wolfe, worked out the first installation requirements for Orac on Windows NT. It seemed almost magical to run a Solaris application on Windows NT for the first time. However the latest builds of ActivePerl for Perl 5.6, with the installed packages of Perl DBI and DBD::Oracle (as described in Chapter 2), should make the running of Orac pretty straightforward. Once the required Perl/Tk DBI system is ready, do the following:

1. Download Orac from one of the CPAN sites listed earlier.

2. Unpack and install Orac into its own directory via an unzip program such as WinZip (see *http://www.winzip.com/*).

3. Set up the environment as required for the ORAC_HOME and ORACLE_HOME environment variables. (See the next section for details.) Once you've started your target Oracle database, the Orac program should now be ready to run out of the box.

4. Double-click on the *orac_dba.pl* icon, and the program should fire right up, as shown in Figure 4-2 (this screen also demonstrates the "one-time-only" initial database configuration).

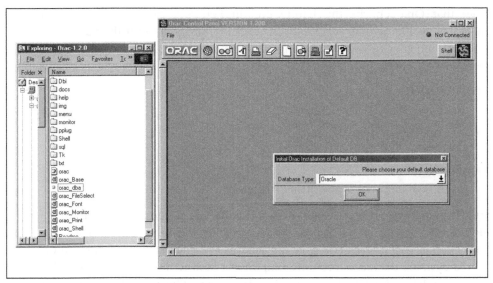

Figure 4-2. Double-clicking on the orac_dba.pl icon

Alternatively, you might like to employ the Win32 command file (written by Thomas Lowery) that comes with the Orac distribution:

```
@echo off
rem
rem Execute orac_dba
rem
start perl -w orac_dba.pl
```

Customizing ORAC_HOME for multiple users on Unix and Windows

The setting of the $ORAC_HOME (or for Windows users, %ORAC_HOME%) environment variable allows Orac to be used on one machine by many different users, with their own personal customizations stored in their own personalized locations. This capability was originally proposed and then coded by Bruce Albrecht. The crucial piece of Perl code is as follows:

```
if ($ENV{ORAC_HOME}) # Generally Non-NT Win32
{
    $main::orac_home = $ENV{ORAC_HOME};
}
elsif ($^O =~ /MSWin/ && $ENV{USERPROFILE}) # Generally NT
{
    $main::orac_home = $ENV{USERPROFILE} . "/orac";
}
```

```
elsif ($ENV{HOME}) # Generally Unix
{
   $main::orac_home = $ENV{HOME} . "/.orac";
}
```

Note that Orac checks the handy built-in Perl $^O operating system variable (which is also known as $OSNAME in other Perl programs) for the value "MSWin", to check whether or not it's running on Win32. Customizations (e.g., personalized menus, etc.) can then go to the following:

$ORAC_HOME

   If already set

%USERPROFILE%/orac

   If on Win32

$HOME/.orac

   As the default on a typical Unix system

Some Win32 systems (e.g., Windows NT systems) automatically set up %USER-PROFILE% so the default always works, creating the required subdirectories and files even if %ORAC_HOME% is not set up on first use. However, other older Win32 systems do not necessarily employ %USERPROFILE%. You must therefore set up %ORAC_HOME% beforehand in something like the *AUTOEXEC.BAT* boot file to make sure the Orac program knows where to store personalized profiles. For example:

```
set ORAC_HOME=C:\Temp\orac
```

On any system, once this is set up (or the default is taken on Unix or Windows NT), any number of users can use the same Orac Perl script, with their personalized preferences (such as screen color) and unique SQL scripts stored under their own allocated home directories. As noted elsewhere, $ORACLE_HOME must always be set up correctly with any Perl DBI program to make sure the DBD::Oracle driver module gets access to the necessary OCI libraries and/or related DLL files (such as *ociw32.dll*).

Using Orac

Now that you're up and running, let's take a look at what Orac can do by examining each of its basic menus:

File menu

   Provides user customizations and general program information.

Structure menu

   Used for current logical and physical setup and to view tables.

Object menu

> Provides hierarchical drill-downs needed to generate the specific Data Definition Language (DDL) needed to re-create every object within the database. You can also use this menu to detect invalid PL/SQL database objects and PL/SQL compilation error messages and perform a variety of other tasks.

User menu

> Provides reporting scripts that let you find out what users are doing in the database, plus drill-downs on specific process addresses and SIDs.

Lock menu

> Generally used in an emergency to find out what's locking the database—also where, when, how, why, and who's to blame.*

Tune menu

> Provides an assortment of scripts used to monitor all aspects of current tuning states within the database (though no time-series tuning is yet available).

SQL menu

> Offers direct access to Thomas Lowery's Orac Shell, which lets you run database transactions directly.

My Tools menu

> Provides a way for users to store personalized and favorite Orac SQL scripts within the standard menu structure.

 The Orac program was designed from the outset to cautiously observe the database rather than to change it. Therefore, except for a very small section where updates are performed to take advantage of Oracle's EXPLAIN PLAN facilities and the Orac Shell module (described later), the main Orac program does not carry out any other database transactions. This basic safety-first philosophy is reflected throughout the entire program's structure wherever possible.

File Menu

Selecting the File menu gives you several options. The leftmost menu available after you select File (shown on the far left of the Orac Control Panel screen in Figure 4-3) gives you a series of customizable user options. These let you modify the visual environment and provide easy viewing access to the various program and configuration files that make up the system.

---

* Sorry, this should read, " . . . which part of the overall system to attach responsibility to for providing us with a proactive challenge in improving our customer service level interface." (We generally find it easier, though, just to blame someone, as long as it's not us!)

File options

Figure 4-3 shows a number of options and also demonstrates the menu tear-off ability, a feature standard across most Tk menu widgets. This enables menu clustering around the main screen for quicker information gathering. The File menu also allows connection to other databases and a straightforward way of exiting the program.

Plain Old Documentation

The Main File Viewer, shown in the lower part of Figure 4-3, can drill up and down the directory structure and allows the user to view source code using either Perl's POD (Plain Old Documentation) capability or straight flat-file text viewing. Most of the Orac source code makes use of Perl's self-documenting POD technique for embedding English language comments within the body of the code. Later on, these comments can be extracted by various programs, formatted, and turned into straightforward documentation without the code getting in the way. The Main File Viewer can do this too, accessing the source code and turning it into (we hope) more readable code descriptions.

If you'd prefer to actually read the source code itself, the POD reader can be turned off, and the straight text and source code, whatever it happens to be, becomes visible instead.

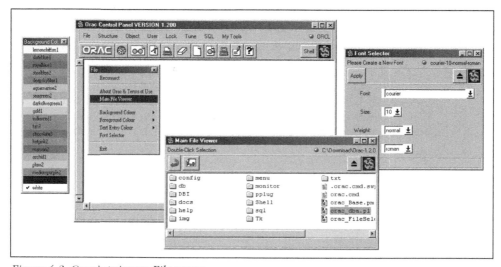

Figure 4-3. Orac's primary File menu

Structure Menu

The Structure menu provides a series of options that allow you to view the current logical and physical structure of the database. This includes two basic graphical reports and several textual reports providing information on tablespaces, datafiles, extent sizing, and free space availability within the extents. Several of the reports are shown in Figure 4-4.

Press me

Figure 4-4 also demonstrates another general feature of Orac. Most of the reports available from this and other Orac menus contain an Alice-in-Wonderland-style "press me" button, generally labeled "SQL." (Notice the icon near the bottom left of the main screen.) If this is clicked, a screen (titled "See SQL" in this figure) usually pops up detailing the exact underlying SQL used to generate the report.

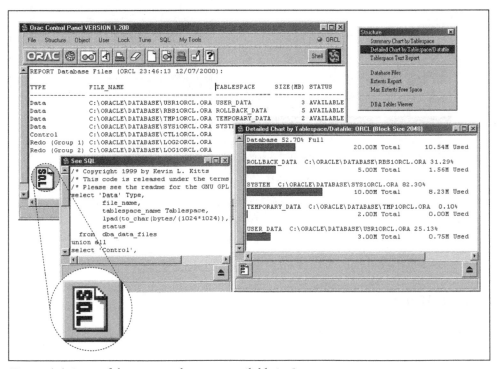

Figure 4-4. Some of the structural reports available in Orac

DBA Tables Viewer

You'll also find the DBA Tables Viewer option available via the Structure Menu. This viewer gives you easy access to all of the information within the general DBA tables. You can navigate as follows:

1. Select the DBA Tables Viewer option, which brings up a scrollable pick-list of DBA tables.

2. Double-click on the selected table to bring up a form where you can enter SQL query lines and the row order in which you wish to bring the results

back. For example, you may want to see all the rows in DBA_TABLES where the owner is the SYSTEM user, and order this by TABLE_NAME.

3. Press the "go" button (the drill-down arrow), to display an ordered slider screen, where you can scroll through every row in the table that matches your original query. This screen can be useful for copying information into a tandem SQL*Plus session.

You can view a cut-down version of this process in Figure 4-5.

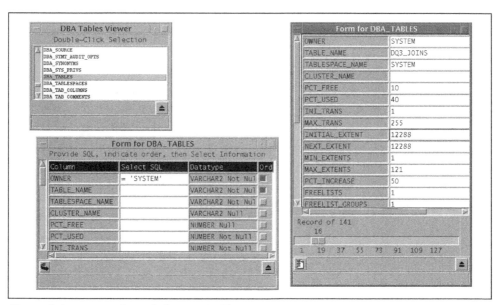

Figure 4-5. Stepping through the DBA Tables Viewer screens

Object Menu

The third menu option, the Object menu, contains drill-downs for accessing the SQL required to re-create all of the objects currently existing within the database.

Tables option drill-downs

The Tables Menu, available via the Object Menu, provides a number of options. Double-click down to the main Tables screen, then drill down through the hierarchical lists of schema owners and tables until you reach your target table. Once you've selected it, a screen pops up, displaying the DDL text that could be used to re-create the table (since this text is provided within a Perl/Tk text widget, full cut-and-paste text facilities are available). The lower menu bar on the table's DDL screen also gives you the following options, from left to right:

SQL

Pops up the SQL used to generate the DDL.

Line Writer

Re-creates the DDL, prefixing each line with its respective line number.

Interactive Form

Similar to the DBA Tables Viewer described earlier, this option allows you to query the table and then scroll through the rows of results. Be careful when using this option; it's not designed for several-thousand-row queries. Although it's possible to perform such queries, doing so may require a huge amount of memory to produce results, especially if the table is a large one and the query SQL is not specifically tailored for a relatively small result set.

Index Builder

Works out the required sizing for any index required on the table.

Index DDL

Generates the DDL necessary to create the table's associated indexes.

Free Space Finder

Works out the free space within the data object.

Constraint

Generates the DDL required for all the table's constraints.

Trigger Finder

Finds any related table triggers.

Comments

If any comments are defined on the table (in DBA_TAB_COMMENTS and DBA_COL_COMMENTS), this button displays the DDL necessary to re-create them.

Figure 4-6 shows a typical subset of the options available in the Tables submenu.

In addition to tables, you can drill down to most of the other Oracle database objects within the various schemas using the options summarized in Table 4-1.

Table 4-1. The Main DDL Drill-Downs Within Orac's Object Menu

Top-Level Menu	Secondary Menu Options	Description
Data Objects	Tables, Indexes, Views, Sequences, Links, Synonyms, Constraints	Access to DDL generating Oracle objects generally controlled by a particular schema
User Objects	Users, UserGrants, Roles, RoleGrants, Profiles	Access to DDL used to re-create schema owners and associated role and profile permissions
Logical Structures	Tablespace, Rollback	Access to DDL used to re-create logical database structures outside of the general schema owner pattern

Table 4-1. The Main DDL Drill-Downs Within Orac's Object Menu (continued)

Top-Level Menu	Secondary Menu Options	Description
PL/SQL	Procedures, Package-Heads, PackageBods, Functions, Triggers, Comments	Grouping of the compiled database objects generally stored within the DBA_SOURCE table
Snapshots	Snapshots, Snapshot Logs	Objects related to replication

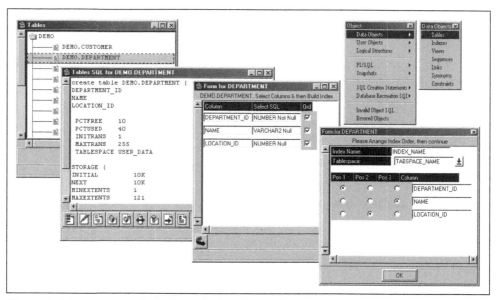

Figure 4-6. Facilities available through the Tables submenu

The PL/SQL drill-down may be the hierarchical submenu most often used. Its use is demonstrated in Figure 4-7, which also shows an example of a "See SQL" pop-up generated from the menu that accompanies every DDL screen, showing the start of the PL/SQL used to generate the DDL. Note that Perl's DBD::Oracle module can make use of Oracle-specific anonymous PL/SQL functionality,* as in the "See SQL" pop-up in Figure 4-7.

The other facilities available through the Object Menu include tools to help generate scripts to re-create the database in its entirety, including a Server Manager (*svrmgrl*)-type script† (a typical example of which is displayed in Example 4-2), as well as other tools to debug PL/SQL objects that fail to compile properly.

---

* Remember from Chapter 2 that the Perl DBI architecture is not universally restrictive. If different database types can provide specific extensions beyond standard SQL/92 usage, the individual drivers (such as DBD::Oracle) can provide access to these extensions via the DBI *func()* method.

† Yes, we know that Server Manager is a cipher in the bit bucket of history, but we'll always love it.

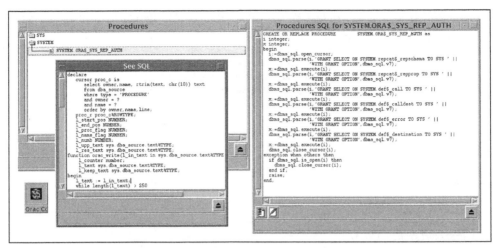

Figure 4-7. Hierarchical drill-down displaying procedural DDL

You will have to do a small amount of customization of the following script, to which we've also added some step numbers. (Note the highlighted lines. At the end of Example 4-2, we'll explain what's happening with them.)

Example 4-2. Typical Orac Script for Regenerating an Entire Database Structure

```
rem  ***********************************************
rem  crdborcl.sql
rem  ***********************************************
rem  Database name         :orcl
rem  Database created      :29-JUL-00
rem  Database log_mode     :NOARCHIVELOG
rem  Database blocksize    :2048 bytes
rem  Database buffers      :100 blocks
rem  Database log_buffers  :8192 blocks
rem  Database ifile        :
rem
rem  Note:  Use ALTER SYSTEM BACKUP CONTROLFILE TO TRACE;
rem  to generate a script to create controlfile
rem  and compare it with the output of this script.
rem  Add MAXLOGFILES, MAXDATAFILES, etc. if reqd.
rem  ***********************************************

spool crdborcl.lst
connect internal
startup nomount

rem -- please verify/change the following parameters as needed

rem Step 1

CREATE DATABASE "orcl"
    NOARCHIVELOG

    REMOVE=>NB: Make sure NOARCHIVELOG/ARCHIVELOG sorted out
```

Example 4-2. Typical Orac Script for Regenerating an Entire Database Structure (continued)

```
/* You may wish to change the following  values,          */
/* and use values found from a control file backed up     */
/* to trace.  Alternatively, uncomment these defaults.    */
/* (MAXLOGFILES and MAXLOGMEMBERS have been selected from  */
/* v$log, character set from NLS_DATABASE_PARAMETERS.*/

/* option start:use control file*/

CHARACTER SET  US7ASCII
MAXLOGFILES    8
MAXLOGMEMBERS  2
rem Step 2

/* MAXDATAFILES   255 */
/* MAXINSTANCES   1 */
/* MAXLOGHISTORY  100 */
/* option end  :use control file*/

DATAFILE
  '/u02/sys1orcl.ora' SIZE 40M

LOGFILE
  GROUP  1 (
  '/u03/log2orcl.ora'
  ) SIZE 100K

  ,
  GROUP  2 (
  '/u04/log1orcl.ora'
  ) SIZE 100K
;

rem -------------------------------------
rem  Need a basic rollback segment before proceeding
rem -------------------------------------

CREATE ROLLBACK SEGMENT dummy TABLESPACE SYSTEM
    storage (initial 500K next 500K minextents 2);
ALTER ROLLBACK SEGMENT dummy ONLINE;
commit;
rem -------------------------------------

rem Create DBA views

@?/rdbms/admin/catalog.sql
commit;

rem -------------------------------------
rem  Additional Tablespaces
rem -------------------------------------

CREATE TABLESPACE ROLLBACK_DATA DATAFILE
    '/u02/rbs1orcl.ora' SIZE 2M
```

Example 4-2. Typical Orac Script for Regenerating an Entire Database Structure (continued)

```
default storage
 (initial 10K
  next 10K
  pctincrease 0
  minextents 1
  maxextents 121
 ) ;
rem ---------------------------------------

CREATE TABLESPACE TEMPORARY_DATA DATAFILE
    '/u03/tmp1orcl.ora' SIZE 2M

default storage
 (initial 10K
  next 10K
  pctincrease 0
  minextents 1
  maxextents 121
 ) ;
rem ---------------------------------------

CREATE TABLESPACE USER_DATA DATAFILE
    '/u04/usr1orcl.ora' SIZE 5M

default storage
 (initial 10K
  next 10K
  pctincrease 0
  minextents 1
  maxextents 121
 ) ;

rem ---------------------------------------
rem  Create additional rollback segments in the rollback tablespace
rem ---------------------------------------

CREATE ROLLBACK SEGMENT DUMMY
 TABLESPACE SYSTEM STORAGE
    (initial 100K
 next 100K
 minextents 2
 maxextents 121
);
CREATE PUBLIC ROLLBACK SEGMENT RB1
 TABLESPACE ROLLBACK_DATA STORAGE
    (initial 50K
 next 50K
 minextents 2
 maxextents 121
 optimal 100K
);
CREATE PUBLIC ROLLBACK SEGMENT RB2
 TABLESPACE ROLLBACK_DATA STORAGE
```

Example 4-2. Typical Orac Script for Regenerating an Entire Database Structure (continued)

```
    (initial 50K
 next 50K
 minextents 2
 maxextents 121
 optimal 100K
);
CREATE PUBLIC ROLLBACK SEGMENT RB3
 TABLESPACE ROLLBACK_DATA STORAGE
    (initial 50K
 next 50K
 minextents 2
 maxextents 121
 optimal 100K
);
CREATE PUBLIC ROLLBACK SEGMENT RB4
 TABLESPACE ROLLBACK_DATA STORAGE
    (initial 50K
 next 50K
 minextents 2
 maxextents 121
 optimal 100K
);
ALTER ROLLBACK SEGMENT RB1 ONLINE;
ALTER ROLLBACK SEGMENT RB2 ONLINE;
ALTER ROLLBACK SEGMENT RB3 ONLINE;
ALTER ROLLBACK SEGMENT RB4 ONLINE;

rem  Take the initial rollback segment (dummy) offline

ALTER ROLLBACK SEGMENT dummy OFFLINE;

rem ----------------------------------------

ALTER USER SYS TEMPORARY TABLESPACE SYSTEM;
ALTER USER SYSTEM TEMPORARY TABLESPACE TEMPORARY_DATA DEFAULT TABLESPACE USER_DATA;

rem ----------------------------------------

rem  Run other @?/rdbms/admin required scripts

commit;

@?/rdbms/admin/catproc.sql

rem You may wish to uncomment the following scripts?

rem Step 3

rem @?/rdbms/admin/catparr.sql
rem @?/rdbms/admin/catexp.sql
rem @?/rdbms/admin/catrep.sql
rem @?/rdbms/admin/dbmspool.sql
rem @?/rdbms/admin/utlmontr.sql
```

Example 4-2. Typical Orac Script for Regenerating an Entire Database Structure (continued)

```
commit;

connect system/manager
@?/sqlplus/admin/pupbld.sql
@?/rdbms/admin/catdbsyn.sql

commit;

spool off
exit

rem EOF
```

Note that you'll have to make the following modifications to this script:

1. You must make sure that the ARCHIVELOG situation is fully resolved before running the script.

2. The MAXDATAFILES, MAXINSTANCES, and MAXLOGHISTORY directions necessary for database creation are held directly within control files. Therefore, the PL/SQL program outputting the Server Manager script (which relies entirely upon the data dictionary) uses defaults that you must uncomment or change, if necessary. To avoid future trace control file trickery adjusting the figure upwards, you might want to make sure that MAXDATAFILES is always set high enough that it won't ever need to be reset, if this is within your database construction guidelines. (We learned this from the hard knocks school of "mistakes you make only once.")

3. After *catproc.sql* is run near the end of the script, you'll have to uncomment or add in any other *@?/rdbms/admin* scripts you may want to run after the initial database creation.

User Menu

The User menu is divided into two main sections. The first offers you ten different reports containing various information on what your users are currently doing with the database. Available submenus include:

User Records
    Current Logged on Users
    Registered Users on Database
    User Activity Summary
User Processes
    What SQL Statements are Users Processing?
    Any Users Updating on Database?
    Any User Processes Performing I/O?
    Current Processes

User Access
> Roles on Database
> Profiles on Database
> Quotas

Typical of the SQL statements driving these reports is the code shown in Example 4-3.

Example 4-3. SQL Behind the Current Logged on Users Report

```
/* Thanks to Andre Seesink for Sid,Serial change to ease */
/* session control */
select s.username "User", s.osuser "OS User",
       s.sid||','||s.serial# "Sid,Serial",
       decode(s.type, 'USER', 'User', 'BACKGROUND',
              'Backgd', s.type) "Type",
       decode(s.status,'INACTIVE','Inact ' ||
                               round((s.last_call_et/60),0) ||
                               ' min',
                    'ACTIVE', 'Active',
           s.status) "Status",
       to_char(s.logon_time,'dd/mm hh24:mi') "Logged On",
       p.spid "Spid",
       s.program "Program", s.module "Module",
       s.server "Server", s.machine "Machine",   s.terminal "Terminal",
       decode(s.command, 0,'',              1,'Create Table',
                    2,'Insert',          3,'Select',
                    4,'Create Cluster',  5,'Alter Cluster',
                    6,'Update',          7,'Delete',
                    8,'Drop',            9,'Create Index',
                    10,'Drop Index',     11,'Alter Index',
                    12,'Drop Table',     15,'Alter Table',
                    17,'Grant',          18,'Revoke',
                    19,'Create Synonym', 20,'Drop Synonym',
                    21,'Create View',    22,'Drop View',
                    26,'Lock Table',
                    28,'Rename',         29,'Comment',
                    30,'Audit',          31,'Noaudit',
                    32,'Cre Ext Data',   33,'Drop Ext Dat',
                    34,'Create Data',    35,'Alter Data',
                    36,'Create Rollback Segment',
                    37,'Alter Rollback Segment',
                    38,'Drop Rollback Segment',
                    39,'Create Tablespace',
                    40,'Alter Tablespace',
                    41,'Drop Tablespace',
                    42,'Alter Session',  43,'Alter User',
                    44,'Commit',         45,'Rollback',
                    46,'Save Point',     47,'PL/SQL',
                    to_char(command))    "Command Type",
       decode(s.lockwait,'','','Yes') "Lock Wait?"
from   v$session s, v$process p
where  s.paddr = p.addr
order by 1, 2, 3, 4, 5
```

As the previous example clearly demonstrates, Orac is not driven by polymorphic 23rd-century science. However, it is nice not to have to type this sort of thing in too often or to need to remember which *afiedt.buf* file you last saw it in (and on which host).

Sids and addresses

The second half of the User Menu gives you two pop-ups with which you can interrogate various Sids and addresses, particularly those of spinning processes or any other processes taking up more than their fair share of CPU time. You may decide that such processes are due for a merciful license-to-kill 007 command. (This part of the User Menu was originally written after a request from a senior sysadmin/DBA within Oracle Corporation, who we hope is still using it.) You can see these two covert partners in action in Figure 4-8.

Figure 4-8. Options to isolate and then kill spinning processes with Orac

Lock Menu

A number of helpful reporting scripts gathered under the Lock menu allow you to check various locking scenarios, particularly in emergency situations. These scripts include the following:

> Locks Currently Held
> Who's holding back Whom
> Who's accessing which objects?
> Rollback locks?
> Top ORACLE Wait events
> Summary of Session Waits & CPU

The use of a specialized Lock Menu was originally suggested by Tim Bunce. The most critical of the submenus available through the Lock Menu is perhaps "Who's holding back Whom?" The driving script for this report is shown below:

```
select substr(s1.username,1,12) "Wait User",
substr(s1.osuser,1,8) "OS User",
s1.serial# "Ser#",
substr(to_char(w.sid),1,5) "Sid",
P1.spid "Pid",
'=>' "=>",
substr(s2.username,1,12) "Hold User",
substr(s2.osuser,1,8) "OS User",
s2.serial# "Ser#",
substr(to_char(h.sid),1,5) "Sid",
P2.spid "Pid"
from v$process P1,v$process P2,
v$session S1,v$session S2,
v$lock w,v$lock h
where h.lmode is not null
and w.request is not null
and h.lmode != 0
and w.request != 0
and w.type (+) = h.type
and w.id1 (+) = h.id1
and w.id2 (+) = h.id2
and w.sid = S1.sid (+)
and h.sid = S2.sid (+)
and S1.paddr = P1.addr (+)
and S2.paddr = P2.addr (+)
```

Every once in a while, with some applications (OLTP applications, in particular), a single user might lock one row on a table, which then blocks every other client. If this user then leaves his client up while he goes for lunch or home for the day, this situation can quickly become a serious problem, especially on a production database.

In normal situations, the driving script shown in the previous section reports no rows. However, if you suspect that a lock situation has occurred, running the report above should reveal it. To demonstrate that case, we'll open a SQL*Plus session and update one row with the following SQL (pressing the Return key, but without committing the update):

```
SQL> select * from dept;

    DEPTNO DNAME          LOC
--------- -------------- -------------
        10 ACCOUNTING     NEW YORK
        20 RESEARCH       DALLAS
        30 SALES          CHICAGO
        40 OPERATIONS     BOSTON
```

```
SQL> update dept set dname = 'ACCOUNTING' where deptno = 10;

1 row updated.

SQL>
```

We then open another SQL*Plus session and attempt the same update:

```
SQL> update dept set dname = 'ACCOUNTING' where deptno = 10;
```

When you press the Return key in this case, however, you will not get the "1 row updated" message; the program will sit there waiting for the first session to commit before it too can carry on (i.e., the row has been locked by the first session). When this occurs, the Orac program will report the situation as in Figure 4-9. As well as providing a basic report, the program also creates a drill-down pick-list within a Perl/Tk text widget that can be used to gain further kill information to help unlock the situation (no prisoners taken in this data shop, we think you'll agree!).

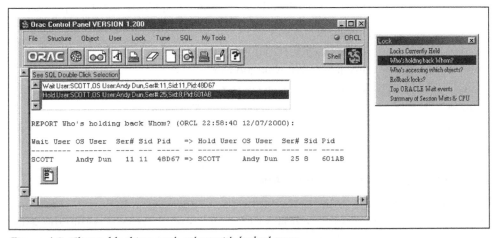

Figure 4-9. Clients blocking each other with locked rows

Tune Menu

There are many different tuning scripts embedded within the Orac program and available from the Tune menu. Most of these scripts were added to the program as a result of user requests for extended functionality with SQL. Many scripts were, in fact, supplied by the users themselves!

Reporting options

Table 4-2 summarizes the options available through the Tune Menu.

Table 4-2. Reporting Options Within Orac's Tune Menu

Top-Level Options	Secondary Options
Hit Ratios	Version 1, Version 2 (various reports on hit ratios et al, displayed in Figure 4-10)
SQL Browser and Explain Plan	The ability to browse through the SQL cache and use the EXPLAIN PLAN tuning facilities (covered in more depth in the following section)
Shared Pool and SQL	Pool Statements, High Disk Reads, All Pool Statements, Pool Fragmentation?, Main SGA Stats, Fuller SGA Stats Info
Rollback	Rollback Statistics, Rollback Sizings, Current States
Parameters	NLS Parameters, Database Info, Version Info, Show Parameters
Mts	Mts User Session Current and Max Memory (Figure 4-11), Mts Busy Time of the Dispatchers, Mts Wait Time for the Dispatcher Queues, Mts Wait Time for a Server, Total Session UGA, Total Session UGA Max
Database Writer	File I/O (also seen in Figure 4-10), ORACLE Session IO (this option also has a rough-and-ready facility to rapidly repeat the report in a 1-second loop, to enable quick visual monitoring), DBWR Monitor, DBWR LRU Latches
Log Writer	LGWR Monitor, LGWR Redo Buffer Latches
DBWR & LGWR	DBWR & LGWR Waits Monitor
Sorts	Sort Monitor, Identifying Sort Users
Latches	Current Latch Wait Ratios, Latch Waiters
Tablespaces	Tablespace Fragmentation, Tablespace Space Shortages
Data Objects	Tables, Indexes, Views, Sequences, Links, Synonyms, Constraints

SQL Browser/Explain Plan menu option

Following a suggestion from Guy Harrison's tuning book about SQL browsing tools, this option browses through all of the SQL currently parsed within the database library cache via the V$SQLAREA data dictionary view.

To get the full Explain Plan capability available via this menu option, the *$ORACLE_HOME/rdbms/admin/utlxplan.sql* script must already have been run by your Orac login user in order to create the necessary PLAN_TABLE. (You may still use the SQL Browser functionality even if PLAN_TABLE has not yet been created, however.)

Merged in with the SQL Browser, the Explain Plan option is only available when looking at cached SQL created originally by the database user logged in via Orac (that is, if you're the SYSTEM user, you can only "Explain" the SYSTEM user's SQL). However, if you clear the screen with the eraser button, you can enter any new

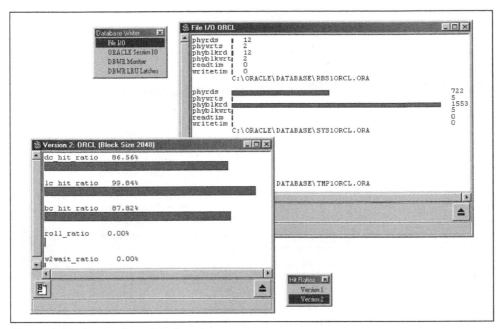

Figure 4-10. A pair of graphical tuning reports

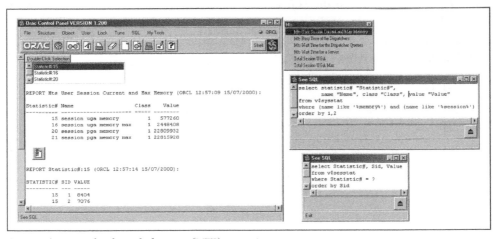

Figure 4-11. Multi-threaded server (MTS) reporting

SQL directly and explain it then and there. To demonstrate the combined Browser/Explain functionality, we'll run a simple SQL statement as our SYSTEM user:

```
SQL> select count(*) from dba_tables;

COUNT(*)
---------
     129


SQL>
```

We can now scroll through the library cache with the Browser slider and find the appropriate SQL. Once we've found it, we press the spot marked "X" to generate the execution plan for this particular SQL statement (Figure 4-12).

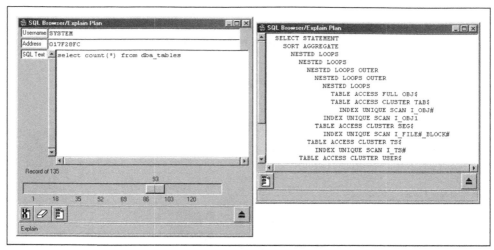

Figure 4-12. The Browser facility to track down and explain SQL

Alternatively, you can clear the SQL text with the eraser button and then enter your own SQL directly before interrogating the execution plan, as shown in Figure 4-13.

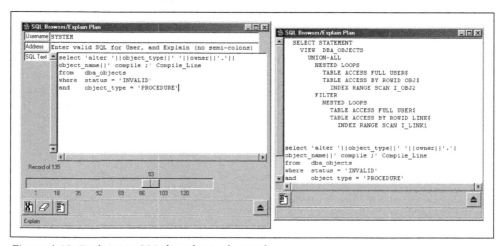

Figure 4-13. Explaining SQL directly via the "X" button

SQL Menu

The SQL menu allows you to invoke the Orac Shell program and perform a number of other SQL-related functions. Orac Shell was developed by Thomas Lowery, who is also a major contributor to the Perl DBI database driver scene (DBD::Ado, etc.). He originally slotted this module directly into the main Orac structure as a GUI form of Perl's *dbish* program. Orac Shell immediately became one of the best features of the program, and its second major functional area (the first, of course, is central DBA interrogation). The third functional area is the program's web interface, which we'll describe at the end of the Orac section later in the chapter.

The Orac Shell interface

As its name suggests, Orac Shell is an interactive shell-like program for interfacing directly with the database and running transactions in a manner similar to SQL*Plus. Although it runs in a window that's separate from the main Orac application, it is often run in tandem with the main window.

Part of Orac Shell's widely interactive use is demonstrated within Figure 4-14. Here we've employed the file selection facility within Orac Shell to pick up the second SQL plug-in file used to fill the SQL Browser feature described earlier. We've then executed it to generate the raw results that are employed by Orac to fill the Browser slider in Figure 4-13. Much more can be achieved through the use of Orac Shell. It's such an interactive tool that we recommend you download it and try it out for yourself, rather than have us try to explain it step by step.

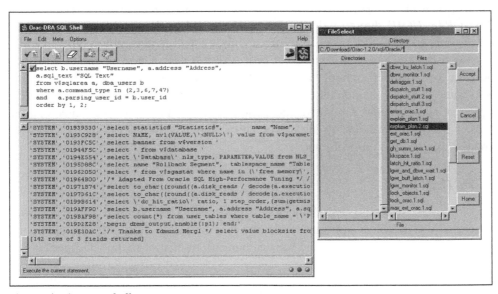

Figure 4-14. Orac Shell in action

Transaction control

Orac Shell is the main place within the Orac program where transactions can take place. You can set whether Perl DBI's AutoCommit facility is On or Off by clicking on a button at the right-hand bottom edge of the main Orac Shell screen. A red button indicates that AutoCommit is Off, a green button that it is On.

My Tools Menu

Suggested originally by Jared Still, Orac's last main menu option adds a personalized feature. The My Tools menu lets you add your own buttons to the menus to allow you to run your own customized SQL statements. To set up this option, follow these steps, which are also fully described within the Help section of the My Tools menu option:

1. Add a cascade menu to the My Tools menu.
2. Add a button to the cascade menu.
3. Add the SQL to the button you wish to run.

Once the SQL has been added, you can then run it immediately, just like any other Orac report. This is demonstrated in Figure 4-15, where we've attached a piece of SQL to a new button and cascade (you can give these cascades and buttons any names you like (we've named ours "tom" and "jerry").

As soon as it's saved, the SQL is available immediately on the fly using Perl's circle-squaring *eval()* capability. The report appears via the main program menu interface as a standard option under the My Tools menu, with the "See SQL" functionality also built in. The cascade-button-SQL combination is also stored directly under the *$ORAC_HOME* directory destination, as described earlier. It remains invisible to other users running this installation of Orac, but it will persistently re-appear each time you run the program (thanks to Bruce Albrecht's creation of multiuser functionality within the program). The cascades, buttons, and accompanying SQL are also fully editable. Incidentally, you may notice in Figure 4-15 that the generated report is automatically formatted into neat columns with no manual intervention. This is the result of some pretty clever DBI coding by Kevin Brannen, who also created the Informix port of Orac.

Icon Bar

The icon bar stretching across the top of the main Orac control panel accesses programs unavailable from the menus and also provides shortcut access to regularly used menu options. (See the bar just beneath the list of menus in Figure 4-3.)

Reconnect
  Brings up the main database login screen.

Database Monitor
  Provides access to the database monitor.

Font Selector
  Allows the display fonts to be configured to any available on the machine.

Print Selection
  Offers a limited printing service.

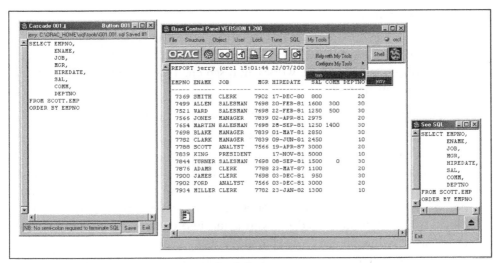

Figure 4-15. Adding a SQL button via the My Tools menu option

Clear Screen

Clears the main control panel screen. Not normally necessary unless manual screen clearance is set, as described below, to enable many reports to be viewed simultaneously.

Auto Screen Clearance

Reports usually clear the screen automatically before they print out. This feature switches between automatic clearance and manual clearance, which requires the eraser button.

Main File Viewer

Allows drill-down access to every file making up the Orac program, including source code files, SQL plug-ins, and everything else (including the image files in the *../img* directory).

Orac Home Viewer

Allows access to files stored separately in your personal *$ORAC_HOME* directory, which may be located on a different directory path from the Orac program directory.

Documentation

Provides access to the development documentation accompanying the program.

Help

Provides help files containing configuration information necessary to set up menus, SQL files, and other parts of the system.

The Print Selection and Database Monitor buttons, described in the following sections, are perhaps the two most interesting options for future development.

Print Selection button

Once the report has appeared on the main control panel report screen, you can press the print icon. It's then transformed into a formatted Perl/Tk canvas widget, which pops up separately on the workstation screen. This window requires you to complete the following tasks:

1. Set the paper size and preferred portrait/landscape orientation.

2. Press the PS button to create a PostScript file in the *$ORAC_HOME* directory or supply an operating system command to send the Perl/Tk canvas directly to a networked PostScript printer. The Help information available via the Print Selection screen should give you some basic details on how to do this on various operating systems; however, printing is not the smoothest facility within the Orac program and could do with some improvement (perhaps linking it more easily to Russell Lang's GSview program?).

3. If the PostScript file is created, you should be able to use any standard Post-Script application to render the Perl/Tk canvas containing the report, as in Figure 4-16.

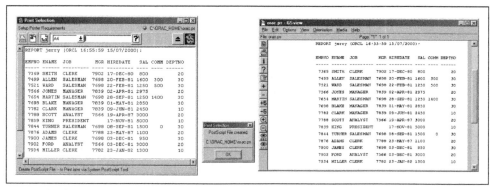

Figure 4-16. Converting an Orac report into a PostScript output file

To learn more about open PostScript applications, check out the following excellent web site for Ghostscript, Ghostview, and GSview (written by Russell Lang):

   http://www.cs.wisc.edu/~ghost/

Database Monitor button

The Database Monitor facility is an experimental part of the Orac program; however, you may wish to make some use of it or possibly expand it to meet your requirements. The ideas behind it are heavily "borrowed" from the Karma program (coincidentally originated by another of your authors, Sean Hull, and described in Chapter 6, *Building Web-Based Oracle Applications*). The Karma program is a far more advanced web database monitoring tool, and its web basis is perhaps a more natural home for such a background monitor. However, if all you require is fairly simple monitoring, Orac's Database Monitor might do the trick.

 The Database Monitor was developed under Solaris 2.6 and has been reported as also working effectively under Win32. However, there was an Oracle OCI bug under Linux that caused disconnection problems for the program. This bug was reported and we hope it will be fixed by Oracle in subsequent versions of Oracle for Linux.

In Figure 4-17, we have set up three databases to be checked by the monitoring program. The program can then be left to run in the background, rechecking the database in a configurable period of 15 seconds to 24 hours. Various red and yellow warning flags are used to indicate particular problems with a target database. You can press these drillable flags for further information. In the following example, we check for the percentage of sorts in memory as opposed to those on disk:

```
Y2KDEV memsorts flag

Red flag given by less than    : 90
Yellow flag given by less than: 95
Last value found               : 95.77


/* This finds out the percentage of sorts occurring in memory */
/* Thanks to Duncan Lawie */
select round((sum( decode( name, 'sorts (memory)', value, 0 ) )
                           / (
          sum( decode( name, 'sorts (memory)', value, 0 ) )  +
          sum( decode( name, 'sorts (disk)', value, 0 ) )
                        ) * 100),2)
from v$sysstat
```

There are currently nine monitoring reports (detailed in Table 4-3) that come preinstalled with the Orac program. There are full configuration instructions for adding many further checks, depending on what you require, with the basic rule being that SQL monitoring plug-ins must report a figure that can be broken down into thresholds. The higher the figure, the better the situation:

- If a figure stays above a particular good threshold, the flag stays green.

- If it drops below this threshold, but stays above danger, it goes to yellow alert.

- If it drops below the danger threshold, the flag goes to red alert.

Here is another example of SQL used to monitor the rollback situation as follows:

```
select 100.00 -
(round((sum(waits) / (sum(gets) + .00000001)) * 100,2))
from v$rollstat
```

You can make up any number of these kinds of checks, which can be easily configured and added into the monitoring loop.

Table 4-3. Pre-Installed Monitoring Scripts Under Database Monitor

Flag	Monitoring Report
redo	Checks the Redo Logs via the V$LOG database view
roll	Checks Rollback Stats in V$ROLLSTAT
w2w	Checks the Willing-to-Wait Stats via Latches
tbsp	Monitors Tablespaces filling up through DBA_DATA_FILES and DBA_SEGMENTS
slow	A rough indicator of slow SQL detected through V$SQLAREA
dchr	Dictionary Cache Hit Ratio (Row Cache)
lchr	Library Cache Hit Ratio
bchr	Buffer Cache Hit Ratio
sort	Percentage of sorts occurring in memory

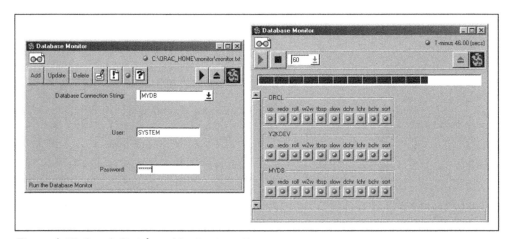

Figure 4-17. Orac's Database Monitor in action

Running Orac over the Web Using Perlplus

By using Frank Holtry's Perlplus plug-in, which we described in Chapter 3, you can set up Orac to run over the Web. Once you've got Perlplus set up (as described in Chapter 3), follow the instructions provided with the Orac program in the *../help/ WebPlugin.txt* file for running it over the Web. An outline of these instructions is provided below (note that here we assume the use of Apache and Orac-1.2.0):

1. Unpack your Orac tarball distribution file in Apache's *../cgi-bin* directory.

2. Rename *Orac-1.2.0/orac_dba.pl* to *Orac-1.2.0/orac_dba.ppl*.

3. Go to the *../pplug* directory.

4. Edit the *orac.html* file by renaming the *Orac-x.y.z* string as follows:

```
<embed src="/cgi-bin/Orac-1.2.0/orac_dba.ppl"
enctype="application/x-perlplus">
```

5. Move *orac.html* to your Apache *../htdocs* directory.

6. Edit the *perlplus-secure.cgi* file by changing the URL_ROOT string to your appropriate host—the one you compiled the Netscape plug-in with, using the *Makefile* SECURE_CGI directive. For our example, we changed this to the following:

```
$URL_ROOT="http://127.0.0.1/cgi-bin";
```

7. Move *perlplus-secure.cgi* directly into Apache's *../cgi-bin* (making sure it's executable).

8. Copy *Orac-1.2.0/img/splash.gif* to your Apache *../icons* directory (it will be accessed here by *orac.html* later on).

9. Under your Apache configuration file, *httpd.conf,* add the following section (and adapt the Oracle DBA user and ORACLE_HOME value, as highlighted):

```
# OracWeb General Environment Variables
SetEnv ORACWEB_SWITCH 1
SetEnv ORACWEB_DB_TYPE Oracle
SetEnv ORACWEB_DBA_USER SYSTEM
SetEnv ORACWEB_BACKGROUND_COL steelblue2
SetEnv ORACWEB_STANDARD_DB pppep
SetEnv ORACWEB_FOREGROUND_COL black
SetEnv ORACWEB_ENTRY_COL white
SetEnv ORACWEB_FONT_FAMILY courier
SetEnv ORACWEB_FONT_SIZE 10
SetEnv ORACWEB_FONT_WEIGHT normal
SetEnv ORACWEB_FONT_SLANT roman

# OracWeb Specific Oracle Required Variable
SetEnv ORACLE_HOME /u01/app/oracle/product/8.1.5
```

10. Shut down your Apache *httpd* program and restart with the new configurations. Then point your browser at the installed Orac program to receive the login dialog over the Web (see Figure 4-18).

This technique can easily be adapted to any Perl/Tk Oracle database programs you write yourself, providing you with a moveable feast of thin Perl GUI applications you won't have to carry around anymore.

Extending Orac

There are plenty of expansion opportunities for the Orac program, particularly in terms of adding new Oracle capabilities. Orac has stagnated for a while because it relied on the efforts of two or three key programmers who took time out to work on other projects (you're holding the results of one of those efforts in your hands).

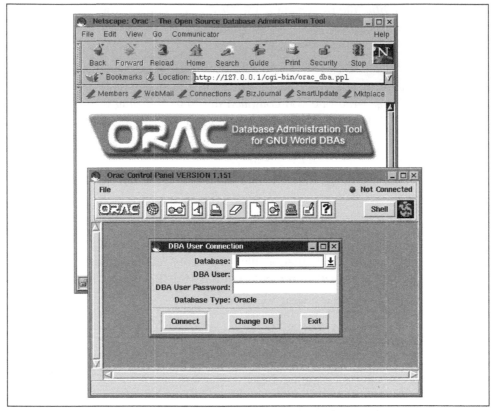

Figure 4-18. The Perlplus plug-in at work with Orac

To help break this logjam, we're going to try to exploit the fluid development model of CVS. If you'd be interested in helping out with this, check out the following SourceForge PerlDBAdmin "parent" project. Further extensions to the Orac program will be developed here before being released on CPAN:

> *http://sourceforge.net/projects/perldbadmin/*

These extensions will include the use of Richard Sutherland's DDL-Oracle Perl module for Oracle developers and DBAs, and Dean Arnold's DBD-Chart graphical facilities (similar to Tcl's BLT, discussed later in this chapter). These two modules are available at the following web sites:

> *http://www.perl.com/CPAN-local/modules/by-authors/id/R/RV/RVSUTHERL*
> *http://home.earthlink.net/~darnold/dbdchart/*

---

dbMan

Hailing from the Czech Republic is dbMan, another Perl/Tk DBI tool designed for use with Oracle. dbMan was created by Milan Sorm and is readily available from the following web sites:

http://dbman.linux.cz
> Home page

http://www.fi.muni.cz/~sorm/dbman/
> Primary mirror

If you've loaded up the required Perl, Perl/Tk, Perl DBI, and DBD::Oracle modules for Orac, as we described earlier, you should be able to run dbMan straight out of the box with the following command:

```
$ perl dbman
```

The dbMan program is an interactive SQL*Plus-like program that provides various plug-in Oracle modules. It also contains other useful tools for accessing and updating information within the database, particularly the table drill-downs and formatted results panels. Download it and check it out.

Oddis

Oddis (Oracle Data Dictionary Information System) is a Tcl/Tk-based graphical user interface for navigating visually throughout the entire Oracle data dictionary (ODD). Oddis follows in the footsteps of Tom Poindexter's Wosql and IUD Maker programs (covered in Chapter 3), but it is a much more comprehensive Tcl/Tk Oracle application, and it provides an excellent example for aspiring Oracle open source developers. The program is based on original work by Rainer Gruetzner and is currently maintained by a team at the University of Hanover in Germany, including Michael Bethke, Axel Schlüter, and Regine Kasten, who have moved the program forward mostly via their computer science projects.

Intended primarily for DBAs, both novice and expert, Oddis aims to make the data dictionary as simple as possible to traverse, while providing the maximum amount of useful information. In addition to providing tools for Oracle DBAs, Oddis also possesses excellent facilities for storing and running SQL files as well as superb EXPLAIN PLAN functionality (including diagrammatic trees), making it potentially useful for developers too.

Oddis is far more than the data dictionary viewer it modestly claims to be. It is also a fully interactive OLTP tool, as well as a general reporting engine. It offers complete facilities for transactions, commits, rollbacks, auto-commits, and so on, in the main interface, all available via its various menus. The program provides an excellent demonstration of what's possible using TclX and Oratcl, and it offers substantial room for expansion in the future. We can't wait to see Oddis 3.0 and any subsequent developments. (Oddis 3.0 is rumored to be nearly ready for release and may even provide some kind of linkup with Java. Stay tuned.)

The large number of Tcl/Tk web plug-ins and other developments from Sun, as well as Oracle Corporation's own efforts to push Oratcl (which we described in Chapter 3) make the future for Tcl/Tk Oracle applications such as Oddis very bright indeed.

The main web site for Oddis is:

ftp://www-b.informatik.uni-hannover.de/ftp/software/oddis/oddis-2.11.html

That central information page will direct you to the latest download, for example, *oddis-2.11.tar.gz*

Installing Oddis

Before you can install Oddis, you will need to install Tcl/Tk, TclX, and Oratcl on your system. These installations are described in Chapter 3. You can then install Oddis by following these steps:

1. Download the latest version of Oddis from the site listed at the end of the previous section.

2. Unpack the Oddis tarball:

   ```
   $ gzip -d oddis-2.11.tar.gz
   $ tar xvf oddis-2.11.tar
   $ cd oddis-2.11
   ```

3. Make sure that the Oratcl side of the equation is happy by ensuring that the correct Oracle libraries are accessible. For example:

   ```
   $ ORACLE_HOME=/u01/app/oracle/product/8.1.5
   $ export ORACLE_HOME
   $ LD_LIBRARY_PATH=/usr/local/lib:$ORACLE_HOME/lib
   $ export LD_LIBRARY_PATH
   ```

4. In case of display difficulty, you may also want to point the appropriate environment variable at your current screen:

   ```
   $ DISPLAY=:0.0
   $ export DISPLAY
   ```

5. Edit the actual Oddis script to make sure you're pointing at the correct version of the *wishx* TclX program on your system:

   ```
   $ vi oddis2.11

   #!/usr/local/bin/wishx
   ```

```
# Program: oddis_v2.0
# Tcl version: 7.4 (Tcl/Tk)
# Tk version: 4.0
```

6. Make sure the Tcl MODULE_PATH variable (described more fully in the *README.FIRST* file in the download) is set to the directory in which you're currently running the Oddis program. This is to ensure that the correct helper Tcl scripts and indexes are picked up correctly:

```
# SET THE RIGHT MODULE_PATH HERE !!!!!
#set module_path /home/tpoindex/src/tcl/oddis-2.11
#set module_path /root/tk/oratcl-2.5/samples/oddis # Local Oratcl
set module_path /root/tk/oratcl-2.5/oddis-2.11 # Local Download
```

7. You should now be ready to run the Oddis program:

```
$ ./oddis2.11
```

Using Oddis

Once you've installed and started up the Oddis program, you'll see the Oddis login screen in Figure 4-19. No surprises here, but as you'll soon see, Oddis does possess several features which we haven't seen in the tools described so far in this book, and it also provides the usual assortment of drill-down goodies (Figure 4-20 also shows the main menus displayed in the Oddis top level menu):

File menu

The usual suspects, plus the ability to open SQL files stored on disk.

Options menu

The most important option is the ability to change the transactional state of the program, but other options are available as well.

SQL-Options menu

Allows several of the more involved SQL types of operations, including LONG data handling and PL/SQL.

User-Objects and All-Objects menus

Allow you to drill down into their respective sets of database objects (e.g., tables, sequences, views, etc.). Roles and other granted privileges can also be accessed from these paired menus.

System menu

Drills down on system-specific details.

Optimize menu

Provides Oddis SQL tuning options.

Help menu

Michael Bethke's extended active help system.

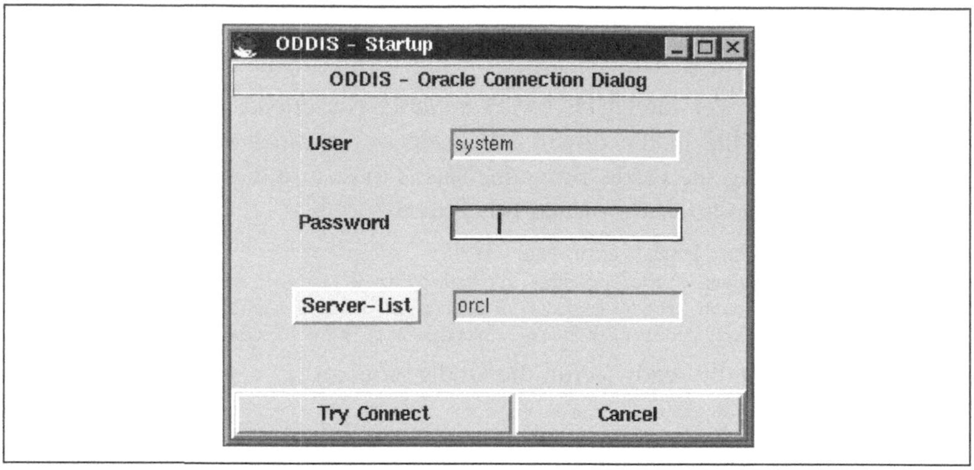

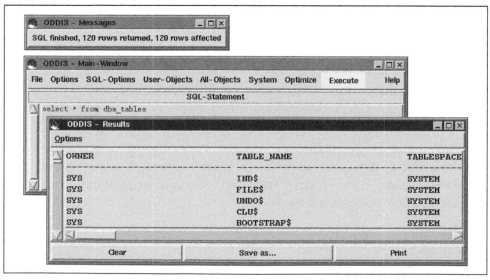

Figure 4-19. The initial Oddis login screen

File Menu

First and foremost, the Oddis program can act as a SQL command and reporting tool, as demonstrated by a familiar selection statement's execution in Figure 4-20. Oddis also lets you read any SQL scripts you might have in your various collections, as in Figure 4-21, and save any new ones you've written.

Figure 4-20. SQL reporting usage via Oddis

To enable these features, the following options are available under the File menu:

New

    Edit any SQL within the main screen and prepare it for file saving.

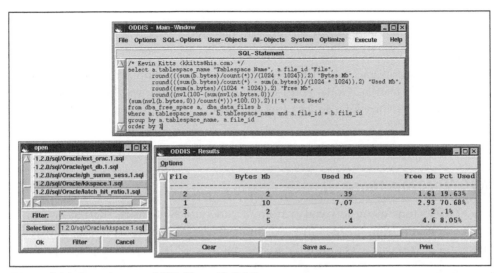

Figure 4-21. Running saved SQL files with Oddis

Open

Pick up a previously saved SQL file and populate the main screen with it.

Save

Save the current SQL into the currently open SQL file.

Save As

Create a new SQL saving file.

Quit

Exit the Oddis program.

The "Execute" button at the right-hand side of the main menu is used to execute any SQL currently within the main screen.

Options Menu

The Options menu provides several options, mostly covering the transactional state of the program:

AutoCommit

This toggles between on and off, determining your transaction commitment status on the SQL statements executed in the main window. This feature is similar to the one available through the Orac program's Orac Shell feature described earlier.

Font
> Offers a range of font sizes for program displays.

Windows
> In contrast to Orac, which is centered around one main screen holding most of the information, Oddis consists of families of windows. You can alter this default behavior with a series of menu options.

Display
> Offers a display choice between color and monochrome.

SQL-Options Menu

The SQL-Options menu lets you perform a variety of SQL tasks, such as writing a LONG column from a file and executing PL/SQL procedures. As shown in Figure 4-22, you can select from the following:

Commit Now
> Available for use when AutoCommit is set to off.

Rollback Now
> Available for use when AutoCommit is set to off.

Write Long Column
> Allows you to insert files into Oracle LONG columns (this process is demonstrated in Figure 4-22).

Read Long Column
> The reverse of Write Long Column.

Procedure Execute
> Enables the binding of variables and the execution of PL/SQL procedures.

User-Objects Menu and All-Objects Menu

The User-Objects menu and All-Objects menu are identical except that the User-Objects menu lets a logged-on user access only his own objects, while the All-Objects menu allows access to all the objects that user can see, either in his own schema or in other schemas. Both menus deliver a full range of options to drill down into the various database objects in a manner that's similar to Orac's Object menu structure.

The general standard format of each drill-down object remains basically the same across all the different types of database objects. You can see this standard format in Figure 4-23, which covers the second option for Columns. This option gives you quick access to all of the columns within the database and shows how they're made up. If you're tired of typing "DESC MY_TABLE" within SQL*Plus to get hold of that table column whose dimensions you keep forgetting, you'll be very happy

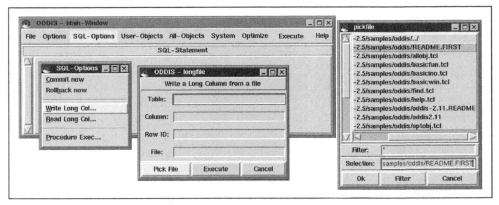

Figure 4-22. Writing LONG columns into the database via Oddis

with this Oddis feature. The following are the available related options on these
two similar menus:

Table
Columns
Indexes
Views
Clusters
Tablespaces
Extents
Sequences
DB-Links
Synonyms
Constraints
Triggers
Procedures
Roles
Privileges
Grants to User
Grants by User

The final remaining option available within this menu structure is Find, which provides a useful search utility for tracking down those elusive objects hiding in the
data dictionary. You can see this option in use in Figure 4-24. A minor difference
between the User-Objects and All-Objects versions is that you can input the object
owner in the latter. You also don't necessarily have to input the correct name for
each object you're after. The standard Oracle search wildcards, such as "%", are
available too.

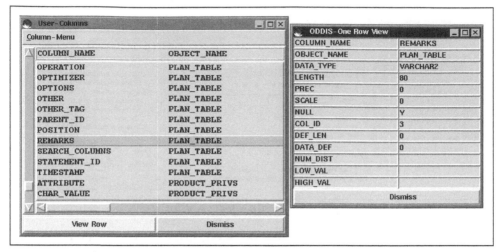

Figure 4-23. Column drill-down information

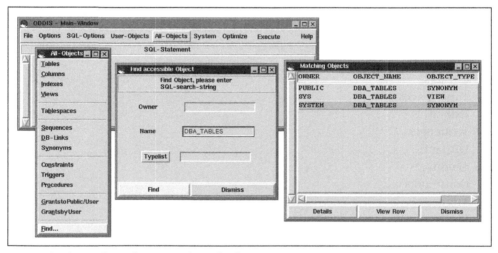

Figure 4-24. Database object searching facility

System Menu

The System menu allows you to examine system-wide information. It provides useful drill-downs in a way that's similar to that of the Columns option within the User-Objects menu. It consists of the following:

> User List
> Tablespaces
> Roles
> Rollback Segments
> Free Space

Data Files

Devices (provides raw operating system information such as disk partitions)

We've displayed a typical usage of the Rollback Segments screen in Figure 4-25.

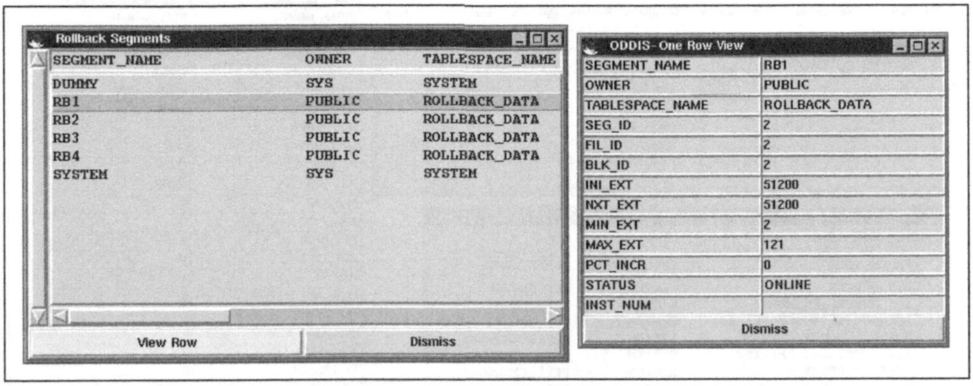

Figure 4-25. Rollback segments under Oddis

Optimize Menu

As far as we're concerned, the Optimize menu is the killer menu with Oddis. It has two main submenus, Analyze and Explain:

Analyze

Allows you to drill down on either tables or indexes and analyze their structure. This option is particularly useful for indexes. You can see this menu option at work in Figure 4-26.

Explain

Provides detailed information on Oracle's EXPLAIN PLAN facility, with numerous drill-downs, as displayed in Figure 4-27.

And if that isn't enough to whet your appetite, if you select the Show Tree option, Oddis will even draw the full execution plan in diagrammatic form, as shown in Figure 4-28.

Help Menu

The Help menu provides a variety of options, most of them making great use of Tcl/Tk's graphical canvas abilities. We've demonstrated a handful of these in Figure 4-29. The "About ODDIS" window is particularly useful. This offers help drill-downs into most of the other menus and areas within the Oddis program. This help system is unlike similar-looking systems you may have come across. Michael Bethke has creatively extended Regine Kasten's original envelope in such a way that every time you navigate through the data dictionary menus, the help function changes its state to show your next options. (We think this is a classic example of good software.)

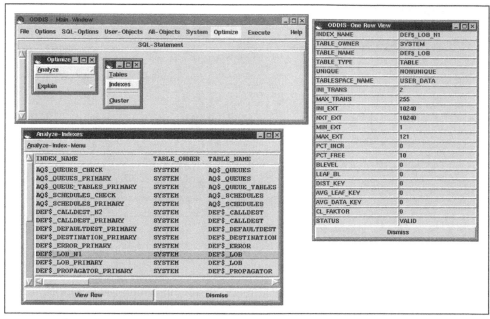

Figure 4-26. Analyze option via the Optimize menu

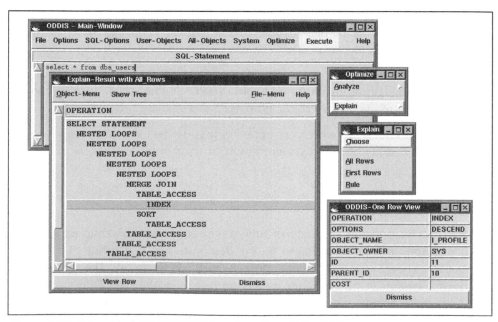

Figure 4-27. Extensive EXPLAIN PLAN functionality within Oddis

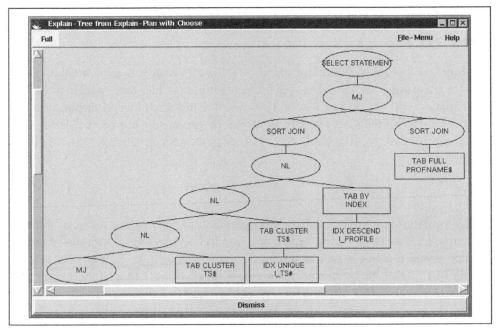

Figure 4-28. Graphical tuning with Oddis

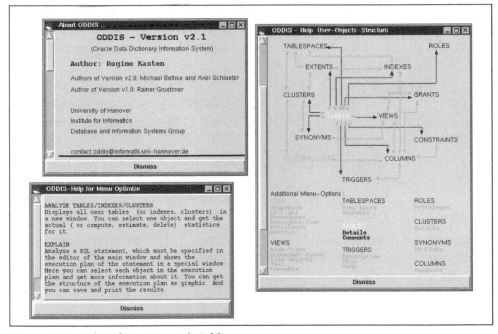

Figure 4-29. Help information with Oddis

Building Applications with Oratcl and BLT

As promised, before we leave the world of Tk, we'll create our own small application for measuring Oracle table space usage. Building this tool, which we'll call TableSpacer, will extend our use of Tk beyond using downloaded applications as is. This example builds on two excellent Tcl/Tk products: George Howlett's BLT, described in this section, and Tom Poindexter's Oratcl, already described in Chapter 3.

BLT

BLT is an extension to Tcl/Tk that adds combinations of plotting widgets (graphs, barcharts, etc.) to Tk canvases, saving you hundreds—possibly thousands—of lines of code when creating a typical on-the-fly graph within a Tk canvas object. (Not only is BLT one of the best chart-making packages around, but also the letters BLT can apparently stand for anything you want them to.)

The following are the main web sites for BLT:

http://www.tcltk.com/blt
> General information on the BLT package, upgrades, latest news, and so on.

ftp://ftp.tcltk.com/pub/blt/
> Central download site for the latest BLT code releases and self-installing pre-compiled Windows executable files.

ftp://tcltk.sourceforge.net/pub/tcltk/blt/
> SourceForge site for all things Tcl/Tk. In this directory you will find two very useful PDF tutorial files (it's the same tutorial in different layouts), *handouts. pdf* and *slides.pdf*.

BLT is also described in Paul Raines and Jeff Tranter's *Tcl/Tk in a Nutshell*, referenced in Appendix C.

Installing BLT on Unix

Before you can install BLT, you must have the basic Tcl/Tk environment set up, as we described in Chapter 3. Then follow these steps:

1. Download BLT from the download site listed earlier in this section.

2. For the standard installation, issue these commands:

```
$ gzip -d bltx.y.tar.gz
$ tar xvf bltx.y.tar (this will create the bltx.y directory)
$ cd bltx.y
$ ./configure --with-tcl=/usr/local/tcl -with-tk=/usr/local/tk
```

There are further switches available for the configuration process. The two shown above assume that you have your previous Tcl and Tk installations in their own directories. (For customized installations, check out the *README* and *INSTALL* files.)

3. Carrying on with the basic installation, run *make* and change directory as follows:

```
$ make
$ cd demos
```

4. Before final installation, check that BLT has compiled correctly by running one or two of the example scripts. For example:

```
$ ./graph3.tcl
```

5. In Figure 4-30, we've run this demo graph under Windows. If this works out OK for you too, carry out the final step:

```
$ make install
```

This final step will install the necessary files in the */usr/local/blt* directory (unless directed otherwise with a customized configuration *–prefix=my_dir* switch).

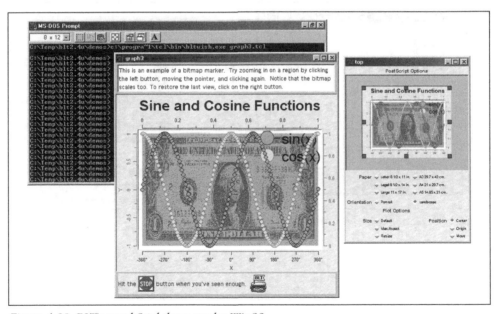

Figure 4-30. BLT's graph3.tcl demo under Win32

Installing BLT on Windows

Windows users can visit the *tcltk.com* site to find self-installing, precompiled versions of BLT, such as *blt2.4u-for-8.3.exe*. You can also compile BLT under Windows using various compilers, such as Microsoft VC++ 6.0 (see the *INSTALL* file again for more details). Before installing BLT on Win32, you must install Tcl/Tk for Win32 first. This is because the key BLT chart-generating program, *bltwish*, relies upon various Win32 DLL files already supplied by Tcl/Tk. If these DLL files are not present, BLT will simply not work.

In Figure 4-30, we've installed BLT under Win32 and then run *graph3.tcl* from the */demos* directory of the standard source code installation tarball, which you may wish to download separately. You can also find these Windows self-installers at:

   ftp://tcltk.sourceforge.net/pub/tcltk/blt/

Using BLT

If you can think of a graph, BLT can probably produce it. BLT's capabilities range from the most complex NASA Mars mission data charts to the simplest tablespace barcharts. However, BLT isn't just about graphs. Figure 4-31 demonstrates what typical spline and barchart graphs look like, and Table 4-4 covers the Tcl extension capabilities of BLT. We're only touching quickly on its capabilities here, though, and we urge you to learn more about this tool.

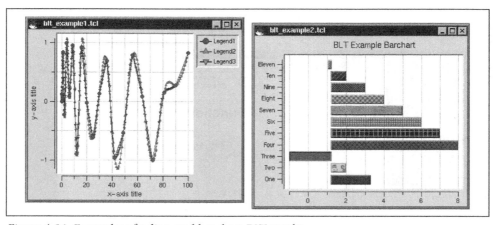

Figure 4-31. Examples of spline and barchart BLT graphs

Table 4-4. BLT Command Summary

Command	Description
graph, barchart, stripchart	Plot various types of highly customizable barcharts that work with BLT vector data objects
hierbox	Produces on-the-fly hierarchical trees
tabset	Generates tearable, notebook-style tabulated widgets in either multitiered or scrollable formats
table	Provides a geometry manager for widget layout
vector	Creates and manipulates vectors, arrays of changing information for creating dynamic graphs

Table 4-4. BLT Command Summary (continued)

Command	Description
bgexec	Enables external programs to be started in the background with monitored output
busy	Locks out windows (preventing user interaction) when required
eps	Provides encapsulated PostScript functionality
drag&drop	Enables dragging and dropping of widgets in Tk
bitmap	Creates bitmaps for use within Tcl
winop	Provides various types of window operation handling
bltdebug	Provides tracing functionality within Tcl/Tk
watch	Enables logging and monitoring of triggered processes
spline	Computes a spline curve, a graphical functionality for tying images to vectors
container	Provides a container for another application's window
cutbuffer	Manipulates properties of X Windows cut buffers
beep	Rings bell on keyboard
htext	Manipulates hypertext widgets, particularly for hyper-linking
tile*command*	A variety of tile widget commands corresponding to their Tk counterparts

Coding TableSpacer

In building the TableSpacer code in Example 4-4, we wanted a simple program based on Oratcl that would provide us with important at-a-glance information on tablespace usage within our database. If possible, we also wanted to be able to drill down on this data. To provide this functionality, we coded the program shown here (the corresponding comments should help you navigate your way through the code). The program performs the following steps:

1. The necessary Tcl extensions are picked up (e.g., Oratcl and BLT are both available under Unix and Win32).

2. Oratcl is used to log into the target database.

3. A SQL cursor supplies the required graphical information.

4. The cursed output information is plugged into graphical elements via BLT.

5. Finally, the graph is displayed.

6. Magical BLT graphical widgets are used to provide zooming capabilities.

Example 4-4. TableSpacer.tcl

```
#!/usr/local/bin/wish8.4

package require Tcl
package require Tk
```

Example 4-4. TableSpacer.tcl (continued)

```
# Step 1 - Pick up the required packages Oratcl and BLT

package require Oratcl
package require BLT

# If we're on Tcl8.x, make use of the namespaces

if { $tcl_version >= 8.0 } {
    namespace import blt::*
    namespace import -force blt::tile::*
}

# Step 2 - Log on to the database

set userid "system/manager"
set env(ORACLE_SID) "orcl"

set handle [oralogon $userid]
set retcode [catch {set handle [oralogon $userid]}]

# Use BLT to initialize our graph.

set graph .graph

option add *graph.xTitle "Percentage Used"
option add *graph.yTitle "Tablespace"
option add *graph.title \
   "$env(ORACLE_SID) Tablespace Space Usage Percentages"
option add *graph.elemBackground white
option add *graph.elemRelief raised

set visual [winfo screenvisual .]
option add *print.background white

# Now create the barchart, and configure the labels

barchart $graph
$graph xaxis configure -command FormatLabel -descending true
$graph legend configure -hide yes

# Build our Oracle SQL cursor

set query_cursor [oraopen $handle]
orasql $query_cursor {
    select a.tablespace_name,
    round((nvl(100-(sum(nvl(a.bytes,0))/
    (sum(nvl(b.bytes,0))/count(*)))*100,0)),0)
    from dba_free_space a, dba_data_files b
    where a.tablespace_name = b.tablespace_name and
    a.file_id = b.file_id
    group by a.tablespace_name, a.file_id
    order by 1
}
```

Example 4-4. TableSpacer.tcl (continued)

```
set row [orafetch $query_cursor]

global names()
global values()

set i 0

# Step 3 - Run through the cursor and fill various arrays

while {$oramsg(rc) == 0} {

    set names($i)   [lindex $row 0]
    set values($i)  [lindex $row 1]

    puts [format "\n%20s %s" $names($i) $values($i)]

    set row [orafetch $query_cursor]
    incr i
}

global numTabsps
set numTabsps [ array size names ]

# Step 4 - Arrays now filled, build up the graph.

for { set i 0} { $i < $numTabsps } { incr i } {
    $graph element create $i \
        -data { { $numTabsps - $i } $values($i) } \
        -bg black \
        -relief raised \
        -bd 2
}

# Step 5 - Finish off the graph

table . \
    .graph 1,0 -fill both

table configure . r0 r2 -resize none
wm min . 0 0

# Step 6 - Add several BLT Graphical goodies :-)

Blt_ZoomStack $graph
Blt_Crosshairs $graph
Blt_ActiveLegend $graph
Blt_ClosestPoint $graph

# Format the column labels and stop them being numeric

proc FormatLabel { w value } {
    global names
```

Example 4-4. TableSpacer.tcl (continued)

```
    global numTabsps
    set i [expr $numTabsps - $value]
    return $names($i)
}
# That's all there is to it!!! 8-)
```

Figure 4-32 shows TableSpacer in action.

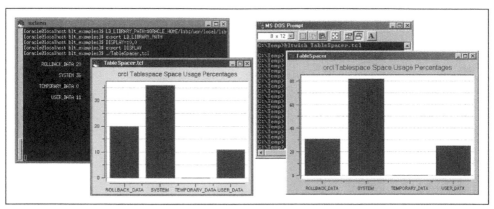

Figure 4-32. TableSpacer in action

Running on Unix

Before running the program, make sure that the standard *wish* Tcl/Tk you're using is able to display the chart, and also be sure that Oratcl can link up to the required Oracle libraries, as described earlier with Oddis:

```
    $ DISPLAY=:0.0
    $ export DISPLAY
    $ LD_LIBRARY_PATH=/usr/local/lib:$ORACLE_HOME/lib
    $ export LD_LIBRARY_PATH
```

Under Unix (or Linux), the program should now run properly:

```
    $ ./TableSpacer.tcl
```

Running on Windows

On Win32 systems, the same code will produce similar results (remember to use the *bltwish* program installed earlier, because the standard *wish* program will simply report errors):

```
    C:\Temp>bltwish TableSpacer.tcl
```

TableSpacer in action

You can see the final TableSpacer program in action in Figure 4-32 for both Linux and Win32. Although the code in Example 4-4 is slightly involved, you may agree with us that this is a lot of bangs per buck. However the real Merlinesque magic of BLT is contained within the following program calls:

Blt_ZoomStack
Blt_Crosshairs
Blt_ActiveLegend
Blt_ClosestPoint

In Figure 4-33, we've demonstrated how, among many other things, these can give you the possibility of zooming in and out of your on-the-fly graphs ad infinitum via either right-clicks or left-clicks of your mouse.

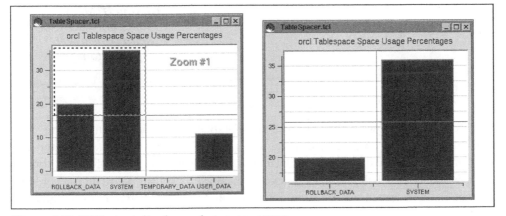

Figure 4-33. BLT's specialized cross-hair zoom option

5

Web Technologies

Web technology powers the Internet, and databases provide the underlying content and the ability to access, display, and manipulate that content. Although the fundamental relationship between databases and the Web is straightforward, building a web site that has an Oracle backend database is no simple matter. There are a great many interactions between a variety of different programming languages, protocols, and components. This chapter tries to demystify these interactions by examining the main technologies used to power the Web, paying particular attention to how these technologies relate to Oracle. We'll discuss the various layers of magic operating between the web server and the database, and we'll touch on the advantages and disadvantages of each approach to building your site. We'll take a little extra time on these basics because they are so crucial to building modern, web-based applications.

Once we've given you a feel for some basic web technologies and concepts, we'll introduce the various open source implementations on which most of the Oracle applications described in this book are based. Here's a brief overview:

Apache

> The web server is the heart of your web application. In this chapter, we'll describe Apache, the most popular web server in use today. Apache is open source, but even large corporations like Oracle are now using it.

Perl and the Web

> Your web applications themselves get served via the web server. The programming can be done in various languages, but Perl is a common choice. The Perl Database Interface module (DBI), discussed in some detail in Chapter 2, *Connecting to Oracle*, and Chapter 3, *Tcl, Perl, and Python*, provides an interface

for accessing data stored in Oracle (or other) databases. In this chapter, we'll also discuss *mod_perl*, an Apache module that can speed up your Perl CGI (Common Gateway Interface) scripts dramatically by incorporating the Perl interpreter directly into Apache.

Java and the Web

Java is an alternative to Perl, though not an open source alternative, for web programming. Although Java itself is not open source, it's important that we look briefly at it here because some Oracle open source web-based applications are built using Java. In this chapter, we'll discuss various ways to develop web applications with Java and Apache. We'll introduce JServ, which is to Java what *mod_perl* is to Perl; it brings a Java interpreter into Apache, allowing us to run Java-based CGI scripts. We'll continue the discussion of JServ in Chapter 7, *Java*, where we'll also describe the relationship between Apache JServ and the Jakarta Tomcat project. We'll also briefly describe Turbine, a framework for building web applications with Java, and the Ars Digita Community System, an open source web development suite of applications based on Oracle's PL/SQL language and Java stored procedures.

HTML embedded scripting and the Web

Embedded scripting is another approach to developing dynamic web sites. This approach differs substantially from CGI-based programming in a few important ways. With CGI, the output of the program is an HTML page. You must follow the rigorous rules of HTML when formatting your various print statements in C, Perl, or Java. With embedded technologies, you leave the HTML formatting to the designers and simply embed snippets of code into your pages, thus making the pages dynamic. In this chapter we'll describe several embedded scripting alternatives: PHP, EmbPerl, Mason, and Aquarium.

Databases and the Web

One of the most exciting developments for databases today is the growing proliferation of backend datastores that drive the Internet's web sites and, indirectly, the world's economy. Everywhere you dig in the fertile ground of the Internet you'll find a hidden database hiding just beneath the surface, from news sites such as *cnn.com* or *nytimes.com* to information archival sites such as *edgar-online.com*. And let's not forget the juggernaut e-commerce sites, such as *amazon.com,* with their trailer loads of product information. Online trading, financial news, search engines, airlines, auction sites, and portals—all of them utilize a database on the back end. Luckily for Oracle developers, that database is very often one emanating from Redwood Shores, California.

An interesting aspect of the backend databases is that, when they access a web site, most end users aren't even aware that they're interacting with a database server. Backend complexity is almost always hidden behind the scenes. Indeed, when it isn't, and the loose wiring becomes frayed and visible, commercial web sites often fail, sparking and fizz-popping into business oblivion. So for the outside viewer, how a web page knows who you are when it recommends the latest Stephen King novel to you is often a complete mystery (a feat of magic, especially if you *are* a Stephen King fan*).

We're aiming to become privileged members of this magic circle, and we need to know what's going on under the hood. So in the rest of this chapter we'll take a look behind the scenes at the various web-based technologies used to build the Oracle applications described in Chapter 6, *Building Web-Based Oracle Applications*, and those you'll need to understand in order to build your own applications. First, though, we'll describe the most important concepts that underlie the connection between the Web and the databases behind it: dynamic content, personalization, CGI programming, and caching.

Dynamic Content

Dynamic content is the programming that enables a web site to change from day to day or hour to hour, as well as between one user and another. These days, most sites are dynamic; there aren't many sites that present only static content—pages that are the same every time you visit them.

Web sites haven't always been based on dynamic content. They've evolved enormously from the mostly static pages available when the Mosaic genie was first released from the bottle back in 1993. Today's web sites are captivating and dynamic, featuring news, searching, shopping, and personalized content. Sites have become ever more compelling with animated GIF images, clever use of JavaScript and Macromedia Flash, and, more recently, streaming audio and video content.

In the early days of web site development, when using the <FONT> tag was the height of sophistication, the first dynamic pages were fairly simple scripted programs sitting quietly on the server, minding their own business, and typically situated in the */cgi-bin* directory. Normally, a URL (Uniform Resource Locator) would refer to a static HTML (HyperText Markup Language) page on the server. However, when a special URL was requested which specified a */cgi-bin* program, the server executed this application and returned the results to the client's browser. Such programs were called Common Gateway Interface (CGI) applications; we'll discuss CGI shortly.

These early web pages retrieved data from the file system, organized the data however they wanted, picked up the current date and time, and then did other

---

* Let's just hope that if you select *The Lawnmower Man* (within the *Night Shift* collection) from a web site book list, all of the mobile WAP phones in the world don't start ringing at once.

useful work to display a page that was *dynamic*—different and tailored specifically for use each time it was requested.

It didn't take long for someone to come up with the idea of plugging these early CGI applications into databases to retrieve useful information. From there, the Web we know today was born. As an example, let's look at today's banking applications. If you have an account at a bank, the bank keeps records about your financial transactions, your various accounts, how much money is where, fees applied each month, checks written against the account, balance, interest earned, and multitudes of related information. With secure online transactions, companies are now able to make this information available to customers via the Web. All you need now is your account number and various pieces of authentication information, and with this you can connect to your financial institution from virtually anywhere in the world, perform transactions, pay bills, and worry about your increasingly negative balance. This trend has been so significant that some banks are closing down entire chains of their old-fashioned real banks and replacing them with jazzy online outlets instead.

For now we'll ignore the effects of this revolutionary type of business on society and focus on how the technologies work. The secret is *dynamic content*, which works in the following way.

When you log in to the site and specify your account number, a generic template is filled with specific information about you and your account. That template has been built with one of a number of technologies we describe in this chapter: PHP, EmbPerl, JavaServer Pages, or the commercial StoryServer or Microsoft ASP. The template specifies the general look of the page, where the images will go, what tables there are to organize content, colors, fonts, and so on. The template is basically HTML, but it has added bits of code that, in turn, query the database. In the case of the banking data we've been discussing, after you've authenticated and verified who you are with the server, requests are made via the bank's backend database for all of your latest financial data. That data is (we hope) encrypted en route, to avoid interception by prying eyes.

News sites work in a way that's similar to online banking (though potentially without the authentication). Go to any site from *http://www.slashdot.org* to *http://www. news.com* or *http://www.cnn.com*, and what do you see? Today's latest news is often moving about in tickertape displays and JavaScript scrollers, trying to grab your attention (as in Figure 5-1), along with pushed advertisements that change every time you reload the page.

Today's dynamic web pages are often built on the fly and customized for your particular request (well, that's not completely true—they've been cached on the server, but more about that later). When you make your request, the page is built based upon the latest articles and news for today's current date. You also know, if

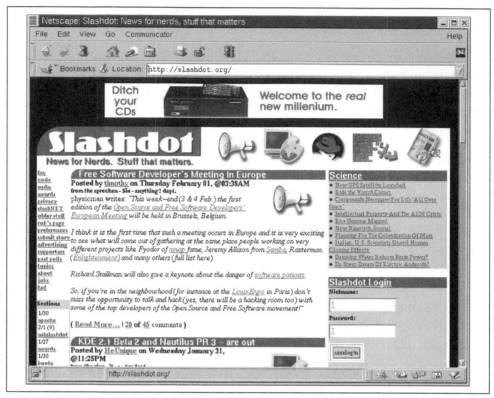

Figure 5-1. A typically busy web news page bursting with information

you've ever searched the archives on such a site, that the old news is still around
too, possibly from many years ago. Again, this is all stored in the database.
Depending on what's requested, the template is filled with different data from the
database.

Personalization

Web page personalization is really just a special form of dynamic content. Go to
http://www.netscape.com, *http://www.themes.org*, or *http://www.yahoo.com* and
you'll find a little button labeled "my" or a preferences area.

How does personalization work? When you visit one of these sites for the first
time and select the "my" section or preferences area, you'll be asked to create a
user ID. When you select one (typically an email address), it will be compared
against other IDs in the database to be sure that it's unique. Once you've done
this, you'll have an identifier with which the site can keep track of you. Later on,
when you visit the site and log in, the site will know what personalized content to
deliver for you. You can also use the various navigational and arrangement controls on the page to customize it to your liking, and your settings will be stored in

the database according to the user ID that you set up previously. The site will then subsequently know just how to deliver the page the way you like it.

Behind the scenes, personalization relies on cookies. The web site sends your browser a cookie that enables the web site to identify you while you're using that site. There are two different kinds of cookies: persistent and non-persistent. By default, friendly sites will typically send you a *non-persistent cookie*, one that will last only while your browser software is left running. It is only stored in memory, not written to your disk. But when you created a user ID and password, if you told the site to "Remember me" (or something similar), the site will actually send you a *persistent cookie*, one written to your hard drive by your browser software. This cookie won't automatically be your user ID, but it will typically be a unique identifier that the site can use to get your ID when you revisit the site.

Even persistent cookies usually have an expiration date, which can be set to one day, one week, one month, or one year (or anything in between). This all depends on the site and the type of cookie policy they have.

Cookie operations typically work as follows:

1. When you visit a web site, it asks your browser for cookies with a particular name. This name might be *netscape.com*, *themes.org*, or *yahoo.com*, for example.

2. Your browser then returns the named cookies.

3. The site looks up your user ID given the unique identifier it retrieves from the cookie.

The use of cookies accounts for why some sites make you log in each time, and why others can remember you from session to session, even if you shut down your machine and revisit the site several days later.

Some people disable cookies for privacy reasons. What happens if you have cookies disabled in your browser? Different sites try in different ways to personalize the web pages presented to you anyway. One way that's been devised is to use hidden tags. Essentially, you go to the site and log in manually, and when you hit the *Submit* button on a form, a hidden tag is added to your returned page with a unique identifier. For each page you view on the site, this hidden tag is added as you browse the site, and the site can keep track of who you are. This is a bit tricky and seems a little puzzling to the end user, but it works, and it is typically contained within a line such as this example:[*]

```
<input type=hidden name=user_id value="sean.hull@pobox.com">
```

---

[*] You can usually find these slinking in your web page HTML code by selecting View → Page Source from a typical browser's drop-down menus.

CGI and Web Programming

How does dynamic content actually work? How do web pages change for each visit or even each reload? And how can this world of dynamic content get served through such a simple little protocol as HTTP? Until recently, most dynamic content has been created via little programs called CGIs that ran on the servers. (We'll describe an alternate method, involving embedded scripting, later in this chapter.)

How do CGIs work? On the client side, the browser calls a CGI in the same way that it would call a static page—by making a request for a file from the web server. By calling a CGI, though, the client is actually telling the server to run a small program. Running that program produces the dynamic content for the web page.

A CGI program can be written to do just about anything, but its output must be an HTML page returned by HTTP. You can write CGI programs in virtually any language that can be made to obey the protocol. CGI files are essentially masquerading as HTML files to the browser. (As far as a browser's concerned, if it gets a standard HTTP response and page, it's a happy bunny.) Binary CGIs are often written in C and then compiled. Most CGI programs today tend to be scripts, usually written in Perl or another popular scripting language, because scripts are quicker to write, develop, and debug, and turnaround speed is what web publishing is all about.

On the server side, the web server sets aside certain directories for CGI files. These special directories are named *cgi-bin* by convention (*bin* stands for binaries, because these directories used to be populated mainly with binaries). The CGI files are programs that, when called, generate an HTML page.

CGI stands for Common Gateway Interface, but even its name doesn't reveal that much about *what* exactly it is. Essentially it's another open protocol. It defines a number of environment variables that will be available to programs called from a browser. Some important pieces of information are passed to the program, including the client's hostname, IP address, username, and browser, as well as the method used (GET, POST, etc), and finally the URI (everything after the protocol and hostname in the URL).

So in come these useful bits of information, which your CGI program may or may not use, and out must come an HTTP 1.0- or 1.1-compliant stream of data—for all intents and purposes to an innocent bystander, a static HTML file.

Let's look at an example of a CGI program. We're going to assume that you have access to a freshly installed Apache web server (we'll describe Apache a bit later in this chapter), and that you've set up the *cgi-bin* directory—via the *httpd.conf* file—where you can run the CGI program:

```
#!/bin/sh
echo Content-type: text/plain
```

```
echo
echo CGI/1.0 test script report:
echo
echo The current date and time is:
date
echo
echo SERVER_SOFTWARE = $SERVER_SOFTWARE
echo SERVER_NAME = $SERVER_NAME
echo REQUEST_METHOD = $REQUEST_METHOD
echo SCRIPT_NAME = "$SCRIPT_NAME"
```

There are a couple of important things you should take note of. One is that this is a shell script. As we mentioned, a CGI program can be written in lots of different languages, as long as it can output an HTML file (or, in Unix terms, as long as it can write to STDOUT). Also, you'll notice that we've output, via the standard Unix *echo* program, the contents of some of those previously mentioned (and highlighted) CGI environment variables. Here's the output:

```
CGI/1.0 test script report:
The current date and time is:
Wed May 24 03:28:09 EDT 2000
SERVER_SOFTWARE = Apache/1.3.11 (Unix) PHP/3.0.14
SERVER_NAME = www.iheavy.com
REQUEST_METHOD = GET
SCRIPT_NAME = /cgi-bin/test.cgi
```

You'll also notice that, each time you run this script, it prints the current date. This is important because it begins to illustrate how dynamic content is made possible. When your browser receives the HTML, it looks like a static page, but the page itself doesn't exist anywhere on the target server. It's generated *by* that target server *when* you request the program via your browser (or when the web server calls the script auto-magically).

Example 5-1 shows what that script would look like in Perl.[*]

Example 5-1. cgi_env.cgi Perl Program to Interrogate the Web Server

```perl
#!/usr/bin/perl -w
use CGI;
my $datestr = `date`;
my $cgivar = new CGI;
my $SERVER_SOFTWARE = $cgivar->server_software ();
my $SERVER_NAME = $cgivar->server_name ();
my $REQUEST_METHOD = $cgivar->request_method ();
my $SCRIPT_NAME = $cgivar->script_name ();
print $cgivar->header,              # create HTTP header
    "CGI/1.0 test script report:<br><br>\n",
    "The current date and time is:<br>\n",
    "$datestr<br>",
    $cgivar->start_html('test');  # start the HTML
```

---

[*] Notice the use of Lincoln Stein's *CGI.pm* Perl module.

Example 5-1. cgi_env.cgi Perl Program to Interrogate the Web Server (continued)

```
print "<br>\n";
print "SERVER_SOFTWARE = $SERVER_SOFTWARE<br>\n";
print "SERVER_NAME = $SERVER_NAME<br>\n";
print "REQUEST_METHOD = $REQUEST_METHOD<br>\n";
print "SCRIPT_NAME = $SCRIPT_NAME<br>\n";
print $cgivar->end_html;            # end the HTML
```

Caching

Dividing content up into static and dynamic types is not the end of the story. There is a third type of content called *cached* content. When you make a request for a particular static page, it may seem that the images are cached on your local machine. Your browser automatically handles this caching for you. What you may not know is that the content may actually be cached elsewhere, between you and the originating server. In essence, when you request a page, your requests may be hitting a caching server that will, in turn, go and request the actual page only if it has *not* already been requested by another user. Caching is an effective method for improving your site's scalability. It can provide one more layer of indirection from the actual backend database, and thus better performance at the front end.

In some cases, even dynamic content can be cached. For instance, news sites may cache content based on requests, so particular current news stories—for example, the latest presidential election news or scandal—will already be put together and made available to you in what look like static pages, which will come whizzing back to you in mere nanoseconds.

Squid is an open source Internet object cache, which means that it can cache data via HTTP, FTP, or gopher protocols. The Squid server then becomes a proxy to the real web server, standing in lieu of it and making requests to the real server only when necessary. The main Squid web site is:

> *http://www.squid-cache.org*

Squid operates on AIX, Digital Unix, FreeBSD, HP-UX, Irix, Linux, NetBSD, Nextstep, SCO, Solaris, and OS/2 platforms.

The Apache Web Server

Apache is a hugely successful piece of open source software. It is the most popular web server in use today—including both open source and commercial web servers. Netcraft reports that over 60% of global Internet sites currently employ Apache.[*]

---

[*] According to Netcraft (*http://www.netcraft.com/survey/*), Apache's share of the web server market was over 60% as of May 2000. Following far behind was IIS, placing second at 21%, and Netscape, placing third at 7%. (Microsoft claims that IIS is the most popular web server in the world, which is true only if you limit the scope of the survey to the commercial domain.)

Apache originally evolved from the HTTP daemon program (*httpd*) developed by
Rob McCool at the National Center for Supercomputing Applications (NCSA),
University of Illinois, Urbana-Champaign. When McCool left NCSA in 1994,
development of the *httpd* program faltered. A group of eight core programmers,
headed up by Brian Behlendorf and Cliff Skolnick, decided to continue McCool's
public domain work, forming the Apache Project (named after "patching," their
standard method of code modification). Other developers in the original core
Apache group included Roy T. Fielding, Rob Hartill, David Robinson, Randy Ter-
bush, Robert S. Thau, and Andrew Wilson.

The Apache group has now become the Apache Software Foundation (ASF),
whose purpose is to provide organizational and legal support for all of the various Apache software projects and to ensure that these projects continue even if
individual volunteers leave.

The main web site for Apache is:

   http://www.apache.org

Apache* runs on virtually every operating system, including Win32, Linux, BSD,
Solaris, and many other varieties of Unix. Apache's modular design allows the
functionality of the basic Apache code to be extended through the use of its easily accessible API; that design greatly enhances Apache's power and flexibility.
Among the important Apache modules are the following:

mod_perl (http://perl.apache.org)
   Provides an interface between Apache and Perl. It allows Perl code to be
   cached in the web server's memory space. This substantially improves performance over standard CGI applications. The use of *mod_perl* also reduces the
   advantage gained by the use of Java servlets (which we'll get to in Chapter 7).

mod_php (http://www.php.net)
   Allows the powerful HTML embedded PHP scripting language to be incorporated directly into the web server's kernel, avoiding the performance problems
   related to running as a separate CGI. We'll describe PHP later in this chapter.

Java Apache modules (http://java.apache.org)
   These include JServ, a Java servlet engine made to serve code written purely in
   Java, and *mod_java,* which allows you to extend the Apache kernel by building modules in Java, rather than C. We'll describe JServ briefly in this chapter
   and in greater detail in Chapter 8, *Building Oracle Applications with Java.*

XML Apache modules (http://xml.apache.org)
   There is also an Apache XML project that, as you might guess, provides an
   XML support layer to Apache.

---

* Apache 1.3.12 is the latest version as of this writing, with Apache 2.0 in alpha testing.

Apache and Oracle

Apache is such a solid web server that Oracle has recently decided to include it in the company's release of the Internet Application Server (*i*AS) product. Essentially, proprietary *i*AS modules are bundled with open source Apache, and the whole has been released as a commercial product. By combining Apache with Oracle's own application servers, *i*AS provides the stability, performance, and scalability required to run the most demanding of web applications. Oracle also claims the following business benefits:

- Apache's proven technology track record and access to the development and support of the large Apache community

- The Apache-driven Secure Sockets Layer (SSL)

- The Apache JServ Servlet engine (described in Chapter 8)

- The ability to employ Perl CGI/DBI programs

- Integration with Oracle's PL/SQL language

- Full Oracle technical support

It's interesting to see how Oracle has not only accepted the use of open source software in its own product set, but also used the ideology of the open source movement (e.g., community support) in its corporate marketing message. What a change from earlier days when acknowledged corporate distribution of open source software would have been unthinkable. You can find out more about Oracle's *i*AS product at:

http://www.oracle.com/ip/deploy/ias/index.html?web.html

Installing Apache

We've provided a basic outline of the installation steps for Apache. However, be sure to read the online documentation for your own platform very carefully:

1. Download the Apache source code from *http://www.apache.org/httpd.html*.

2. Once you've got the source, you should be able to build the latest Apache version straight out of the box with the Apache Autoconf-style Interface (APACI), contained within the download. If you are determined to compile Apache manually, you can check out the *README* and *INSTALL* files for most of the relevant platforms. For Unix systems, the manual installation (which requires a C compiler such as *gcc*, available at *http://www.gnu.org/software/gcc/gcc.html*) tends to follow this pattern:

```
$ ./Configure
$ make
```

This will usually place the required files in the */usr/local/apache/* directory (for a totally standard install). We'll run through a non-standard install in Chapter 7.

3. Edit the configuration files, as described by the full installation instructions you will get with the download. This often involves altering the critically important *httpd.conf* file.

4. Run the server:

```
$ /usr/local/apache/bin/httpd -f /usr/local/apache/conf/httpd.conf
```

In a perfect world, the server should now be running; if you're anything like us, you'll encounter one or two slight problems. But by crossing fingers, touching wood, saying three hail Marys, and oh, by actually reading and following the directions in the *INSTALL* and *README* files, you should get to the screen shown in Figure 5-2. (Alternatively, do as the *README* file says, and use the automatic installation.)

You may find the following site a very useful place for quick tips on configuring Apache (and many other pieces of open source software):

http://www.refcards.com

Once you really start pushing Apache (be sure to follow all the available online documentation when you do so), you'll be amazed at what you can do with it.

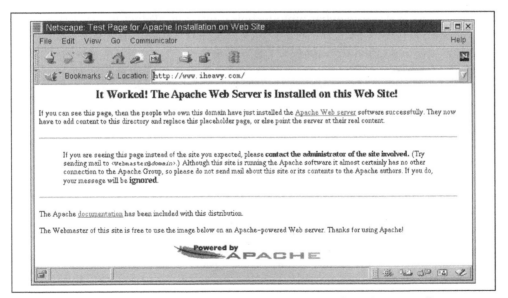

Figure 5-2. The default page that runs under Apache directly after a basic installation

Apache and HTTP

To understand how Apache and other web servers work, you need a basic understanding of the HTTP protocol.

When you type a URL into your browser, you're probably used to typing something like *http://www.somesite.com*. The "http" at the beginning tells your browser that you're requesting an HTTP-based web page. There are a few other possibilities—for example, you might be making an FTP request (e.g., *ftp://ftp.ora.com*) or a Telnet request (e.g., *telnet://ora.com*). The point is that the name before the colon specifies the protocol to your browser. This convention is used largely because the first browsers back in the NCSA days did more than just view web pages.

What is HTTP? It's a stateless protocol, which means that you make a request and get results, and later make another request and get results, but there is no continuity between these requests. HTTP is built to be lightweight and fast, lending itself well to a distributed web of documents (following the original, inspirational work of Web pioneer Tim Berners-Lee; see *http://www.w3.org/People/Berners-Lee/*). HTTP requests return various pieces of data in multiple streams. One static HTML request might contain many images and, if frames are used, other HTML pages, all of which are fetched and returned to the requesting program or the browser that originated the request.

Let's take a look at a somewhat more technical example. Telnet to port 80 of your favorite web server as in Example 5-2. We've highlighted key statements that we'll explain at the end of the example.

Example 5-2. Connecting to the Internet via Telnet

```
$ telnet www.apache.org 80
Trying 63.211.145.10...
Connected to www.apache.org.
Escape character is '^]'.
GET / HTTP/1.0

HTTP/1.1 200 OK
Date: Tue, 23 May 2000 08:24:20 GMT
Server: Apache/1.3.9 (Unix) ApacheJServ/1.1 PHP/3.0.12 AuthMySQL/2.20
Connection: close
Content-Type: text/html
<!DOCTYPE HTML PUBLIC "-//W3C//DTD HTML 3.2 Final//EN">
<HTML>
 <HEAD>
  <TITLE>Index of /</TITLE>
 </HEAD>
 <BODY>
<H1>Index of /</H1>
<PRE><IMG SRC="/icons/blank.gif" ALT="      ">
```

Example 5-2. Connecting to the Internet via Telnet (continued)

```
<A HREF="?N=D">Name</A>
       <A HREF="?M=A">Last modified</A>
       <A HREF="?S=A">Size</A>   <A HREF="?D=A">Description</A>
<HR>
<IMG SRC="/icons/back.gif" ALT="[DIR]">
 <A HREF="/">Parent Directory</A>          18-Mar-2000 20:09       -
<IMG SRC="/icons/folder.gif" ALT="[DIR]"> <A HREF="dev.apache.org/">dev.apache.org/</
A>
        20-May-2000 19:27       -
<IMG SRC="/icons/folder.gif" ALT="[DIR]"> <A HREF="search.apache.org/">search.apache.
org/</A>
       22-May-2000 05:33       -
<IMG SRC="/icons/folder.gif" ALT="[DIR]"> <A HREF="www.apache.org/">www.apache.org/</
A>
        20-May-2000 19:23       -
</PRE><HR>
<ADDRESS>Apache/1.3.9 Server at locus.apache.org Port 80</ADDRESS>
</BODY></HTML>
Connection closed by foreign host.
$
```

Try this example yourself and see what happens. Be sure to hit the Return key twice after the GET line, and type everything exactly as you see it above. That's HTTP in a nutshell—well, it's a GET request, at least. GET requests are used when you're receiving information from the Web—for example, when you've requested your favorite news site.

You should also understand a bit about POST commands, which are used when you want to send information to the server—for instance, when you enter a string at a search engine and click "Search". You're really sending a POST command to the HTTP web server that is handling requests for that URL.

There are also some very useful nuggets of information in the response from the server shown in Example 5-2. First of all, take a close look at the "Server:" line. It's telling us not only that it's using Apache (of course), but also the version number and that a number of modules are compiled into the kernel, including JServ, PHP, and MySQL authentication. Now glance down a bit more and you can see the subsequent requests for additional items, a number of GIF images. When the browser receives and interprets this page, it will notice these and send them back as further requests to the server. It will then construct the web page you see in your browser.

The instructions for putting this page together, the exact layout of image and text, size, color, and alignment are all determined by the HTML tags in the page. A text-based browser like Lynx (*http://lynx.browser.org*) will simply ignore these image tags and build the page based on the text and HTML markup.

Apache Security

Apache can also protect the security of HTTP transactions via the module *mod_ssl*. Encryption is an important aspect of any web server, especially if you want it to have secure pages and forms, which are encrypted in transit between the user and your server. This security layer essentially protects data sent over such connections from being intercepted in transit and read by prying eyes. Any time you wish to send credit card information, for example, you'll want to encrypt the data in transit.

The *mod_ssl* module implements strong cryptography through the Secure Sockets Layer (SSL) and Transport Layer Security (TLS) protocols. The implementation is based on the open source program OpenSSL, which uses SSLeay, a project by Eric Young and Tim Hudson. This module is actually based on Ben Laurie's code developed for the Apache-SSL web server. It can be used free outside the U.S. for commercial and non-commercial purposes, and inside the U.S. for non-commercial purposes. However, if you wish to use it inside the U.S. for commercial purposes, you'll need to obtain a license from one of the following sites:

> *http://www.apache.org/related_projects.html#apachessl*
> *http://www.rsasecurity.com*

You may also be interested in the commercial versions of the *mod_ssl* module (known as Raven) and the web server (known as Stronghold). By getting the commercial product, you also get a license to use this software in the U.S. Check out:

http://www.covalent.net/raven/ssl/
  Raven

http://www.c2.net/products/sh2/
  Stronghold in the U.S. and Canada

http://www.int.c2.net/products/sh2/
  Stronghold outside the U.S. and Canada

Using Perl with Oracle Web Applications

Perl is an excellent language for enabling web communication with an Oracle database. Perl DBI, which we describe in some detail in Chapter 2, is the interface you'll use for this communication. Chapter 3 contains more general information about installing and using Perl.

You will be reassured to know that connecting to the database via your Perl CGI scripts is much the same as connecting to the database via a standalone Perl program. You open a database handle and connect to the database, open a cursor or statement handle, specify a query, parse or prepare the statement, and then execute it. If the statement is a SELECT, you then fetch rows (perhaps the user's favorite books, as generated the previous night by your monster data warehouse).

When you're all done spitting back the information, you close down your cursor and disconnect from the database.

Historically, there have been some performance problems with this approach, however. Whenever a Perl program is run, the rather sizeable Perl interpreter must first be brought into memory before it can interpret and execute your Perl program. Unfortunately, this can be *Ssssslowwwwwww* with a capital S. (Java servlet fans have pointed to this slowness of Perl in advocating that their technology be used instead of Perl—via *ConnectionPool.class* and *PoolManager.class* statically instantiated objects, as we describe later in this book).

Has Perl taken this challenge from the Java evangelists lying down? Certainly not. The *mod_perl* module, developed by Doug MacEachern and available at *http://perl.apache.org*, brings the Perl interpreter directly into the heart of the Apache kernel, thus avoiding the overhead of loading the interpreter into memory for each script executed on the server. As well as doing memory caching, this incredible module also allows you to extend the Apache server in the Perl language itself. In the following sections we'll describe how to install *mod_perl* and use it to connect to an Oracle database.

The main web site for *mod_perl* is:

http://perl.apache.org

You'll find extensive online documentation for the module at:

http://perl.apache.org/#docs

Installing mod_perl

There are a few steps you'll need to follow to successfully install *mod_perl* on your system. Here is the outline of what you need to do:

1. Download the latest source code from *http://perl.apache.org*.

2. Untar the source and build the *Makefile*.

   This process prompts you for the location of the Apache source code and even invokes *configure* to build the Apache daemon for you.

3. Next, you'll run *make* to install *mod_perl*, following the usual Perl standard:

   ```
   $ perl Makefile.PL
   $ make
   $ make test
   ```

4. Then issue the following as *root*:

   ```
   $ make install
   ```

For information about each of these steps, see the basic description of Perl installation in Chapter 2.

Connecting to the Database

When you access the database with your Perl scripts, you have to open a connection to Oracle via the DBD::Oracle module. As we discussed in Chapter 2, DBD:: Oracle is the Oracle-specific driver that interfaces to the database-independent Perl DBI database interface module. This login process has a substantial cost overhead and is something you should avoid whenever possible. Many applications run the same set of Perl scripts over and over again, logging in as the same user each time. In these cases, your application can benefit tremendously by *not* having to log in to Oracle each time. Caching the connections between subsequent runs of different scripts can be a very powerful performance enhancement, and one you'll want to look at closely.

These cached connections amount to cached database handles in Perl, but in the web server world as a whole they're called *persistent connections*, because the connection to the database is kept persistent between sessions. To get this functionality, you'll need to install the Apache::DBI module, which will give you persistent connections to your database when you're using Perl DBI. This module is an example of an extension to the Apache kernel written in Perl, and, as such, it requires *mod_perl*.

The Apache::DBI module essentially keeps your database handles in memory between sessions or between executions of a particular script. The builders of this module have done some really cool stuff with Apache to make it virtually transparent to your applications that Apache::DBI is being used. You must add the following to your Apache *httpd.conf* file:

```
PerlModule Apache::DBI    # this comes first !!
...                       # other ApacheDBI modules
```

And that's it. You don't have to change any of your Perl scripts. You don't even have to add a *use* statement to them.

When Apache encounters either of the following:

```
$dbh = DBI->connect
$dbh->disconnect
```

and Apache::DBI has been loaded already, the flow of control goes through Apache::DBI instead. This is how the caching of persistent database connections is handled transparently. Apache::DBI essentially overloads the *connect* routine and stores the handle in a hash which is kept persistent by the magic of *mod_perl*.

Using Java with Oracle Web Applications

Java provides an alternative approach to Perl for enabling web communication with an Oracle database. In this section, we'll provide a rough outline of using

Java for web applications. Refer to Chapters 7 and 8 for much more detail about Java and its use with Oracle.

Java has its own version of an embedded HTML language, aptly called JavaServer Pages (JSP), and its *.jsp* pages are analogous to Microsoft's *.asp* Active Server Pages. Using JSP, you add code to an HTML template page, rather than write a script that generates an HTML page, as is the case with Perl. The Java approach is similar to that of other embedded scripting languages such as PHP, which we'll describe later in this chapter. In addition to accessing pure Java, a web page can also access precompiled Java Beans, which facilitates component-based code and interoperability and allows you to encapsulate functionality outside the page.

JavaServer Pages and Java Servlets

JavaServer Pages, like the various embedded scripting technologies discussed later in the chapter, allow you to embed code in your HTML pages. The code is preprocessed, and a complete HTML page is then returned by the web server.

Java *servlets* are bits of code which run on the server machine and are invoked by the web server. Java servlets are an alternative to JSPs. They operate in much the same way that other CGI programs do. But to make Java servlets work, you need a special module—namely, JServ for Apache, which we'll describe in a moment.

We prefer using Java servlets for web work with Java, since JavaServer Pages can get messy pretty quickly when you need to embed an entire Java program within an HTML template. However, if you especially like Java, you might want to give JSP a try. Typical directives include the following:

- Import an appropriate Java package:

    ```
    <%@ page import="java.util.*" %>
    ```

- Use that package to provide required information:

    ```
    Date: <%= new java.util.Date() %>
    Hostname: <%= request.getRemoteHost() %>
    ```

- Run an entire program code segment within your template:

    ```
    <%
    String queryData = request.getQueryString();
    out.println("Attached GET data: " + queryData);
    %>
    ```

For more complete information about Java, refer to the books referenced in Appendix C, *For Further Reading*.

The main web sites for JavaServer Pages and Java servlets are:

> *http://www.sun.com/software/embeddedserver/index.html*
> *http://java.sun.com/products/OV_jservProduct.html*

For much more, see the excellent JavaServer Pages tutorial at:

http://www.apl.jhu.edu/~hall/java/Servlet-Tutorial/

JServ

Apache JServ is another Apache extension for running Java CGI-like servlet scripts. (We'll explain JServ's ongoing relationship with Tomcat in Chapter 7.) JServ implements a 100% pure Java servlet engine. Standalone servlets (conceptually similar to Perl CGI scripts), which you create in Java and connect to a database using JDBC (Java DataBase Connectivity), can then be called up from the Web. Obviously, in order to be useful, those servlets need to generate HTML. We'll be covering an example of JServ in Chapter 7, where we'll dig more deeply into JDBC.

The main web site for Jserv is:

http://java.apache.org/jserv/index.html

Turbine

If you want to get started building a web application with Java, look no further than Turbine, the Java servlet-based framework. Based on the FreeEnergy approach to web application development, Turbine provides a modular way to do web development.

There's plenty going on with the Turbine project (which is also linked to Tomcat) See the following sites:

http://java.apache.org/turbine/
http://jakarta.apache.org/turbine/

We make use of Turbine in Chapter 8, when we discuss DB Prism and Cocoon.

Ars Digita Community System

The Ars Digita Community System (ACS) is a suite of web-based solutions that provide dynamic web-based content management. ACS offers facilities for web publishing, calendaring, site management, personalization, collaboration (through discussion boards, messaging, and chat), transactions, and aggregation of content. Based on Java and PL/SQL stored procedures, ACS connects to Oracle8*i* databases and uses AOLServer or Apache as the web server. This project is the contribution of a commercial entity that provides regular updates of their open source software. Ars Digita explains the project as follows:

> If you had enough time, patience, and money, you might be able to cobble together a set of standalone commercial and freeware applications that collectively approach the cumulative functionality of the ACS. But why bother? Systems

integration is not a multibillion dollar business because it is easy or fun. The ACS is a comprehensive set of functional modules, all integrated in a single collection of Oracle tables that reference each other. It's fast, stable, field-tested, and free.

The ACS suite of solutions is too extensive to explain in detail here, but we find it very impressive and urge you to check it out. The main web site is:

http://www.arsdigita.com/pages/toolkit/

Using HTML Embedded Scripting with Oracle Web Applications

So far in this chapter, we've looked at how you can build open source web-based applications with Perl and Java technologies that use CGI scripts. Another approach to dynamic web programming is to use embedded scripting. With the embedded scripting approach, you embed snippets of code in your HTML pages, rather than writing CGI programs that output HTML pages. This is an elegant way to separate web and database programming from web page design (though the separation works well only if the embedded language is a simple and straightforward one).

There are various web programming solutions loosely based on the idea of embedding code into HTML pages and then preprocessing it. With Java, for example, you use JavaServer Pages (JSP), as we mentioned in the previous section. Microsoft's version of this technology is known as Active Server Pages (ASP). There are also a number of excellent open source solutions. In this section we'll take a look at four exciting and widely used open source solutions: PHP, EmbPerl, Mason, and Aquarium.

PHP

PHP is a powerful embedded scripting language that supports an extensive set of Oracle functions. PHP differs from CGI scripting in a fundamental way. With CGI scripting, you return an HTML page that's generated directly as the result of running your script. PHP lets you generate dynamic web pages simply by embedding pieces of PHP code inside your HTML. PHP is similar to JavaServer Pages, Active Server Pages, and Cold Fusion technologies, but PHP is easier to use. With JSP, for example, you must have a fair amount of familiarity with the considerably more complex Java language.

PHP was conceived and developed by Rasmus Lerdorf, who started work on the project back in 1994. By 1995, PHP was known as Personal Home Page Tools and had grown rapidly into a large collection of scripts. It then became PHP/FI as an HTML Form Interpreter and other modules were added. Gradually, as the download rate of PHP across the Internet became exponential, the toolset became known as PHP: Hypertext Processor. The tool has now morphed from its rewritten PHP3 incarnation into PHP4 (driven by the Zend scripting engine, *http://www.zend.com*), and it is simply known as PHP (try searching for "Personal Home Pages" on the Internet, and you may realize why). For much more on the history of this incredible set of parsers, scripts, and tools, see:

http://www.php.net/manual/en/intro-history.php

PHP offers a clean and straightforward means of generating dynamic web content. Unlike Perl and C programs, which make you do the work of generating an HTML page from possibly complex code, PHP provides an easy interface. Special tags allow you to jump into the PHP code and then back out into HTML in a very simple fashion. When a PHP page is requested, it is preprocessed, and the web server runs the embedded code output framed *within* the flat HTML template.

There are actually two different ways to use PHP for web development:

- One way is to run it as a CGI—that is, when a PHP3 page is requested from the server, Apache invokes a CGI interpreter which preprocesses the page. The resulting page is then returned to the browser.

- The other way, which is more powerful and efficient, is to incorporate the *mod_php* module into your Apache kernel, just as we earlier described how to incorporate the *mod_perl* module for Perl programming. This way, Apache has the PHP interpreter and can directly preprocess the pages itself, without having to invoke an external CGI.

The main web site for PHP is:

http://www.php.net

Installing PHP

Follow these basic steps to install PHP (for details, see the online PHP installation files):

1. Download the source code for PHP from *http://www.php.net*.
2. Run *configure* to build a fresh *Makefile* for your system.
3. When prompted, let PHP know where your Apache source tree is located.
4. Finally, run *make*, and install.

Here is an example of the commands you might use:

```
$ ./configure --with-mysql
$ make
$ make install
```

Using PHP

Now let's take a look at a very basic PHP example. This simple example code actually produces some very impressive output:

```
<html><head><title>PHP Test</title></head>
<body>
<?php echo "Hello World<P>"; ?>
<?php phpinfo() ?>
</body></html>
```

For a more typical use of PHP, take a look at the somewhat more complex example in Example 5-3.

Example 5-3. date.php3 PHP Web Server File

```
<HTML>
<HEAD>
<TITLE>Date/Time Functions Demo</TITLE>
</HEAD>
<BODY>
<H1>Date/Time Functions Demo</H1>
<DL>
<DT>Functions demonstrated</DT>
<DD><CODE>&lt;?date($format,$time)?&gt;</CODE>
<DD><CODE>&lt;?gmdate($format,$time)?&gt;</CODE>
<DD><CODE>&lt;?time()?&gt;</TT>
</DL>
<P>The <CODE>date()</CODE> function is used to display times and
dates in various ways. The function takes a format string and a time
as arguments.  If the time argument is left off, the current time
and date will be used.  The time argument is specified as an integer
in number of seconds since the Unix Epoch on January 1, 1970.
The format string is used to indicate which date/time components
should be displayed and how they should be formatted.
<P>For example, if we wanted to print the current date and time,
we might use a tag like:
<CODE>&lt;?echo date("D M d, Y H:i:s")?&gt;</CODE>.
This looks like: <EM><?echo date("D M d, Y H:i:s", time())?></EM>
<P>In the above you will find that the various characters in
the formatting string were replaced with a date/time component.
Any characters not replaced with anything were displayed verbosely.
The valid formatting characters are:
<CODE>
<UL>
  <LI>Y - Year eg. <?echo date("Y")?>
  <LI>y - Year eg. <?echo date("y")?>
  <LI>M - Month eg. <?echo date("M")?>
  <LI>m - Month eg. <?echo date("m")?>
  <LI>D - Day eg. <?echo date("D")?>
  <LI>d - Day eg. <?echo date("d")?>
  <LI>z - Day of the year eg. <?echo date("z")?>
  <LI>H - Hours in 24 hour format eg. <?echo date("H")?>
  <LI>h - Hours in 12 hour format eg. <?echo date("h")?>
```

Example 5-3. date.php3 PHP Web Server File (continued)

```
<LI>i - Minutes eg. <?echo date("i")?>
<LI>s - Seconds eg. <?echo date("s")?>
<LI>U - Seconds since epoch eg. <?echo date("U")?>
</UL>
</CODE>
<P>The <CODE>gmdate()</CODE> function is identical to the
<CODE>date()</CODE> function except that it uses Greenwich Mean
Time instead of the current local time.
<P>The <b>time()</b> function simply returns the current local
time in seconds since Unix epoch.  It is equivalent to calling
<CODE>date("U")</CODE>.
</BODY>
</HTML>
```

Figure 5-3 shows the results of running the list part of this script. You can see how simple routines in PHP give us enormous potential for developing dynamic web pages.

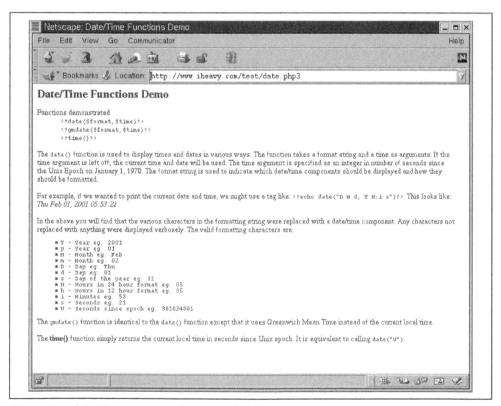

Figure 5-3. date.php3 in action, back in July 2000

PHP and Oracle

PHP offers one major advantage for Oracle users doing web development: it supports an excellent Oracle API. The main Oracle functions, along with their parameters, are summarized in Table 5-1. For detailed information about all Oracle functions, check out the following web site:

http://www.php.net/manual/ref.oracle.php

PHP supports many different datatypes, including arrays, floating-point numbers, integers, objects, and strings. It also supports *type juggling*, which allows the context of use in a program to change a variable. For example, if a string is assigned to an integer variable, that variable becomes auto-magically a string (a similar thing occurs in Perl). The *mixed* indicator shows that it is acceptable to put various variable types in this position, depending on field type (VARCHAR2, NUMBER, etc.).

Table 5-1. The PHP/Oracle API

PHP/Oracle Function	Description
int Ora_Bind (int cursor, string PHP variable name, string SQL parameter name, int length [, int type])	Binds a PHP variable to an Oracle parameter
int Ora_Close (int cursor)	Closes an Oracle cursor
string Ora_ColumnName (int cursor, int col)	Gets the name of a column
string Ora_ColumnType (int cursor, int col)	Gets the column type
int Ora_Commit (int conn)	Commits a transaction
int Ora_CommitOff (int conn)	Disables automatic commit
int Ora_CommitOn (int conn)	Enables automatic commit
string Ora_Error (int cursor_or_connection)	Gets an Oracle error message
int Ora_ErrorCode (int cursor_or_connection)	Gets an Oracle error code
int Ora_Exec (int cursor)	Executes a parsed statement
int Ora_Fetch (int cursor)	Fetches a row of data
mixed Ora_GetColumn (int cursor, mixed col)	Gets data from a fetched row
int Ora_Logoff (int connection)	Closes an Oracle connection
int Ora_Logon (string user, string password)[a]	Opens an Oracle connection
int Ora_Open (int connection)	Opens an Oracle cursor
int Ora_Parse (int cursor, string sql, int defer)	Parses a SQL statement
int Ora_Rollback (int connection)	Rolls back a transaction

[a] As in *$dbb = Ora_Logon("scott@mydb", "tiger");*.

As with the Perl DBI, you can use all of the PHP/Oracle API functionality to connect to your Oracle database and use its content to generate dynamic web pages. It's a wonderful facility.

EmbPerl

Like PHP, EmbPerl (developed by Gerald Richter) is an embedded scripting language, but EmbPerl uses Perl instead of PHP's Perl-like language. The main advantage of using EmbPerl over PHP is that it gives you automatic access to the hundreds of Perl modules available on CPAN.

The main web site for EmbPerl is:

> *http://perl.apache.org/embperl/*

Installing EmbPerl

In order to install EmbPerl, you must have the following installed on your system:

- Perl.

- The Perl DBI and DBD::Oracle modules.

- The Apache *mod_perl* module (optional).

- EmbPerl-1.2b1 (or higher).

- A number of nonstandard Perl modules (see the discussion of the security modules in Chapter 6). Actually, the following Perl modules are required for the *make test* step to work, but are not, in fact, required for a fully working installation. Nevertheless, it's usually best to make sure that *make test* works correctly. That way, if you have any problems later, you will at least be able to exclude all the things the *make test* step has been designed to weed out:

      URI
      MIME::Base64
      HTML::Parser
      HTML::HeadParser
      Digest::MD5
      libnet
      libwww
      libwin32 (only on Win32)

You can install EmbPerl on a Unix system as follows:

1. Download the EmbPerl source code from *http://perl.apache.org/embperl*.

2. Once you've downloaded the appropriate files, perform the standard Perl install:

```
$ perl Makefile.PL
$ make
$ make test
$ make install
```

EmbPerl is usually installed to be run under the *mod_perl* module (currently, *mod_perl-0.96* or higher), and this will certainly make it run faster; however, use of *mod_perl* is not required. The *mod_perl* module simply allows Apache to optimize the running of Perl code.

EmbPerl is fully supported under Win32. However, the Win32 installation differs slightly from the Unix one; detailed instructions are available within the download package or online at *http://perl.apache.org/embperl/*.

Using EmbPerl

Example 5-4 demonstrates a typical EmbPerl HTML template page with embedded Perl DBI programming, which we have highlighted (see this output in Figure 5-4).

Example 5-4. mother_embperl.pl, EmbPerl Template Construction

```
<HTML>
<HEAD>
<TITLE>EmbPerl Template Usage</TITLE>
</HEAD>
<BODY BGCOLOR="#FFFFFF">
<CENTER>
<H1>DBI Example</H1>
[-
$url = 'dbi:oracle:mydb';

use DBI ;

# connect to database
$dbh = DBI->connect($url, 'scott', 'tiger') or
   die "Cannot connect to '$url'" ;

# prepare the sql select
$sth = $dbh -> prepare ("SELECT EMPNO, ENAME FROM EMP") or
   die "Cannot SELECT EMPNO, ENAME FROM EMP" ;

# excute the query
$sth -> execute or die "Cannot execute SELECT EMPNO, ENAME FROM EMP";

# get the fieldnames for the heading in $rs
$rs = $sth -> {NAME} ;
-]
<TABLE BORDER=2 WIDTH="100%">
<TR>
[$ foreach $h @$rs $]
<TH>[+ $h +]</TH>
[$ endforeach $]
</TR>
[$ while $row = $sth -> fetchrow_arrayref $]
<TR>
[$ foreach $v @$row $]
<TD>[+ $v +]</TD>
[$ endforeach $]
```

Example 5-4. mother_embperl.pl, EmbPerl Template Construction (continued)

```
</TR>
[$ endwhile $]
</TABLE>
</CENTER>
</BODY></HTML>
```

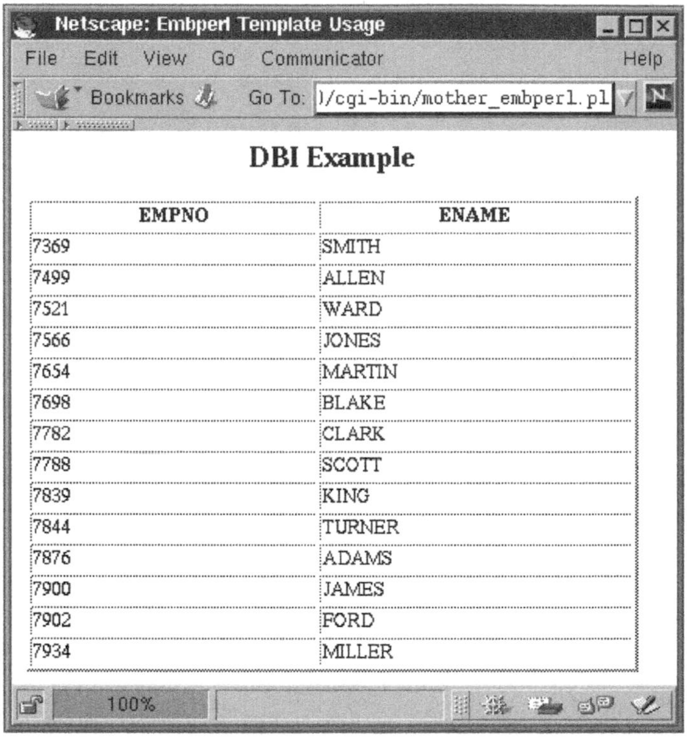

Figure 5-4. mother_embperl.pl output

Mason

Mason is becoming a powerful new force in the world of embedded scripting languages, and it's definitely worth a good look. Developed by Jonathan Swartz, Mason is built on some other technologies we've discussed in this chapter. Like PHP and EmbPerl, Mason uses Apache. It also takes advantage of *mod_perl*, the Apache module that brings the Perl interpreter into the Apache process, speeding up Perl-based scripts. Mason is essentially implemented as a Perl module, providing similar functionality to EmbPerl. It is different from EmbPerl in that it builds on it with component-based reusable code. Mason's other advantages over EmbPerl include its object orientation, caching, and expiration of individual components, its sophisticated previewing, and best of all, its staging and production modes that optimize production development and speed.

The main web site for Mason is:

http://www.masonhq.com

Aquarium

Aquarium is similar in functionality to the Turbine project mentioned in our discussion of Java technologies earlier in this chapter. Developed by Shannon -jj Behrens, Aquarium provides another modular web application development system based on FreeEnergy, a modular approach to the development of web applications. Unlike Turbine, Aquarium is based on Python, not Java. Fans of Python, which was described in Chapter 3, will be excited about this project.

The main web site for Aquarium is:

http://aquarium.sourceforge.net

6

Building Web-Based
Oracle Applications

The world of web-based Oracle applications is bursting at the seams these days, with a well-rounded and growing list of tools ranging from snapshot-based performance monitoring tools and database administration gizmos to data browsing and remote online transaction processing (OLTP) systems.

What are web-based applications? We loosely define such applications as those whose output or interface is viewed through a web browser. Some of these applications are Perl-based CGI scripts; others are just SQL scripts whose output is HTML. Chapter 5, *Web Technologies*, describes the fundamental technologies on which these applications are built. If you've read that chapter, you will have a solid foundation for understanding the web-based Oracle applications described in this chapter.

The advantage to employing a web solution is that you need to deploy it only once, at one web address, and thereby provide a tool that anyone with a web browser can access from anywhere on the network. This is a powerful application paradigm indeed, especially for busy administrators who may manage dozens of databases and who want to maintain a satellite's-eye view of what's going on. If you deploy over the Internet, as well as over your corporate intranet (with the appropriate security measures, of course), you'll be able to administer your systems much more simply and effectively, especially if you're away from your base system, need instant access, and sometimes have difficulty remotely logging in to your intranet. Web-based applications are also useful to the many non-technical people at your site who need different levels of access to browse the database, but who don't want to know, or don't need to know, SQL.

There are many different types of web-based applications available in the Oracle world. In this chapter, we'll focus on a number of excellent applications, highlighting those that help demonstrate a variety of open source implementation strategies.

Check out the web sites mentioned in the preface for pointers to other helpful open source web-based applications for Oracle. We'll cover the following applications in this chapter:

Karma

A robust Oracle database monitoring application, Karma offers the ability to notify the DBA by email when database problems occur, and it provides a single place to keep track of many different databases. Karma is written in Perl, but unlike some of the other Perl-based applications described in this chapter, it's not a CGI. Instead, it runs as a daemon, or background process, generating HTML pages in a specified location.

Oracletool

This tool focuses on performance monitoring, but it also provides other database administration features. It is written in Perl and implemented as one CGI script. It uses the Perl DBI and, like other Perl CGI scripts, can take advantage of the *mod_perl* module with Apache.

OraSnap

OraSnap provides snapshot-based performance monitoring and statistics gathering. OraSnap works somewhat like Oracle's own *utlbstat* and *utlestat* utilities, but it provides much more sophisticated reports, and it's all presented in a web browser. This application stands out from the others in that it does not use any web-based programming technologies per se. OraSnap's ingenious approach is simply to wrap the various SQL scripts in printable HTML tags, so the resulting output is valid HTML that can be understood by a web browser.

DB_Browser

This tool provides a way to browse tables, search for columns, and add data to a database. DB_Browser was built using the Perl DBI and provides an interesting example of how to build a database-independent application. As a Perl CGI script, it takes good advantage of the *mod_perl* Apache module.

PhpMyAdmin and PhpOracleAdmin

PhpMyAdmin provides a simple way to browse a schema, modify a table, add and delete rows, and run SQL queries against your database. PhPMyAdmin is a PHP-based MySQL database administration tool. Work is just beginning on PhpOracleAdmin, the long-awaited Oracle version of this tool.

WWWdb

WWWdb provides a mechanism for searching for text inside database tables. It is somewhat like Oracle's ConText (now renamed Intermedia) product, but it is a CGI-based script written in Perl.

Big Brother

Big Brother is essentially a general network monitoring tool that includes support for monitoring Oracle databases. Big Brother is particularly useful to those of us who have system administration, as well as Oracle database administration, responsibilities. Big Brother is written in C and uses various Unix networking technologies to monitor a disparate network of computers and the services running on them.

Karma

Karma is an open source tool that can help Oracle DBAs with their daily work. The program is especially helpful in automating the tracking of important but tedious-to-collect information—information that you need to know but are too busy to gather personally. Karma's comprehensive configuration capabilities let you select the particular features and database events to monitor and how often and how strictly to monitor them. You can also break up your many databases into groups, each with their own monitoring criteria and thresholds.

Even if you don't have the time to keep checking Karma's continuously updated web page, the product's new email notification capability will email you with alerts about potential database problems. This way, you'll find out when something goes wrong before anyone else notices it (and the suits need never know!).

The Karma project has been in development since July 1999, when Sean Hull, your faithful author, first started work on it, and it has grown exponentially in popularity since its first release. Its feature list has expanded too, as well as its stability, driven particularly by the comments and bug fixes of its ever-widening group of users. Karma is written in Perl and runs as a daemon, generating HTML pages in a location you can specify.

The main web site for Karma is:

> *http://www.iheavy.com/karma/*

Installing Karma

Karma's installation follows the pattern of many Perl-based tools, so if you're familiar with the *perl Makefile.PL* drill described in Chapter 2, *Connecting to Oracle*, you shouldn't have too much trouble installing Karma. Before you install Karma, you must make sure that the following are installed on your system:

- Perl

- The Perl DBI and DBD::Oracle modules

- The Mail::Send Perl module (if you will be using Karma's email notification facilities). Mail::Send is part of the MailTools module on CPAN; it can be found under Graham Barr's Perl CPAN site at:

  > *http://www.perl.com/CPAN-local//authors/id/G/GB/GBARR/*

To install Karma, follow these steps:

1. Download Karma from one of the sites listed previously.

2. Unzip the zipped Karma file and install it. There is a standard Perl *Makefile.PL* included with Karma, so the actual installation should be fairly simple:

   ```
   $ perl Makefile.PL
   $ make test
   ```

3. Issue the following as *root*:

   ```
   $ make install
   ```

4. Once that's done, Karma's scripts should be installed in */usr/bin, /usr/local/ bin*, or wherever you've configured Perl to put its scripts. You can find the main Karma script like this:

   ```
   $ which karmad
   ```

Karma provides a wide variety of configuration options. Once you've installed Karma, you can select these options by editing the program's configuration file. The *karma.conf* file included with Karma should go a long way towards explaining the intricate features of the product and how to configure it, but you might want to get started quickly and easily with the simpler default *basic.conf* file.

The two important lines in the *basic.conf* file are these:

```
karma:*:UNA:karma:amrak
doc_root:/home/shull/karma/karma098/doc_root
```

Edit these lines as follows:

1. The first line specifies the individual database to monitor. Edit the third field on that line, UNA, to be the same as the equivalent name in the *tnsnames.ora* file of the database you'll be monitoring, as in:

   ```
   UNA =
     (DESCRIPTION =
       (ADDRESS_LIST =
         (ADDRESS =
           (COMMUNITY = UNA)
           (PROTOCOL = TCP)
           (Host = 127.0.0.1)
           (Port = 1521)
         )
       )
       (CONNECT_DATA = (SID = UNA)
       )
     )
   ```

   The last two fields on the first line specify your username and password respectively.

   If you want to add more databases to monitor, simply add more lines. Copy the line provided and change the appropriate names to protect the innocent.

2. Now edit the second line in the configuration file, the *doc_root* line, to indicate where you want *karmad* to generate the *karma.html* file—the watershed HTML file, from which all the other drill-downs start. If this isn't the default, note that there are many supporting files that you will have to copy manually to that location. These are currently stored within your default Karma install directory, */doc_root*.

3. Once you've done all this, you should be able to use the *karmactl* utility to ignite the daemon:

   ```
   $ karmactl -s
   ```

4. You may also want to specify the location of the configuration file like this:

   ```
   $ karmactl -s -c /home/oracle/karma.conf
   ```

5. Make sure that Karma is running. You can use the Unix *ps* command (or an equivalent command on your system) to do this. If there are environment variables that aren't set, you may need to debug things by checking the *karma.log* file. You can also check the status by typing:

   ```
   $ karmactl -t
   ```

   You should see a small report about what is being monitored, how often, and what the current status is for each item monitored.

You can configure many different aspects of Karma, and we won't go into all of them here, but the *karma.conf* file provided with the product should serve as a good example. Notice that you can separate your various databases into groups, each with their own preferences. The *basic.conf* file simplifies all this by just using the default "*" group. This may be all that you will need for your own system. If not, check out the product's documentation.

There is no shortage of documentation with Karma. If you click on the help "?" link, you'll find various links to online documents, as we'll show later.

Using Karma

Karma lets you monitor a great many database statistics and characteristics. Table 6-1 summarizes these and specifies the names used to request them. Later in this section we'll show some examples illustrating how to interpret these statistics.

Table 6-1. Karma Monitorables

Name on Screen	Full Name	Description
alog	*alert log*	Monitors errors in the alert log file (*karmagentd*)
hitr	*hitratios*	Regularly checks the buffer cache hit ratio
rdlg	*redo log*	Monitors redo log file switching contention
rlbk	*rollback*	Reports on rollback segment contention

Table 6-1. Karma Monitorables (continued)

Name on Screen	Full Name	Description
ssql	*slow sql*	Monitors for slow SQL (by number of disk reads)
exts	*max extents*	Checks objects nearing their maximum extents
ltch	*latch contention*	Checks latch contention
frag	*fragmentation*	Monitors tablespaces for fragmentation
mts	*multi-threaded server*	Looks for multi-threaded server contention
tbsp	*tablespace quotas*	Supervises tablespace quotas (not user quotas)
repq	*replication queue*	Monitors deferred transaction queue
rper	*replication errors*	Monitors deferred transaction error queue
os	*os statistics*	Monitors load average of target database machine (*karmagentd*)
up	*up/down status*	Checks that the target database is up and running

Karma can be very simple to use for DBAs who have straightforward administrative needs, but it offers an enormous amount of flexibility for those with complicated configurations. As we've mentioned, two of the most important features of Karma are the following:

- Email notification about database problems. Getting email from Karma gives you early warning of problems and the chance to solve them before anyone else even notices them. This feature can be an absolute godsend to the DBA.

- The ability to monitor multiple databases.

We'll describe these features in the following sections.

Like the Big Brother tool, described later in this chapter, Karma allows you to collect statistics about a number of different entities (i.e., your databases) and present them all in one simple table. This table then becomes your central command bunker, your first point of defense against the underwater sea wolves menacing the convoys of information tracking across your databases.

Figure 6-1 shows Karma's main screen in all its glory. Here, Karma is monitoring seven different databases in five different cities!

Using Karma for email notification

Email notification is fairly simple to configure, and the facility is very flexible, so if you have different DBAs responsible for different groups, Karma can handle that as well. In this example, we're configuring for the default group:

```
notify_email:full:shull@myhost.com,dba@myhost.com
notify_alert:1:fragmentation,up,hitratios,alertlog
notify_warn:1:hitratios,fragmentation
```

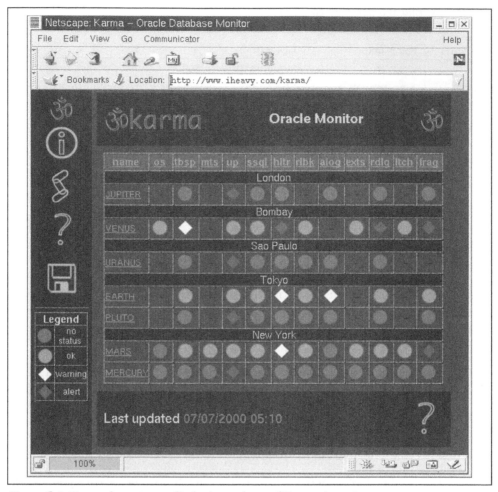

Figure 6-1. Karma home page, displaying a demo of Karma in action

In the first line, notice that the users *shull@myhost.com* and *dba@myhost.com* will receive email messages. Notice too that the size of the email message is specified as *full*. This means that a full-length message will be sent to those email addresses.

In the second line, we're asking that *alert* messages be sent only if there are problems with specified types of statistics: *fragmentation, up/down status* (whether the database is up or not), *hitratios,* and *alertlog* (see Table 6-1 for a description of these and other database statistics). If those specified statistics hit only the *warning* level threshold, Karma will not send email.

In the third line, however, we see that for *hitratios* and *fragmentation,* warning threshold messages will be mailed.

If you want a short message instead (which is potentially useful for email addresses of text pagers or small-screen PDAs, for those handling 24×7 support), you could configure the *notify_email* line like this:

```
notify_email:short:2223333@pager.net,4445555@pager.net
```

Running Karma on Windows

Given the cross-platform nature of Perl, it is fairly simple to get most programs to work on the Win32 platform. With a few exceptions, this is also true of Karma. Unfortunately, there are a few Unix-only system facilities used to make the *karmactl* tool work that currently don't translate well to the Win32 world. Those include various *kill* signals, as well as the *fork* system call (to allow *karmad* to run in the background). True, there are ways to implement these on Win32, but they haven't yet been been implemented within Karma. For now you run *karmad* directly on Win32 like this:

```
DOS> perl karmad -c karma.conf
```

See the various Karma online documents (available for download) for more Win32-specific information. These documents, along with many other help files, are accessible via the question mark (?) drill-down, as shown in Figure 6-2.

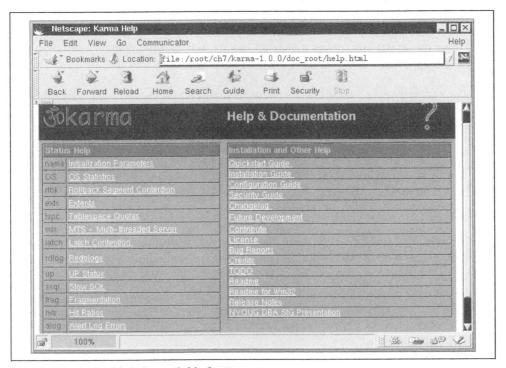

Figure 6-2. Browsable help available for Karma

If the web-based online documentation isn't sufficient, you may be happy to find the */pod* directory in the Karma installation directory. It contains all the various original documents that eventually turn into text and HTML; these documents started life as Perl POD documents (Plain Old Documentation).

Using Karma with multiple databases

Let's look at an example of using Karma with multiple databases. In the following example we'll use the absolute basic setup, as provided via the *basic.conf* file, and run Karma through some initial simple trials:

1. Create two databases under Linux.*

2. After saving the original, more complex *karma.conf* file as *karma.conf.old* (which may be useful later on), add the following lines to the *basic.conf* file, and then save it as *karma.conf*:

   ```
   #
   # karma line specifies database to connect to
   # The "*" means use the default preference group, and "UNA" is the
   # name of the db (tnsnames.ora), then user and password are specified
   #
   karma:*:orcl:system:manager
   karma:*:mydb:system:manager

   doc_root:/root/ch7/karma-1.0.0/doc_root
   ```

3. These two database entries match up to our two complementary entries in the *$ORACLE_HOME/network/admin/tnsnames.ora* file, as follows:

   ```
   orcl =
     (DESCRIPTION =
       (ADDRESS = (PROTOCOL= TCP)(Host= localhost.localdomain)(Port= 1521))
       (CONNECT_DATA = (SID = orcl))
     )

   mydb =
     (DESCRIPTION =
       (ADDRESS = (PROTOCOL= TCP)(Host= localhost.localdomain)(Port= 1521))
       (CONNECT_DATA = (SID = mydb))
     )
   ```

   The *doc_root* line points to the place where we want our HTML files to be created. (In a web server situation, this might be something like */usr/www/site. karma/docs*.)

4. Make sure that the ORACLE_HOME environment variable is set correctly for Perl DBI.†

---

* See Appendix A, *Oracle8i on Linux*, for instructions.

† We've assumed here that you've already set up Perl and Perl DBI. This particular Karma installation is not using notification, so in this case the MailTools module is not required.

5. Finally, run the Karma program:

```
$ cd /root/ch7/karma-1.0.0
$ ORACLE_HOME=/u01/app/oracle/product/8.1.5 ; export ORACLE_HOME
$ bin/karmactl -s -c karma.conf
```

This program can now repeatedly generate appropriate HTML files in timed loops, which you can use either in conjunction with a web server such as Apache or, as in this basic example, merely by pointing a browser at the files directly (as detailed in the *README, INSTALL,* and *QUICKSTART* setup files). This gives us our output, as shown in Figure 6-3.

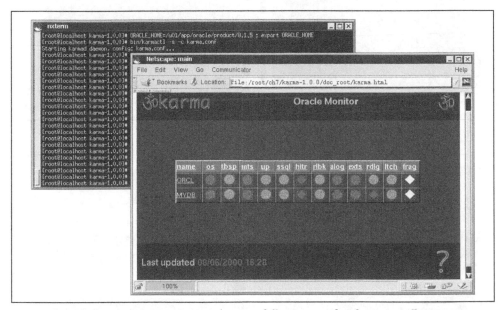

Figure 6-3. The Karma program's initial screen following our first basic installation

The first screen provides numerous drill-downs into further information. You may notice from the key in Figure 6-1 that several of the checks are set to "No Status." This is because we are using the minimal configuration. If you read through the documentation listed in Figure 6-2 and follow the various instructions, you'll learn how to activate many more of these configurable checks. For now, in Figure 6-4, we've drilled down into the *ORCL* address to see what that gives us, plus the first green flag, *tbsp,* for tablespace figures.

Finally, to wrap up our Karma example, we've drilled down on the first red flag (on *bitratios*) as generated by our example code, and also on our first yellow flag (for a fragmentation report) to find out what *alert* and *warning* figures will reveal, as shown in Figure 6-5.

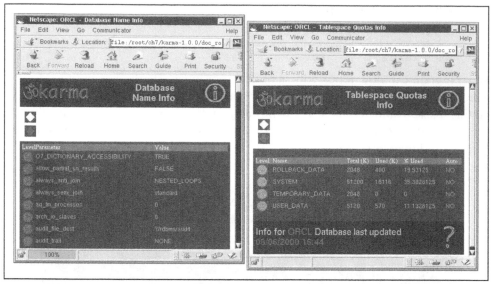

Figure 6-4. Drilling down into the Database Name address and the tbsp green flag

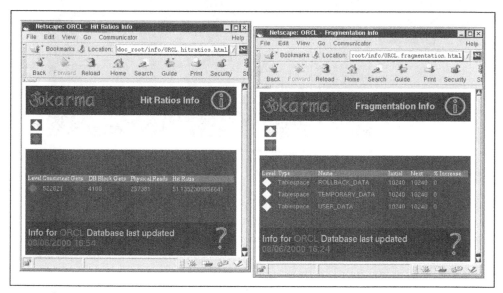

Figure 6-5. Drilling down on hit ratios and fragmentation flags

Extending Karma

Karma is a good tool, but there is plenty of room for improvement. It has been some time since Version 1.0.0 was released, and development is just beginning on Version 2.x. Sean would certainly like to hear from potential contributors, especially those who have experience programming Perl under Win32. That is where the biggest problems with Karma remain.

Oracletool

Oracletool is a serious piece of weaponry in our Oracle and open source armory. This program is an excellent tool for maintaining Oracle databases. You can use it to help with performance tuning and to perform a variety of database administration functions. Oracletool provides a simple web-based interface to many of the day-to-day maintenance tasks a DBA needs to carry out in order to keep a typical database in good working order. And for those developers who can pluck a SELECT ANY TABLE privilege from the tight clutches of their DBA (good luck!), Oracletool is also a highly useful development utility.

Adam vonNieda first started work on Oracletool in 1997, and it had its first major release in March of 1999. Oracletool enjoys regular releases and maintains independence from any web server–specific modules. Written in Perl, it is completely CGI-driven and makes use of a number of great Perl modules, including Perl DBI and DBD::Oracle. Oracletool is a very straightforward program; its entire wealth of functionality is contained in a single CGI script. This implementation makes Oracletool easy to install and configure.

Oracletool provides a reasonable degree of security as a default, but it also gives you the ability to configure more rigorous security. You can choose your level of security based on your own site's requirements. The faint of heart will be glad to hear that Oracletool does *not* modify your database. You can create a user with the SELECT ANY TABLE privilege and rest assured that running Oracletool won't break your database. Not that you'll need to worry in any case—Oracletool is well written and behaves consistently.

The main web site for Oracletool is:

http://www.oracletool.com

Installing Oracletool

Before you install Oracletool, you must make sure that the following are already installed on your system:

- Perl

- The Perl DBI and DBD::Oracle modules

- The appropriate Perl security modules for performing cookie encryption. You will need to install these in order for Oracletool to run securely. If you haven't installed the appropriate modules, Oracletool will send cookies with your Oracle username and password unencrypted. If there is any chance that someone might walk up to your workstation and read that cookie file, you'll have a security problem.

For moderate security and at least some level of cookie encryption (which might be appropriate on a reasonably secure intranet), Oracletool is preconfigured for use with the following two Perl security packages:

Digest::MD5
> Used with the MD5 Message Digest algorithm

Mime::Base64
> Used to encode and decode Base64 strings (specified in RFC 2045, MIME [Multipurpose Internet Mail Extensions])

For stronger measures on a full-blown Internet security setup, we advise you also to install these Perl encryption packages:

Crypt::IDEA
> Used to access the International Data Encryption Algorithm (IDEA) block cipher

Crypt::CBC
> Used to encrypt data with the Cipher Block Chaining (CBC) mode

See the Oracletool *INSTALL* and *SECURITY* documentation files for details.

Once you've installed Perl and the other prerequisite files, you can install Oracletool itself and prepare your system to run it, as follows:

1. Download the latest stable version of Oracletool from *http://www.oracletool. com/download.html.* Click on the link appropriate to your current platform.

2. Unpack the files and read all of the instructions.

3. As with the other web-based tools, you need to make sure that you have Apache or another suitable CGI-capable web server up and running. Apache is a particular winner because its *mod_perl* module really makes Perl code fly.

4. Copy the *oracletool.pl* and *oracletool.sam* files into a valid *cgi-bin* directory (while doing this, rename *oracletool.sam* to *oracletool.ini*).

5. Be sure to edit the *oracletool.ini* file in order to modify the ORACLE_HOME and TNS_ADMIN environment variables as appropriate for your installation.

In the following steps, we'll run through a fairly simple initial test installation, just to see how easy it is to get Oracletool up and running, with its wide variety of out-of-the-box functionality:

1. Create a new Apache site in the following directory:

   /usr/www/site.oracletool

2. Configure the Oracletool configuration file, */usr/www/site.oracletool/conf/httpd. conf,* to contain the following key values (the *cgi-bin* directory line is particularly important):

```
ServerRoot "/usr/www/site.oracletool"
PidFile /usr/www/site.oracletool/logs/httpd.pid
ScoreBoardFile /usr/www/site.oracletool/logs/httpd.scoreboard
DocumentRoot "/usr/www/site.oracletool/htdocs"
ScriptAlias /cgi-bin/ "/usr/www/site.oracletool/cgi-bin/"
ErrorLog /usr/www/site.oracletool/logs/error_log
CustomLog /usr/www/site.oracletool/logs/access_log common
Port 8666
```

3. Run the following commands:

```
cd /root/ch7/oracletool-1.2.0
cp oracletool.pl /usr/www/site.oracletool/cgi-bin/
cp oracletool.sam /usr/www/site.oracletool/cgi-bin/oracletool.ini
cd /usr/www/site.oracletool/cgi-bin/
chmod +x oracletool.pl
```

Note that the *oracletool.sam* file gets renamed to a new *oracletool.ini* file.

4. Alter the *oracletool.ini* file with some necessary changes:

```
# Alter as appropriate
ORACLE_HOME = /u01/app/oracle/product/8.1.5

# Comment out if not required (default: $ORACLE_HOME/network/admin)
#TNS_ADMIN = /home/oracle/admin/sqlnet
```

In this case, because the value of our TNS_ADMIN environment variable matches the default, we comment it out. There are many other parameters, including important encryption parameters, in the initialization file, but the pair above are the two main Oracle parameters, so for testing purposes you can probably accept the other defaults. Later on, when you reset the configuration for production purposes, you will want to reset other parameters as appropriate for your own environment. Most of the parameter settings are fairly self-explanatory, and the documentation is thorough, so you should be able to configure Oracletool without too much difficulty.

5. Once you have performed the other installation and configuration steps, fire up the Apache *httpd* daemon with the following command:

```
/usr/local/apache/bin/httpd -d /usr/www/site.oracletool
```

Now you're ready to start up Oracletool.

Using Oracletool

Oracletool lets you perform the following tasks:

- Watch sessions for database waits
- Check the sessions that are the busiest
- Check out datafiles and see how busy *reads* and *writes* relating to each file are
- Examine currently held locks and various other types of contention

- Examine Oracle system security and see with crystal clarity which users have which privileges and which roles, and basically just make sure everything is configured as it should be

- Generate DDL for the existing tables in your database

 If you're running these web-based applications with a web server on the local machine and your browser is not behaving correctly, this may be because TCP/IP isn't running for your local loopback device. In this case, for a quick fix, run the following commands as *root*:

```
# Assign loopback (lo) to the standard IP address
/sbin/ifconfig lo 127.0.0.1

# Point a route at the loopback device
/sbin/route add 127.0.0.1
```

To get started with Oracletool, follow these steps:

1. To run Oracletool from your favorite browser, simply point the browser to your CGI script, using a URL like this one:

   http://*yourhost.com*/cgi-bin/oracletool.pl

2. Next we need to log in to our target database, as shown in Figure 6-6.

3. Once you have logged into the database successfully, just drill down via the Schema list to check out our SYSTEM user, as shown in Figure 6-7.

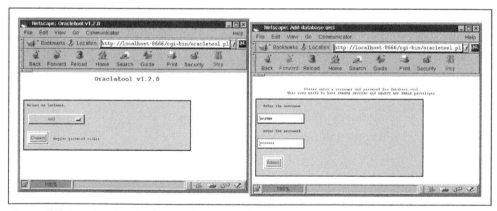

Figure 6-6. Logging in via the Oracletool interface

In this discussion of Oracletool, we won't try to explain every menu option displayed on the left side of Oracletool's extensive user interface. Since there are so many different functions and screens, we'll just cherry-pick a few favorites; you can check out the others on your own.

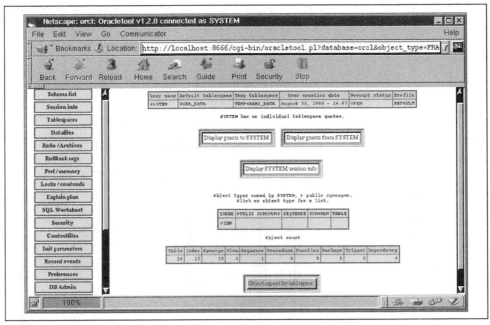

Figure 6-7. Oracletool drilling down into the SYSTEM user's schema

One Oracletool function we particularly like is the Datafiles graph shown in Figure 6-8, which shows the I/O for your datafiles.

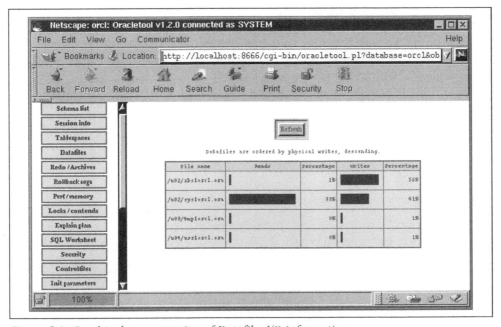

Figure 6-8. Graphical representation of Datafiles I/O information

Another cool feature is the SQL Worksheet, with which you can run SQL*Plus-like commands over the Web. This feature is a very handy way of getting out of some sticky situations. Simply enter the required SQL and press *Execute*, and the results pop right back within a neatly formatted HTML table!

In Figure 6-9, you can see the generic SQL query execution window on the left side and the results on the right.

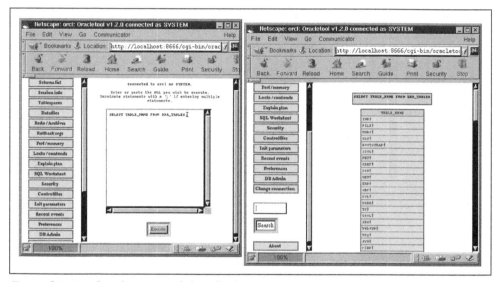

Figure 6-9. Oracletool's SQL Worksheet facility

Perhaps the most useful of Oracletool's menu options is DB Admin, which provides a variety of database administration and reporting features. Administration features include the following menu choices:

> User administration
> Session administration
> Rollback segment administration
> Generate table DDL
> Invalid object administration

Reporting features include the following menu choices:

> Space report by user
> Space report by tablespace/user
> Datafile fragmentation report
> Object extent report

You can see the DDL generation drill-down in Figure 6-10. We needed to traverse several screens to get to the actual DDL screen shown here, and we haven't tried to show them all. Those screens give you the ability to scroll through all of a schema user's objects, ticking off the ones required for DDL generation.

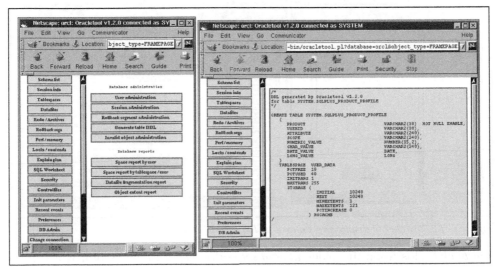

Figure 6-10. Generating database DDL via DB Admin

Oracletool also provides a really neat Explain Plan facility. If your user doesn't have PLAN_TABLE installed, Oracletool installs it automatically for you. For example, if you type the following statement:

```
select count (*) from dba_tables
```

Oracletool brings back another neatly formatted HTML table, which you can see in Figure 6-11.

You may sense from our enthusiastic discussion here that we just love Oracletool. It's a great tool bursting with helpful features—we only wish we'd thought of it first! If this section doesn't persuade you that it's worth your time and energy to download and install Oracletool, take a look at the live demo on the Oracletool web site to try out the program first hand.

OraSnap

OraSnap provides Oracle snapshot-based[*] performance monitoring and statistics gathering. It takes a very different approach to database administration and tuning from the tools we've looked at so far. OraSnap consists of a set of specialized SQL scripts that produce HTML output that can be used by a web browser. The product works somewhat like *statspack*, Oracle's own new snapshot-based tool;

---

[*] We use the word "snapshot" here to mean a moment in time; it's not a reference to Oracle's snapshot objects.

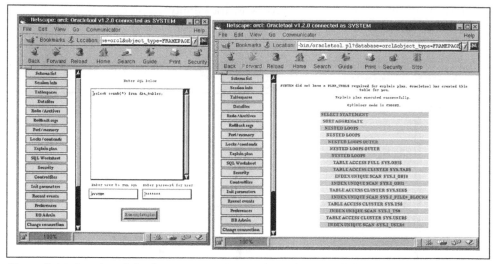

Figure 6-11. Oracletool displaying some of its Explain Plan capabilities

statspack builds upon the older *utlestat.sql* performance tuning script, which provides report-based functionality.

Stewart McGlaughlin, the author of OraSnap, started work on this program back in 1998. The first version of OraSnap was released in December 1998, and, after various revisions and changes, the hallowed 1.0.0 version was quickly released to great acclaim. The latest OraSnap version (v2.2.1) was released in April 2000, and that version is compatible with Oracle Versions 7.3 through 8.1.5. The program will continue to be updated to keep the data dictionary views and other information up to date as Oracle9*i* reaches release. As of January 2001, the latest release of OraSnap, v2.3.3, is available with lots of new features.

The main web site for OraSnap is:

   http://www.stewartmc.com/oracle/orasnap/

You'll find a lot of other useful Oracle links and references at this site as well:

   http://www.stewartmc.com

Installing OraSnap

This out-of-the-box tool is really Win32-based, but with a little work it can be made to run under Unix too. That's because OraSnap basically consists of a wrapper around a large collection of clever SQL scripts. These need to be executed to create the right reports, but this doesn't necessarily make OraSnap Windows-bound. The modifiability and simplicity of OraSnap is what gives it such elegant power. Figure 6-12 illustrates OraSnap's display of shared pool usage.

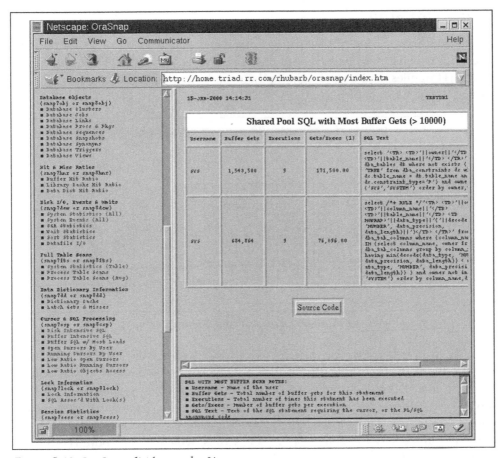

Figure 6-12. OraSnap display under Linux

Installing OraSnap is very straightforward:

1. Download the OraSnap file from the web site mentioned earlier.

2. Unzip the downloaded file (or, if you are copying the files over to your Unix box or Linux partition, stick with the same directory structure). See the instructions on the web page for details.

3. Run *snap7.sql* (for Oracle7) or *snap8.sql* (for Oracle8) from SQL*Plus.

4. Point your browser at the *index.htm* file in the installation directory (under Windows, *C:\OraSnap*).

Windows-based users will be happy to know that there is an *OraSnap.exe* self-extracting archive, so installation is even easier than dealing with the straight zip file. As a bonus, the *OraSnap.exe* program adds all the right options to the Windows menu structure. This makes updating the snapshots on a regular basis and viewing the latest reports very straightforward.

Using OraSnap

Figure 6-13 shows a log of OraSnap generating snapshots of all of its HTML files. The main OraSnap web page is a set of frames. Along the left are links to the generated HTML files, and on the right, in the main body frame, the contents of these various HTML files are displayed.

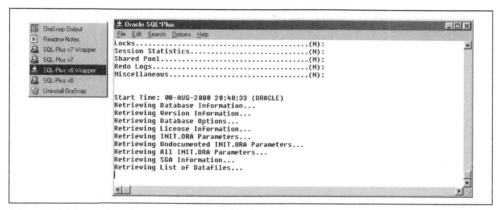

Figure 6-13. Running the main snap8.sql file from the Windows menu

If you're wondering how this magic box of tricks works, take a look at the various scripts in the */sql* directory for a hint. OraSnap is essentially a collection of tried-and-true DBA SQL scripts—from tablespace, rollback segment, and user reports to performance statistics and contention checks. The typical user doesn't need to know this level of detail, however. The clarity of OraSnap with the hood down lies in the spooled output of the SQL scripts, which creates pure HTML. The gateway *index.htm* file is merely a linked conduit to the collection of these generated HTML files. We think that's a pretty cool implementation.

OraSnap is very easy to get going, and it provides a top-notch collection of SQL scripts that can be run against your database. What's more, the resulting reports are so handsomely presented that we doubt you'll ever again go back to hand-typing SQL*Plus substitution variable values.

To provide a full-blown web solution based on OraSnap, you might want to consider wrapping the *snap8.sql* command into some sort of *cron* process or web server daemon, to regularly update a web page. For extra marks, you could archive old information into drillable web pages and then create even more web pages on the fly to analyze these archived data patterns over time to get some meaningful information on the growth of your database. (Hey, we've got to get out more . . .)

In Figure 6-14, OraSnap displays its main frameset, listing foreign key constraints on various tables.

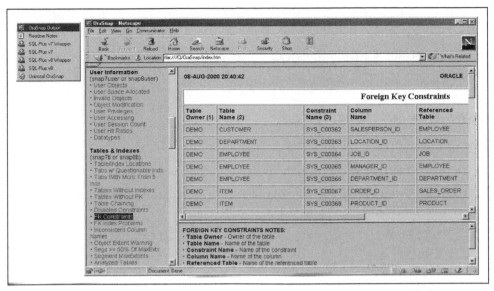

Figure 6-14. Accessing the newly regenerated OraSnap information tables via the main Windows Start menu

Extending OraSnap

OraSnap consists of a collection of specialized SQL scripts that dump HTML output. The product could be extended by writing additional scripts and integrating them into the main screen's frameset. The architecture is ready-made for someone to make such an addition without having to dive into a lot of programming. If you do this successfully, try sending the author your contributions. Maybe they will be adapted into a new OraSnap release. Even if you don't ever enhance OraSnap, you'll learn a lot about Oracle performance tuning and administration by looking through the OraSnap code.

Another welcome extension to OraSnap might be web server functionality, as we mentioned in the previous section. Stewart McGlaughlin himself may add some sort of web server functionality, but he has said that he wants to keep the number of moving parts down to a bare minimum to ensure clean future maintenance.

DB_Browser

DB_Browser is a web interface that lets you browse database tables, search for columns containing particular content, and add new data to a database.

Created by Chris Hardie, DB_Browser was last updated in January 2001. The product, a Perl CGI script that uses the *mod_perl* Apache module, is definitely worth a look. It provides a good illustration of how to use Perl DBI and its various drivers to build a tool that works on various databases, including Oracle. It may provide a good starting point for building your own web-based application.

The main web site for DB_Browser is:

http://www.summersault.com/software/db_browser/

Installing DB_Browser

If you are using DB_Browser with Oracle, follow these steps:

1. Download DB_Browser from the web site mentioned earlier.

2. Edit the *browse_lib.pl* file for your site. At a minimum, you will need to correctly set the following variables:

   $orahome
   $dbtype
   $dbuser
   $dbpass
   $database

   In the following example, we altered the variables at the top of the *browse_lib. pl* file. Also make sure that the *$orahome* variable (which is a bit lower down in the file) is set correctly for ORACLE_HOME. Notice our default table:

   ```
   # User defined variables
   $database = "orcl";
   $dbtype = "Oracle";
   $dbuser = "scott";
   $dbpass = "tiger";
   $default_table = 'EMP';
   $compname = "Oracle and Open Source Technology";

   # Oracle Home
   $orahome = '/u01/app/oracle/product/8.1.5';
   ```

3. Copy the *.cgi* files and *browse_lib.pl* to a valid */cgi-bin* directory.

4. Open *http://yourhost.com/cgi-bin/search.cgi* and you're off and running.

Let's assume that, after having unpacked the DB_Browser download in a */root/ch7* directory, we decided to "borrow" the Oracletool Apache web site we'd set up earlier. We copied the appropriate DB_Browser files into its */cgi-bin* directory and made them executable as follows:

```
$ cd /usr/www/site.oracletool/cgi-bin
$ cp /root/ch7/db_browser1.30/browse_lib.pl .
$ cp /root/ch7/db_browser1.30/search.cgi .
$ cp /root/ch7/db_browser1.30/add.cgi .
$ cp /root/ch7/db_browser1.30/edit.cgi .
$ chmod +x *.pl
$ chmod +x *.cgi
```

Finally, we started up our dormant *httpd* web server daemon again and went once more unto the breach as follows:

```
$ /usr/local/apache/bin/httpd -d /usr/www/site.oracletool
```

Once DB_Browser has been installed properly, fire up your favorite browser, as you do with all of the web-based applications we describe in this chapter. Point the browser to the location of your *search.cgi* script, and you'll see the main window on the left side in Figure 6-15.

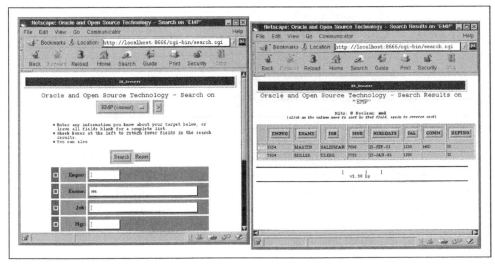

Figure 6-15. Our first DB_Browser screen, and a search for MILLER using M

In this figure, you can see that because we set *$default_table* to EMP, our first screen defaulted to it. In Figure 6-16, poor old MILLER gets the mace in the neck again.[*]

PhpMyAdmin and PhpOracleAdmin

PhpMyAdmin is a very helpful tool that can be used to browse existing tables, select, insert, and update rows, and add and drop columns. You can also use it to run SQL queries against your database: you simply dump the creation SQL and the data from the table to a flat file, separated by commas or some other delimiter. This is certainly a very useful bunch of features; however, the original PhpMyAdmin can only be used only with the MySQL database.[†]

---

[*] Since Oracle's earliest days, this character has been the unfortunate target of many such slings and arrows of outrageous fortune, but we dare not oppose such a sea of traditions.

[†] You can obtain MySQL and learn about this fast and highly popular database at *http://www. mysql.com*. We also recommend reading *MySQL & mSQL* by Randy Jay Yarger, George Reese, and Tim King; see the references in Appendix C, *For Further Reading*.

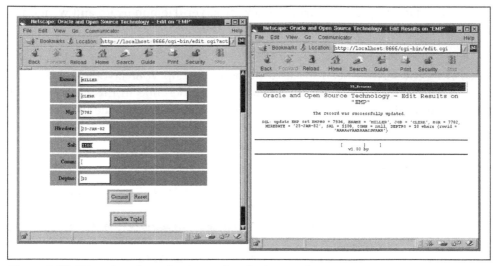

Figure 6-16. Using the salary-altering update facilities within DB_Browser

The PhpMyAdmin project was started back in 1998 by Tobias Ratschiller, as a result of the author's increasing frustration with other tools. The PhpMyAdmin project has grown phenomenally in the past few years, benefiting from contributions from the user community in the form of many diffs and patches. The 2.0.5 version of the tool has been downloaded more than 150,000 times. Version 2.1.0 was released in August 2000.

As this book was going to press, news came that work on a port to Oracle had finally begun. Anton Bangratz started the work on PhpOracleAdmin, and Thomas Fromm is performing active development. The most recent pre-release was in January 2001, and we hope to see the port completed soon. PhpOracleAdmin development is still in its infancy, but the demo certainly looks promising.

Learn more about PhpMyAdmin at the following web sites:

http://www.phpwizard.net/projects/phpMyAdmin/index.html
> The main web site for PhpMyAdmin

http://www.phporacleadmin.org
> Keeps track of what's happening with the embryonic PhpOracleAdmin project

http://www.php.net/manual/ref.oracle.php
> Information on the Oracle PHP library

http://www.mysql.com
> Information on MySQL

Installing PhpMyAdmin

Install PhPMyAdmin as follows:

1. Make sure you have PHP installed with Apache before attempting to install PhpMyAdmin.

2. Download PhpMyAdmin from the main web site mentioned earlier.

3. Untar its gzipped TAR file into a directory within your Apache document root.

4. Edit the file *config.inc.php3* and specify the hostname, port, username, and password for access to your MySQL database.

5. Point your browser to *http://yourhost.com/phpMyAdmin/index.php3*.

Using PhpMyAdmin

Figure 6-17 shows the main window you'll see when you start up PhpMyAdmin. The frame on the left side of the main window shown in the figure lists the databases available. Click on the + and the program will open to show all the tables in that database.

In the world of MySQL, a "database" is sometimes more like an Oracle schema.

Figure 6-17 also shows the table edit page. You can alter columns, their datatypes, and their contents. You can also can add new columns, browse the tables for particular columns, and insert and delete rows of data. There is even a facility to dump a table's data to a CSV (comma-separated values) file—a very useful feature indeed.

PhpMyAdmin gives you many of the features you use on a day-to-day basis to administer a database, and all in a simple browser-based GUI.

WWWdb

WWWdb gives you a way to search for text inside database tables. It provides facilities similar to those of Oracle's interMedia product (formerly known as ConText). Klaus Reger has been working on WWWdb for about a year now, with the most recent release in April 2000. WWWdb is still in beta, but when it's ready for prime time, it could be quite a tool.

The main web site for WWWdb is:

http://wwwdb.org

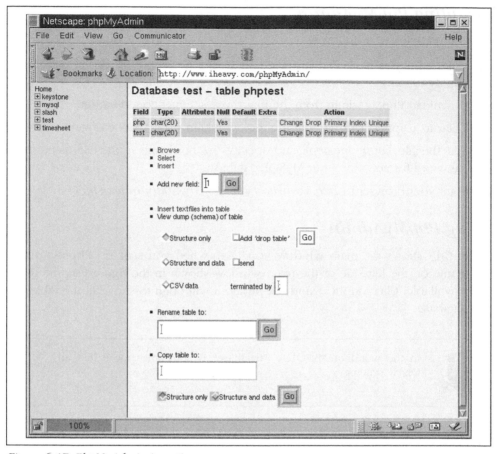

Figure 6-17. PhpMyAdmin in action

Installing WWWdb

WWWdb installation is currently a bit of a long and winding road, but we think performing this installation provides a good learning experience for those interested in Perl web technology.

Before you install WWWdb, make sure that the following are already installed on your system:

- Perl
- The Perl DBI and DBD::Oracle modules
- Additional Perl modules, described next

Installing special Perl modules

Like the Oracletool program described earlier in this chapter, WWWdb requires several non-standard Perl modules (such as LWP::UserAgent) to be in place, and

you might not already have these modules on your system. You can get all of
these modules from various places within CPAN.

 These nonstandard modules are required only for testing purposes
and are not essential to create your new *httpd* program, configured
for *mod_perl*. The wise thing to do, however (as with most Perl
installs), is to run the *make test* step properly, as we'll describe in the
following instructions.

You can get the first set of special Perl modules from the CPAN pages of Gisle Aas
and Graham Barr at the following web sites:

> *ftp://ftp.funet.fi/pub/languages/perl/CPAN/authors/id/G/GA/GAAS/*
> *ftp://ftp.funet.fi/pub/languages/perl/CPAN/authors/id/G/GB/GBARR/*

These special modules include the following:

Digest::MD5
  MD5 Message Digest algorithm

HTML::HeadParser
  Used to parse sections of an HTML document

MIME::Base64
  Used to encode and decode Base64 strings

Net::FTP
  FTP Client class (contained within the *libnet* library)

URI
  Uniform Resource Identifiers

You will also need to download and install LWP itself. You can get LWP from the
libwww-perl library, which you can also pick up from Gisle Aas's CPAN site. LWP
installs in the usual Perl manner.

To run WWWdb, you will also need to download and install the following additional non-standard Perl modules, available from the Perl contributions to CPAN of
Gerald Richter, Rich Bowen, Michael G. Schwern, Norman Walsh, Mike Shoyher,
and Steffen Beyer at:

> *ftp://ftp.funet.fi/pub/languages/perl/CPAN/authors/id/G/GR/GRICHTER/*
> *ftp://ftp.funet.fi/pub/languages/perl/CPAN/authors/id/R/RB/RBOW/*
> *ftp://ftp.funet.fi/pub/languages/perl/CPAN/authors/id/M/MS/MSCHWERN/*
> *ftp://ftp.funet.fi/pub/languages/perl/CPAN/authors/id/N/NW/NWALSH/*
> *ftp://ftp.funet.fi/pub/languages/perl/CPAN/authors/id/S/ST/STBEY/*

The following are the modules in this set:

DBIx::Recordset
The basic mechanism employed for database access

Carp::Assert
A security package

Delim::Match
Needed for scanning expressions more than one line long

Locale::PgetText
Special text handler

Date::Calc
Used for date calculations

You may also require the following:

Config::IniFiles
A module for reading *.ini*-style configuration files (WWWdb cats together several configuration files, on the fly, to mimic a *.ini* file)

Installing WWWdb itself

Once you've installed all the necessary Perl modules, follow these steps to install WWWdb (first, though, check through the *INSTALL* file in the WWWdb distribution—and remember that this is beta, so check it well):

1. Download WWWdb from *http://linux.twc.de/wwwdb/*.

2. Configure your *../conf/httpd.conf* file by appending WWWdb's *ApacheConfig. addon* file to it. The contents of this file are shown here (note the *PerlTransHandler* directive we enabled when configuring *mod_perl*):

   ```
   # <IfDefine PERL>  # For SuSE 6.2
   # URI-Translation for WWWdb/<Database>/<Table>
   PerlTransHandler        Apache::WWWdb_TransUri
   # </IfDefine>     # For SuSE 6.2
   ```

3. Follow the instructions in the *INSTALL* file for copying the *Apache::WWWdb_ TransUri.pm* packaged module, also mentioned earlier, to the correct destination. This will be something like the following:

   ```
   ../perl/lib/site_perl/5.005/my_OS_architecture/Apache
   ```

4. Copy *WWWdb.cgi* to your */cgi-bin* directory. Make sure that the call to Perl on the top shebang line is pointing at the right version of Perl on your system, for example:

   ```
   #!/usr/local/bin/perl
   ```

5. Within your *http.conf* Apache configuration file, you may want to add the following Oracle environment variable directives (tailored appropriately to your

environment), which the Apache server will pick up when it's daemonized. The first of these is based on the location of your WWWdb unpacked download directory:

```
SetEnv WWWDB_BASE_PATH /home/oos/apache/cgi-bin/WWWdb
SetEnv WWWDB_DATABASE Oracle
SetEnv ORACLE_HOME /u01/app/oracle/product/8.1.5
SetEnv TNS_ADMIN /home/oos/
SetEnv ORACLE_SID orcl
SetEnv TWO_TASK orcl
```

(This back-door environment variable setup via Apache is cheating a bit, so don't tell anyone!)

6. Set your local host in the *lib/WWWdb/Pre.rc* file, for example:

```
[WWWdb]
Hostname = "localhost"
```

7. Go to the *lib/WWWdb/Db/Oracle.rc* configuration file and set the contained values appropriately (note that you must always set *Driver=Oracle*), as in the following:

```
Driver   = Oracle
Username = scott
Password = tiger
OraSid   = orcl
OraHost  = localhost
```

8. You may also wish to add these values:

```
Database = orcl
DbHost   = localhost
```

9. To complete your Oracle configuration setup for WWWdb, edit *lib/WWWdb/Db/Oracle.pl* to ensure that the Perl version is set correctly on the top line, as with the *WWWdb.cgi* executable described earlier.

10. When setting up the required DBIx::Recordset Perl module, ignore all the databases you're asked about except Oracle, by entering a single period or full stop character (.), as in the following:

```
ADO [dbi:ADO:test].
Multiplex [dbi:Multiplex:test].
Oracle [dbi:Oracle:test]dbi:Oracle:orcl
    Username []scott
    Password []tiger
Proxy [dbi:Proxy:test].
```

The other Perl modules needed by WWWdb have no such complications.

Just a few more steps now, and we'll be ready, promise!

11. Now go to your Apache */htdocs* directory, and symbolically link in the WWWdb download directory, which has numerous associated files (e.g., images) that the main *WWWdb.cgi* script will be looking for. These are located

within the download (alternatively, copy the entire directory structure across). We did this symbolic link within the */cgi-bin* directory too:

```
$ cd ../apache/htdocs
$ ln -s /home/oos/WWWdb-0.0.7 WWdb
$ cd ../cgi-bin
$ ln -s /home/oos/WWWdb-0.0.7 WWdb
```

12. Now, we actually prepare WWWdb for action. Run the standard Perl configuration steps to install WWWdb's many Perl packages (check out the *INSTALL* file for theme variations):

```
$ perl Makefile.PL
$ make
$ make test
$ make install
```

Once you've got the software installed, walk through the remaining steps.

13. Prepare your target database for the searchable information capabilities of WWWdb by running the *CreateNewDb.sh* script.

We recommend that for this evaluation, you employ an Oracle database that is *strictly* for testing purposes.

14. This *CreateNewDb.sh* script executes the *InstallDB.pl* program, which creates the necessary WWWdb tables within your Oracle test database and fills them with all of WWWdb's required information. (You may have to alter the CSV files, which *InstallDB.pl* calls, to ensure that dates insert correctly into your Oracle database.)

15. Indicate that you require all rows to be inserted for all tables, for at least your own language requirement (either *en* for English or *de* for German).

16. You may also want to change any calls to IniConf in your *WWWdb.cgi* Perl CGI script to Son-of-IniConf, Config::IniFiles. (Once WWWdb moves out of beta, this will be covered; the IniConf Perl package has only recently been retired, to be replaced by Config::IniFiles.)

17. Finally, we're ready to run our new application. Assuming that you have already configured and started up Apache, you can start up WWWdb by firing up your browser and pointing it to:

http://localhost:8080/cgi-bin/WWWdb.cgi

This should flip auto-magically to something like this:

http://localhost:8080/wwwdb/0000000000000000/Oracle/
WWWdb:System:Login

Using WWWdb

Figure 6-18 shows the WWWdb main login screen you'll see when you start up.

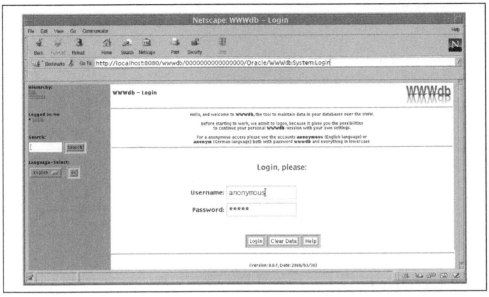

Figure 6-18. The initial WWWdb login screen

Once you've logged in, you can experiment with WWWdb by searching for various data. For example, we tried a search on the word "Database" with the original downloaded information, and you can see our result in Figure 6-19.

Extending WWWdb

WWWdb is a general web-based database tool. We mention it here because it works with Oracle, but more importantly because it is tailor-made to be extended. It is almost like a library you could use to enhance other web database applications you're already building. As such, it could very well be a good jumping-off point for someone wishing to stake out another open source database project. We feel sure that WWWdb will become a major tool once it has been developed to its full potential.

WWWdb isn't a completely finished product; the current software is still in beta, and its author expects to add features and make further changes to the configuration files. Nevertheless, even now, WWWdb is definitely worth a good look.

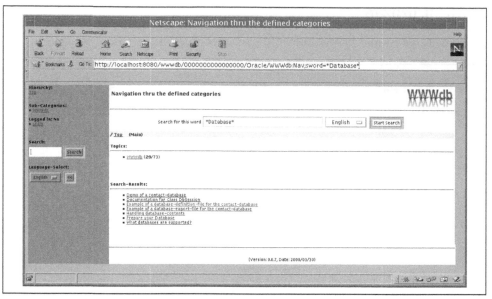

Figure 6-19. Information retrieval with WWWdb

Big Brother

Big Brother is an enormously successful product in the server hardware monitoring world. Although it's not a database-centric application, it does allow you to monitor the status of all your network services, including all the Oracle databases on your network. Big Brother is a very helpful tool for those who need to perform system administration as well as database administration. Among its other features, Big Brother allows you to configure email notification, a feature that's increasingly necessary for 24×7 support staff.

In addition to its Oracle support, Big Brother also provides almost unlimited modifiability, so we feel that it's worth including in this chapter. We also mention Big Brother because its development has been ongoing for quite some time; it provides a good model for open source software development, as well as for development of a potentially lucrative after-care support market. If you want to your software to cover your rent, Big Brother is where you learn how. It's also the tool Karma was modeled after.

Sean MacGuire has been developing and enhancing Big Brother since 1998, and it is still very much in active development, with downloads by both Oracle Corporation and Sun Microsystems (among literally hundreds of thousands of others). For proof of how useful a tool Big Brother can be, check out some of the demos on Big Brother's web site.

The main web site for Big Brother is:

http://bb4.com

To see a demo, check out:

http://bb4.com/demo.html

 Big Brother has a very professional look and feel, and numerous high-profile corporations download and use the software. In some ways, it's a great example of open source software. The source code is there for all to see and review, and it has a rich and extensible feature set. The product is not, however, free for commercial use, so we wouldn't say it's open source in the strictest sense. But it's close enough, and good enough, that we want you to know about it anyway.

Installing Big Brother

Big Brother is all about checking large networks, servers, and databases; it's not really designed to run on a small configuration. But it doesn't play favorites, so if you want to evaluate this product on a non-networked PC (we did our testing on Linux), do the following:

1. Download Big Brother from *http://bb4.com*.

2. Unpack the downloaded file as a non-*root* user.*

3. Set the BBHOME environment variable to your unpacked source directory for Big Brother, and then invoke the configuration utility:

   ```
   $ BBHOME=/home/bb ; export BBHOME
   $ cd $BBHOME
   $ cd install
   $ ./bbconfig
   ```

4. Big Brother's configuration utility then asks you questions about your setup, as follows:

   — Do you intend to use the recommended FQDNs (fully qualified domain names)?

   — Which hosts are you going to use for web display?

   — Which hosts are you going to use for paging services?

---

* For security reasons, making use of a new *bbuser* (for Big Brother) rather than *root* is particularly recommended.

— Which URL do you intend to view Big Brother with (e.g., *http://localhost: 8666/bb*)?

— What is the destination of the Big Brother CGI scripts (e.g., */usr/www/site. bb/cgi-bin*)?

5. Big Brother is now compiled and installed. Type the following to edit the Big Brother hosts file, *bb-hosts*:

```
$ cd ../src
$ make
$ make install
$ cd ../etc
$ vi bb-hosts
```

6. Following the various *README* files' instructions, we went for an absolute super-basement configuration and added the following single line. We tried to make it even simpler, but this was as good as we could get it:

```
#
# THE BIG BROTHER HOSTS FILE
#
# THIS FILE SHOULD BE THE SAME ON ALL SYSTEMS RUNNING BIG BROTHER
# CHANGE THIS FILE TO REFLECT YOUR ENVIRONMENT!
#
127.0.0.1      localhost.localdomain # BBPAGER BBNET BBDISPLAY
```

7. Configure your new Big Brother user and set the appropriate file permissions, as described in the *README* files.

8. Link your web server to the Big Brother WWW pages:

```
$ ln -s $BBHOME/www /usr/www/site.bb/htdocs/bb
```

This gives your web server access to the continuously updated HTML report pages.

9. Finally, run the Big Brother startup process, which fires up all the required daemons:

```
$ $BBHOME/runbb.sh start
```

Using Big Brother

Figure 6-20 shows an example of Big Brother's main monitoring screen. Like Karma, Big Brother allows you to monitor various services—in this case, network services such as FTP and HTTP access to a server, disk partition usage, and so on. Big Brother provides a nice way to check what's going on on your network, with colored symbols indicating different types of activities.

Our super-minimal installation carried this out in just a handful of commands and gave us our output, as shown in Figure 6-21. You'll find more detailed instructions in the Big Brother download in the */www/help* directory for extending all of

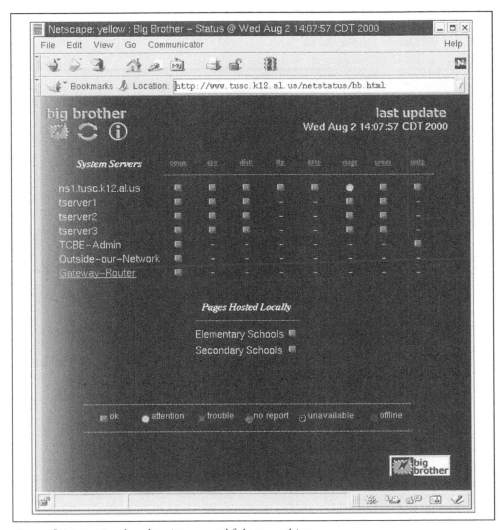

Figure 6-20. Big Brother, keeping a watchful eye on things

the available services within your own required customization and configuration sets. This includes any number of tests for checking on your Oracle servers, both in hardware and software terms. It may even be possible to say that, if something is capable of being monitored, then Big Brother *can* monitor it.

In Figure 6-21 we show Big Brother running on our local box. As you can see, all disks are OK and *conn* (as in *ping*) is working, but the CPU is quite busy. In a real case, you'd want to take a look at the CPU usage before a serious problem occurred.

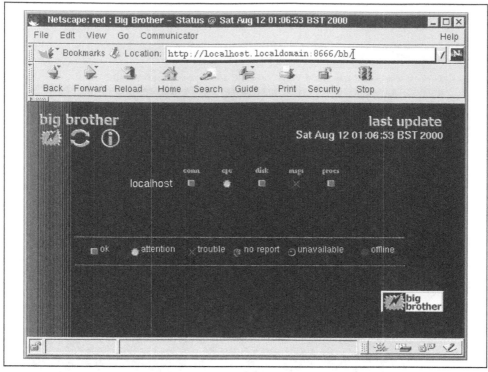

Figure 6-21. A very simple Big Brother system

Java

Java is becoming an increasingly important technology for Oracle Corporation and for Oracle developers. Java is not a base open source technology—as Perl is, for example. However, developers are starting to release fully-formed Java applications and development frameworks that adhere to the open source philosophy. Instead of simply providing wrapped-up executable *.jar* files for download (as has been customary in the Java world), they're starting to release the full source code of their applications in *.java* source files. In this chapter and the next, we'll take a look at some of the new open source applications built upon the Java platform. We'll also examine the new developmental links between Java and Oracle, especially in light of Oracle's incorporation of the Apache JServ web server in its suite of Internet products.

First, though, we'll introduce just enough Java so you'll be able to begin using the new generation of Oracle/Java open source applications. We'll focus on building Java GUI applications, running Java servlets on the Web, and using JDBC to connect your Java applications to Oracle.

There is a lot more to learn about Java. We'll reference a number of web sites in this chapter. Appendix C, *For Further Reading*, contains a list of the Java-related books that we've found most helpful.

Java Foundations

Java is a programming language that was designed from the ground up with networking and portability in mind. It's intended to run on many different or heterogeneous platforms, including PCs running Windows, Macintosh computers, the full gamut of Unix machines (including Solaris and Linux), and even the new breed of Internet appliances. As you might expect, there are many web sites full of useful

Java information. Here are two of the best-known general Java portals, plus a source for Oracle-specific Java information:

http://www.javasoft.com
  API documentation and extensive language information reference

http://www.gamelan.com
  Developmental news and other breaking information

http://technet.oracle.com/tech/java/
  Oracle/Java resources and information

The Road to Java

If you've worked with Java for any length of time, you probably know something about its origins. Java is a fairly new language, at least in comparison to C. It's been in development since 1991, when Bill Joy (who donated many BSD-Unix gifts to open programming before joining Sun Microsystems) gathered together a high-powered team in the woods of Aspen, Colorado. Under James Gosling, the Green team (later renamed FirstPerson) there created the Oak language for controlling set-top boxes and working with the cable television industry and other complex networks.

The television people failed to jump at the original idea, but (in yet another Stephen Jay Gouldian example of successful evolutionary preadaptation), Oak proved to be in the right place at the right time for something that may have surprised its original designers. A quick marketing re-shuffle, a new name and—presto!—Java, the new language for the Internet generation, rose up from the burning timbers and sacrificial pyre of Oak.

At this point, the Web already possessed the ability to move text and graphics among heterogeneous systems. On top of this existing functionality, Java promised the potential for small interactive applications (or *applets*) to be delivered straight over the Internet to the desktop—which to a Java program is just another kind of complicated network needing connectivity. Because of Java's bytecode nature, these small applications could be written on any operating system, yet still produce identical bytecode *.class* files. These could then be delivered onto any other operating system via the Internet, and as long as the Java Virtual Machine (JVM) scaffolding framework was available at the other end, they could then be executed like any other program. All the browser companies had to do was build the JVM directly into their products, and, instead of the browser being "on" the desktop, it had the potential to "become" the desktop (much to the consternation of certain quarters).

The HotJava browser, created by Patrick Naughton and Jonathan Payne, contained such a JVM and was first demonstrated at the TED (Technology, Entertainment, and Design) conference in 1995. It wowed the audiences. At SunWorld in March of that year, a last-minute deal was made with Netscape allowing Java applets to run in their new JVM-powered browsers. As a result, Java's wildfire popularity spread rapidly throughout the globe as it drove the burgeoning Internet beyond the treacle pool world of static HTML files and anonymous FTP downloads.

Heavy built-in security within the Java development model helped the new browsers lock every applet within a demarcated *sandbox*, to keep them from interfering with the target client browsers or mutating into viruses and Trojan horses. Without powerful servers and high-speed connectivity links, however, many of us at the time found that, although Java applets were relatively safe, they were often just an overly complicated way to make web graphics spin on a page. Indeed, the Berlin wall seemed to come down more quickly than the download time of your average calculator applet.

In addition, with Netscape's subsequent introduction of JavaScript (renamed from LiveScript to pick up on the Java hype), a different type of client-side programming embedded directly within the old flat HTML files became possible. Allied with the increasingly sophisticated use of animated GIF files, web designers gained all the flexibility they craved without requiring Java, which had kicked off the interactive revolution in the first place.

In the background however, many C++ programmers had discovered Java's virtues and become evangelists for its use. Developers at Sun were also hard at work extending the Java envelope, pushing its machine independence and networking abilities into server-side programming, as well as into its client-side uses. With Oracle Corporation itself realizing the unrestricted-platform potential of Java, it was not long before Java moved into the enterprise arena, especially once JDBC (Java DataBase Connectivity) really got going. (We'll discuss JDBC shortly.)

Installing Java

Many books, as well as the online Java documentation itself, have been written to help with the installation of Java onto various different platforms. We'll give a quick summary of the steps here, but be sure to check the documentation for specific details.

The first thing to do is download the Java Developers Kit (JDK). There are many different versions of the JDK and many other Java-related products that you may be interested in. The main web site* for the JDK is:

http://java.sun.com/products/jdk/1.2/

---

* These pages are very fluid. If you simply go to *http://java.sun.com* and try searches from there, you can usually find everything you need, including all the relevant documentation, particularly for the standard classes. This home page will also direct you to regular news updates and the latest downloads.

The JDK is available in a range of downloads for different operating systems, including a self-extracting file for building the JDK on Windows. The JDK should also contain virtually everything you need for your first Java programs, even packages that previously were separate, like those making up the Java Swing GUI environment. These became part of the core JDK distribution when Java Version 1.1 evolved into Java 1.2 (or Java2 as it is often known, even at beta Version 1.3).

Unix-specific downloads

If you're planning to install Java on a Unix system, you may want to look at the following sites for specific operating systems. Each of these has its own independent JDK download, so distributions from these sites are often more specifically tailored for the particular OS than the matching generic JDKs direct from Sun:

http://www.ibm.com/java/jdk/download/
 IBM's AIX version of Unix

http://www.unixsolutions.hp.com/products/java/index.html
 Hewlett-Packard's HP-UX

http://www.blackdown.org/java-linux.html
 The Blackdown work on Java is the de facto Linux standard

http://www.freebsd.org/java/
 Java resources for the FreeBSD Project

All these self-extracting downloads come with the necessary unpack and install instructions, which you should follow for your own particular operating system.

Installing Java on Unix and Linux

For the typical Unix-like installation from a full JDK download, follow these steps:

1. Download the correct file for your setup.

2. Unzip this file to create the tar file, using an unzip utility such as the *gunzip* or *bunzip2* utilities available under Linux. Run these commands:

   ```
   $ su - root
   $ bunzip2 /tmp/jdk1.2pre-v2.tar.bz2
   $ cd /usr/local/
   $ tar xvf /tmp/jdk1.2pre-v2.tar
   ```

3. You might also create symlinks to make the various executables accessible from your standard path, like this (or alternatively, add */usr/local/jdk1.2/bin* to your default path):

   ```
   $ cd /usr/local/bin
   $ ln -s /usr/local/jdk1.2/bin/appletviewer .
   $ ln -s /usr/local/jdk1.2/bin/java .
   $ ln -s /usr/local/jdk1.2/bin/javac .
   $ ln -s /usr/local/jdk1.2/bin/jdb .
   ```

```
$ ln -s /usr/local/jdk1.2/bin/javadoc .
$ ln -s /usr/local/jdk1.2/bin/javap .
```

Most other Unix-like installations will be similar (Sun's Solaris often comes complete with the latest JDK, depending on version). Other non-Unix operating systems will vary slightly in terms of their command-line interfaces for the installation process, but the commands and their usage should be pretty similar.

Installing Java on Windows

Self-extracting downloads are also available for Win32 platforms and are generally the best way to install Java on Windows. These downloads usually carry out most of the grunt work for you, installing everything in the appropriate places and interrogating you for possible alternative directories. Simply do the following:

1. Download the latest self-extracting JDK executable file (such as *jdk-1_2_2_006-win.exe*) from *http://java.sun.com/j2se/*.

2. Double-click on this file to install Java (as in Figure 7-1).

Your Java installation should complete itself in just a few minutes.

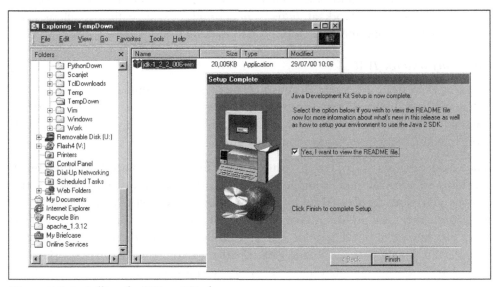

Figure 7-1. Installing the JDK on Windows

Java Programming

Because Java is much more of a 3GL programming language than Tcl, Perl, or Python is, we'll spend a little more time working our way through the basics, before we get to the really important subjects of JDBC, Oracle database connectivity, and combining Java and Oracle technologies. Current Java users may wish to skip ahead while we carry out our whistle-stop tour through the earlier stages of Java development. We certainly won't cover all the details—we'll just mention a number of areas that may be especially helpful as you get into Java/Oracle development.

Java programming can appear complicated (in comparison to something like Python), and there are many hundreds of books out there to help you master its intricacies. Consult Appendix C for a list of our own personal favorites. For online tutorial and development information, check out the following sites:

http://java.sun.com/docs/books/tutorial/index.html
> Excellent Java tutorials

http://java.sun.com/jdc/
> The Java Developer Connection

http://java.sun.com/docs/books/jls/html/index.html
> The Java Language Specification (by James Gosling, Bill Joy, and Guy Steele); if these three don't know the answers, the rest of us are in real trouble

Information on all aspects of Java technologies of particular relevance to Oracle (e.g., SQLJ and JDBC), and other Oracle technologies as well, is available via the Oracle Technology Network at *http://technet.oracle.com*. Use the excellent OTN search facilities to find the exact topic you're looking for.

Portability and the JVM

Java was built from the ground up as an object-oriented language. It shares intellectual roots with Bjarne Stroustrup's C++[*] but is also related to John McCarthy's venerable Lisp (still one of the best languages around, especially for artificial intelligence, natural language, and vision research).

When you program with Java (as with C, C++, and other compilable languages), you have source code and compiled code. You don't have just interpreted script files, as you would with Perl and Tcl. With Java, you develop your source code, store it in *.java* files, and then compile these into *.class* files via the JDK-supplied *javac* program. One big difference with Java, though, is that these generated *.class* files are not strictly executable and object-native to your own particular operating system. Instead, they are "intermediate bytecode" files which are later handed off, via the supplied native *java* interpreter program, and translated on the fly to the native machine code for your platform, via the JVM. (Note that the Java Virtual Machine itself is based on work by Niklaus Wirth, who created virtual machines for the Pascal language.)

---

[*] You can find out more of the history of C++ at Bjarne Stroustrup's home page, *http://www.research.att.com/~bs/homepage.html*.

Bytecode versus object code

To demonstrate the difference between bytecode and ordinary object code, let's compile a *.java* file under Linux and then examine it:

```
$ javac MyCode.java
```

The resulting output will be called *MyCode.class*. This output is not executed directly from the command line.* Let's check this with the Linux *file* command:

```
$ file MyCode.class
MyCode.class: compiled Java class data, version 45.3
```

A normal binary executable looks like this:

```
$ file gcc
gcc: ELF 32-bit LSB executable, Intel 80386, version 1,
```

If you compile a Java program from identical *.java* source on two different operating systems, the generated *.class* files will also be identical on the different operating systems (unless you're using direct native methods in Java, but we think this kind of takes away the point of using it in the first place). This doppelgänger effect means that the code can be transferred from one operating system to another with impunity and executed there under the appropriate JVM. This OS portability is the "write once, run anywhere" Java paradigm (or, as seasoned Java hackers will tell you, the "write once, debug everywhere" paradigm). In this way, Java provides something precious—the ability to run identical programs on disparate platforms.

We demonstrate the Java development system in Figure 7-2. Note that it doesn't matter which operating system we're using; from the same *MyGraph.java* file FTPed from one platform to another, we should be able to create an identical *MyGraph.class* file. After compilation, no matter which operating system we transfer this *.class* file to, it should produce the same graphical GUI (as long as the platform possesses a valid JVM that's accessible via the *java* program).

 Java GUIs will be similar in form and function, though not absolutely identical down to the last pixel, because each windowing system has its own display variations. Note, though, that Java Swing is increasingly able to make these appearance differences almost negligible except for the decorative window borders.

Later, we'll demonstrate this portability in a simple STDOUT program in Example 7-3, and then a GUI in Example 7-6.

---

* Unless we've compiled our Linux kernel to handle Java bytecode—not a job for the faint of heart.

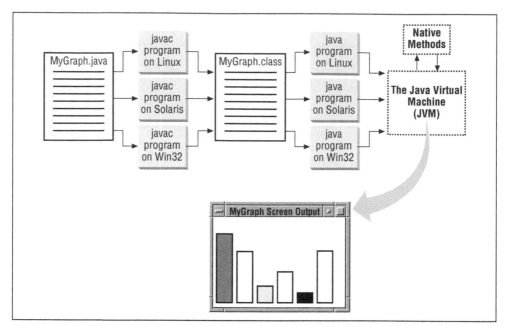

Figure 7-2. The OS-portable approach of the JVM

Running applets

Writing applets is the first step for most Java programmers. Let's suppose you want to run a *.class* file as an Internet applet. You can embed the applet within an HTML file and run it from either your browser or the Java-supplied *appletviewer*, which should come along with the JDK (for example, *c:\jdk1.2.2\bin\appletviewer.exe* under Win32).

First, put together an HTML file like the one shown in Example 7-1.

Example 7-1. MyCode.html, for Use with appletviewer

```
<HTML><HEAD>
<TITLE>MyCode</TITLE>
</HEAD><BODY><HR>
<APPLET CODEBASE="." CODE="MyCode.class" WIDTH=400 HEIGHT=100>
<PARAM NAME=outputMessage VALUE="Hello Applet">
</APPLET><HR>
<A HREF="MyCode.java">The MyCode.java source file</a>
</BODY>
```

This calls the *MyCode.class* applet file we're about to compose and sends it a string parameter called "outputMessage" (we've also provided an HREF drill-down, so we can look at the code under a real browser later).

Next, save the HTML file as *MyCode.html* and then create the Java file shown in Example 7-2.

Example 7-2. The MyCode.java File

```java
import java.awt.*;
import java.applet.Applet;

public class MyCode extends Applet {
    Font f = new Font("TimesRoman",Font.BOLD,36);
    String outputMessage;

    public void init () {
        setBackground(Color.white);
        outputMessage = getParameter("outputMessage");
        if (outputMessage == null){
            outputMessage = "No message parameter";
        }
    }
    public void paint (Graphics g){
        g.setFont(f);
        g.drawString(outputMessage,100,50);
    }
}
```

This loads the AWT (Abstract Windowing Toolkit) Java graphics packages, available automatically within the JDK. It also imports everything needed for becoming an applet via the special *java.applet.Applet* package (this approach hides the need for a main initializing program start point). The program then paints the required message into the graphical output box designated by the <APPLET> tag in the HTML file.

Finally, compile this Java source into the related *MyCode.class* file and then run it with *appletviewer*:

```
$ javac MyCode.java
$ appletviewer MyCode.html
```

The resulting program should pop up, as shown in Figure 7-3 (where you can also see what the applet looks like in a "real" browser).

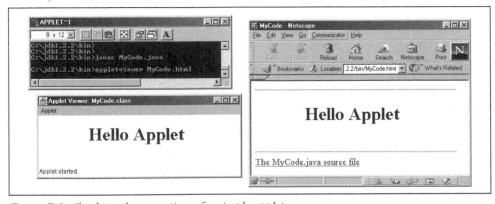

Figure 7-3. Checking the execution of a simple applet

There are many different ways to run applications these days, employing Java technology well beyond applets. However, starting with them can be the most fun, especially once you start spinning graphics! You'll also find plenty of interesting applet examples under your initial JDK download, in *../jdk1.2.2/demo/applets*, and you can use these to help build your own.

Writing a full Java program

In the previous section, we ran our first Java applet. That's a start, but we'd like to get to proper database programming as quickly as possible and take a real look at portability. As a next step, we need to write a "real" program with a *main()* function in it. Once we've got this going, we can then climb directly towards JDBC and the Olympus peak of Enterprise Java. Before we get there, we'll need to know how many gods and goddesses are living on the mountain, so that when we arrive, we'll be prepared. We'll do this with a short but fully-formed Java program, as shown in Example 7-3.

Example 7-3. Apollo.java

```java
public class Apollo
{
    public static void main(String[] args)
    {
        // Declare the main variables
        int numGoddesses = 6;    // Number of Goddesses
        int numGods = 6;         // Number of Gods
        int numOlympians = 0;    // Total of Olympic Spirits

        numOlympians = numGoddesses + numGods;   // Count the Total

        // Output
        System.out.println("Total Olympians: " + numOlympians);
    }
}
```

Here's what we'll do:

1. Once we're inside the *main()* module, we can work out the total of how many Olympic powers reside on Olympus.

2. We then output this information via the *System.out.println()* object-oriented-style print function.

3. After completing the coding, we compile it using *javac* on the command line.

4. Then we run it by calling it with the *java* program.

This resulting output is shown in Figure 7-4. We can also copy the *Apollo.class* file to Linux and execute it there unchanged via the Linux JDK downloaded from the *blackdown.org* site. In this way, we'll neatly demonstrate Java's OS independence.

Figure 7-4. Compiling and running the Apollo Java program

Although admittedly unsophisticated, in this section we have demonstrated the development of a real Java program. Note, however, that the example illustrated is a very simple case in which the *.class* file was in the current working directory. This is not the usual pattern in Java development. Often, we need to let the JVM know where all of our handcrafted class files are via the special Java CLASSPATH environment variable. This is especially true when they're collected into transportable *.jar* files. In more advanced Java programming, we also need to let the JVM know where any special libraries are, such as the ones provided by Oracle under OCI for use with the Fat JDBC client (described later), which can be used to access the database. We do this through the much more generic LD_LIBRARY_PATH environment variable (also used under Tcl, Perl, etc.). Before we get to these two environment variables, however, let's discuss what these mysterious *.jar* files are all about.

JAR files and the jar utility

The *jar* utility is a very handy way to compress all your Java classes into a single zip-like file. It works somewhat like the *tar* utility in Unix. Because of Java's object orientation, Java programs often consist of several related class files. The JAR file is a particularly useful device for shipping a complete program system to a production site, or over an Internet connection, to a remote client. For more on JAR (the Java ARchive), see:

http://java.sun.com/products/jdk/1.2/docs/guide/jar/jarGuide.html

The *jar* program provides a number of options. The following are the main, *tar*-like options:

-*c*   Creates a new JAR file.

-*t*   Lists the contents of a JAR file.

-*u*   Updates a current JAR file (adds new files or replaces existing ones).

-*x*   Extracts files from a JAR.

There are also five command options:

-f   Indicates that the next command-line argument will be the JAR file's name.

-m   Indicates that the MANIFEST file name will be supplied after the JAR file name. This file holds the content and authentication information for the JAR file and is usually created automatically.

-M   Indicates that a MANIFEST file should not be created. This option is not often used.

-v   Outputs verbose comments when the *jar* command is executed.

-0   Prevents file compression (the zero option is not often used).

As well as being cleverly named (continuing in the noble Unix tradition of *bin* for keeping your binary files in, and *tar* for sticking your files together), *jar* is an excellent way to store all of your golden-baked class files in one handy chocolate-chip repository. In the following piece of code, let's create a new *jar* repository from the two class files we've compiled so far. We can then examine its contents.* (Note that, as with the *tar* command, hyphen switches are not essential, with *cvf* being equivalent to *-cvf*.)

```
$ jar cvf MyJar.jar MyCode.class Apollo.class
added manifest
adding: MyCode.class(in = 837) (out= 635)(deflated 24%)
adding: Apollo.class(in = 596) (out= 379)(deflated 36%)
$ jar tvf MyJar.jar
     0 Sat Jan 13 16:44:10 GMT 2001 META-INF/
    68 Sat Jan 13 16:44:10 GMT 2001 META-INF/MANIFEST.MF
   837 Sat Jan 13 16:43:08 GMT 2001 MyCode.class
   596 Sat Jan 13 16:09:18 GMT 2001 Apollo.class
```

To ship our two class files to any other JVM system in the world, all we have to do now is FTP *MyJar.jar* to the desired site and then add the *.jar* file to the remote CLASSPATH variable. Thus:

```
$ CLASSPATH=$CLASSPATH:/usr/local/jarfiles/MyJar.jar
$ export CLASSPATH
```

Java environment variables

As we mentioned in passing, the following are the two most often used environment variables with Java:

CLASSPATH

A standard Java environment variable used to tell the JVM where your class files are. It works in a similar way to the ordinary PATH environment variable, which points to executables, though you don't only name directories

---

* It is a standard convention that JAR files are given the *.jar* suffix, as in *MyJar.jar*. The other suffix generally seen is *.zip*, especially when used to store JDBC drivers and packages.

where classes descend from; you can also specify named *.jar* files. The standard classes used by Java, such as *java.applet.Applet*, do not need to be specified in the CLASSPATH variable. They're already built into the JVM.

LD_LIBRARY_PATH

This environment variable is similar in form to CLASSPATH. It points at directories containing required native library files (such as OCI) and is divided with colons or semicolons, depending on operating system.

Here's a typical example of setting up these variables for use with Java and Oracle:

```
$ export CLASSPATH=/java/MyClasses:$ORACLE_HOME/jdbc/classes12.zip
$ export LD_LIBRARY_PATH=/usr/local/lib:$ORACLE_HOME/jdbc/lib
```

If you're using special character sets with Oracle, you may also want to add on the appropriate *.zip* files containing special character set classes (we cover exactly where to get *classes12.zip* and *nls_charset12.zip* shortly):

```
$ export CLASSPATH=$CLASSPATH:nls_charset12.zip
```

Suppose you've written a new program and stored it in the *MyProgram.class* file, which is available under the *myJava.event* package. This class file is then stored in */java/MyClasses/myJava/event/MyProgram.class*.

The following call can now run that Java program from any part of your system, because the JVM now knows to look for it under */java/MyClasses* (already set up earlier in CLASSPATH):

```
$ java myJava.event.MyProgram
```

Alternatively, you can add to the CLASSPATH variable directly, when you run the Java program with the special *-classpath* switch:

```
$ java -classpath \
/java/MyClasses:$ORACLE_HOME/jdbc/classes12.zip myJava.event.MyProgram
```

JDBC: Java DataBase Connectivity

At this point, we've installed the JDK, and we have a little experience using HTML, applets, standalone Java programs, *.jar* files, and the standard environment variables. Let's get on with the real business of doing useful work with Oracle. First, we need to acquire the drivers needed to connect Oracle and Java via JDBC (Java DataBase Connectivity). JDBC, which we described briefly in Chapter 2, *Connecting to Oracle*, is Java's answer to ODBC (Open DataBase Connectivity).

java.sql Drivers for JDBC and Oracle

The first thing we need to do is to get hold of the appropriate Oracle connectivity drivers. Because the download pages for these drivers tend to be quite fluid, the best way to get the code is to first access the Oracle Technology Network (OTN).

(You may need to register there beforehand as a developer, if you haven't done so already, as described in the preface.) Visit the following site, and search for "Java" and/or "JDBC". The download pages for the relevant Oracle JDBC drivers should reveal themselves in any search results:

> *http://technet.oracle.com*

Types of drivers

There are four types of drivers for generic JDBC database use, two Fat and two Thin. Fat drivers for any database type require access to native code libraries, such as OCI, at the client end. Thin drivers are entirely encapsulated and do not require anything outside of themselves to connect Java to a target database (these differing characteristics are displayed in Figure 7-5). This makes them especially useful with Thin clients, such as browser platforms or workstations provided by diskless network computers.

The following are the four types of JDBC drivers:

JDBC-ODBC bridge driver (Type I)
> Automatically available within the JDK releases, this Fat driver bridges over the standard ODBC API gateway to access the database via another separate ODBC driver (which itself then uses OCI). Using this driver system is an inelegant solution that requires the appropriate ODBC and OCI software to be preloaded onboard the client. We don't hear of it being used much for Oracle work. You can find out more about ODBC-related drivers here:
>
> > *http://java.sun.com/products/jdbc/driverdesc.html*
> > *http://java.sun.com/j2se/1.3/docs/guide/jdbc/getstart/bridge.doc.html*
> > *http://technet.oracle.com/software/utilities/software_index.htm*

Native API driver (Type II)
> Another Fat solution, though far more acceptable and often used with Oracle, especially when high performance outweighs the need for Thin client usage. Database-specific interface software (such as OCI) is required on the client. This software also uses native methods to access the database. This kind of driver is perhaps the easiest to install and use on a home system and is similar to the DBD::Oracle driver for Perl we discussed in Chapter 2. In Oracle terms, this is the Fat JDBC/OCI driver you often hear about. You can read more about these kinds of drivers and download two of the most popular examples from these sites:

> *http://technet.oracle.com/software/tech/java/sqlj_jdbc/software_index.htm*
> > For more information

> *http://download.oracle.com/otn/utilities_drivers/jdbc/817/jdbc817jdk12-sol.zip*
> > Download site for Solaris

http://download.oracle.com/otn/utilities_drivers/jdbc/817/jdbc817jdk12-nt.zip
Download site for Win32

Generic network API driver (Type III)

A partially Thin client that uses sockets to connect to specific software on the database server. That software translates the various API calls from the client. This solution is particularly effective because it enables multiple database access, as well as allowing the client to remain software-free. However, we have not heard of this methodology being used with Oracle because of the easy availability of the direct database socket driver (the next method discussed). However, you may be able to find out more here:

http://technet.oracle.com/docs/products/oracle8i/doc_library/817_doc/java.817/

Direct database socket driver (Type IV)

An extremely slim driver that uses sockets (typically TCP/IP ones) to connect directly to the heart of the database SQL engine via Net8 and a Two-Task Common (TTC) presentation layer. This is an excellent solution, especially for applets. In Oracle terms, this is the standard 100% Thin JDBC driver type. The latest generation of this driver we came across could be downloaded from the following location:

http://download.oracle.com/otn/utilities_drivers/jdbc/817/classes12.zip

Now we have to figure out how to decide between our two main choices: the Fat and the Thin drivers supplied by Oracle (the second and fourth solutions above). Let's look at the capabilities of those drivers:

NLS

Both driver types have National Language Support, which enables you to use various international languages in your Oracle database. Both support all of the many Oracle datatypes, including ROWIDs, REFCURSORs, and the various types of LOBs. In addition, both support PL/SQL stored procedures, since callable statements are part of the standard JDBC definition. Another download from OTN you may be interested in, to complement any NLS-specific work, is this one:

http://download.oracle.com/otn/utilities_drivers/jdbc/817/nls_charset12.zip

Applets

The JDBC/OCI driver doesn't support Java applets since it relies on OCI code being locally available under ORACLE_HOME. Thus, if you're planning on writing Java programs to be called from within an HTML page, you must choose the Thin driver. (If you're building any Java application where Oracle software is not installed on the client, you'll have to stay Thin.)

Networking

Skinniness has its price. The Thin driver supports only TCP/IP, whereas the JDBC/OCI driver supports all Net8 formats, including IPC, DECNet, TCP/IP, and Named Pipes. In addition, the JDBC/OCI driver supports Oracle's new encryption technology available though the Advanced Networking Option (ANO).

OS independence

Another reason for choosing Thin clients is that the *.zip* files containing them remain identical for all operating system platforms, neatly sidestepping any need for OS dependence. If you use Fat clients, you will need compiled code libraries that are native for each individual platform (this is the reason that there is both a Fat Solaris *and* an NT download above, for Fat driver usage on different operating systems).

Which driver?

In choosing a driver, the tradeoff is between performance and platform independence. For reasons of client platform independence, you may want to stick with the JDBC Thin clients to start with. These can be found in the classic *classes111.zip* file (or its latest derivative, such as *classes12.zip*) in your JDBC download from OTN. However, if you're building a non-independent, standalone application and need to take advantage of some of the more complex features available with OCI, or if you require relatively high server performance, you may need the JDBC/OCI driver types. For more information on these kinds of tradeoffs, check out the documents at these sites:

> *http://technet.oracle.com/tech/java/*
> *http://technet.us.oracle.com//tech/java/sqlj_jdbc/htdocs/jdbc_faq.htm*
> *http://technet.oracle.com/tech/java/jroadmap/jdbc/listing.htm#998321*

The Thin driver is generally slower than the Fat one because it has to carry around with itself a cut-down set of OCI-type commands under Java bytecode control. These commands are relatively slow in comparison to the fast, C-compiled native OCI commands accessed directly by the Fat driver. We illustrate this difference in Figure 7-5, along with the extra middleman requirement of ODBC.

Connecting Oracle and Java

The *java.sql* package, which contains the JDBC classes, comes as part of the standard JDK release and does not require anything beyond the appropriate driver for connecting to the Oracle database. Installation is pretty painless:

1. Download the driver *.zip* file from *http://technet.oracle.com* (as previously described).

2. Add the downloaded file to designated directories (e.g., *$ORACLE_HOME/jdbc*).

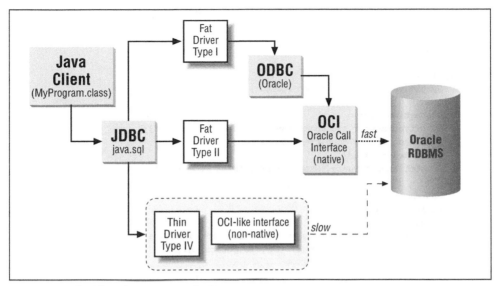

Figure 7-5. The Thin driver versus the Fat ones

3. Modify the CLASSPATH environment variable, for example:

```
$ cp classes12.zip $ORACLE_HOME/jdbc
$ export CLASSPATH=$CLASSPATH:$ORACLE_HOME/jdbc/classes12.zip
```

We won't try to present all the specifics here. Check out the documentation in the downloaded files for current details. The following file contains good instructions on how to install and use the driver within your Java code:

http://technet.oracle.com//tech/java/info/jdbc_doc.htm

We'll cover the JDBC API shortly, but for now, let's show a quick example of JDBC connection using the fatter driver. In Example 7-4, we've employed the Native API (OCI) driver to connect to a local Oracle database on a PC running Windows. We'll describe the highlighted statements at the end of the example.

Example 7-4. Dionysus.java, a Simple JDBC Connection

```
import java.sql.*;  // Pick up JDBC
import java.math.*; // Import for occasionally required decimal classes

public class Dionysus
{
   public static void main(String[] args)
   {
      String url = "jdbc:oracle:oci7:ORCL";  // Connection string
      try {
         DriverManager.registerDriver (
            new oracle.jdbc.driver.OracleDriver());
      }
      catch (Exception e) {
```

Example 7-4. Dionysus.java, a Simple JDBC Connection (continued)

```
        System.out.println("Failed to load driver");
        return;
    }
    try {
        System.out.println("Driver loaded");

        Connection conn =
            DriverManager.getConnection(url, "scott", "tiger");
        Statement stmt = conn.createStatement();
        ResultSet rs =
            stmt.executeQuery("SELECT EMPNO, ENAME FROM EMP");

        boolean gainedResults = false;
        while( rs.next() ){
            gainedResults = true;
            System.out.println("Number = " + rs.getString(1) + "   " +
                               "Name = " + rs.getString(2)
                              );
        }
        if (!gainedResults){
            System.out.println("No rows found");
        }
        stmt.close();  // Always close stmt/pstmt statements to avoid
        conn.close();  // too many open cursors oracle errors.
    }
    catch (Exception e) {
        e.printStackTrace();
    }
    finally {
        System.out.println(
            "Program Shutting Down");  // Useful for tidying up
    }
  }
}
```

The first thing to notice in Example 7-4 is that, in addition to including the standard JDK *java.sql* package at the top of the file, we also included the built-in *java.math* package in order to pick up some objects and datatypes, such as *BigDecimal,** which we've included in this program for potential use later. Once we've imported the correct packages, we set our connection URL. We then register the driver, establish the connection, and, finally, run our SQL code. We've displayed the results in Figure 7-6.

---

* This Java object can hold FLOAT-type numbers of an almost unlimited precision, which is often useful with Oracle and mathematical operations. However, what it gains in size it makes up for in lack of speed. *BigDecimal* tends to take up a lot of processing power.

It is always a good idea to close all *CallableStatement, PreparedStatement,* and *Statement* cursors opened up within JDBC programs as soon as they are no longer required. This prevents difficult-to-track problems that occur because the database thinks that too many cursors are open. This situation sometimes occurs on heavily loaded, Java servlet–driven web sites with hundreds (or even thousands) of concurrent data requests.

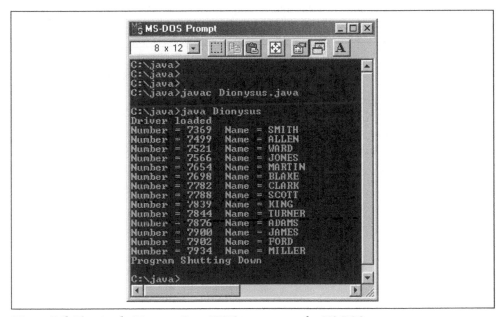

Figure 7-6. The simple Dionysus Java JDBC program under MS-DOS

The JDBC API

The JDBC API is similar to both ODBC and the Perl DBI; all three interfaces sit between their client programs and target databases and try to solve the same problems of getting their data in and out as cleanly as possible. We'll provide an example shortly that illustrates combining Java GUI techniques with JDBC. First, though, Table 7-1 demonstrates how JDBC fulfills its requirements.

Table 7-1. Basic JDBC Functionality

Conceptual Requirement	How JDBC Achieves It
Database driver	Vendors provide driver software to translate specific JDBC API calls into appropriate database operations on the specified data sources.
Manage drivers	JDBC loads and manages the specified driver.

Table 7-1. Basic JDBC Functionality (continued)

Conceptual Requirement	How JDBC Achieves It
Connect to database	JDBC allocates a *Connection* object to begin the database session.
Execute SQL statements	JDBC prepares a *Statement* (or *PreparedStatement*[a]) object from the *Connection* object and then executes it.
Retrieve data	When the SQL statement is executed, the *ResultSet* object, consisting of sets of rows and columns of data, is returned.
Retrieve metadata (column names, etc.)	This information can be mapped into the *ResultSetMetaData* object (itself obtained from *ResultSet*).
Clean up after SQL statement completed	JDBC closes the *ResultSet* object, the *Statement* object, and, finally, the *Connection* object.

[a] *PreparedStatement* itself is an object-oriented extension of the *Statement* JDBC class object.

Datatypes

JDBC also maintains a range of datatypes that conform to the SQL/92 database standards. Unfortunately, Oracle usage is not exactly the same as standard usage. Table 7-2 maps out these differences for you. These various datatypes are picked up in related, appropriately-named JDBC functions, such as these:

> *getBigDecimal()*
> *getBinaryStream()*
> *getBoolean()*
> *getDate()*
> *getFloat()*
> *getInt()*
> *getString()*
> *getTimestamp()*

You can also mix-and-match these functions. JDBC will try its best to translate for you, where it can. For example, if you use a *getString()* on an integer field with a number value of 200, JDBC will return a "200" string for you. The code to do this would be:

```
String myStr = rs.getString( "MY_INTEGER_FIELD" );
```

Table 7-2. Mapping Oracle's Datatypes to JDBC

Oracle Datatypes	Matching JDBC Datatypes
NUMBER	BIGINT, TINYINT, SMALLINT, INTEGER, FLOAT, REAL, DOUBLE, NUMERIC, DECIMAL
CHAR, VARCHAR, VARCHAR2	CHAR, VARCHAR
LONG	LONGVARCHAR

Table 7-2. Mapping Oracle's Datatypes to JDBC (continued)

Oracle Datatypes	Matching JDBC Datatypes
LONGRAW	LONGVARBINARY
RAW	VARBINARY, BINARY
DATE	DATE, TIME, TIMESTAMP

Preparing SQL and using cache optimization

In addition to providing the basic datatypes, JDBC also needs to be able to prepare and execute our SQL to fill them. The three main objects used, the latter two in the majority of cases, are *Statement, PreparedStatement,* and *CallableStatement:*

Statement

> This object is the basic SQL call interface in Java. You build up a single string and then execute it, for example:
>
> ```
> Statement stmt = con.createStatement();
> Stmt.executeUpdate("UPDATE EMP SET SAL = (SAL/3) " +
>                    "WHERE ENAME = 'MILLER' ");
> con.commit();
> stmt.close();
> ```

PreparedStatement

> This object allows you to prepare a single statement and then execute it many times, saving you the overhead of having to do the SQL parsing again and again. It also provides the benefit of bind parameters, which can be cleared and reused:
>
> ```
> PreparedStatement pstmt = con.prepareStatement(
>     "UPDATE EMP SET SAL = (SAL / ? ) WHERE ENAME = ? ");
>
> pstmt.setInt(1, 2);
> pstmt.setString(2, "BLAKE");
> pstmt.execute();
> con.commit();
>
> pstmt.clearParameters();
>
> pstmt.setFloat(1, 1.5);
> pstmt.setString(2, "CLARK");
> pstmt.execute();
> con.commit();
>
> pstmt.close();
> ```

CallableStatement

> This object is similar to *PreparedStatement* (and is derived from it), allowing you to call stored procedures residing within the database:
>
> ```
> CallableStatement cstmt =
>     con.prepareCall("{ CALL SCOTT.myProc(?, ?) }");
> ```

```
cstmt.setInt(1, 666);
cstmt.setString(2, "The Beast");
cstmt.execute();
con.commit();

cstmt.close();
```

Notice that in the *CallableStatement* call above, we don't use *EXECUTE* as you might have expected. Instead, we use *CALL*, wrapped in braces, which is generic across JDBC for all database types when calling stored procedures.

These three different extended object ways of executing SQL within JDBC usually provide what we need.

Java GUIs

Now that we've looked at the basics of the JDBC API, let's do something interesting with GUI clients. Our goal is to figure out how Java works at this level, as well as to provide an example along the lines of the Wosql and OraExplain programs (see the discussion of Tcl/Tk and Perl/Tk, respectively, in Chapter 3, *Tcl, Perl, and Python*). Most of the open source Java projects described in Chapter 8, *Building Oracle Applications with Java*, also involve GUIs, so it will be helpful to look at how you can use Java to build such applications. First we'll build a basic GUI, and then we'll blend some JDBC into it so we will be able to connect to an Oracle database.

Java Swing

The quickest way to get going with a Java GUI is to use the Java Swing library. Java Swing is an extension of AWT, and these two GUI toolkits are intimately related:

AWT

    AWT, the original Abstract Windowing Toolkit, comes with the standard JDK distribution. It handles simple graphics, widgets, and layout managers for different native formats.

Swing

    Although it relies on AWT, Swing is entirely Java-based and covers a far more generalized and flexible set of GUI capabilities through its Java Foundation Classes (JFC). It used to come in a separate package from Java Version 1, but it's now entirely integrated within the Java2-based JDKs.

The main web site for Java Swing is the Swing Connection, where you can find out about Swing and all of its many component GUI widgets:

    http://java.sun.com/products/jfc/tsc/index.html

There are also many GUI builders available to help create your Java Swing applications, including these:

http://www.inprise.com/jbuilder/
   Borland's JBuilder

http://www.webgain.com/Products/VisualCafe_Overview.html
   Webgain's Visual Café

http://www.sun.com/forte/
   Sun Microsystems' Forte

http://www7.software.ibm.com/vad.nsf/data/document2590/
   IBM's Visual Age

Interestingly, the Forte product seems to be evolving into an open code project called NetBeans. Although NetBeans is still entirely controlled by Sun, you are able to download the source. While NetBeans does not qualify as true open source, as we defined it in Chapter 1, *Oracle Meets Open Source*, it's getting close. It will be interesting to see if Sun can be persuaded to drop all of its restrictions and signed disclaimers and turn this into a *real* open source project. For now, if you want to download an integrated development environment (IDE) with which to build your Java GUIs, you might want to check it out:

   http://www.netbeans.org

This full-featured IDE is displayed in Figure 7-7.

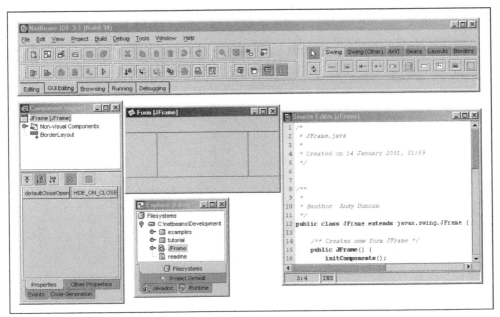

Figure 7-7. Running the NetBeans IDE after download

With all of these GUI tools available to you, you might not even need to know the APIs very well, but, heck, we've got to have some hacker fun. Let's try to develop a Java GUI (though a fairly primitive one) the good old-fashioned way, by editing a text file the way Noah did it on the Ark.

Developing the GUI Program

Our first Java GUI will allow us to pick our favorite mythological gods and goddesses. We'll divide this program into two classes. The first class (Example 7-5) contains the screen elements for building a simple menu. The second one (Example 7-6) holds the *main()* function, which calls up our screen elements for display. For an explanation of what's going on in the various steps of this program (note the step numbers in the comments), see the corresponding notes at the end of the code listing.

Example 7-5. OlympusFrame.java, Containing Menu Construction Elements

```java
import javax.swing.*;  // Step 1
import java.awt.*;

public class OlympusFrame extends JFrame {  // Step 2

   public OlympusFrame() {

       setTitle("Mount Olympus");
       setDefaultCloseOperation(WindowConstants.DISPOSE_ON_CLOSE);

       setJMenuBar(menuBar);

       JMenu fileMenu = new JMenu("File");
       JMenu godsMenu = new JMenu("Hellenic Gods");

       exitItem = fileMenu.add("Exit");

       fileMenu.addSeparator();

       aboutItem = fileMenu.add("About");

       // Begin Main Menu Options to select our favorite Gods

       godsMenu.add(ZeusItem =                             // Step 3
          new JRadioButtonMenuItem("Zeus", false));
       godsMenu.add(PoseidonItem =
          new JRadioButtonMenuItem("Poseidon", true));
       godsMenu.add(HadesItem =
          new JRadioButtonMenuItem("Hades", false));

       godsMenu.addSeparator();

       godsMenu.add(AtheneItem =
          new JRadioButtonMenuItem("Athene", false));
       godsMenu.add(AphroditeItem =
```

Example 7-5. OlympusFrame.java, Containing Menu Construction Elements (continued)

```
              new JRadioButtonMenuItem("Aprhodite", true));
          godsMenu.add(HeraItem =
              new JRadioButtonMenuItem("Hera", false));

        menuBar.add(fileMenu);
        menuBar.add(godsMenu);
    }
    private JMenuBar menuBar = new JMenuBar();  // Step 4
    private JMenuItem exitItem, aboutItem;
    private JRadioButtonMenuItem ZeusItem, PoseidonItem, HadesItem,
                               AtheneItem, AphroditeItem, HeraItem;
}
```

These are the most important elements of the *OlympusFrame.java* file:

1. The *java.awt.** and *javax.swing.** class libraries are imported at the top of the file to handle all the GUI widgets and API calls.

2. The *OlympusFrame* object extends the hidden *JFrame* object (buried in Swing) and picks up its 200-plus methods for GUI frame handling.

3. We then create our two main top-level menu selections and drop our various options down from them, before adding them to the frame's menu bar.

4. Finally, we must declare all the variables that we've used to build up this simple menu.

Now that we have our menu bar component, we need our *main()* container to cocoon it in. This is shown in Example 7-6. See the explanations of the various steps in the notes following the code listing.

Example 7-6. Olympus.java, Main Parent Class for Our Program

```
import java.awt.*;  // Step 1

public class Olympus {

    static OlympusFrame window;  // Step 2

    public static void main(String[] args){

        window = new OlympusFrame();
        Toolkit toolKit = window.getToolkit();
        Dimension winSize = toolKit.getScreenSize();

        window.setBounds(winSize.width/4,
                         winSize.height/4,
                         winSize.width/2,
                         winSize.height/2);

        window.setVisible(true);  // Step 3
    }
}
```

Note the following about Example 7-6:

1. Only *java.awt.** is required for import, because all of the objects requiring the Swing libraries are in the subservient *OlympusFrame* object.

2. The parent *Olympus* class builds a window out of the previously declared *OlympusFrame* object.

3. Once the window is defined and sized, the parent class pops it up on the screen and makes it visible.

Compiling and Running the GUI Program

Now we have to compile and run the GUI. Once you've completed both Java files, you only need to compile the top-level one. The *javac* compilation process automatically picks up and compiles any other Java files in the same directory required beneath it. (Because we're using packages automatically built into Java2, we do not need to worry about CLASSPATH for the moment.) Let's do the following:

1. Compile and run on Linux:

```
$ $JAVA_HOME/bin/javac Olympus.java
$ $JAVA_HOME/bin/java Olympus
```

2. To demonstrate portability, FTP the same class file to Windows:

```
%JAVA_HOME%\bin\java Olympus
```

You can see the final GUI screen generated from the same class file in Figure 7-8 running under both Linux and Windows. Notice how, although the GUIs differ at a pixel level because of the different native windowing systems used by the JVM, the form and functions of the two GUIs remain extremely close.

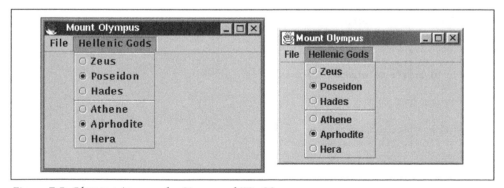

Figure 7-8. Olympus.java under Linux and Win32

Combining Java Swing with Java JDBC

Now that we understand the basic structure of JDBC and Java Swing, we'll run through a somewhat lengthy example. Example 7-7 demonstrates several aspects of combining Java GUI application techniques with the information available from the Oracle database via JDBC. This time, we'll point a Thin driver at our local host (127.0.0.1). Hang onto your metadata!

 Much of the actual GUI handling is outside the scope of this book. For much more on this topic, consult the Java tutorials and Swing books listed in Appendix C.

As with the other examples in this chapter, see the explanation of each step in the notes following the code listing.

Example 7-7. Hermes.java, a SQL*Plus-like Java Program

```java
import java.awt.*; // Step 1
import java.awt.event.*;
import javax.swing.*;
import java.sql.*;
import java.math.*;

public class Hermes extends JFrame implements ActionListener // Step 1
{
    public static void main(String[] args)
    {
        Hermes theApp = new Hermes();
    }
    public Hermes() {

        setBounds(0, 0, 1000, 1000);
        setDefaultCloseOperation(DISPOSE_ON_CLOSE);

        addWindowListener(new WindowHandler());
        enterSQL.addActionListener(this);            // Step 2

        getContentPane().add(enterSQL, BorderLayout.NORTH);
        getContentPane().add(helpText, BorderLayout.CENTER);

        font = new Font("Monospaced", Font.BOLD, 10);
        resultStrB = new StringBuffer();
        workBuf = new StringBuffer();

        textOutput.setFont(font);
        textPane = new JScrollPane(textOutput);
        getContentPane().add(textPane, BorderLayout.SOUTH);

        JMenu fileMenu = new JMenu("File");
```

Example 7-7. Hermes.java, a SQL*Plus-like Java Program (continued)

```java
        eraseMenuItem.addActionListener(this);
        exitItem.addActionListener(this);

        fileMenu.add(eraseMenuItem);
        fileMenu.add(exitItem);

        menuBar.add(fileMenu);
        setJMenuBar(menuBar);

        String url = "jdbc:oracle:thin:@127.0.0.1:1521:ORCL"; // Step 3
        String user = "SCOTT";
        String password = "TIGER";

        try {
            DriverManager.registerDriver
                (new oracle.jdbc.driver.OracleDriver());  // Step 3
        }
        catch (Exception e) {
            System.out.println("Failed to load driver");
            return;
        }
        try {
            con =
                DriverManager.getConnection(url, user, password); // Step 3
        }
        catch (Exception e) {
            System.out.println(e);
        }
        pack();                 // Step 4
        setVisible(true);
    }
    public void byeBye(){
        try {
            con.close();
        }
        catch (SQLException e) {
            System.out.println(e.getMessage());
        }
        dispose();
        System.exit(0);
    }
    class WindowHandler extends WindowAdapter {
        public void windowClosing(WindowEvent e){
            byeBye();
        }
    }
    public void actionPerformed(ActionEvent e){    // Step 5
        Object objectSource = e.getSource();
        if (objectSource == enterSQL){
            executeQuery();                         // Step 6
        } else if (objectSource == eraseMenuItem) {
            enterSQL.setText("");
```

Example 7-7. Hermes.java, a SQL*Plus-like Java Program (continued)

```
        } else if (objectSource == exitItem) {
          byeBye();
        }
    }
    public void executeQuery(){
        String query = enterSQL.getText();
        if (query == null){
            return;
        }
        try {
            resultStrB.setLength(0);

            pstmt = con.prepareStatement(query);          // Step 7
            ResultSet rs = pstmt.executeQuery();
            ResultSetMetaData metaData = rs.getMetaData();

            int cols = metaData.getColumnCount();
            int length = 0;
            int[] colLengths;
            colLengths = new int[cols];

            for (int i = 1; i <= cols; i++){
                length = metaData.getColumnDisplaySize( i );
                resultStrB.append(
                    padder(metaData.getColumnLabel(i),(length + 1))
                            );
                colLengths[(i - 1)] = length;
            }
            resultStrB.append("\n\n");

            int rows = 0;
            while(rs.next()){
                rows++;

                for (int i = 1; i <= cols; i++){
                    length = colLengths[(i - 1)];
                    resultStrB.append(
                        padder(rs.getString(i),(length + 1))  // Step 8 (a)
                                );
                }
                resultStrB.append("\n");
            }

            workBuf.setLength(0);
            workBuf.append(resultStrB.toString());
            workBuf.append("\n\n");
            workBuf.append(rows);
            workBuf.append(" row(s)");
            textOutput.setText( workBuf.toString() );   // Step 8 (b)

            pstmt.close();
        }
```

Example 7-7. Hermes.java, a SQL*Plus-like Java Program (continued)

```
        catch (SQLException e){
            textOutput.setText(e.getMessage());
        }
    }
    public String padder (String inStr, int reqLength){
        if (inStr == null){
            inStr = "";
        }
        for (int i = inStr.length(); i < reqLength; i++){
            inStr += " ";
        }
        return inStr;
    }
    Connection con;
    PreparedStatement pstmt;
    Font font;
    StringBuffer resultStrB;
    StringBuffer workBuf;

    JTextField enterSQL = new JTextField();
    JLabel helpText = new JLabel("Enter SQL and Press Enter");
    JTextArea textOutput = new JTextArea(20, 30);
    JScrollPane textPane;

    JMenuBar menuBar = new JMenuBar();
    JMenuItem eraseMenuItem = new JMenuItem("Erase");
    JMenuItem exitItem = new JMenuItem("Exit");
}
```

The most important elements of the program are described here:

1. First of all, we import our usual collection of packages to run a Java GUI SQL program. Notice, however, that we also import the *java.awt.event.** packages, which later will allow us to get the program to listen to event requests and carry out work for us. In a related move, this class implements *ActionListener*, which means that a listener is set up in the background to deal with our mouse and keyboard requests.

2. If you look at the main class variables, set out at the end of the program, you'll see that we've set up a text entry field called *enterSQL*. We make sure that this field is attached to the listener, so that when we enter SQL, the SQL statements are picked up and dealt with.

3. After building up the screen with a text entry box, an information label, and a scrollable results screen, we then attach the program to the Oracle database. Although this attachment is hard-coded in this example, it could easily be soft-coded, via parameters, allowing access to all the databases in your environment. Alternatively, it could read your *tnsnames.ora* file directly, via a base object, or it could use a configuration file-driven call to a fixed Oracle Names

server to get all the soft-coded information required to access all the databases on your system via a drop-down list.*

4. Finally, the screen is packed and displayed to the waiting world.

5. The *actionPerformed()* method then sits in an infinite loop, waiting for our requests. (This is similar to the way the *MainLoop()* function in Perl/Tk works, as we described in Chapter 3.)

6. If we've entered some SQL, the program calls the most important method in the program, *executeQuery()*, which is where the real action is.

7. Using JDBC, this function takes the *PreparedStatement* variable, *pstmt*, and executes the inputted SQL through it. It gets the results back via a *ResultSet* object and also picks up valuable metadata, such as column names and maximum display lengths, via a *ResultSetMetaData* object.

8. The program uses this information to print out the column names resulting from the SQL, and all the formatted rows of information (if any) are delivered by the database over the JDBC link. The program then outputs these, or any SQL errors, into a scrolling pane we set up earlier.

Sample output from this program is shown in Figure 7-9.

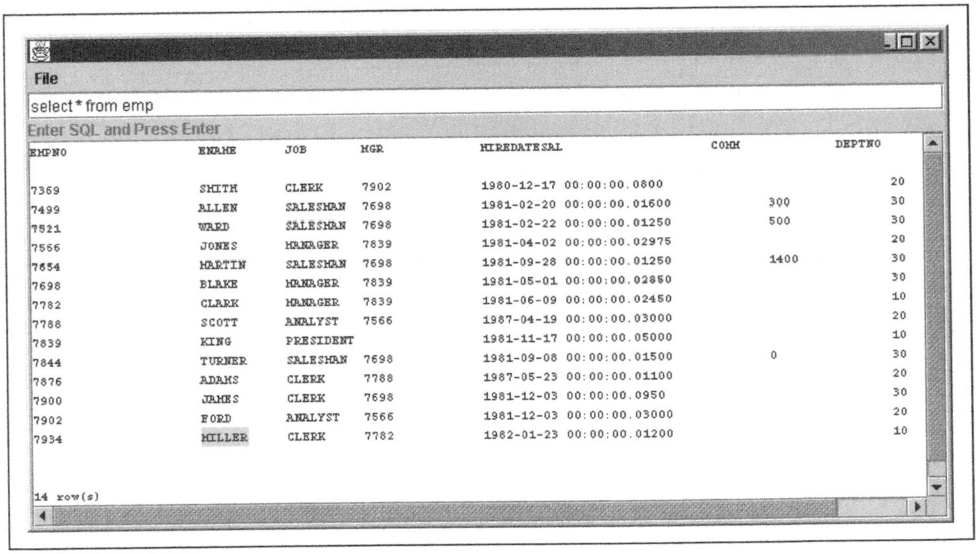

```
File
select * from emp
Enter SQL and Press Enter
EMPNO     ENAME     JOB        MGR    HIREDATE SAL             COMM      DEPTNO

7369      SMITH     CLERK      7902   1980-12-17 00:00:00.0800          20
7499      ALLEN     SALESMAN   7698   1981-02-20 00:00:00.01600   300   30
7521      WARD      SALESMAN   7698   1981-02-22 00:00:00.01250   500   30
7566      JONES     MANAGER    7839   1981-04-02 00:00:00.02975          20
7654      MARTIN    SALESMAN   7698   1981-09-28 00:00:00.01250  1400   30
7698      BLAKE     MANAGER    7839   1981-05-01 00:00:00.02850          30
7782      CLARK     MANAGER    7839   1981-06-09 00:00:00.02450          10
7788      SCOTT     ANALYST    7566   1987-04-19 00:00:00.03000          20
7839      KING      PRESIDENT         1981-11-17 00:00:00.05000          10
7844      TURNER    SALESMAN   7698   1981-09-08 00:00:00.01500     0   30
7876      ADAMS     CLERK      7788   1987-05-23 00:00:00.01100          20
7900      JAMES     CLERK      7698   1981-12-03 00:00:00.0950          30
7902      FORD      ANALYST    7566   1981-12-03 00:00:00.03000          20
7934      MILLER    CLERK      7782   1982-01-23 00:00:00.01200          10

14 row(s)
```

Figure 7-9. The Hermes.java program in action

---

* Most servlet engines usually run with a config file, typically named *servlet.properties*, which contains required hard-coded information (such as the NameServer address information). This means that you can move your servlet classes around the world in handy *.jar* files and simply do a quick edit of the config file at each web server site, in order to get each site up and running without further editing and compilation of the source Java files. This approach is useful in tight, unscheduled situations.

Several important open source Java/Oracle applications make heavy use of Java Swing and JDBC in combination, and we'll cover these in Chapter 8.

Java and the Web

To round off our discussion of Java, especially those aspects of special interest to Oracle developers using Java on the Web, we'll take a look at servlets, JavaServer Pages, and servlet runners in the following sections.

Java Servlets

A *Java servlet* is nothing more than a Java program that sits on a web server delivering web content, doing much the same thing that a Perl CGI program might do. In fact, Java servlets are essentially just "Java CGI" programs. The name "servlet" itself is a sort of pun on "applet." If it weren't such a tongue-twister, applets might have been called "clientlets" (try saying *that* after a glass of Chardonnay).

Java servlets are becoming hugely important in the world of Oracle web applications, and in servlets Java has found itself a valuable niche, especially within the realm of the Apache JServ web server covered later in this chapter. Servlets have some advantages over traditional CGI scripting techniques, in particular:

They are highly portable.
> Java servlets written on your Windows NT machine can be transferred later to your Solaris or Linux machines without any code changes.

They avoid the areas where Java is weak.
> For example, they don't require the AWT (Abstract Windowing Toolkit).

They benefit from the strengths of the core Java APIs.
> These strengths include JDBC, multi-threadability, networking, and so on.

They are remarkably efficient.
> Servlets usually remain as object instances in memory until the web server is shut down. If they are written properly with connection pools,* pool managers, and synchronized threading control, Java servlets are highly scalable. They make multiple concurrent connections possible, especially across the more esoteric web server architectures, such as RMI (Remote Method Invocation)

---

* A *ConnectionPool* is usually a base Java object that sets up a pool of static database connections for use by servlets. When it needs to make a database connection, a top-level servlet generally asks a higher *PoolManager* object for an already created database connection. The *PoolManager* then takes one connection from the *ConnectionPool* object and lends it to the servlet, which hands it back when its task is complete. This process prevents the constant need to make time-consuming connections as servlets drop in and out of use. Database responses can reach lightning speed, dipping in and out of these pools like thirsty swallows on the wing.

and CORBA (Common Object Request Broker Architecture). For more, particularly on CORBA, check out these web sites:

http://www.omg.org
http://www.corba.org

There is a growing link between the operating system–independent structure of Java and the database-independent structure of XML. In the next few years, it's possible that Java XML coding work, tied to an Oracle back end, could become the mainstay of the software development industry. Such a development would drive the evolution of Internet business even further. (For that reason alone, Java servlets are probably worth keeping on top of.) For some other interesting servlet and XML links, check out the following:

http://www.jguru.com/jguru/faq/faqpage.jsp?name=Servlets
A servlets FAQ from Alex Chaffee, a co-founder, along with Nova Spivack, of Gamelan (*http://www.gamelan.com*), itself a highly popular Java resource; Alex is also a popular writer and promoter of Java

http://www.jdom.org
An open source attempt to provide a low-cost entry point into XML with Java

http://www.openxml.org
The OpenXML organization

http://www.oasis-open.org/cover/sgml-xml.html
XML Cover Pages

http://technet.oracle.com/tech/xml/
OTN information on Oracle and XML

JavaServer Pages (JSP)

JavaServer Pages (JSP) is a server-side scripting language that is similar to embedded Perl (Embperl) or PHP. Essentially, it lets you embed bits of Java code into an HTML page in order to access a database and generate dynamic content. JSP diverges from EmbPerl and PHP, though, in that JSP code actually gets compiled into Java servlets on the fly. In this chapter, we'll mention JSP only briefly; since we're unaware of any open source JSP projects, we won't dwell on the details. You may wonder, however, why anyone would want to use JSP instead of running servlets directly. There are two main reasons:

With JSP there is a particular emphasis on the HTML.
JSP functionality is structurally built around making the HTML more flexible. Although servlets can output HTML, doing so is more difficult and tedious to maintain and update since the capability lies within the code, rather than within a template.

It's easier to make changes in a JSP page.
> You can let the Java web server handle the compilation of your JSPs into servlets, rather than handcrafting it all.

If you want to learn more about JSP, see these very useful web sites:

http://www.esperanto.org.nz/jsp/jspfaq.jsp
> The JavaServer Pages FAQ

http://java.sun.com/products/jsp/
> JSP from the horse's mouth

Installing JSDK

Servlets and JSP do not yet come automatically with the ordinary JDKs, so you may be wondering where you can obtain the necessary software. To begin with, you'll need the *javax.servlet.** classes, which are part of the Java Servlet Development Kit (JSDK), an extension to the basic JDK:

http://java.sun.com/products/servlet/
> The main servlet information page from Sun

http://java.sun.com/products/jdk/1.2/
> The download page for JSDK2 and various Unix flavors

http://java.sun.com/products/jdk/1.2/download-windows.html
> The Win32 JSDK download page

Once you have downloaded the software bundle appropriate to your operating system, the installation is virtually identical to the basic JDK installation carried out earlier. You'll need to preinstall the JSDK for the installation of Apache JServ that we'll explain later in this chapter.

Servlet Runners and Other Web Servers

Servlet runners are cut-down developmental web servers, which typically run only Java servlets. In this way, they are similar to the original *appletviewer* programs designed to run only applets. You can download servlet runners from many of the following web sites; you can also download more mainstream web servers that are able to deliver servlets as well as other content:

http://www-uk.hpl.hp.com/people/ak/java/nexus/
> Nexus, a freely available Java web server

http://java.apache.org
> All the latest on combining the Apache web server with Java

http://jakarta.apache.org

> The download site for the Tomcat Server project, along with most of the other software and information related to the many Apache Java projects; many of these projects are now migrating from other related sites within different parts of the Apache software sphere

http://java.sun.com/products/servlet/download.html

> The latest Sun servlet downloads

http://www.servlets.com

> A useful site created by Jason Hunter, coauthor (along with William Crawford) of *Java Servlet Programming*

Apache JServ

Apache JServ is one of the most popular web servers running Java servlets. It is based on the basic Apache web server and is so good that Oracle Corporation itself has decided to incorporate it into its product set. The Apache JServ web server now lies at the heart of Oracle's *i*AS (Internet Application Server). For more on this open source development at Oracle, check out the following web site:

> *http://www.oracle.com/ip/deploy/ias/*

In this section, we'll run through two separate JServ installations, one for Unix and the other for Windows. Both are more involved than our usual installations, because there are a lot of bits and pieces making up the whole. Before carrying out this installation, make sure that you have already installed the JDK and then the JSDK, as described above.

 You may want to follow our steps in order to install your own version of Apache. However, treat them only as general guidelines; for the most up-to-date information, check the *README* files and installation notes that come with the distribution.

Apache JServ, the Jakarta Project, and Tomcat

As we went to press, the older Java Apache project (*http://java.apache.org*) was being merged and migrated into the newer Jakarta project (*http://jakarta.apache. org*), which already includes the development team of the original Apache JServ web server product. The complete Jakarta project is itself an umbrella grouping of many smaller Apache subprojects; the general goal is to produce commercial-quality server solutions based on the Java platform.

The flagship project of Jakarta is Tomcat, which is the official reference implementation for the Java Servlet 2.2, JavaServer Pages 1.1, and other complementary technologies. The main web site for Tomcat is:

> *http://jakarta.apache.org/tomcat/*

Tomcat will eventually replace Apache JServ, and all related development will switch at some point, from one to the other. (See the sidebar for a sampling of other Jakarta development work.)

Nevertheless, we've chosen to describe the latest version of Apache JServ, rather than the early implementations of Tomcat, in this chapter and in Chapter 8. JServ is currently an important component of Oracle Corporation's *i*AS product, and at the time we went to press, it is still the main web server for the latest version of the DB Prism application we could download (1.1.0). (DB Prism is described in Chapter 8.) DB Prism itself will be upgraded to use Tomcat in version 1.1.1 and all subsequent versions.

Once you have cut your teeth on the slightly simpler Apache JServ, you will have a relatively straightforward migration path upwards to the fuller implementation of Tomcat. Full installation and user documentation is also online and available here:

> *http://jakarta.apache.org/tomcat/index.html*
> *http://jakarta.apache.org/site/faqs.html*
> *http://jakarta.apache.org/tomcat/jakarta-tomcat/src/doc/index.html*

Installing Apache JServ on Unix

Download Apache JServ from the main web site:

> *http://java.apache.org*

This will clearly signpost the current download pages.[*]

Setting up Apache JServ is a bit more complicated than setting up straight Apache. This is mainly because we need to tell the configuration about our Java setup. Remember that these details may change, so always check the latest *INSTALL* file at the *http://java.apache.org* portal site for up-to-date information and more details. If you encounter a problem while performing the installation, the solution will generally be hiding somewhere in this file.

Before getting into JServ specifics, you need to make sure that Apache itself is installed on your system. If you haven't installed it already, get it from this site:

> *http://www.apache.org/dist/*

---

[*] When installing Apache JServ on Linux, make sure that you're using at least Apache 1.3.9 and Version 2.1 of *glibc* over your Linux kernel.

Apache Jakarta Open Source Projects

In addition to Tomcat, other Apache Jakarta open source projects include the following:

http://jakarta.apache.org/ant/index.html

Ant is a Java-based build tool (which incidentally is also used by the ViennaSQL Java GUI program described in Chapter 8).

http://jakarta.apache.org/avalon/index.html

Avalon is a common framework for Java server applications.

http://jakarta.apache.org/ecs/index.html

The Element Construction Set (ECS) is an API for generating the various markup language elements in Java.

http://jakarta.apache.org/james/index.html

The Java Apache Mail Enterprise Server (JAMES).

http://jakarta.apache.org/jetspeed/site/index.html

Jetspeed is an enterprise information portal project, employing Java and XML, that makes network resources available via web devices.

http://jakarta.apache.org/jmeter/index.html

Apache JMeter is a Java desktop application used to measure and test the performance of other programs. It was initially designed and built with Apache itself in mind, but its functionality has since been transferred to other applications.

http://jakarta.apache.org/log4j/docs/index.html

Log4j is a project intended to deliver switchable detailed logging information in production code with minimal performance effects.

http://jakarta.apache.org/oro/index.html

ORO provides a full-featured regular expression set of classes for Java.

http://jakarta.apache.org/regexp/index.html

Regexp is another regular expression package for Java.

http://jakarta.apache.org/slide/index.html

Slide is a content management and integration system.

http://jakarta.apache.org/struts/index.html

Struts provides a framework for building Java server solutions.

http://jakarta.apache.org/taglibs/index.html

Taglibs aims to provide custom tags to help separate presentation from implementation.

—Continued—

> *http://jakarta.apache.org/turbine/index.html*
> Turbine is a servlet-based framework for building secure applications; it is also used by DB Prism (see Chapter 8).
>
> *http://jakarta.apache.org/velocity/index.html*
> Velocity is a web page template engine.
>
> *http://jakarta.apache.org/watchdog/index.html*
> Watchdog provides validation for Java server solutions.

Like us, you might not want JServ to affect your main Apache web server and may want only to experiment with it. This is not a problem. All you have to do is install Apache under your local *$HOME* directory. You can do this as follows:

1. Download Apache from the above site (our distribution was *apache_1.3.12*) into *$HOME*.

2. Move and unpack that file into a newly created *$HOME/apache_jserv* directory (in our example, *$HOME* was */home/oos*):

   ```
   $ cd $HOME
   $ mkdir apache_jserv
   $ mv apache_1.3.12.tar.gz $HOME/apache_jserv
   $ cd apache_jserv
   $ gzip -d apache_1.3.12.tar.gz
   $ tar xvf apache_1.3.12.tar
   $ cd apache_1.3.12
   ```

3. We're going to build shared object support into Apache JServ.[*] To do this, you first need to make sure that the version of Apache you build has the required DSO (Dynamic Shared Object) support. You turn on shared object support with the *enable* switch, as shown below. Install into a new *$HOME/apache* directory:

   ```
   $ mkdir $HOME/apache
   $ ./configure --prefix=$HOME/apache --enable-shared=max
   ```

4. To ensure that you've loaded the DSO option, check for a message like the following when you run the *./configure* program:

   ```
   Creating Configuration.apaci in src
    + enabling mod_so for DSO support
   ```

5. We're now ready to install the "DSO and JServ Ready" version of Apache into our local user space on the server:

---

[*] The arguments for and against using shared object support are discussed in detail in the Apache JServ download installation notes. For a static build, follow the appropriate steps (which are similar to those shown here) in the download installation files.

```
$ make
$ make install
$ vi $HOME/conf/httpd.conf
```

6. Set the *ServerName* variable within the *httpd.conf* file:

```
# ServerName myhost.mycountry.myorg.com
ServerName localhost
```

7. Start up the Apache Server:

```
$ $HOME/apache/bin/apachectl start
```

This gives us access to our first web page, as displayed in Figure 7-10.

8. We're now ready for Apache JServ proper. Unpack the appropriate download from *http://java.apache.org* into our *$HOME/apache_jserv* directory, first creating a *$HOME/jserv* directory as a target to contain the actual installation:

```
$ cd $HOME
$ mkdir jserv
$ mv ApacheJServ-1.1.2.tar.gz apache_jserv
$ cd apache_jserv
$ gzip -d ApacheJServ-1.1.2.tar.gz
$ tar xvf ApacheJServ-1.1.2.tar
$ cd ApacheJServ-1.1.2
```

9. For the configuration of JServ proper, we need to tell the configuration program where the required *apxs* files are (the Apache Extension is a built-in Apache program module that helps build DSO modules outside of the main Apache source tree). We also need to tell the configuration process where to install JServ, where to find the newly installed JSDK servlet JAR file *jsdk.jar*, and other optional items, such as SSL (the Secure Sockets Layer). Finally, we need to switch the debugging option to the desired state. In our installation, we therefore employed the following switch commands for our JServ configuration:

```
$ ./configure \
   --prefix=$HOME/jserv \
   --with-apache-src=$HOME/apache_jserv/apache_1.3.12 \
   --with-JSDK=$HOME/jsdk/jsdk.jar \
   --disable-debugging
```

10. The Apache JServ configuration program may now click and whir for quite a while, checking to make sure that your setup is as it should be. If it reports any problems, you will need to sort them out. However, the installation is usually quite painless, and it should run entirely smoothly on a plain vanilla Unix-like operating system. Once the configuration operation is complete, carry out the following familiar steps, which use the newly configured *Makefile*:

```
$ make
$ make install
```

Once the last step completes successfully, the installation should be complete.

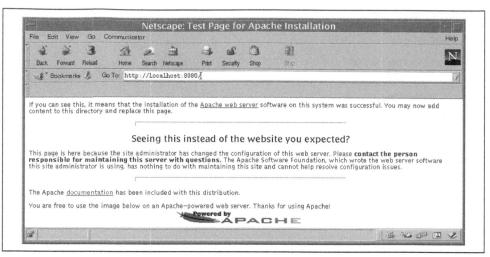

Figure 7-10. Checking that our base Apache is working correctly

Installing Apache JServ on Windows

Because the Windows installation uses self-extracting executables, it is a little less involved than the Unix setup. The steps remain essentially the same, however:

1. First of all, get hold of Apache for Windows and the related documentation from the following web sites:

    http://httpd.apache.org/docs/windows.html
       The central information page for Win32

    http://httpd.apache.org/dist/binaries/win32/
       The main download page, where you can obtain self-installers such as the *apache_1_3_12_win32.exe* download file

2. Install in the normal Windows binary fashion, accepting the defaults. Once Apache is installed, edit the following file:

    C:\Program Files\Apache Group\Apache\conf\httpd.conf

    Make sure that the *ServerName* variable is set appropriately in this file:

    ```
    ServerName localhost
    ```

3. On the Windows Start menu, you should be able to find the relevant options to start up Apache. Once you've done this, fire up your local browser and enter *http://localhost/* or *http://127.0.0.1/* to bring up a Windows version of what you saw in Figure 7-10. If this does not work as expected, see the excellent troubleshooting help available at the central Apache Windows page listed previously.

4. If all has gone well, shut down the web server. Do this from the Windows Start menu. Now get the latest Apache JServ Win32 executable download from the following site (we downloaded *ApacheJserv-1.1.2-2.exe*):

> *http://java.apache.org/jserv/dist/*

5. Again, simply double-click on this file to install it. This time, however, you will be asked several questions. First, you'll be asked where the Java Virtual Machine (JVM) is located. Simply enter the directory where your JDK-installed *java.exe* program is living, such as:

```
C:\jdk-1.2.2\bin
```

6. Next, the JServ install will ask where the JSDK is located. This actually means, "Tell me where the *jsdk.jar* file is." The location is typically something like this:

```
C:\JSDK2.0\lib
```

7. Finally, you'll be asked if you want the installation process to update the base Apache's *httpd.conf* file. You do. Therefore, enter the directory where this is located:

```
C:\Program Files\Apache Group\Apache\conf
```

8. The installation should then complete with no further questions. Once this is completed, start up Apache again and enter the following address into your browser (note the trailing slash):

```
http://localhost/jserv/
```

If you see a screen something like Figure 7-11, Apache JServ is installed and running as nature intended, on Windows.

Running JServ on Unix

We now need to make sure that our base Apache will run with servlets and the JServ option. We'll check this first for Unix.

Testing the configuration

To start off with, make sure that the right daemon version of *httpd* comes first within our execution pathway (especially if there are any others lurking around your system):

```
$ PATH=$HOME/apache/bin:$PATH ; export PATH
$ httpd -l
```

This listing should look something like this:

```
Compiled-in modules:
  http_core.c
  mod_env.c
  mod_log_config.c
  mod_mime.c
```

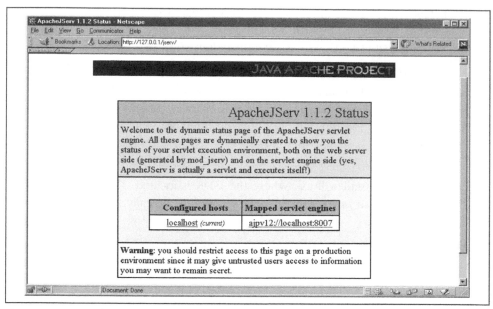

Figure 7-11. Apache JServ running on Win32

```
mod_negotiation.c
mod_status.c
mod_include.c
mod_autoindex.c
mod_dir.c
mod_cgi.c
mod_asis.c
mod_imap.c
mod_actions.c
mod_userdir.c
mod_alias.c
mod_access.c
mod_auth.c
mod_setenvif.c
mod_jserv.c
```

If everything looks OK, we'll deal next with our JServ configuration files. At this point, there are three that concern us directly:

> *jserv.conf*
> *jserv.properties*
> *example.properties*

If you've mirrored our installation so far, you can find examples of this triumvirate under the following directory:

> *$HOME/apache_jserv/ApacheJServ-1.1.2/example*

Now follow these steps:

1. Copy all three of these files to the *$HOME/apache/conf* directory. This assumes that you wish to have a servlet zone called "example", a default we'll accept for the moment. See the next section, "Setting up servlet zones," for a discussion of these zones.

   ```
   $ cd $HOME/apache/conf
   $ cp $HOME/apache_jserv/ApacheJServ-1.1.2/example/jserv.conf .
   $ cp $HOME/apache_jserv/ApacheJServ-1.1.2/example/jserv.properties .
   $ cp $HOME/apache_jserv/ApacheJServ-1.1.2/example/example.properties .
   ```

2. The standard Apache *httpd.conf* file requires that we include a directive to pick up the *jserv.conf* file. Therefore, add the following line to *httpd.conf*:

   ```
   # httpd.conf
   Include /home/oos/apache/conf/jserv.conf
   ```

   The *jserv.conf* file, will, in turn, point to *jserv.properties* and so on, in a sort of linked list of files.

3. We then edit the three JServ configuration files. Follow closely the commented instructions, which you'll find within each of the three files. Again, these instructions will change regularly, so we won't cloud matters by being too specific here. The following are the ones we paid particular attention to in our example *jserv.conf* file:

   ```
   # jserv.conf
   ApJServProperties /home/oos/apache/conf/jserv.properties
   ApJServMount /example /example
   ApJServMount /servlets /example
   ApJServMount /servlet /example
   ```

   The first one continues our configuration file chain, this time pointing towards the general JServ *properties* file. The last three directives determine what's acceptable for our later web addresses when they pick up servlet requests from our calling browsers. Notice that our servlet zone is pointing generally towards the *"example"* zone specified earlier.

Setting up servlet zones

One of the beauties of JServ, as compared to several of the other servlet runners out there, is that you can have as many separate servlet zones as you need. Use of multiple zones gives your development projects excellent separation and modularity.

Unfortunately, using separate servlet zones requires further directives within the *jserv.properties* file, our next configuration file target; *jserv.properties*, in turn, points towards the *example.properties* file. Let's deal with them one at a time:

```
# jserv.properties
zones=example
example.properties=/home/oos/apache/conf/example.properties
```

We now need to edit the *example.properties* zone file, which we point towards *Hello.class*, a Java class file already prepared for us by those nice JServ development people. This comes automatically with the JServ download, along with its matching *Hello.java* file. You'll find both of these files in the *$HOME/jserv/servlets* directory. You can check out the Java code in Example 7-8.

Example 7-8. JServ Reconnaissance with the Hello.java File

```java
import java.io.*;
import javax.servlet.*;           // Required servlet classes
import javax.servlet.http.*;

/**
 * This is a simple example of an HTTP Servlet.  It responds to the GET
 * and HEAD methods of the HTTP protocol.
 */
public class Hello extends HttpServlet
{
    /**
     * Handle the GET and HEAD methods by building a simple web page.
     * HEAD is just like GET, except that the server returns only the
     * headers (including content length) not the body we write.
     */
    public void doGet (HttpServletRequest request,
                       HttpServletResponse response)
                       throws ServletException, IOException
    {
        PrintWriter out;  // The crucial HTTP output variable.
        String title = "Example Apache JServ Servlet";

        // set content type and other response header fields first
        response.setContentType("text/html");

        // then write the data of the response
        out = response.getWriter();

        out.println("<HTML><HEAD><TITLE>");
        out.println(title);
        out.println("</TITLE></HEAD><BODY bgcolor=\"#FFFFFF\">");
        out.println("<H1>" + title + "</H1>");
        out.println("<H2> Congratulations, ");
        out.println("ApacheJServ 1.1.2 is working!<br>");
        out.println("</BODY></HTML>");
        out.close();  // Always close.
    }
}
```

Follow these steps:

1. Make sure that you have at least the following lines in your *example.properties* zone file:

```
# example.properties
repositories=/home/oos/jserv/servlets
```

```
servlets.startup=hello
servlet.hello.code=Hello
```

This tells the servlet runner which servlets should be available for initialization inside the "example" zone and what the Java classes are called. Now let's test our configuration.

2. Again, fire up Apache, which should now pick up all our new configurations:

```
$ $HOME/apache/bin/apachectl stop
/home/oos/apache/bin/apachectl stop: httpd stopped
$ $HOME/apache/bin/apachectl start
```

3. If you now point your local browser at *http://localhost:8080/*, the default servlet host and port combination, you should get the same screen displayed as in Figure 7-10 earlier. (However, you may have to disable browser proxy server usage if you're using *localhost* rather than your network-aware host name.)

4. If this screen *does* upload as expected, move on to *http://localhost:8080/example/hello*. You should now see the Unix-style screen, shown on the left side of Figure 7-12.

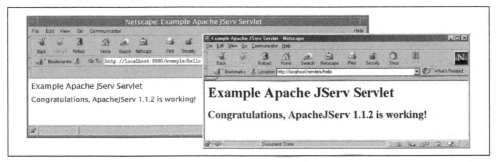

Figure 7-12. The servlets have landed on Solaris and Win32

Success! Now that you've made a detailed run through JServ, there's just time to go lie down for 10 minutes with a lavender-steamed flannel over your face. It will help get you ready for the next phase, after we've quickly run through the Windows version of a similar servlet generation check.

Running JServ on Windows

Next, we'll make sure that Apache will run with the Jserv option on Windows. Follow these steps:

1. Add the following line to the *C:\Program Files\Apache JServ 1.1.2\conf\jserv. conf* file:

```
ApJServMount /servlets /root
```

2. Add the following line to the *C:\Program Files\Apache JServ 1.1.2\conf\jserv. properties* file:

```
# jserv.properties
zones=root
root.properties=C:\Program Files\Apache JServ
(continued from line above) 1.1.2\servlets\zone.properties
```

3. Edit the *C:\Program Files\Apache JServ 1.1.2\servlets\zone.properties* file:

```
# zone.properties
repositories=C:\Program Files\Apache JServ 1.1.2\servlets
servlets.startup=hello
servlet.hello.code=Hello
```

4. Copy *Hello.class* from the *example* directory to the *servlets* directory:

```
> cd C:\Program Files\Apache JServ 1.1.2
> copy example\Hello.* servlets
```

5. Finally, restart Apache, and go to the following web address:

   http://localhost/servlets/hello

6. You should now see the Win32 screen shown on the right side of Figure 7-12.

Running an Oracle Servlet

Next we'll attempt to compile and run a relatively straightforward Oracle servlet, which you can find in Example 7-9, our first step towards total Java servlet world domination. For an explanation of what's going on in the various steps of this servlet (note the step numbers in the comments), see the corresponding notes at the end of the code listing.

Example 7-9. The HelloOracle.java Java/Oracle Servlet

```
import java.io.*;
import java.util.*;
import java.text.*;

// Step 1 - Import the JDBC package.
import java.sql.*;

import javax.servlet.*;
import javax.servlet.http.*;

/**
 * This is a simple example of an HTTP Servlet connecting to Oracle.
 * It responds to the GET and HEAD methods of the HTTP protocol.
 */
public class HelloOracle extends HttpServlet
{
    /**
     * Step 2 - SQL Connection and main command.
     */
    Connection con = null ;
```

Example 7-9. The HelloOracle.java Java/Oracle Servlet (continued)

```java
    StringBuffer commandSQL = null ;

/**
 * Initialize, Captain.  This init() function only runs once, when
 * the Java servlet is first called by the web server.  Afterwards
 * it remains in memory for all new instantiations of the servlet,
 * thus greatly aiding scalability.
 */
public void init(ServletConfig config)
        throws ServletException {

    super.init(config);

    // Step 3 - Now get the database connection.

    String connString =
       "jdbc:oracle:thin:@localhost:1521:ORCL";
    String user = "SCOTT";
    String password = "TIGER";

    // Step 4 - Now set up the main constant SQL command.

    commandSQL = new StringBuffer ();

    commandSQL.append( "SELECT EMPNO" );
    commandSQL.append( ",ENAME" );
    commandSQL.append( ",JOB" );
    commandSQL.append( ",TO_CHAR(MGR)" );
    commandSQL.append( ",TO_CHAR(HIREDATE,'DD/MM/YYYY') " );
    commandSQL.append( "FROM EMP " );
    commandSQL.append( "WHERE JOB = ? " );
    commandSQL.append( "ORDER BY 2" );

    try {

        // Step 5 - Load (and therefore register) the Oracle Driver

        Class.forName("oracle.jdbc.driver.OracleDriver");

        // Get a Connection to the database
        con = DriverManager.getConnection(
                    connString,
                    user,
                    password
                                        );
    }
    catch(ClassNotFoundException e) { }
    catch(SQLException e) { }
}

/**
 * Handle the GET and HEAD methods by building a simple web page.
 * HEAD is just like GET, except that the server returns only the
```

Example 7-9. The HelloOracle.java Java/Oracle Servlet (continued)

```
 * headers (including content length) not the body we write.
 */
public void doGet (HttpServletRequest request,
                   HttpServletResponse response)
                   throws ServletException, IOException
{
    PrintWriter out;
    String title = "Example Apache JServ Oracle Servlet";

    // set content type and other response header fields first
    response.setContentType("text/html");

    // then write the data of the response
    out = response.getWriter();

    out.println("<HTML><HEAD><TITLE>");
    out.println(title);
    out.println("</TITLE></HEAD><BODY bgcolor=\"#FFFFFF\">");
    out.println("<CENTER>");
    out.println("<H1>");
    out.println(title);
    out.println("</H1>");
    out.println("<H2> Congratulations, ");
    out.println("Oracle Servlets are working!<br>");

    try {

        // Step 6 - Execute an SQL query, get a ResultSet.

        PreparedStatement pstmt =
           con.prepareStatement( commandSQL.toString() );

        pstmt.clearParameters();
        pstmt.setString( 1, "SALESMAN" );

        ResultSet rs = pstmt.executeQuery();

        out.println("\n<TABLE ALIGN=CENTER BORDER=1 ");
        out.println("CELLPADDING=0 FRAME=\"BOX\">");

        out.println("\n<TR>");
        out.println("<TH>Employee No</TH>" );
        out.println("<TH>Name</TH>" );
        out.println("<TH>Position</TH>" );
        out.println("<TH>Mgr</TH>" );
        out.println("<TH>Hired</TH>" );
        out.println("</TR>\n");

        int i = 0;

        // Step 7 - Run through the result set cursor
        // (always close the prepared statement when finished)
```

Example 7-9. The HelloOracle.java Java/Oracle Servlet (continued)

```
            while( rs.next() ) {
                out.println("\n<TR>");

                for (i = 1; i < 6; i++){

                    out.println("<TD>" );
                    out.println( rs.getString ( i ) );
                    out.println("</TD>" );
                }
                out.println("</TR>\n");
            }
            pstmt.close();

            out.println("</TABLE></CENTER>\n");
        }
        catch(SQLException e) {
            out.println("SQLException caught: ");
            out.println(e.getMessage());
        }

        out.println("</BODY></HTML>");
        out.close();
    }

    public void destroy() {
        // Step 8 - Always close the database connection.
        try {
          if (con != null) con.close();
        }
        catch (SQLException ignored) { }
    }
}
```

Here we'll explain briefly what's going on in this example:

1. The most important step is loading JDBC via the *java.sql* package.

2. Prepare the connection and SQL handler variables.

3. Here, we're using the Thin driver to pick up the Oracle database connection.

4. Avoiding slow string concatenation, we build up the necessary SQL.

5. Next, we register the driver and establish the JDBC connection.

6. The heart of the program is reached and the SQL is prepared.

7. The cursor loop operation takes place, gathering the information and always making sure that the *PreparedStatement* object is closed as soon as it's dispensed with.

8. Finally, the database connection is released.

After we've compiled the *HelloOracle.java* servlet within the *$HOME/jserv/servlets* directory, we need to shut down the web server and modify our configuration once more.

Configuring the Oracle servlet on Unix

We can now modify our entries again within the *example.properties* configuration file:

```
# example.properties II: The Final Countdown
repositories=/home/oos/jserv/servlets
servlets.startup=hello,hellooracle
servlet.hello.code=Hello
servlet.hellooracle.code=HelloOracle
```

Before restarting the web server, we must also alter the notional CLASSPATH variable that was created for Apache JServ via its configuration files. At the time of initial setup, the *./configure* program determined for us the location of two essential JAR files, *ApacheJServ.jar* and *jsdk.jar*. Because we're now writing Oracle servlets, we also need to tell JServ where our Oracle JDBC drivers are located. This is done via the WRAPPER.CLASSPATH variables specified in the *$HOME/apache/conf/jserv.properties* file. Here are the entries we made to ensure that the necessary CLASSPATH environment variable was set correctly for our web server to run our Java Oracle servlets:

```
wrapper.classpath=/home/oos/jserv/libexec/ApacheJServ.jar
wrapper.classpath=/home/oos/jsdk/jsdk.jar

# Oracle JDBC drivers contained within the classes111.zip file
wrapper.classpath=/home/oos/classes12.zip
```

Configuring the Oracle servlet on Windows

Follow these steps to configure the Oracle servlet on Win32 systems:

1. This time, modify the *zone.properties* file:

   ```
   servlets.startup=hello,hellooracle
   servlet.hello.code=Hello
   servlet.hellooracle.code=HelloOracle
   ```

2. Also modify the *jserv.properties* file with the latest driver file you have for this platform:

   ```
   wrapper.classpath=C:\Oracle\jdbc\classes12.zip
   ```

3. Now, simply compile the *HelloOracle.java* servlet and make sure the *.class* output file resides in the same directory as the *Hello.class* servlet.

Running the servlet

Now we're all set to turn our usual flood of replicant *httpd* daemons loose. Restart Apache under either Unix or Windows. The compiled Java servlet should then respond via your browser, as displayed in Figure 7-13. Mission accomplished!

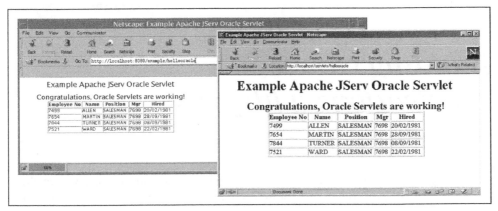

Figure 7-13. HelloOracle.java in wildly impressive action

8

Building Oracle Applications with Java

Although Java itself isn't an open source technology, more and more Java developers are building open source environments and applications with this popular language. In this chapter, we'll focus on two main areas of Java open source activity as they relate to Oracle open source applications. First, we'll look at three JDBC-based Oracle GUI applications:

jDBA

Provides Oracle database administrators with a complete toolkit of DBA tools for browsing and manipulating database objects. jDBA is similar in concept to the Orac tool, which is based on Perl/Tk and described in Chapter 4, *Building Oracle Applications with Perl/Tk and Tcl/Tk*. jDBA provides a familiar set of functions that allow you to browse tablespaces, synonyms, views, tables, and other objects, and to manipulate the data within these objects.

VieunaSQL

A Java GUI built with the very latest Java Swing components. VieunaSQL provides an excellent Java-based substitute for SQL*Plus. Like jDBA, this tool lets you examine and manipulate objects in an Oracle database.

DBInspector

A client for Oracle that allows you to browse the data in your Oracle database and to execute SQL.

Later in the chapter, we'll turn our attention to a trailblazing open source project that combines the best of Oracle and Java:

DB Prism

An open source framework, DB Prism is a servlet engine that can work either as a standalone servlet or plugged into Cocoon. It makes use of Apache JServ, Oracle, PL/SQL, and Java. Using DB Prism, applications built using the older

Oracle Web Application Server (OWAS) PL/SQL cartridge can coexist with those using Oracle's new Internet Application Server (*i*AS).

Cocoon

When DB Prism is plugged into the Cocoon publishing framework, it provides a new way to make Internet applications work with technologies such as XML and XSLT. DB Prism serves as a database web content provider for Cocoon, generating dynamic XML from the database.

jDBA

jDBA (Java Database Administrator) is a complete GUI toolkit for the Oracle DBA. It provides a set of tools that let you browse and manipulate tables and other Oracle database objects.

Like so many other Oracle open source projects, the genesis of jDBA was heavily intertwined with the initial Oracle port to Linux and the realization that there were essentially no existing, usable tools for Oracle database administration on this new platform. Most available applications (even the freeware ones) were only Windows-based. In a situation similar to the one that brought about the development of the Perl/Tk Orac program (described in Chapter 4), Ezra Pagel turned necessity to invention. Starting with the goal of automating his use of Oracle's character-based SQL*Plus, he ultimately built a complete GUI toolkit that makes the lives of Oracle DBAs quite a bit easier.

In the summer of 1999, Oracle8*i* on Linux was maturing nicely, and the volunteers from *blackdown.org* were porting Sun's Java Development Kit (JDK 1.2) to Linux. Although there was little other real support for Java on Linux, Ezra had been using JDK 1.1.x for application development and liked the robust database API that JDBC offered, with its single Thin driver requirement and its general OS portability. He enlisted the help of Dain Caldwell, an Oracle coworker and OCI code guru. Over the next few months, they threw themselves into learning everything they could about how Oracle and Java could work together, and eventually they developed the initial version of jDBA.

The application subsequently moved out of the hobby stage in the spring of 2000, when there was enough support for Java on Linux to make jDBA into a living, breathing project. Ezra and Dain were joined by Michael Salmon of *collab.net*, who shared many of their views on the state of databases, Java, and open source.

jDBA is still a work in progress. Currently, the underlying structure for jDBA is in place, with much of the basic functionality developed and many new features promised in the future. As with many other similar projects, the unfortunate necessity of day jobs keeps interrupting development, but the future of jDBA still looks bright.

All of jDBA's classes are written exclusively in Java. As with most other Java/Oracle tools, when you run jDBA you'll need to have access to one of the JDBC drivers described in Chapter 7, *Java*; these can generally be found lurking within the latest generation of Oracle's *classes12.zip* file.

These are the main web sites for jDBA:

http://sourceforge.net/projects/jdba/
   The development project web site

http://www.jdba.org
   jDBA's general web site

Installing jDBA

To build jDBA successfully, you must have at least a Java2 JDK (Java Development Kit) on your system, as described in Chapter 7. You can download jDBA from any one of the following sites:

   http://www.jdba.org
   http://sourceforge.net/projects/jdba/

Installing jDBA on Unix and Linux

For Unix and Linux, follow these instructions to install jDBA:

1. Download the latest jDBA *jDBA.xx.tar.gz* file from one of the sites just listed (we installed *jDBA.0.41.tar.gz*).

2. Unpack the tar file:

   ```
   $ gzip -d jDBA.0.41.tar.gz
   $ tar xvf jDBA.0.41.tar
   ```

3. Run the following command to compile jDBA:

   ```
   $ /usr/local/bin/javac jDBA/*.java
   ```

   That's all the compilation you'll require for jDBA (honest!). We're now almost ready to run the program.

4. Make sure you include the correct Oracle JDBC drivers zip file within your CLASSPATH environment variable specification; you can set this variable either directly within the environment or via the command line, as we've done below:

   ```
   $ /usr/local/bin/java -cp \
   $CLASSPATH:$ORACLE_HOME/jdbc/lib/classes111.zip jDBA/MainFrame
   ```

5. The jDBA setup screens should appear, as shown in Figure 8-1 (this particular version of jDBA was generated under Solaris).

Installing jDBA on Windows

The installation process is virtually identical on Windows. To compile and run the jDBA program, just remember to use backslashes for the path to *javac* and then forward Unix-style slashes to tell *javac* where the appropriate Java files are:

```
C:\> C:\java\bin\javac jDBA/*.java
C:\> C:\java\bin\java -cp $CLASSPATH:classes111.zip jDBA/MainFrame
```

This should produce a Windows-style screen that's very similar to the Solaris output in Figure 8-1.

Figure 8-1. jDBA alias screen under Solaris

Configuring JDBC

On the screen shown in Figure 8-1, you'll note a selection of database types appearing under the Database Type field. Although this list includes Sybase and Informix, jDBA is designed with Oracle very much in mind. After the main application entry screen appears, you'll be able to drill down to the appropriate alias screen to register your first chosen Oracle database.

To configure your first database connection, do the following:

1. Click on the Aliases menu. This will display a drill-down list.

2. Drill down to Add. This will display the alias addition screen; there you can fill in the connection details for your selected database.

3. Go back to the main screen. Once you have set up your alias on the main screen, you can double-click on it to get a typical login screen, as shown in Figure 8-2. Fill this in with your username and password, and then press the

Submit button. (You may have to restart the program to pick up the alias, but we're told that this problem will be rectified in later versions of jDBA.)

4. If you're running standard output to your console screen, you may see a message flash by, informing you which Oracle connection you've just made, for example:

```
jdbc:oracle:thin:SYSTEM/MANAGER@localhost:1521:ORCL
```

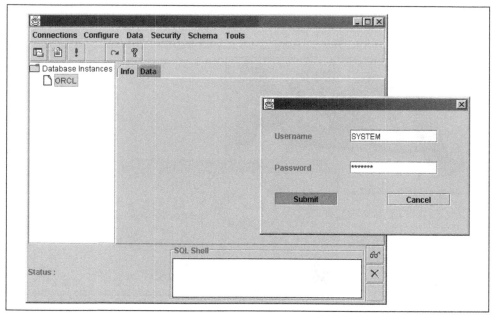

Figure 8-2. jDBA's main login screens under Win32

Using jDBA

Once you finish configuring JDBC, you should see a screen similar to the one in Figure 8-3, providing a full selection of drill-down objects. From here on, the program is reasonably intuitive. You can drill down on the various layers of table information (as shown in Figure 8-3), examine indexes, or continue down through the hierarchy for many other options. jDBA currently allows you to examine any of these objects (additional objects will be available in future versions of the program):

Tables
Views
Sequences
Synonyms
Tablespaces
Triggers
Indexes
Procedures

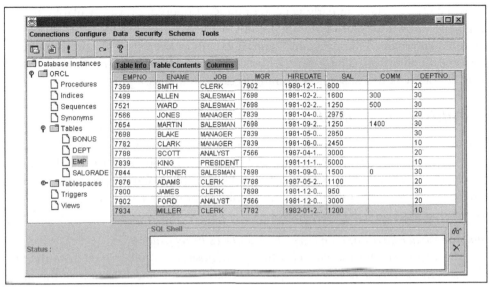

Figure 8-3. jDBA layered panes of table information

We'll leave you to have fun exploring the rest of jDBA's functionality at your leisure.

ViennaSQL

ViennaSQL is another superb open source Java GUI tool that provides numerous Oracle SQL data drill-downs into the database. It is useful for both developers and DBAs. ViennaSQL comes with a GNU license, excellent functionality, and the very latest Java look-and-feel.

The following are the main web sites for ViennaSQL:

http://sourceforge.net/projects/vienna/
    The development project web site

http://vienna.sourceforge.net
    ViennaSQL's general web site

Early in 1999, Mike Wilson was working on a large project with Oracle on the back end, and he needed a GUI query tool to overcome the limitations of the character-based SQL*Plus. He originally wrote a server-based tool in Tcl/Tk, but this X-based tool wasn't up to doing the job over slow international connections— hence the need for a local client that could work on various operating systems. In order to both brush up on his Java skills and get the tool he needed—and in the tradition of many other open source developers—Mike decided that necessity was the mother of invention. He started building his tool in July 2000, with plenty of helpful advice from Andrei Lenki.

By September of 2000, an early version of the GUI query tool was available. It was originally known as vsql (Visual SQL), but because an earlier tool had the same name, Mike renamed the program ViennaSQL both to keep the "V" and to follow a personal tradition of naming server hosts after famous cities. (The famous 1980s song by Ultravox had absolutely nothing to do with it, alas.)

Installing ViennaSQL

You can install ViennaSQL using the executable JAR file, *vienna.jar*, provided with the various downloads for Windows and Linux, or, if you want to use the entire development environment, you can build the tool from source yourself. The following downloads are useful if you are building from source (if you just want to use *vienna.jar*, you don't need these):

http://developer.java.sun.com/developer/techDocs/hi/repository/
> The access site for the Sun Java Images Repository, a full collection of the latest Sun Java toolbar button graphics available in the latest version of the *jlfgr-1_0.jar* file.

http://jakarta.apache.org/ant/index.html
> The download site for Ant, the Java-based build tool we mentioned in Chapter 7 in the discussion of Jakarta.

http://www.wilson.co.uk/xml/minml.htm
> You may also need MinML, a Java XML configuration file processor created by John Wilson. It can be downloaded directly from the ViennaSQL web site, and it is also available from *http://freshmeat.net/projects/minml/*.

Install ViennaSQL as follows:

1. Download the executable *vienna.jar* file or build it from source.

2. Put the precompiled or locally compiled *vienna.jar* file in a location such as *C:\Local\Vienna* for Win32 or */usr/local/lib* for a Unix-style install.

3. Execute this file directly. Either double-click via a windowed frontend or run the following command within the directory:

   ```
   $ java -jar vienna.jar
   ```

4. This "easy" method under Win32 also requires that you put the *classes12.zip* Oracle driver file in the *../ext* directory (e.g., *C:\Program Files\JavaSoft\JRE\1.2\lib\ext*) so the automatic Java processes there can pick up the relevant JDBC connection code.

5. You can also run the *java* program on the command line in the more traditional Unix style, if you wish. For example, you may wish to choose the following alternatives (we've split the command here, to fit in the margins of this book, but it must be on one long line):

Unix:

```
$ java -classpath $CLASSPATH:/some/directory/vienna.jar
    uk.co.whisperingwind.vienna.MainController
```

Win32:

```
> java -classpath "%CLASSPATH%;\some\directory\vienna.jar"
    uk.co.whisperingwind.vienna.MainController
```

6. Once the program starts up, you should see a screen similar to the one shown in Figure 8-4.

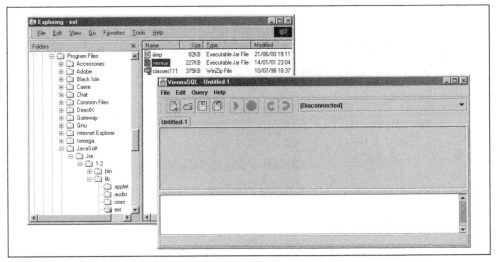

Figure 8-4. ViennaSQL via a Win32 double-click

Using ViennaSQL

On the ViennaSQL startup screen you'll see the familiar JDBC connection setup, but there's a difference with this program. Before accepting your new ViennaSQL configuration, you can test the connection, as shown in Figure 8-5. ViennaSQL also possesses an excellent system for saving and retrieving SQL files. You can view the system at work in Figure 8-6, which also shows the Win32 look-and-feel.

Since ViennaSQL is a SQL tool, it naturally has a full range of facilities to browse and execute SQL. We particularly like the spreadsheet-like panes, which are automatically generated via SQL*Plus-like input statements. These are tabulated and neatly formatted, with all the SQL*Plus and SQL commands you'll require (note the Execute choice on the screen in Figure 8-7).

Schema objects

As well as providing full SQL facilities, ViennaSQL also provides a schema option that lets you drill down on many of the database's objects (see Figure 8-8). As this

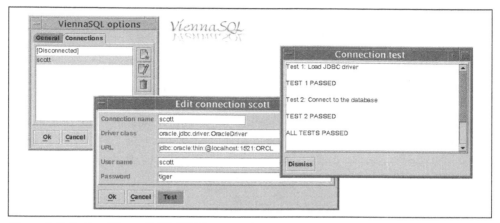

Figure 8-5. Testing ViennaSQL's JDBC connection

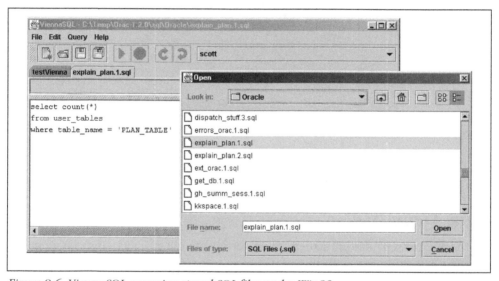

Figure 8-6. ViennaSQL accessing stored SQL files under Win32

example shows, for such a recently developed program, ViennaSQL already displays a high level of elegance and stability, with intuitive buttons and commands, a clear system for connecting to target databases, and a fresh clean structure.

ViennaSQL and XML

The ViennaSQL configuration system is based on XML, and we expect the XML-ization of ViennaSQL to continue apace. When you set your JDBC connection, the necessary configurable information is stored automatically in your home directory, in the *vienna.xml* file, as demonstrated in Example 8-1.

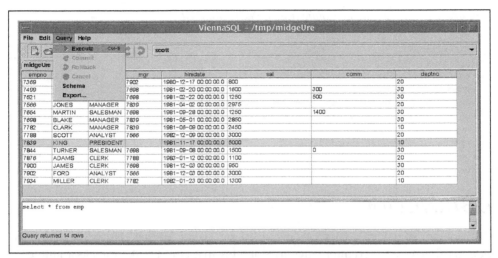

Figure 8-7. SQL execution under ViennaSQL

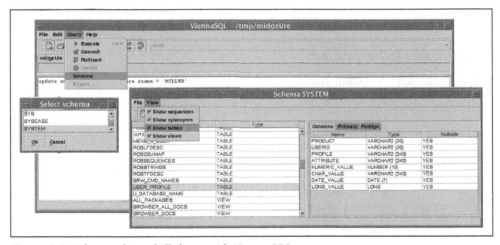

Figure 8-8. Schema object drill-down with ViennaSQL

Example 8-1. The vienna.xml Configuration File

```xml
<vienna>
  <options>
    <savepassword>true</savepassword>
    <maxrows>500</maxrows>
    <tablefont>
      <family>dialog</family>
      <style>plain</style>
      <size>12</size>
    </tablefont>
    <textfont>
      <family>monospaced</family>
      <style>plain</style>
```

Example 8-1. The vienna.xml Configuration File (continued)

```
      <size>14</size>
    </textfont>
  </options>
  <connection>
    <name>scott</name>
    <url>jdbc:oracle:thin:@localhost:1521:ORCL</url>
    <driver>oracle.jdbc.driver.OracleDriver</driver>
    <username>scott</username>
    <password>tiger</password>
  </connection>
</vienna>
```

DBInspector

DBInspector is a Java GUI tool developed by David Moffett. He wanted to provide another Java-based alternative to SQL*Plus that could make Oracle a little easier to use. The main web site for DBInspector is:

http://dbinspector.com

Installing DBInspector

Follow these steps to install DBInspector:

1. Download DBInspector from the web site just listed.

2. Unpack the tarball, for example (under Unix):

   ```
   $ tar xvf dbi.93.tar
   ```

3. Once this is done, running the main program is a straightforward step. Simply add the resultant *dbi.jar* file to your CLASSPATH, as well as the standard file that stores your Oracle JDBC drivers.

4. Execute something similar to the following step (under Win32):

   ```
   > java -classpath C:\dbi.jar;C:\classes12.zip dbi.ui.DBInspector
   ```

   A screen similar to the one in the center of Figure 8-9 should then appear. Note, however, that there is no preexisting database entry. We'll add our first entry in the next section.

Using DBInspector

Configuring and using DBInspector is a straightforward operation:

1. When the first main screen appears, click on the *Add* button. This will bring up the screen shown on the left in Figure 8-9.

2. Add your target JDBC connection information and press *Save*.

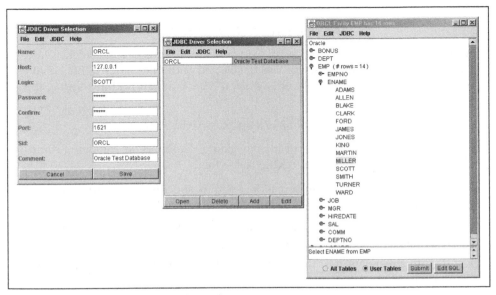

Figure 8-9. DBInspector probing the evidence

3. You should now see the main screen again, this time with your newly entered database available as a target. Select this and press *Open*. The SQL drill-down screen should then appear (see the screen on the right in Figure 8-9), giving you access to your target database.

Although this project was still very much in a beta-development stage when we downloaded it, David told us that DBInspector would soon move out of this stage to become a fully active open source project.

DB Prism

Now we're going to move away from Java GUIs and into the realm of one of the most astonishing success stories of Java, Oracle, and open source cooperation. This is DB Prism, created by Marcelo F. Ochoa. DB Prism was originally built on Version 3.0 of an earlier product, OWSKiller, itself created by Martin Kuzela. Marcelo took this project over and changed its name (partially in response to a suggestion from Steve Muench of Oracle Corporation). The application has since gone from strength to strength, riding on the Apache JServ web server system (before *i*AS itself got there).

DB Prism is an open source framework designed to generate dynamic XML from an Oracle database (other databases are expected to be supported in the future). The DB Prism servlet engine works in two different modes: it can be run as a standalone servlet, or it can be plugged into the Cocoon publishing framework. When

---

Java Database Explorer

Another Java GUI tool you may want to investigate is Bernard Van Haecke's Java Database Explorer. This program was developed under the older JDBC 1.1 API (which is currently heading towards Version 3.0). You can find this tool at the following web site:

> *http://www.geocities.com/RodeoDrive/1620/jexplorer.html*

Java Database Explorer is a tool for navigating databases. It runs as a stand-alone application and lets you do the following:

- Display various DBMS information, such as specifications and supported features

- Drill down and explore most types of database objects, including catalogs, tables, and stored procedures

- Investigate relational information, including primary, imported, and exported keys for all tables

Java Database Explorer also provides an interactive SQL query and update tool that displays its SQL results in tabular formatted output.

---

used with Cocoon, DB Prism provides a new way to make Internet applications work with technologies like XML and XSLT.

DB Prism can also be used both to emulate the old Oracle Web Application Server PL/SQL cartridge, and to work with the latest Oracle *i*AS products, in conjunction with the *mod_plsql* Apache module (which extends Apache to handle PL/SQL web content).

DB Prism is also a fully open source project, with Apache style licensing. You can use it to drive web output via either Oracle PL/SQL or Oracle8*i* Java stored procedures. The most exciting avenue for DB Prism is perhaps the Oracle database support it provides for the emerging XML-based Cocoon CMS (Content Management System). We'll describe Cocoon, a very exciting open source project from the Java Apache Project, later in this section. Look for this 100% Java project to ultimately change the way that XML content is managed and displayed over the Web.

DB Prism is a triumph. It is, however, a fairly complicated triumph, because it relies necessarily upon so many different elements. In this chapter, we'll try to provide an outline of how to hook up those elements. Fortunately, we installed the difficult parts in the last chapter: the Java JDK and JSDK modules and the Apache JServ web server. What remains here is to set up the correct environment and install DB Prism itself.

You can find out much more about DB Prism and related software from the following web sites:

http://www.plenix.com/dbprism/doc/Home.html
> The main DB Prism home page.

http://xml.apache.org/cocoon/
> The main Cocoon web page.

http://www.total-knowledge.com/downloads/mod_plsql/
> The *mod_plsql* download page.

http://jakarta.apache.org/tomcat/
> The home page for Tomcat, which is described in Chapter 7. Version 1.1.1 of DB Prism will make much more use of Tomcat, as the switch from Apache JServ accelerates.

Installing DB Prism

The DB Prism site itself provides excellent documentation covering all its application areas, which extend well beyond the Oracle database. We'll concentrate on one of its main areas of most relevance to Oracle developers, the emulation of the PL/SQL cartridge in use with the older OWS/OWAS products and the more recent *i*AS. Once we've got this running, we'll then tackle Cocoon integration.

DB Prism is itself undergoing rapid advancement. Version 2.0 is expected to take much larger steps towards taking full advantage of Cocoon; this version will also greatly enhance the use of the Tomcat Java web server technology, following from its DB Prism 1.1.1 introduction, as we mentioned previously, in order to supplement JServ. For up-to-date information on all these exciting projects, we recommend that you check out the main DB Prism web site at regular intervals.

Required HTP, HTF, and OWA packages

Before you can run DB Prism with Oracle PL/SQL, your target database schema needs to have access to the Oracle HTML Toolkit Procedures, including the HTP, HTF, and OWA packages. Those packages usually come with OWS, OWAS, and *i*AS installations, so you may already have them installed in your Oracle database for use with current PL/SQL web content production. If they are not already installed, you need to install them in order for DB Prism to be able to run Oracle PL/SQL web programs. For installation details, refer to the online documentation at *http://technet.oracle.com*.

Version 8.1.7 of the Oracle database should have these HTP packages already preinstalled under the SYS user. In our example, however, we'll use an Oracle 8.1.5

database in order to show that it's possible to use DB Prism with slightly older databases.

Installing DB Prism on Unix

As we said earlier, we've already carried out the most difficult part of getting DB Prism running on Apache JServ. This section describes the installation of DB Prism itself on top of JServ on Unix systems. For Windows, the installation is almost identical except for the differing full file path names:

1. Assuming you have already installed the necessary, interrelated HTP packages, download the latest version of DB Prism. As well as the all-important *Prism.jar* file, all the *.java* source code files are downloaded too. Once you have upacked the download, you can find these under *../src/com/prism*, with the important Oracle classes under *../src/com/prism/oracle*. We downloaded DB Prism 1.1.0 and unpacked it to form the */home/oos/apache/prism* base directory (following on from our Unix Apache JServ install in the last chapter).

2. Shut down Apache JServ if it is currently running:

   ```
   $ apachectl stop
   ```

3. Make sure that the following lines exist in the */home/oos/apache/conf/jserv. conf* file, both to pick up *jserv.properties* later and to set up our servlet zones, which we'll be using to drive our PL/SQL programs:

   ```
   ApJServProperties /home/oos/apache/conf/jserv.properties
   ApJServMount /servlets /root
   ApJServMount /servlet /root
   ```

4. Similarly, ensure that the root zone itself is covered in *jserv.properties*, with its own properties file pointer:

   ```
   zones=root
   root.properties=/home/oos/apache/conf/root.properties
   ```

5. In *jserv.properties*, you also need to ensure that the new *Prism.jar* servlets file is properly accessed by CLASSPATH, to get hold of the main *ServletWrapper. class* embedded file later (that program encapsulates our PL/SQL):

   ```
   wrapper.classpath=/home/oos/apache/prism/bin/Prism.jar
   ```

6. Next, we move on to the *root.properties* file, which we've just pointed to. Create this by copying it from a default *servlets.properties* file (or the *example. properties* file from the last chapter), and then make sure that the following line occurs somewhere within it:

   ```
   servlet.plsql.code=com.prism.ServletWrapper
   ```

   This will wrap up the intended database PL/SQL output within the *ServletWrapper.class* file (which resides in *Prism.jar*).

7. Also, point to another file, which we're just about to create. The *prism. properties* entry will shortly hold the PL/SQL DADs (Database Access

Descriptors). These are the sets of configured information used to direct DB Prism to the correct schema of a target database:

```
servlet.plsql.initArgs=properties=/home/oos/apache/conf/prism.properties
```

8. Copy a default *prism.properties* file from the DB Prism install directories. This creates your new *prism.properties* file in your own local Apache JServ setup:

```
$ cd /homs/oos
$ cp apache/prism/conf/prism.properties apache/conf/prism.properties
```

9. Edit this new *prism.properties* file, first setting three highly important global variables, as we'll describe below.

First, any Java error reporting should go to yourself, rather than to Marcelo Ochoa (this gets you extra bonus points, especially, we suspect, from Marcelo Ochoa):

```
global.webmaster=my_name@my_corp.com
```

Second, set the *global.behavior* variable to zero:

```
global.behavior=0
```

Later on, if you should experience connection problems with your PL/SQL DADs, you may want to change *global.behavior* to either 1 or 2. This makes DB Prism parse your web addresses slightly differently and look for different DADs as a result. For example, with a web address of *../servlet/plsql/ myprocedure* and a *global.behavior* setting of 1, DB Prism may extract a connection descriptor of "servlet", which then returns a database connection error (because we won't be creating a DAD for it). On the other hand, with a *global.behavior* value of 0, parsing the same web address can return a connection descriptor of "plsql", which is exactly what we *are* after. Different systems will vary in their response to this flag, so just try the full range of the three variable values (0, 1, or 2), until one of them works out for you.

Third, set *global.alias* to point DB Prism at the soon-to-be-created "plsql" DAD values:

```
global.alias=plsql
```

10. Having created the "plsql" alias listing, we now need to fill in the actual DAD database details for it. The following paired value sets, aimed at our usual target database, worked for us:

```
plsql.dbusername=scott
plsql.dbpassword=tiger
plsql.connectString=jdbc:oracle:thin:@localhost:1521:ORCL
plsql.errorLevel=2
plsql.errorPage=http://localhost:8080/error.html
plsql.toolkit=4x
plsql.compat=8i
plsql.producerarg=pass
plsql.dbcharset=8859_1
plsql.clientcharset=8859_1
```

We note the most important of these here:

— The *plsql.connectString* is our familiar JDBC URL.

— The *plsql.errorPage* setting is the location where DB Prism will return any errors, either from the servlets or from the database itself. Getting this information back is an invaluable aid in configuring DB Prism correctly.

— Our PL/SQL toolkit was OWAS Version 4. The other main OWS alternative for *plsql.toolkit* is "3x".

— The *plsql.compat* is important. This can be either "7x" or "8i". Again, the *prism.properties* comments will help clarify this, but basically, if your target is not an Oracle8*i* database, use "7x".

— On every other *plsql.** value, we either accepted the defaults or left the values commented out, as in the original file.

11. Finally, start up Apache JServ again:

```
$ apachectl start
```

Using DB Prism

DB Prism should now be fully up, running, and ready to respond to your PL/SQL requests. To test this, either run one of the current PL/SQL web packages from within your target database, or compile Example 8-2 within your target schema. (Note the use of the HTP package in this example.)

Example 8-2. The HelloDBPrism.sql Procedure

```
create or replace procedure HelloDBPrism as
   cursor emp_c is
      select a.ename,
             a.job,
             a.sal,
             b.dname
      from emp a, dept b
      where a.deptno = b.deptno
      order by a.ename;
   emp_r emp_c%ROWTYPE;
begin
   htp.p('<html><head><title>');
   htp.p('DB Prism, Oracle and Open Source PL/SQL Web Server');
   htp.p('</title></head><body><center>');
   htp.p('<h1>Hello DB Prism!</h1>');
   htp.p('<hr>');

   htp.p('<table border="1" frame="box"><tr>');
   htp.p('<th>Name</th><th>Job</th>');
   htp.p('<th>Salary</th><th>Department</th>');
   htp.p('</tr>');
```

Example 8-2. The HelloDBPrism.sql Procedure (continued)

```
   open emp_c;
   loop
      fetch emp_c into emp_r;
      exit when emp_c%NOTFOUND;

      htp.p('<tr>');
      htp.p('<td>'||emp_r.ename||'</td>');
      htp.p('<td>'||emp_r.job||'</td>');
      htp.p('<td align="right">'||emp_r.sal||'</td>');
      htp.p('<td>'||emp_r.dname||'</td>');
      htp.p('</tr>');

   end loop;
   close emp_c;

   htp.p('</table><hr></center></body>');
end;
/
```

This test procedure creates a simple HTML table filled with selected employee information from the SCOTT/TIGER schema. Once *HelloDBPrism.sql* is compiled into your schema, you can call it with the following web address:

http://localhost:8080/servlet/plsql/hellodbprism

If you're going through a proxy server, you may have to switch this proxy service off, or alternatively use your network-aware host name to replace *localhost*. This should bring up a screen similar to the one displayed in Figure 8-10.

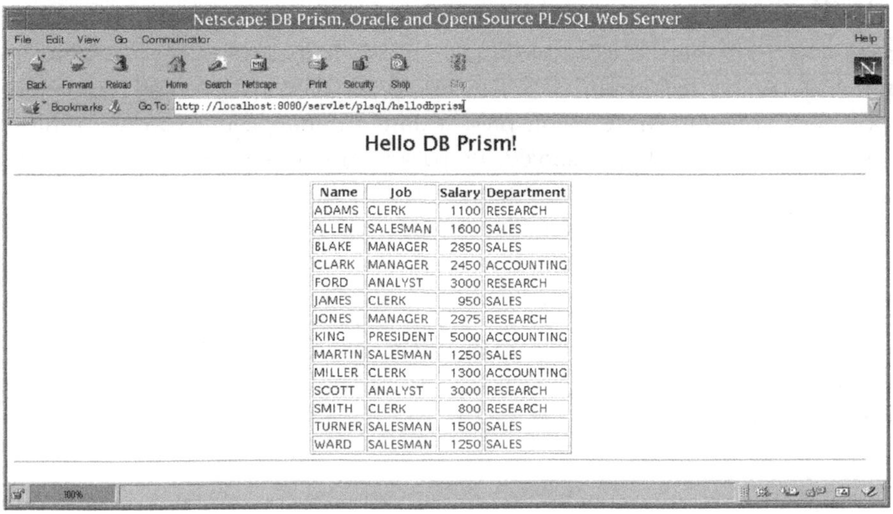

Figure 8-10. DB Prism directing PL/SQL to the Web

Oracle Adapters for DB Prism

The source code that arrives with DB Prism is the real treasure, carefully crafted according to a rigorous architectural concept. Some of the more important Java classes for use with Oracle are the "adapters" linking DB Prism's Java to the Oracle database. Standard Oracle adapters are the following:

DBConnPLSQL

Initially connects DB Prism to your schema-targeted PL/SQL and removes any database version dependency problems.

SPProcPLSQL

Gathers all the information relating to a particular stored procedure just before the required screen is generated. This is also where many of the *plsql.** variables covered previously become crucially important.

DBConnJava

Similar to DBConnPLSQL. Carries out a similar function for Java stored procedures.

The following are the Oracle8*i* adapters:

DB8iFactory

Supports Oracle8*i* PL/SQL objects.

DBConn8i

Deals with Oracle stored procedures within Oracle8*i.*

Cocoon

Cocoon is a 100% pure Java publishing framework that relies upon various new World Wide Web Consortium (W3C) technologies (e.g., DOM, XML, and XSL) to provide web content. The Cocoon project aims to change the way web information is created, rendered, and served. Its paradigm is based on the fact that document content, style, and logic are often created by different individuals or working groups. Cocoon aims for a complete separation of these three layers, to allow them to be independently designed, created, and managed. The goal of all this is to make the whole web content delivery process much easier to manage.

Cocoon can also be made to rely upon a database provider backbone driven by DB Prism. To demonstrate this, we'll install Cocoon over DB Prism to show you what it might be capable of.

Installing Cocoon

Download the latest Cocoon version from the Apache Software Foundation:

http://xml.apache.org/cocoon/index.html

We downloaded the following tarball into our local Apache install directory:

/home/oos/apache/Cocoon-1.8.2.tar.gz

Cocoon is quite a large download, because it contains many leading edge *.jar* and other related files from various XML/Java Apache projects. Once our own download had completed after a few minutes, we unpacked Cocoon within our Apache JServ development directory structure as follows:

```
$ cd /home/oos/apache
$ gzip -d Cocoon-1.8.2.tar.gz
$ tar xvf Cocoon-1.8.2.tar
$ cd cocoon-1.8.2
```

Configuring Cocoon

What follows is another rather complex configuration exercise, and another large step onward from our original Apache JServ installation. Although this process may seem complex, we think it's worth going through so you can appreciate what Cocoon is all about. Here goes:

1. First of all, shut down Apache JServ again:

    ```
    $ apachectl stop
    ```

2. In */home/oos/apache/conf/jserv.conf*, find the following line:

    ```
    #ApJServAction .xml /dev/org.apache.cocoon.Cocoon
    ```

    Add the following lines. These point Cocoon at the right web addresses, including its XSL content generation:

    ```
    Action cocoon /servlet/org.apache.cocoon.Cocoon
    AddHandler cocoon xml
    Alias /xsl/ /home/oos/apache/prism/xsl/
    ```

3. Edit the *jserv.properties* file, adding the following lines to CLASSPATH (watch out for version number changes between different versions of Cocoon, especially on *fop_0_15_0.jar*). Also make sure the Xerces *.jar* file comes before *cocoon.jar* (this works around certain DOM presentation-level problems caused by having these the wrong way around):

    ```
    wrapper.classpath=/home/oos/apache/cocoon-1.8.2/lib/xerces_1_2.jar
    wrapper.classpath=/home/oos/apache/cocoon-1.8.2/bin/cocoon.jar
    wrapper.classpath=/home/oos/apache/cocoon-1.8.2/lib/fop_0_15_0.jar
    wrapper.classpath=/home/oos/apache/cocoon-1.8.2/lib/xalan_1_2_D02.jar
    wrapper.classpath=/home/oos/apache/cocoon-1.8.2/lib/turbine-pool.jar
    ```

4. Next, edit */home/oos/apache/cocoon-1.8.2/conf/cocoon.properties* and add the following lines to link up Cocoon to its database content access via DB Prism (for this book, we've had to split the longer lines across two, but each should be specified on one long line):

    ```
    producer.type.db = com.prism.CocoonWrapper
    producer.db.properties = /home/oos/apache/conf/prism.properties
    ```

```
processor.type.http = com.prism.HeaderProcessor
formatter.type.application/vnd.ms-excel =
    org.apache.cocoon.formatter.TextFormatter
formatter.application/vnd.ms-excel.MIME-type = application/vnd.ms-excel
processor.xsp.logicsheet.connection.java =
    resource://com/prism/xsp/connection.xsl
```

5. Also change the following line:

```
producer.default = file
```

to:

```
producer.default = db
```

6. Now that we've altered *cocoon.properties*, we need to pick it up in the DB Prism/JServ system. Do this by editing */home/oos/apache/conf/root.properties*. Look for the following line:

```
#servlet.org.apache.cocoon.Cocoon.initArgs=properties=
    /usr/local/prism/conf/cocoon.properties
```

Replace this with:

```
servlet.org.apache.cocoon.Cocoon.initArgs=properties=
    /home/oos/apache/cocoon-1.8.2/conf/cocoon.properties
```

7. Also in this *root.properties* file, find the line:

```
servlet.plsql.code=com.prism.ServletWrapper
```

Beneath this, to run the DB Prism XML demos later, add the following:

```
servlet.demo.code=com.prism.ServletWrapper
servlet.xml.code=org.apache.cocoon.Cocoon
servlet.xmld.code=org.apache.cocoon.Cocoon
```

8. Also look for the line we added earlier in the basic DB Prism install:

```
servlet.plsql.initArgs=properties=
    /home/oos/apache/conf/prism.properties
```

Beneath this, add the following lines:

```
servlet.demo.initArgs=properties=/home/oos/apache/conf/prism.properties
servlet.xml.initArgs=properties=
    /home/oos/apache/cocoon-1.8.2/conf/cocoon.properties
servlet.xmld.initArgs=properties=
    /home/oos/apache/cocoon-1.8.2/conf/cocoon.properties
```

9. We now need to move on to the *prism.properties* file and add some new DADs. First, update the *global.alias* value from:

```
global.alias=plsql
```

to:

```
global.alias=plsql demo xml xmld org.apache.cocoon.Cocoon
```

10. Once this is done, add in the new DADs. The following are the lines we used; they are essentially copies of the "plsql" DAD set up earlier, with one or two

slight amendments (you'll find most of these already preset, except for the JDBC URLs):

```
#DAD demo
demo.dbusername=scott
demo.dbpassword=tiger
demo.connectString=jdbc:oracle:thin:@localhost:1521:ORCL
demo.errorLevel=2
demo.errorPage=http://localhost:8080/error.html
demo.compat=8i
demo.toolkit=4x
demo.producerarg=pass
demo.StateLess=false

#DAD xml
xml.dbusername=scott
xml.dbpassword=tiger
xml.connectString=jdbc:oracle:thin:@localhost:1521:ORCL
xml.errorLevel=2
xml.errorPage=http://localhost:8080/error.html
xml.compat=8i
xml.toolkit=4x
xml.producerarg=ignore

#DAD xmld, use with demos to show dynamic login
xmld.connectString=jdbc:oracle:thin:@localhost:1521:ORCL
xmld.errorLevel=2
xmld.errorPage=http://localhost:8080/error.html
xmld.compat=8i
xmld.producerarg=ignore
xmld.toolkit=4x
```

11. Getting away from JServ configuration for a short while, edit the */home/oos/apache/prism/plsql/demo.sql* program, making sure that the final few lines contain the URL you require. In our case, this is:

```
BEGIN
    -- where can I find xml stylesheets
    url_server := 'http://localhost:8080';
END demo;
```

You may also want to alter the modifiable *authorize()* function to be something simpler, like this:

```
function authorize return boolean is
begin
    return true;
end;
```

You can modify this to something more rigorous when you move into production.

12. We now need to add some new tables under the SCOTT/TIGER schema. If you can't find the Oracle Corporation *summit2.sql* demo script under your

own Oracle OWAS/*i*AS distribution, get hold of a similar SQL script from the following site:

> *http://www.telecomrg.com/darylcollins/prism/*

13. Download this *SUMMIT2.SQL* file to provide the database object and insert statements required by a DB Prism demonstration later. Once you've checked that the SQL in this file is acceptable, install *summit2.sql* (or *SUMMIT2.SQL*) onto the SCOTT/TIGER schema.

14. Now we run an *xtp.sql* SQL file, also provided by DB Prism within its *../prism/ plsql* directory. This installs the XML procedures required by DB Prism. This is followed, in turn, by *demo.sql* (recently altered), which makes immediate use of the XTP calls provided by *xtp.sql*:*

    ```
    SQL> @xtp
    Installing DB Prism Xml Toolkit Procedures (xtp)
    Package created.
    Package created.
    Package body created.
    Package body created.
    SQL> @demo
    Installing DB Prism Xml Demos
    Package created.
    Package body created.
    SQL>
    ```

15. The penultimate step is to fire up Apache JServ (the ultimate step is to enjoy a well-deserved drink!):

    ```
    $ apachectl start
    ```

Testing Cocoon

The first thing you'll want to do is make sure Cocoon is up and running. To do this, simply enter the following address into your browser:

> *http://localhost:8080/Cocoon.xml*

A screen similar to Figure 8-11 should appear.

Demonstrating Cocoon and DB Prism

Now we get to the money (and as Woody Allen said, money is good, if only for financial reasons). Let's run the demo thoughtfully provided by Marcelo Ochoa. To do this, enter the following address into your browser:

> *http://localhost:8080/servlets/demo/demo.startup*

---

* An alternative file, *xtp_public.sql*, is supplied; it installs the XTP calls under a user such as SYS and then makes these accessible to all via public synonyms. See the DB Prism downloaded installation instructions for more details on this approach.

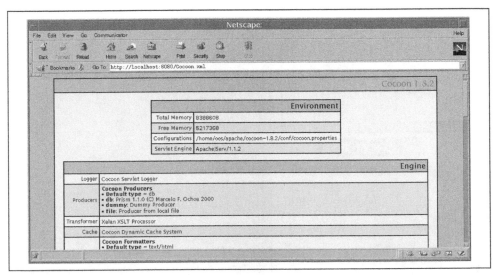

Figure 8-11. Checking that Cocoon is running properly

This should provide a range of example items. You can check this menu out in Figure 8-12. We've also shown some of the available drill-downs in Figure 8-13; these are generated directly from the target Oracle database.

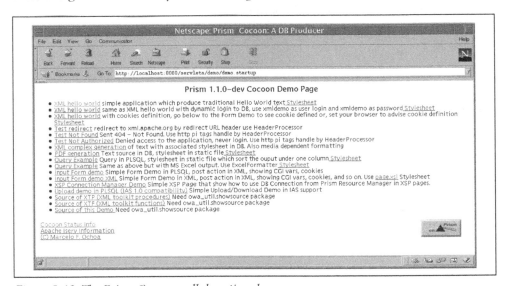

Figure 8-12. The Prism-Cocoon collaboration demo

We hope this coverage of DB Prism has whetted your appetite for more. DB Prism is heading towards the eagerly awaited 2.0 version and is definitely an application worth watching. In linked combination with something like the J2EE Enterprise

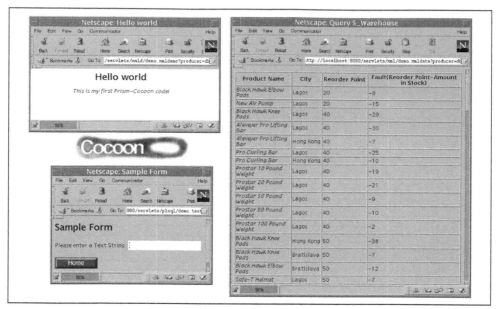

Figure 8-13. Just some of the Prism-Cocoon demo examples

Java Beans (EJB) server framework, provided by the open source JBoss project (*http://www.jboss.org*), it could help supply all your future Enterprise Java Oracle requirements.

9

GNOME and GTK+

When the Linux operating system exploded on the open source landscape, it was greeted with great enthusiasm. But Unix users, however much they loved the Linux command line, with its power, simplicity, speed, and elegance, still longed for a graphical user interface with which they could run all their other software: WYSIWYG word processors, load monitors, notepads, browsers, and image editors. For a long time, the only option on any free Unix system was the X Windows System, with its myriad of window managers (e.g., *twm*, *fvwm*, etc.). Enter GNOME.

The GNOME project is a Linux-based effort to build the world's best desktop environment, one that combines the power and functionality of Unix-like systems with the visual elegance of Macintosh and Windows-type desktops. Not only did the GNOME developers set out to build a better-looking desktop environment, they also wanted to create a framework for easily building applications—applications whose GUIs would share a common, flexible look and feel, and whose activities would be integrated with other desktop operations. With the advent of GNOME, Oracle on Linux, which has in recent years become an important platform for database backend solutions, is now becoming a viable desktop solution as well. As the benefits of Linux become more widely appreciated, we anticipate that Linux could eventually become the platform of choice for many of the world's developers and global software corporations. In fact, Sun Microsystems has already announced that they'll be retiring CDE (the Common Desktop Environment) and replacing it with a version of GNOME, which complements the growing use of Linux on SPARC chips.

This chapter introduces the GNOME Project and some of its most interesting components. Because our focus in this book is on building Oracle applications, we'll spend most of our time looking at GTK+, GNOME's graphical toolkit, which underlies such applications. In Chapter 10, *Building Oracle Applications with*

GNOME and GTK+, you'll read about some of the excellent Oracle applications developed using GTK+. We'll start here with a look back at the origins of the windowing technologies that inspired GNOME and GTK+. Then we'll look briefly at GTK+'s capabilities and at the use and programming of GTK+ applications.

Why GNOME and Not KDE?

Although similar in appearance, the GNOME and KDE (Kool Desktop Environment, *http://www.kde.org*) projects are not interchangeable. GNOME uses the GTK+ library to draw all of its windowing elements; that library is licensed under the GNU LGPL (Lesser General Public License) label. Although the GNU Project prefers that you use the full GNU GPL, you can use the LGPL to develop commercial solutions freely, from those libraries covered by this license. Chapter 1, *Oracle Meets Open Source*, introduces the GNU Project and its licenses. You can read more about the LGPL license at this site:

>   *http://www.gnu.org/copyleft/lesser.html*

The KDE alternative uses the Qt library from Troll Tech for its windowing elements. This library comes under the commercial QPL license, which contains certain prohibitions on commercial usage. Read about this license at this site:

>   *http://www.trolltech.com/products/download/freelicense/license.html*

If you want to develop commercial solutions using Qt (and ultimately KDE), you have to pay to use the professional license:

>   *http://www.trolltech.com/products/purchase/pricing.html*

Because of the financial restrictions on KDE, we recommend that you do your Linux GUI development using the GNOME environment to avoid licensing issues. GNOME has other advantages as well, including the fact that Solaris has adopted it as its main windowing environment, that GNOME has been ported to Win32, and that the whole tide of Linux development seems to be moving GNOME's way. In the end, GNOME could become the single windowing environment we've all been looking for.

Windowing Foundations

Even in today's brave new world of the Internet, graphical user interfaces (GUIs) are still the front ends to most of the world's desktop applications. The GUI model is a vastly different model from the web-based model. Web-based interfaces, such as the ones we described in Chapter 5, *Web Technologies*, and Chapter 6, *Building Web-Based Oracle Applications*, require a browser, a reliable network, a web server, and a number of other components to work effectively. GUI-based interfaces, on the other hand, provide a much simpler mechanism (at least when they're implemented correctly) for allowing the end user to interact with your application and do useful work, even if it's done only on a single, isolated machine.

The typical GUI builds on a number of components that are invisible to the end user, but that the programmer needs to be aware of. These components are available in different forms on different types of platforms. In the Macintosh world, for example, the lowest level is the *toolbox*, a set of routines that Apple has designed, developed, and burned into its ROM chips. The toolbox is essentially a low-level library that presents a consistent interface across all Macintosh applications. At the top level, programmers often work with various object-oriented class libraries (generally in C++) or with other wrappers that provide an object-oriented interface to that low-level library.

In the world of Unix, the X Windows System is the main graphically oriented interface. X Windows has been around for more than 15 years, fighting off its commercial challengers to become a ubiquitous graphical solution for Unix.[*] X Windows grew up at the Massachusetts Institute of Technology[†] as part of Project Athena. The original purpose of Project Athena, formed in 1984, was to take all the different and incompatible graphical workstations then available on the market and develop a system that would allow users to display their applications (either locally or remotely) on any one of these workstations and use either local or remote resources. In essence, the developers at Project Athena sought to create a windowing environment that was independent of vendors and hardware. (At the time, the arguments for such an environment were similar to those for products like Java Swing today.)

These days, X Windows is best known for its connections with the various Unix workstations and Linux, but the X Windows project also spawned a wide variety of excellent graphical libraries:

Xt
> The X Toolkit, the low-level graphics library for the X Windows System. Xt is the library around which GTK+ was built.

Motif
> Like GTK+, a wrapper built around the X Toolkit. Motif was a product of the Open Software Foundation, a consortium of companies including DEC, HP, and IBM.

---

[*] The main challenger to the X Windows System was Sun Laboratories' proprietary NeWS (Network Extensible Window System). James Gosling, who later led the development of Java, was one of the major movers behind NeWS. By all accounts superior to X Windows, NeWS never took off because it remained closed, whereas X Windows was spectacularly open. This lesson has not been lost on Sun, which subsequently made Java far more open (and thus far more successful) than it might otherwise have been.

[†] For specific X Windows information for GNOME systems, from MIT, see *http://www.gnu.ai.mit.edu/directory/X.html*. For more general information about MIT, check out *http://web.mit.edu*.

OpenLook

> Another wrapper built around the X Toolkit. OpenLook was a product of Sun and AT&T.

Athena

> The original testing library for the X Toolkit. Athena is available on most X Windows systems.

Tk

> The graphics toolkit first developed for use with the Tcl scripting language (described in Chapter 3, *Tcl, Perl, and Python*); Tk now works with Perl and Python as well and is the heart of modern-day scripted GUI solutions.

These toolkits, often called *widget sets*, are libraries of routines that you can call to perform various types of graphical functions—for example, to create scroll bars, radio buttons, check boxes, pop-up menus, scrolling listboxes, and all the other familiar graphical items that work together to create a friendly user interface.

You can learn much more about the X Windows System and its history at this site:

> *http://www.x.org*

The GNOME Project

The GNOME (GNU* Network Object Model Environment) open source project is a highly ambitious project that owes much to the legacy of the X Windows System. GNOME started exclusively as a Linux project, but, as we'll describe later in this chapter, ports are underway for other operating systems. The purpose of GNOME is twofold:

- To build a completely free, easy to use, graphical desktop for end users (along the lines of the Macintosh and Windows models)

- At the same time, to build a powerful GUI application framework for those on the development side who are building desktop applications

Some people think of GNOME as being simply a window manager. But the GNOME Project is really a whole group of projects under one vast umbrella, including many sophisticated and technically interesting projects that make extensive use of XML. GNOME started up as a discrete project around 1997, with an initial call for participation by Miguel de Icaza. Since then, many excellent developers have joined forces under the GNOME umbrella.

The GNOME development framework focuses on GTK+ (the GIMP Toolkit) and GDK (the GIMP Drawing Kit); we'll describe these in the following sections. Many

---

* GNU, of course, stands recursively for "Gnu's Not Unix," but you knew that already from Chapter 1!

applications have already been developed for GNOME, including an image-manipulation tool, an image viewer, a word processor, various types of audio players, and various database applications. For information about these database applications—in particular, the excellent Orasoft applications suite—see Chapter 10.

GNOME

As we mentioned, GNOME is a window manager, but it's also an entire framework within which you can build your own GUI applications. GNOME uses an object model based on CORBA (Common Object Request Broker Architecture) that allows distributed objects to communicate with one another. This capability allows GNOME to integrate its applications with the desktop and synchronize their activities in some very sophisticated ways.

GNOME's capabilities include the following:

GNOME Desktop

The desktop provides various control panels, including the control center shown in Figure 9-1 and the desktop itself, which offers drag-and-drop functionality, support for icons, copy and paste between applications, and more.

Standard look-and-feel

This is implemented via themes, providing commonality across applications with a consistent set of buttons, menus, and various other design elements. GNOME's standard look-and-feel also means that you can build applications that have common menus for consistency across applications, something Mac users are familiar with.

Multi-language support

Applications using GNOME can be written with different language bindings.

Robust session management

This feature allows the state of desktop applications to be saved and restored.

The main web site for GNOME is:

http://www.gnome.org

GTK+

GTK+ is the main widget library for GNOME, and it's the heart of the GNOME application development framework. GTK stands for the GIMP (GNU Image Manipulation Program) Toolkit. The original toolkit, GTK, got its name because it was developed as a widget toolkit for the GIMP project (described in the next section). Peter Mattis and Spencer Kimball, who also developed GIMP, developed the original version of GTK. Josh McDonald developed a newer version, which was

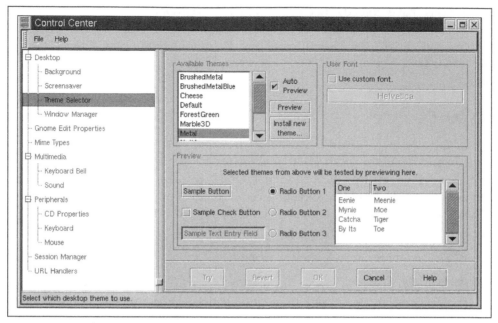

Figure 9-1. Displaying the GNOME Control Center

dubbed GTK+ to distinguish it from the earlier version. Although developed originally for use with GIMP, GTK+ is now used by many different types of applications, including the Oracle applications described in Chapter 10.

For information on GTK+, see the following sites:

http://www.gtk.org
> The main web site for GTK+

ftp://ftp.gtk.org/pub/gtk/
> The GTK+ tutorial, which provides a step-by-step tour of GTK+ with an intro-
> duction to widgets, datatypes, signal handlers, and more

http://www.gtk.org/tutorial/
> The main download site for GTK+

GIMP

The GIMP is a GTK+-based application that was developed by Peter Mattis and
Spencer Kimball (the original authors of GTK+). The GIMP is mainly an image
manipulation program, although its many plug-ins allow it to perform a wide variety of functions, such as photo retouching, image composition, and image authoring. The goal of the GIMP project is to develop an open source alternative to
Adobe's commercial Photoshop product. Figure 9-2 shows the GIMP's welcome
screen.

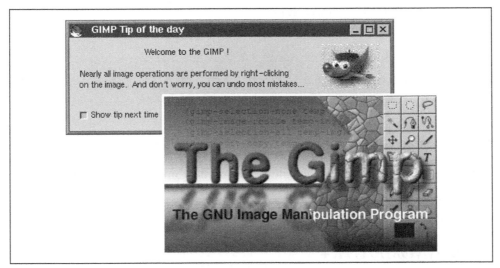

Figure 9-2. The GIMP's welcome screen

For more information on the GIMP, see the following sites:

http://www.gimp.org
    The main web site for the GIMP

http://www.gimp.org/download.html
    The main download site for the GIMP

http://manual.gimp.org
http://gimp-savvy.com/BOOK/index.html
    Online access to a comprehensive GIMP tutorial and to another popular alternative

http://www.adobe.com/products/photoshop/main.html
    For more information on Photoshop, which the GIMP seeks to supplant

Installing Gnome/GTK+

If you're running on a system without GNOME already installed, you'll need to get a copy. The recommended, and by far the simplest and quickest, way to get up and running is to install from binaries. If you're running any of the systems listed here, you can find precompiled binaries at this site:

http://www.ximian.com/desktop/download.php3

Follow the specific directions for your platform:

- Solaris 2.7 on UltraSparc
- LinuxPPC 2000

- Debian GNU/Linux 2.3 (Woody)

- TurboLinux 6.0

- Yellow Dog Linux Champion Server 1.2

- RedHat Linux 6.0, 6.1, or 6.2

- SuSE Linux 6.3 or 6.4

- Linux Mandrake 6.1, 7.0, or 7.1

- Caldera OpenLinux eDesktop 2.4

The more ambitious can certainly choose to install from source; the GNOME web site has a page designed just for you. Find out all about installing from source at:

   http://www.gnome.org/start/source.html

Using GNOME/GTK+

You can use the extensive set of widgets available in the GTK+ library when you build GNOME GUI applications. If you write a program using GTK+, it will have the consistent look and feel of all GNOME applications; for example, your buttons, scroll bars, and pop-up menus will have a consistent, standard look. The GNOME Desktop itself was built using the GTK+ library, and through the GNOME Control Center shown earlier in Figure 9-1, you can set such properties as screensaver, background image, themes, desktop sound events, and URL handlers.

You don't even have to be limited by GNOME's standard look and feel. Take a look at the XMMS application in Figure 9-3. XMMS is an audio player that lets its users play CDs and MP3 files. As you can see, its Preferences dialog looks like fairly standard GTK+ widgets, but its main window is reminiscent of a Macintosh application.

GNOME and GTK+ also provide your applications with capabilities that extend beyond widgets. If you're using GNOME as your desktop environment, you'll be able to control all of your GNOME applications in quite remarkable ways. You'll be able to change the "theme" of your desktop and have all GNOME applications listen to those commands and respond accordingly. Figure 9-1 shows the "Theme Selector" option currently selected; that demonstrates a scrolling listbox, radio buttons, checkboxes, and so on.

GNOME does a fine job of synchronizing application activities and integrating them with desktop operations. For example, when you use GNOME as your window manager, your desktop applications will be able to respond to GNOME when you attempt to shut down your machine, log out, or restart your PC. Each application, in turn, will be sent a message to quit and take appropriate action. In some cases, your application will die gracefully; in other cases, the application will ask the user if it should save changes to a document. The point is that the window manager has knowledge of all your applications and can coordinate their activities.

 This behavior may not seem so impressive, but back before GNOME, window managers (whether *twm*, *fvwm*, or *mwm*) knew nothing of the programs that were running. Shutting down the X Windows System would simply pull the rug out from under a user's applications without prompting her to save changes, possibly causing the loss of data. So GNOME's behavior represents a significant leap in the direction of a consistent platform on which to develop coordinated applications.

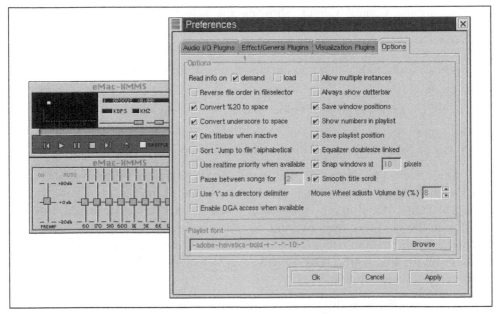

Figure 9-3. XMMS, showing a nonstandard GTK+ user interface

Figure 9-4 shows a snapshot of a Linux desktop running some of the great GTK+-based applications that are currently available. From the upper left corner, running roughly clockwise, you'll find these applications:

gkrellm
   A CPU, disk, and Ethernet monitoring tool that provides constant feedback about the performance of your machine

abiword
   A word-processing program capable of reading all your old Word documents (and you thought you were chained to Windows forever?)

everybuddy

AOL Instant Messenger, IRC, and Yahoo!, all rolled into one client

gzilla

A GTK+ and Gnome-compliant browser

gnumeric

A GTK+ and Gnome-compliant spreadsheet

Gnome Mines

You guessed it . . . the excellent game

xmms

An MP3, CD, and general audio player

gnomecc

The Gnome Control Center, showing the screen saver (see Figure 9-1 for more)

Electric Eyes

An image editor for when you fancy a change from the GIMP

Color Selector

Finally, an easy way to pick colors under Unix

File Manager

A way to list files, drag and drop to folders, and perform related functions

What more could you want? The free world of GNOME is evolving so rapidly that you'll soon have no excuses left for sticking with your Win32 PC. For now, you're limited to Linux, but in a very short time, you'll be in a far wider world, as we'll describe in the next few sections. And, as more applications are ported, and more commercial vendors start using GNOME and GTK+, support for these products will surely grow until GNOME/GTK+ is viewed as being a complete, stable, and high-performing desktop solution.

And, of course, if you're thinking of developing your own Oracle GTK+ applications, you have a chance to do so before the rest of the market catches on. You too could become part of this exponential growth. See the section titled "Programming with GTK+" later in this chapter, and see Chapter 10 for examples of the first generation of GTK+ applications for Oracle.

GTK+ on Windows

Despite its Linux roots, GTK+ is currently being ported to the Win32 platform. The project is spearheaded by Tor Lillqvist. Tor had trouble getting a Minolta Slide Scanner to work under Linux, so he decided that the solution was to port the GIMP to Windows. Before getting the GIMP to work, however, he had to move

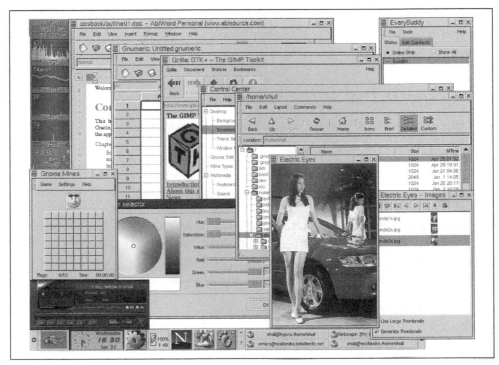

Figure 9-4. The world of GTK+ applications

the foundation—the GTK+ library—to Windows. Work on the port is proceeding well. To keep up with progress on the Windows port, check out this site:

http://user.sgic.fi/~tml/gimp/win32/

GTK+ on BeOS

As if a Windows port of GTK+ isn't exciting enough, the GTK+ folks are also tackling a port to the BeOS operating system.

BeOS is a very interesting operating system, especially appropriate for those doing broadband digital media work. If you are interested in storing audio and video files directly in an Oracle database and then pumping them out to the Internet, BeOS provides an excellent operating environment. Once the GTK+ port is ready for general release, you'll be able to take advantage of the various open source applications built on GTK+. We describe a number of these, including the excellent Orasoft suite of applications, in Chapter 10.

The BeOS project is apparently much further along than the Windows project, and the GTK+ port was in alpha release as we went to press. To find out more about the status of the GTK+ port for BeOS, check out this site:

http://www.gtk.org/beos/

For complete information about BeOS and to obtain a free download, go to the Be web site:

http://www.be.com

Programming with GTK+

Let's take an initial look inside a GTK+-based application. We recommend that you download and install GTK+ first so you can try this out. If you have a recent version of Linux, you may already have GTK+ installed.

Sample Program

In this section, we'll run through Example 9-1, a quick "Hello World" program that's a simple demonstration of a one-button window. When you click the button, "Hello World" is printed to your shell, and then the program exits. We've highlighted the program elements we'll describe later on.

Example 9-1. GTK+ helloworld.c

```
#include <gtk/gtk.h>

/* This is a callback function. The data arguments are ignored
 * in this example. More on callbacks below. */
void hello( GtkWidget *widget,
            gpointer   data )
{
    g_print ("Hello World\n");
}

gint delete_event( GtkWidget *widget,
                   GdkEvent  *event,
                   gpointer   data )
{
    /* If you return FALSE in the "delete_event" signal handler,
     * GTK will emit the "destroy" signal. Returning TRUE means
     * you don't want the window to be destroyed.
     * This is useful for popping up 'are you sure you want to quit?'
     * type dialogs. */

    g_print ("delete event occurred\n");

    /* Change TRUE to FALSE and the main window will be destroyed with
     * a "delete_event". */

    return(TRUE);
}

/* Another callback */
void destroy( GtkWidget *widget,
              gpointer   data )
```

Example 9-1. GTK+ helloworld.c (continued)

```c
{
    gtk_main_quit();
}

int main( int    argc,
          char *argv[] )
{
    /* GtkWidget is the storage type for widgets */
    GtkWidget *window;
    GtkWidget *button;

    /* This is called in all GTK applications. Arguments are parsed
     * from the command line and are returned to the application. */
    gtk_init(&argc, &argv);

    /* create a new window */
    window = gtk_window_new (GTK_WINDOW_TOPLEVEL);

    /* When the window is given the "delete_event" signal (this is given
     * by the window manager, usually by the "close" option, or on the
     * titlebar), we ask it to call the delete_event () function
     * as defined above. The data passed to the callback
     * function is NULL and is ignored in the callback function. */
    gtk_signal_connect (GTK_OBJECT (window), "delete_event",
                        GTK_SIGNAL_FUNC (delete_event), NULL);

    /* Here we connect the "destroy" event to a signal handler.
     * This event occurs when we call gtk_widget_destroy() on the window,
     * or if we return FALSE in the "delete_event" callback. */
    gtk_signal_connect (GTK_OBJECT (window), "destroy",
                        GTK_SIGNAL_FUNC (destroy), NULL);

    /* Creates a new button with the label "Hello World". */
    button = gtk_button_new_with_label ("Hello World");

    /* When the button receives the "clicked" signal, it will call the
     * function hello() passing it NULL as its argument.  The hello()
     * function is defined above. */
    gtk_signal_connect (GTK_OBJECT (button), "clicked",
                        GTK_SIGNAL_FUNC (hello), NULL);

    /* This will cause the window to be destroyed by calling
     * gtk_widget_destroy(window) when "clicked".  Again, the destroy
     * signal could come from here, or the window manager. */
    gtk_signal_connect_object (GTK_OBJECT (button), "clicked",
                               GTK_SIGNAL_FUNC (gtk_widget_destroy),
                               GTK_OBJECT (window));

    /* This packs the button into the window (a gtk container). */
    gtk_container_add (GTK_CONTAINER (window), button);

    /* The final step is to display this newly created widget. */
    gtk_widget_show (button);
```

Example 9-1. GTK+ helloworld.c (continued)

```
    /* and the window */
    gtk_widget_show (window);

    /* All GTK applications must have a gtk_main(). Control ends here
     * and waits for an event to occur (like a key press or
     * mouse event). */
    gtk_main ();

    return(0);
}
```

The example doesn't provide a sophisticated interface, but it does demonstrate the basic GTK+ concepts (events, callbacks, signals, and widgets) and a number of GTK+ datatypes; we'll touch on these in the following sections.

You can compile this program as follows:

```
$ gcc -Wall -g hello.c -o hello \
`gtk-config --cflags` `gtk-config --libs`
```

Then run it like this:

```
$ ./hello
```

Figure 9-5 demonstrates this program in action.

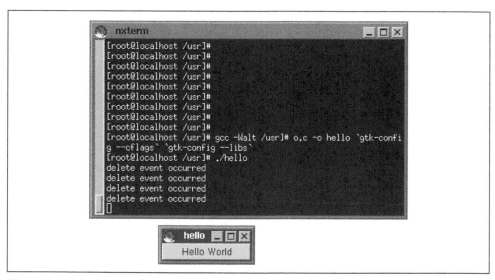

Figure 9-5. Running our first GTK+ program

Events

When you build a program with the GTK+ library, calling *gtk_main* is pretty much the last thing you do in your *main()* function, as you can see in Example 9-1. Your program will happily spin inside this routine loop until something happens.

What is that something? An event, of course. Clicking on a menu, button, or other control, or even dragging over some types of widgets, generates an event. Through the use and magic of signals and callbacks (described in the following sections), these events direct the flow of your program so it behaves the way you want it to.

Callbacks

Whenever an event occurs, GTK+ directs the program flow through a special callback routine. This callback routine encapsulates whatever special behavior should occur as a result of the given event. The program in Example 9-1 illustrates the use of callbacks—in this case, to override the functionality of the close box. Click on the X (or whatever the icon is in your window manager), and the "Hello World" program reports back, "delete event occurred." That's because the *delete_event* routine gets called in the place of the normal GTK+ behavior. The highlighted parts of the example show you this logic.

Signals

Signals are closely associated with the callback routine. A signal is a message that GTK+ generates as the result of an event. Different events generate different signals.

Widgets

Widgets are the good stuff. They're the visible things that make up your interface, objects like buttons, labels, and list items. Widgets also include objects for a window, the more generic containers (an abstraction), a widget that holds other widgets, and so on. The program in Example 9-1 demonstrates two simple widgets: a window widget and a button widget. We then do the following:

1. Place the button inside the window widget.

2. Attach the various callback routines.

3. Show the window.

4. Call *gtk_main*.

Classes

Every widget derives from the *GtkObject* class. Other top-level types just below that highest-level class are *GtkWidget*, *GtkData*, and *GtkItemFactory*. From this second level, most objects derive from *GtkWidget*. The types of *GtkWidget* objects fall into a usual handful of categories:

GtkMisc
GtkContainer
GtkCalendar
GtkDrawingArea

    GtkEditable
    GtkRuler
    GtkRange
    GtkSeparator
    GtkPreview
    GtkProgress

The hierarchy continues to many levels of depth, like a Tolkienesque mithril mine. Consult the GTK+ documentation for detailed information about this hierarchy and all the various objects in it.

Datatypes

When you write applications with GTK+, you'll find it helpful to use GTK+ pre-defined datatypes. One category of GTK+ datatypes (*gint*, *gchar*, and *gpointer*, for example) are essentially *typedefs* to C's corresponding datatypes. For example, the GTK+ *gint* datatype maps to the C *int* datatype, and the GTK+ *gchar* datatype maps to the C *char* datatype. Note that we used some of these datatypes in our "Hello World" program in Example 9-1.

Another category of predefined datatypes, including *guint8*, *guint16*, *guint32*, *guint64* (yes, really!) are integer datatypes with a guaranteed size, no matter what platform you're on, from a 32-bit x86 machine to an Alpha where an integer might be 64 bits. Whenever possible, you should stick with these predefined GTK+ datatypes.

Although GTK+ can sometimes be confusing, the nuts and bolts boil down to the basic concepts we've described here. Once you understand these concepts and the special properties of a program that executes in a framework like GTK+, you'll be well on your way to building a full-fledged desktop GUI for your application. Later, you can move on to plugging in Oracle-specific drop-downs, pop-ups, XML, and the rest.

User Interface Builders

A number of interface builders have been developed for GTK+. Designed for use by both novice and advanced GTK+ developers, these tools help jump-start your GTK+ applications. Using one of the following interface builders makes the first steps of putting together a GTK+ interface faster, easier, and more graphical. Most of the tools listed below work by generating a skeleton of code around the inter-face that you design graphically. The list of such tools is growing rapidly, but the following are the main tools available as we go to press:

http://glade.pn.org

    Glade, the GTK+ User Interface Builder, can generate code in such languages as C, C++, Ada95, Python, and Perl.

http://www.epita.fr/~theber_s/epingle/epingle.html

> Epingle sports yet another recursive name (EPIngle is Not GLadE) and supports various language bindings.

http://www.penguin.cz/~grad/

> GRAD (GTK+ Rapid Application Development) is being developed as a visual programming solution similar to Delphi or C++Builder.

http://www.guest.net/homepages/mmotta/VDKHome/vdkbuilder.html

> VDKBuilder is a RAD (Rapid Application Development) tool based around the VDK (Visual Development Kit) library, an object-oriented wrapper around GTK+.

We hear the most about Glade, and its development seems to be the furthest along, so we'll use it as our example.

Glade (as shown in Figure 9-6) allows you to create a construct, known as a *project*, that will, roughly speaking, become the GUI application you're building. The generic application it gives you has File, Edit, View, Settings, and Help menus, as well as *New, Open,* and *Save* buttons. Other than that, it's a blank slate. You're given a palette, and it's up to you to lay out your interface. Briefly, this is what you do:

1. Place various widgets down like cards on a table, lining up each control where you'd like it to be. The Properties panel allows you to customize the size and shape of the selected object, as well as some of the events it responds to, how it will respond to the resizing of its parent view, and so on. The Properties dialog is of utmost importance: the more functionality you can set up now, the less programming you'll have to do later.

2. Build your application code. The fun part is clicking the *Build* button. Given the layout you specified and the controls you created, Glade writes out some pretty slick skeleton code for you. By default, you'll find this in the */home/username/Projects/project1/* directory. Glade creates the real beginnings of your application, complete with empty *AUTHORS, NEWS,* and *README* files, as well as some semblance of an *autoconfig* file, and places the source code in the *src* directory. You can pick up the generated code there and use it as a foundation for building your application.

Glade is not limited to generating C code. You can also generate code in other languages: C++, Eiffel, Ada, and our old favorite, Perl. All this is done through the magic of XML. Under the hood, the Glade project file is just an XML file that allows you to define markup languages. In this case, the XML is used to generate code in the various programming languages. For example, you can generate Perl code by installing the *glade2perl* module.

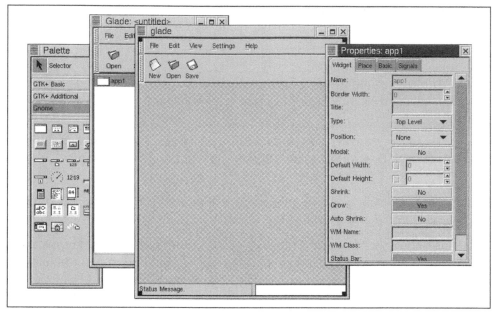

Figure 9-6. Glade in action

GTK+ Language Support

GTK+ itself is a C library, but it's not just for C programmers. There are now bindings available for many other popular programming languages. So, if your programming background doesn't include C (and if the very thought of linked lists makes you want to lie down in a dark room with an ice pack on your forehead), you're in luck—especially if you're an object-oriented C++ programmer of the Bjarne Stroustrup school. There are several object-oriented class libraries available, wrapped around the basic GTK+ library:

GTK--

Yet another wrapper (this time built around GTK+), GTK-- provides a more purely object-oriented approach to UI development.

> *http://gtkmm.sourceforge.net*

VDK

Another C++ class library. It works in conjunction with the code generator VDKBuilder (mentioned in the "Interface Builders" section).

> *http://www.guest.net/homepages/mmotta/VDKHome/vdkbuilder.html*

wxWindows

Yet another C++ library. WxWindows is is actually a wrapper for a couple of different libraries, including GTK+; it is intended to provide a common look and feel across all platforms, including Linux and Windows. You can also find bindings for Python. (We described this library briefly in our discussion of Python in Chapter 3.) There does not seem to be a home page for this project, but you can download it from the following site:

> *ftp://ftp.gtk.org/pub/gtk/python/*

GTK+/Perl

Let's not forget Perl. You can find bindings for Perl through the Perl/GTK+ project. Basically, the *gtkplusperl* package allows you to call all of the standard GTK+ routines from Perl. There doesn't seem to be a home page for this project either, but you can obtain the software from the following site:

> *http://www.rit.net/sporter/gtkplusperl/*

Note, however, that the main documents available there are from the standard GTK+ documentation library, because, as we said, *gtkplusperl* simply provides an interface for Perl programs calling the GTK+ library routines.

If those mainstream languages don't suit you, and you're looking for something a bit more exotic, check out these options:

Ada

Named after Ada Lovelace (who worked with Charles Babbage on the Difference Engine, the world's first computer), Ada is a programming language that not only provides object-oriented features, but also attempts to implement many other modern software engineering principles, including reliability, portability, modularity, and reusability.

> *http://gtkada.eu.org*

Dylan

Dylan is a new object-oriented language. It can be used as a rapid prototyping language or as a more efficient compiled language.

> *http://gwydiondylan.org/gui.phtml*

Eiffel

Dubbed "a software engineer's dream," Eiffel is a language whose purpose is, like other object-oriented languages, to reuse software. What makes it different is that it is more than just a language: it also includes a method and an environment in which to program.

> *http://www.netlabs.net/hp/richieb/gtk_eiffel.html*

Guile

Guile is actually an interpreter that works with code written in the Scheme programming language (Scheme is a Lisp-like programming language).

> *http://www.ping.de/sites/zagadka/guile-gtk/*

Haskell

Unlike C, C++, Java, and Pascal, which are known as imperative programming languages, Haskell is a purely functional programming language. More like Prolog from our days as computer science undergrads, Haskell doesn't require you to tell the computer what to do, but rather to describe the relationships, and build an expression to evaluate.

http://www.cse.unsw.edu.au/~chak/haskell/gtk/

Objective-C

Like a bridge between C and C++, Objective-C is an object-oriented language whose compiler is still friendly with C programs.

ftp://ftp.gtk.org/pub/gtk/objc-gtkkit/

Pascal

Here is one of our old favorites. Back in the Macintosh's early days, Pascal was the language of choice. It's a standard imperative programming language like C, but with stricter typing and some unfriendly ways of handling strings.

http://agnes.dida.physik.uni-essen.de/~gnu-pascal

Python

An imperative programming language, Python, like Perl, is able to provide rapid prototyping, but Python is a more serious language, offering object orientation and other features for large software projects. In Chapter 3, we discussed Python and its use in building Oracle applications.

http://www.daa.com.au/~james/pygtk/

10

Building Oracle Applications with GNOME and GTK+

Now that Oracle Corporation has ported Oracle to the Linux operating system, Linux is rapidly becoming an important platform for backend solutions employing Oracle databases. What's even more exciting is that Linux, coupled with the GNOME and GTK+ technologies we described in Chapter 9, *GNOME and GTK+*, has become a viable desktop solution, too. The number and quality of GTK+ applications is growing fast. Suddenly, the world of Linux-based Oracle applications is bursting at the seams. In this chapter, we'll cover what we consider to be the best database applications built on GNOME and GTK+:

Orasoft

A set of Oracle applications built on GTK+ that's intended to be an open source replacement for the commercial Oracle Enterprise Manager (OEM). This application suite provides a variety of database administration tools, including Object Manager (to browse database objects), SQLWork (to run SQL), Procedit (to edit PL/SQL), Session Monitor (to browse SQL execution by users), and Table Browser (to view tables and attributes).

GNOME-DB

A framework for building GTK+ database applications. The GNOME-DB distribution also includes plug-ins to different databases (including Oracle) and sample applications that provide excellent examples of how to build your own database applications.

gASQL

A tool that shows graphically an entity relationship diagram (ERD) of the tables in a database (Oracle and others are supported). gASQL gives you an easy view of tables, primary and foreign keys, and sequences.

Gnome Transcript

A tool that allows you to easily create, browse, and edit the contents of tables in a database.

Gaby

This tool started out as a simple GTK+ address book application, but it has grown to be a generic data-handling application that's somewhat like a specialized notepad.

Orasoft Applications Suite

As with so many other open source projects, Orasoft came into existence because the database applications its author wanted weren't already available on Linux. In 1998, Matthew Chappee found himself in a new position as an Oracle DBA. Since he didn't have any Linux-based applications to work with, he decided to create his own. Shortly thereafter, Paul Flinders joined the project, and development picked up speed. In addition to Matt and Paul, the project now also includes Brent Gilmore and Tony Likhite.

The Orasoft applications suite consists of the following major Oracle applications:

Object Manager

Browses objects in your Oracle database or schema—from tables, indexes, and sequences, to views and database links, they're all accessible from this GUI tool.

SQLWork

Provides what's essentially a GUI version of a SQL*Plus or SQL Worksheet character-mode interface to the database. With this tool you can save, edit, and run SQL scripts and view the results.

Procedit

Allows you to edit PL/SQL stored procedures, functions, and triggers. You can use it to easily view, edit, save, and compile your stored procedures.

Session Monitor

Provides a powerful way to keep track of current sessions in the database by browsing the SQL that's currently being executed by database users. You can find out when a session was started, whether it is currently active, and what SQL query it is currently executing.

Table Browser

Examines database objects and their attributes. You can use this GUI tool to view tables, columns, and their properties. Keep it in your arsenal of database tools so it's available when you want to graphically view tables at a glance.

You can expect many more excellent program developments to emerge from the Orasoft stable in the future.

The main web site for Orasoft is:

> *http://www.orasoft.org*

You might also want to check out the Advantio web site; Advantio is a for-profit company that provides support and consulting for users of the Orasoft software:

> *http://www.advantio.com*

Installing Orasoft

There are two ways you can install the Orasoft applications:

- Download the Red Hat Package Manager (RPM)[*] packages for Orasoft.
- Download the source code and compile it yourself.

Installing Orasoft with an RPM

You can obtain the RPM packages for the Orasoft applications suite from *http://www.orasoft.org*. Downloading RPMs is certainly the easiest way to install the Orasoft applications. If you do have problems with the RPM process, we recommend that you compile everything yourself directly from the source. This way you'll know that every brick and crossbeam has been correctly laid in place, without having to rely on prefabrication. (As well as gaining maximum bonus points, you may also find it more satisfying if you roll your own.)

If you run into problems with the RPM prebuilt packages, these might relate to code dependencies or varying library versions. Some RPMs run checksums against the libraries they expect to be preinstalled, so even if they're on the right version, the RPM still won't install. If you do want to give it a go but are having trouble, you may want to try using the *-force* and *-nodeps* options. However, please check the RPM man page for your own flavor of Linux before going down this route. As with issuing a ROLLBACK FORCE statement, this approach might work, but it's not ideal.

Installing Orasoft from source

If you don't have any luck with the RPMs, or if you're simply a fan of installing from source, you can follow the instructions presented in this section. Although the overall compilation method is probably familiar to you by now from similar

---

[*] RPMs have become very popular in the Linux world. They are not restricted to Red Hat's distribution of Linux, and they are also not the only package management system out there. If you're looking for RPMs for your favorite programs, visit *http://rpmfind.net*.

discussions in this book, there are slight variations from our typical *perl Makefile.PL* pattern. As always, remember that these instructions are general guidelines. For the most up-to-date information on installation, see the online documentation.

You will have to build each of the major applications separately; the following instructions demonstrate how to build Table Browser, but all of the applications follow the same pattern:

1. Download the source code from *http://www.orasoft.org*.

2. Unpack the source file:

   ```
   $ tar xvzf tablebrowser-3.0.tar.gz
   ```

3. Now go into the resulting directory and build the required *Makefile* with the *configure* program. Note that *configure* can take various options when you run it. Issue the following command to see a list of these:

   ```
   ./configure --help
   ```

4. Next, get the compiler configuration prepped. If there are any features for which your particular Linux system is not preconfigured, you may be able to use the *configure* program to screen them out (this isn't possible if you are using RPMs, and it might be a reason for choosing not to use them). For example, to remove any potential MySQL features which you don't want or need, use this:

   ```
   $ ./configure --disable-mysql
   ```

   This will build the correct *Makefile* for later program compilation:

   ```
   $ cd tablebrowser-3.0
   $ ./configure
   ```

5. If all goes well, you'll now have the correct *Makefile* for your particular plat-form and previously installed libraries. Do an *ls -l* just to be sure that it was created in the previous step.

6. Finally, simply *make* the final program:

   ```
   $ make
   ```

7. If *make* succeeds without error, log in as *root* and carry out the installation:

   ```
   $ su - root
   Password: xyz
   $ cd /path/to/tablebrowser-3.0
   $ make install
   ```

8. Now exit out of *root* and, as a regular Linux user, run your chosen program (in this case, Table Browser). You'll be prompted with a typical database login screen and be asked to specify the following:

   — Username

   — Password

— Tnsname (the alias you gave your target database in the *tnsnames.ora* file)

Once these are correctly entered, you'll be ready to run.

Using Orasoft

The following sections explain briefly how to use the major Oracle applications available in the Orasoft suite.

Object Manager

New Oracle users will find Object Manager an especially excellent application to have available in their own Oracle systems. It provides a GUI to browse and create objects, including all our old favorites:

Datafiles
Database links
Functions
Packages
Procedures
Triggers
Tables
Indexes
Synonyms
Types
Views

Figure 10-1 shows the initial Object Manager screen. Note that the Page 2 tab displays the current query being executed by this session.

The standard SQL syntax for creating some of the Oracle objects via direct commands in a command-line program like SQL*Plus can often be nonintuitive, especially for users new to Oracle (or, indeed, to experienced users on *any* ANSI-compliant database who have left their DBA manuals at home).

This is especially true if you need to use one of the many confusing options for specifying obscure attributes on a particularly complicated object.* One solution is to carry around a large trunk full of Oracle DBA syntax manuals and third-party books. Another is to make use of Object Manager. It displays all the relevant options right in front of you, so you'll know what's possible, be able to ask the right questions, and easily figure out what to set and what to leave at the default setting.

---

* If anyone knows of a surefire method for remembering the syntax for adding a complex FOREIGN KEY CONSTRAINT to existing table columns (without looking at a manual or ripping out their hair, that is), please send it to us!

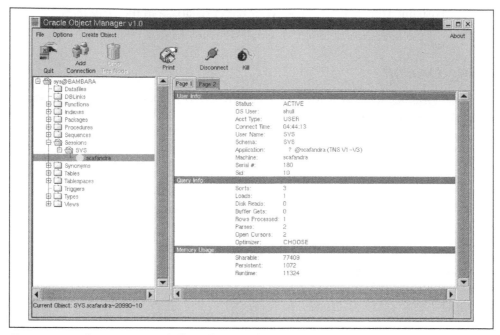

Figure 10-1. Object Manager drilling down and reviewing session information

As you can see in Figure 10-2, Object Manager provides various tabs for table-related data that enable you to edit the object and all its associated properties. This type of presentation is very helpful to a novice Oracle user or developer and is quite a bit like the features available from Oracle's own Enterprise Manager product—except, of course, that no license fee need be paid, and you can modify the code either to fix any bugs you find or to make the program do something new and specific to meet your own requirements.

Our last snapshot of Object Manager in Figure 10-3 demonstrates another feature that would be harder to achieve using a command-line interface such as SQL*Plus. Here, Object Manager illustrates the browsing of a view. The source code of the view, retrieved from the TEXT column in DBA_VIEWS, is displayed as well as the pseudo-columns, as a kind of ersatz table. You can now click on the View Contents tab to see what the view actually contains.

Of course, a view object doesn't really contain anything; it's merely a virtual query window on a series of other objects. The graphical display in Object Manager does help convey the nature of a view, as well as provide the required window view parameters. These characteristics make Object Manager a valuable tool.

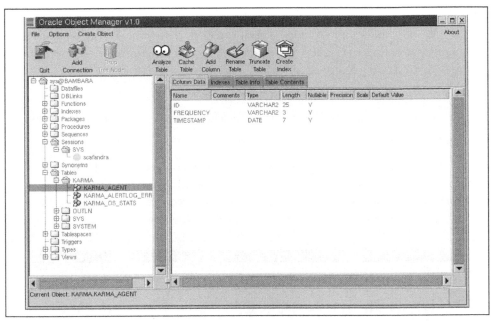

Figure 10-2. Object Manager displaying drill-down column data

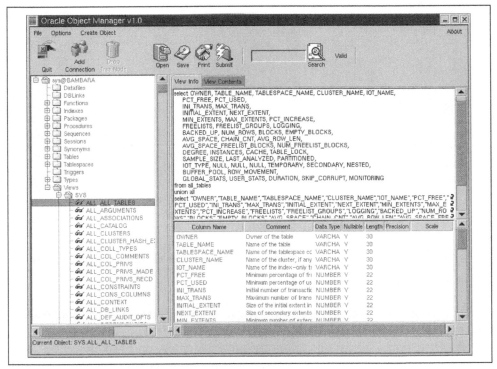

Figure 10-3. Object Manager browsing a complex view

SQLWork

The SQLWork application provides a tool you'll find helpful if you want to edit and enter SQL scripts over and over again until you get them right. SQLWork also provides the following features, all easily accessible via menu items:

- Features for loading and saving SQL scripts to disk
- The ability to launch other Orasoft applications from various menu options
- Configurable printing features

Figure 10-4 illustrates a running query. One great characteristic of the SQLWork application, which you don't get with character-based SQL tools, is a sense of how far along your requested query is. Even better is the ability to halt it halfway through execution while knowing how far you've progressed.

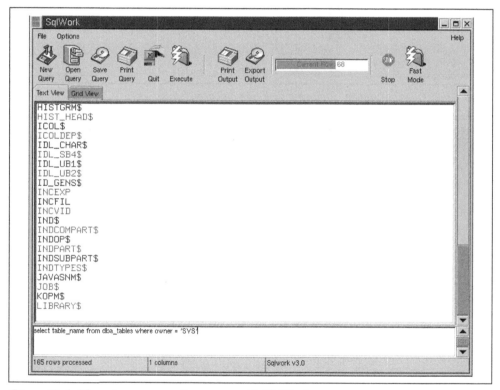

Figure 10-4. Observing an executing query with SQLWork

Newer versions of SQLWork are being released all the time, with ever-increasing functionality programmed in by the committed Orasoft developers. Some recently introduced features are MySQL support, query planning, and font selection. You can expect this list to expand as Orasoft development work continues.

Procedit

The Procedit application provides a procedure editor for all your PL/SQL source code programs found in the DBA_SOURCE data dictionary view. You can browse your schema for procedures, functions, and packages, and view and edit the source code. You can then submit your changes to update the database. Procedit is a wonderful tool!

As Figure 10-5 illustrates, you can edit triggers, procedures, and functions, and drill down directly into the target objects from a menu on the left side of the screen. If you take a look at the selected Oracle function, SEAN_TEST_FUNC, you'll see that its invalid state is displayed at the bottom of the screen on the help bar. You can display errors by clicking on the *Errors!* button.*

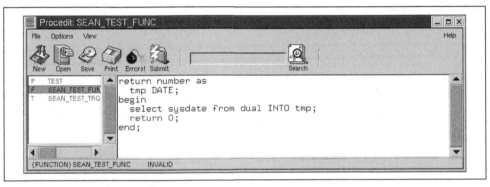

Figure 10-5. Procedit at work

A feature we'd love to see added to Procedit is one to deal with compilation dependencies. Often, we have packages that rely upon other packages, and procedures that have complex and intricate relationships with other objects in the database, such as tables, sequences, and so on. If an object changes (so Oracle flags it as INVALID) or is dropped, this change can create a cascading effect on compromised stored procedures and packages. These INVALID packages and procedures should ideally be recompiled; however, the proper order is important, and this is where an understanding of the dependency tree can come in handy. Perhaps by the time you read this book, this idea will have been seized upon by the Orasoft development team. They love a challenge, and if you have any similar ideas, we know they'd love to hear from you too. It's that sort of a project.

In the meantime, you may want to use a couple of hoary old SQL scripts we often carry about for doing a much cruder version of the above; this method detects *all* INVALID objects and then provides a rough-and-ready recompilation script to

---

* As users from the Macintosh generation, we like the graphic here for *Errors!*, which takes us on a nostalgic trip down memory lane.

sledgehammer them all into clean compilation mode. Example 10-1 is a somewhat tedious and primitive algorithm, but it does do the job,* as long as you have
the patience to work through all the invalidated PL/SQL programs one at a time
and figure out what's causing the problem via the DBA_ERRORS table.

Example 10-1. Script for Invalid Object Recompilation, invalided_out.sql

```
select 'alter '||object_type||' '||owner||'.'||object_name||
' compile ;'
from    dba_objects
where   status = 'INVALID'
and     object_type not in ('PACKAGE BODY','PACKAGE')
union
select 'alter PACKAGE '||owner||'.'||object_name||
' compile BODY ;'
from    dba_objects
where   status = 'INVALID'
and     object_type in ('PACKAGE BODY')
order by 1
```

The SQL code in Example 10-2 can also be used to track down the errors causing
the invalidation. Simply substitute the object owner and object name (which you
previously discovered with *invalided_out.sql*) for the two bind parameters, *:err_
owner* and *:err_name*.

Example 10-2. Script for Finding Object Errors, errors_out.sql

```
select type "Type",
sequence||':'||line||':'||position "seq:ln:pos", text
from    dba_errors
where   owner = :err_owner and
name   = :err_name
order by type,sequence,line
```

Session Monitor

The Session Monitor application lets you review the currently logged-in sessions
and obtain detailed information about an individual session. It can tell you when
the user connected, whether she is active or inactive, and, best of all, the current
SQL she's executing. This SQL may range from nicely tuned SQL masterpieces all
the way up to overbloated memory monsters that deserve the full ALTER SYSTEM
KILL treatment (and possibly a fistful of stiff emails if you're feeling really mean).
In Figure 10-6 you can see the application in action. Notice the *Kill* button, fourth
from the left on the main menu. We'll leave to your imagination what this does;
it's nasty, but someone's got to do it.

---

* It's often useful at 3:00 a.m. when the *just* upgraded production database is due back online at 7:00 a.m.
  Panic? Us? *Je ne comprende pas.*

The only downside of the Session Monitor application is that it's not really built to act in real time as a monitoring tool per se. Instead, it takes a user snapshot. If a new user logs in, or if others log out while the application is still up and running, Session Monitor won't automatically update the relevant information. You'll have to reconnect to have the data updated. Then you can click on the *Users* or *Machine* button shown on the menu in Figure 10-6 to cause the application to update appropriately.

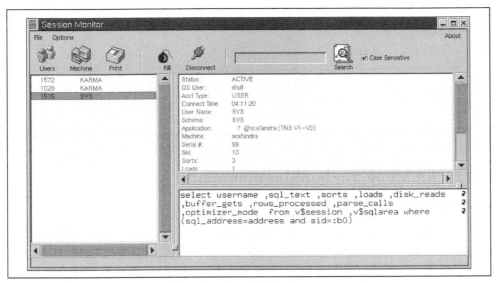

Figure 10-6. Recursive SQL tracking from Session Monitor

Table Browser

The Table Browser application is essentially a specialized version of Object Manager, with extra functions designed especially with table objects in mind. In Figure 10-7 you can see that the SEAN_TEST table has an index on its ID column. You'll also see the storage parameters associated with this table, including these:

PCT Free
PCT Used
Minimum Extents
Maximum Extents
Initial Extent
Next Extent

You could, of course, extract all of this information via a command-line interface, but there is something to be said for a clean GUI and its simple representation of a complex set of data, created in negligible time with a single mouse-click. Maximum gain, minimum effort.

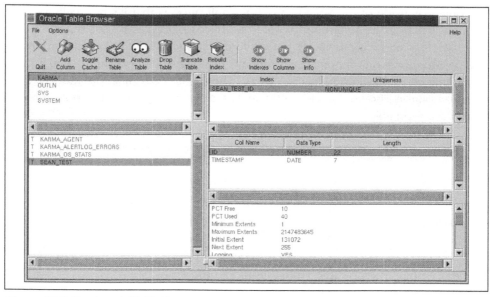

Figure 10-7. Serving up Table Browser

Extending Orasoft

The Orasoft applications have come a long way in just a couple of years (especially considering that Orasoft competes favorably against programs having multimillion dollar budgets and decades of development). With continuing user feedback, these applications will get even better. We're looking forward to seeing what the Orasoft development team achieves in the next decade with an ever-expanding feature set and a growing critical mass of enthusiastic volunteer developers.

If you want to take an active part in Orasoft development, feel free to send any bug reports and suggestions for enhancements to the project team. (We've already provided one suggestion in the Procedit section.) Let them know exactly what it is you'd like their tools to do, and they may surprise you with how fast they'll turn your ideas around. We also know they'll appreciate hearing both that you're using their software and that you're interested in contributing towards helping them improve it, either by making suggestions or by joining the development team directly.

GNOME-DB

If you think, after reading Chapter 9, that writing applications in GTK+ is a formidable challenge—and that the idea of then having to learn the Oracle Call Interface (OCI) in order to get proper Oracle interaction is even worse—don't lose hope. GNOME-DB was written partially to avoid just such aggravation. The development project was started back in 1998 by Michael Lausch, Rodrigo Moya, Stephan Heinze, Vivien Malerba, Nick Gorham, Chris Wiegand, and Alvaro del Castillo.

GNOME-DB provides a plug-and-play framework for GTK+ programmers to wrap database applications around. Essentially, it provides a framework for such applications: a base program and a set of libraries you can use to build your own applications. You can obtain backend plug-ins for various databases, including Oracle, Sybase, MySQL, PostgreSQL, Interbase, and Solid; there is even an LDAP driver. GNOME-DB also comes with a number of sample database applications that you can use as examples of what you might want to create yourself. All in all, GNOME-DB is an impressive product.

The main web site for GNOME-DB is:

http://www.gnome.org/gnome-db/

Installing GNOME-DB

We suggest that you install GNOME-DB from source. There are RPMs available for GNOME-DB, but you're probably going to run into missing libraries or version conflicts with this program, so you're better off just giving the source a try.

Before you can install GNOME-DB, you'll need to install the following modules:

- *libgda*, which in turn relies on *glib*, ORBit, OAF, Gconf, *libxml*, and the database libraries for Postgres, Oracle, and/or MySQL

- GNOME, with all of its associated libraries: Bonobo, Gnome Application Library, and *gtkhtml*

We could devote an entire chapter to the intricacies of installing all these different libraries—and possibly still miss some details—because there are so many different types of configurations and systems. We strongly advise you to read carefully all the online documentation files for these libraries; Chapter 9 provides a starting point.

When you are installing *libgda*, be sure to tell the *configure* program where your database software resides, for example:

```
./configure --with-oracle=directory
```

or:

```
./configure --with-mysql=directory
```

These preliminary installation and configuration steps can be complicated. We advise you to check the *README* documents closely for compatibilities between versions and to keep a block of time free to do the job in one sitting. (You might also want to look around for an RPM.)

As with many open source projects these days, GNOME-DB itself comes with an *autoconfigure* script. This will help get the program installed without a hitch. The basic steps you'll need to follow to install GNOME-DB are shown here:

1. Download the source code from *http://www.gnome.org/gnome-db/*.

2. Unpack the tar file like this:

   ```
   $ tar xzvf gnome-db-0.2.0.tar.gz
   ```

3. Let *configure* do the magic of creating a *Makefile* on your system as follows:

   ```
   $ cd gnome-db-0.2.0
   $ ./configure
   ```

4. Use *make* to build the executables from the source. There may be many different libraries, executables, and dependencies, but if you successfully created a *Makefile* for your system, *make* should take care of all of this for you:

   ```
   $ make
   ```

5. Now that you've built all the libraries and executables, you'll need to install them in the right places on your system. This step, of course, needs to be done as *root*, because those directories are only accessible by the *root* user:

   ```
   $ make install
   ```

6. Once you've successfully installed the software, fire it up, specify the data source, username, and password in the Open Connection dialog, as shown in the next section, and you'll be off and running.

The *./configure* step is the key. If you get past that, you're probably going to have good luck getting the whole thing compiled successfully. If you're not installing in the usual location, be sure to use the *-prefix* option.

Using GNOME-DB

Like most Gnome applications, GNOME-DB uses CORBA for communication among its various components. The code distribution available from the GNOME-DB web site even includes some excellent starter database applications. The following applications are built with GNOME-DB and are included in the distribution:

gda-rolodex
 A simple rolodex application

gda-fe
 The frontend to GNOME-DB

Figure 10-8 shows the look and feel of the types of database applications you can build with GNOME-DB. As is typical of applications that support multiple databases, you'll find a dialog for specifying the database connection information:

* Database driver or plug-in

* Data source

- Username

- Password

The figure shows the main GNOME-DB manager window, along with the database plug-in configuration dialog. Next to it is the GNOME-DB frontend example application, *gda-fe*.

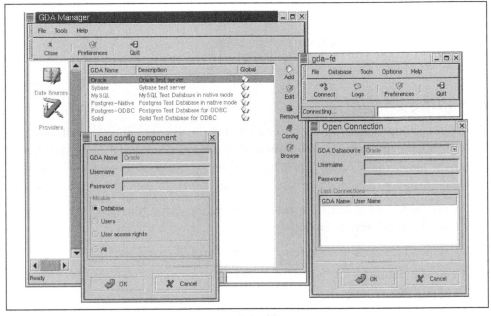

Figure 10-8. A typical GNOME-DB program (gda-fe) in action

Extending GNOME-DB

GNOME-DB is tailor-made for extension; it's built with the budding open source developer in mind. If you're interested in extending this tool, we recommend that you start with *gda-fe* or *gda-rolodex* and extend those applications, or simply use the code as a model for building your own. The almighty mantra here is "use the code." That's what it's there for, so refer to it, learn from it, and build upon it.

gASQL

In addition to working on GNOME-DB, Vivien Malerba is contributing to an embryonic project with Gerhard Dieringer called gASQL. The gASQL application is a GTK+-based relational modeling tool that works with all of the GNOME-DB compatible databases, including, of course, Oracle. gASQL graphically represents an entity relationship diagram (ERD) of the tables in your database. It provides you with an easy-to-understand view of your tables and their primary keys, foreign keys, and sequences.

 In order to demonstrate gASQL's database independence (and for some variety), we've used the PostgreSQL database for the examples in this section.

The main web site for gASQL is:

> *http://malerba.linuxave.net*

Installing gASQL

gASQL is an application based on GNOME-DB, so refer to the GNOME-DB section for preliminary installation information. Actually, GNOME-DB is the hard part. After you finish installing it, you'll have all the libraries and associated software you need installed. You can install gASQL from source or use an RPM as we did.

If you do decide to install from source, follow the basic format of other source-based installations. Here is an outline:

1. Download the source code from *http://malerba.linuxave.net*.

2. Expand the tar file:

   ```
   $ tar xvzf my_code.tar.gz
   ```

3. Build the *Makefile*:

   ```
   $ cd my_code
   $ ./configure
   ```

4. Run *make* to build libraries and executables:

   ```
   $ make
   ```

5. Install the libraries and executables in the proper directories on your system. You must be the *root* user to perform this step:

   ```
   $ cd /path/to/my_code
   $ make install
   ```

6. Once you have gASQL installed, you can fire it up and configure it for the database you'd like to connect to, just as you did with GNOME-DB. After you specify the data source, username, and password, you'll be ready to run.

Using gASQL

Figure 10-9 shows all the important pieces of the gASQL application, including the Tables & Views, Sequences, and Queries sections.

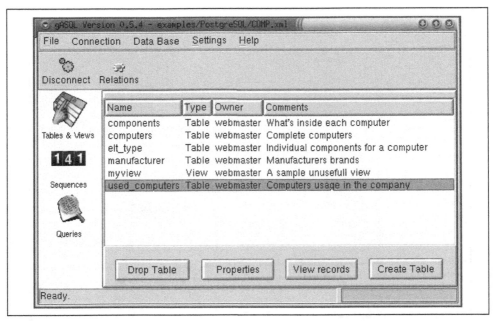

Figure 10-9. Starting up gASQL

The really exciting part of gASQL comes with the relational browser, pictured in Figure 10-10.

This example shows clearly how a graphical interface can offer something well beyond what a command-line interface provides. By depicting the primary key and foreign key relationships, as well as a bird's eye view of all the tables, gASQL can quickly represent your database in its entirety. This tool is also helpful in showing the relationships you've created, or in spotting those that are missing.

Extending gASQL

You get two excellent things from the gASQL application. First, you get the application itself—a full-featured data modeling program, filling a basic need among database developers. Second, and possibly more importantly, you get an excellent model for building your own software. With gASQL, it's easy to look under the hood and figure out *exactly* how it works.

Gnome Transcript

Now let's turn our attention to a relatively new project called Gnome Transcript (in the world of GTK, "ancient" is about 16 months, "modern" about 16 nanoseconds). Since its first release in late 1999, Matias Mutchinick and Jose Miguel Ronquillo have been putting their energies into building a generic database application for

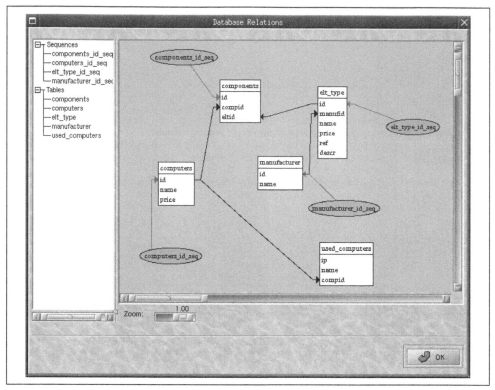

Figure 10-10. Relational modeling with gASQL

managing tables. With Gnome Transcript, you can easily create, browse, and edit the contents of the tables in your database.

The main web site for Gnome Transcript is:

http://gtranscript.sourceforge.net

Gnome Transcript is a database-independent application that requires plug-ins for the various databases it supports. Currently, only MySQL and PostgreSQL have plug-ins available. Since there isn't yet a plug-in for Oracle, you may wonder why we've included Gnome Transcript in this book. There are two reasons:

- A plug-in for Oracle could very well be written, and the exercise of doing so would teach the people involved a lot about OCI and/or Pro*C.

- The existing architecture provides an excellent model for building your own GTK+-based database applications, especially those involving the graphical display of tabulated information.

Installing Gnome Transcript

Installing Gnome Transcript itself is fairly straightforward, as long as you use the relevant RPM package. Before you install Gnome Transcript, you will have to obtain the following:

- The *libgtrans_ifase module*, a separate package that provides access to the Gnome Transcript plug-in system. This module is a part of the Gnome Transcript distribution.

- A plug-in for MySQL or PostgreSQL. (Eventually, we hope to add Oracle to this list.)

Feeling ambitious (and in order to provide the visual example in Figure 10-11), we downloaded PostgreSQL and installed it from an RPM.* Installation and configuration were surprisingly easy and pleasant, and we soon had a sample database up and running. Here are the main installation steps for Gnome Transcript:

1. Download the source code from *http://gtranscript.sourceforge.net*.
2. Install the MySQL or PostgreSQL plug-in for Gnome Transcript.
3. Start the Gnome Transcript application. You'll see the windows shown in Figure 10-11.
4. Select a plug-in for the type of database you wish to connect to, and the dialog on the left side of Figure 10-11 pops right up.
5. Specify the following database connection information:
   — Machine
   — Database Name
   — Port
   — User Login Info

   Once this information has been entered correctly, the application then connects you to your target database.

Using Gnome Transcript

Once Gnome Transcript has connected successfully to your target database, the main window opens, as shown in Figure 10-12. You'll see each table in the database, displayed graphically as a folder.†

---

* We won't try to explain how to install PostgreSQL in this book. That really would be going too far. Check out the *http://www.postgresql.org* site to find out more about this open source database, the main friendly rival to MySQL.

† Shades of HAL's file system in Stanley Kubrick and Arthur C. Clarke's 2001?

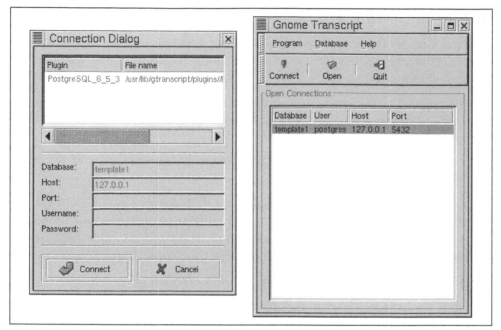

Figure 10-11. Connecting Gnome Transcript to the target database

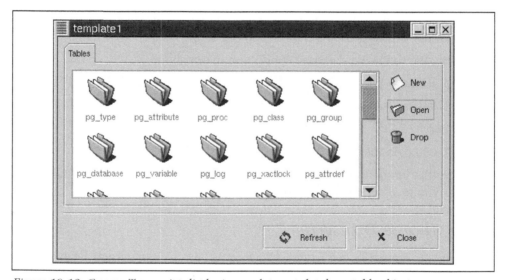

Figure 10-12. Gnome Transcript displaying each target database table object

Let's run through the new table dialog displayed in Figure 10-13. Note that:

- You must specify the table name and columns, one by one.
- The attributes and datatypes shown are specific to your particular database.

- You can specify indexes and index names for columns, data length, and defaults.

Once you have created your new table, or if you wish to browse other tables in your database, you can click on the *Open* button on the table dialog for your database. You'll now see a spreadsheet-type dialog appear, with columns for fields, rows of table data, and a scrollbar, if necessary, as shown in Figure 10-14.

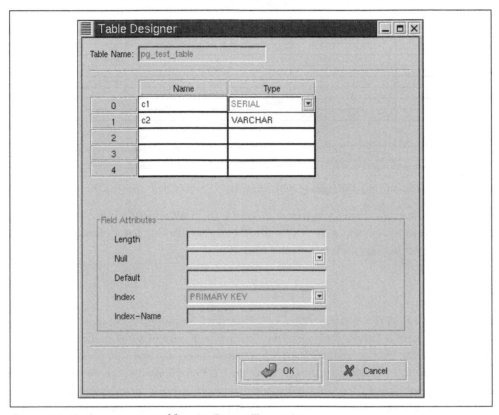

Figure 10-13. Creating new tables via Gnome Transcript

One nice aspect of using a powerful and feature-rich toolkit like GTK+ is that the columns in this display are all easily adjustable (as with various commercial spreadsheet programs). You can also click on any field and then edit its contents directly.

Extending Gnome Transcript

Gnome Transcript is an extremely useful application and will be even more so when a brave code warrior out there provides us with an Oracle plug-in. This application gives us a quick way to get acquainted with a database, its tables, and

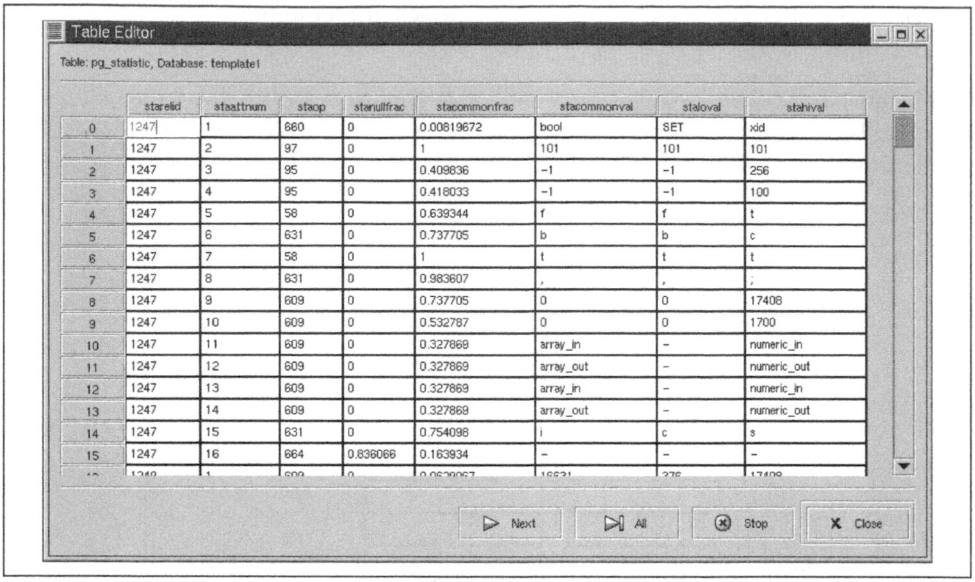

Figure 10-14. Examining and editing individual rows of data with Gnome Transcript

the attribute specifications you need in order to create further new tables. Even more importantly for us, it provides another great model for building our own Oracle open source applications in the future.

Gaby

Gaby stands for GTK Address Book of Yesterday. Names can be deceiving, however—Gaby isn't a product of yesterday, and development work is actively going on today. Gaby is a straightforward application used to store generic records of data, for example, books, addresses, and notes. Gaby got its start in 1998, when Frederic Peters started to build a Python-based telephone number/address book application. (Subsequent problems with Python GTK+ bindings prompted a port to C.) Gaby has grown to be a generic data-handling application that's somewhat like a specialized notepad.

New versions of Gaby are still coming out regularly. In the future, Frederic has plans to support various SQL database backends such as PostgreSQL and ODBC.

The main web site for Gaby is:

http://gaby.netpedia.net

Like Gnome Transcript, Gaby is not an Oracle-specific application—in fact, it's not even really a client/server application that connects to MySQL or PostgreSQL, as is common with open source applications. So why describe it at all? Because Gaby is an application that shows off GTK+ well and, in the process, builds a simulated database for storing simple records such as a contact or book database. You provide simple files describing the fields, and Gaby provides you with an interface to create, edit, and delete records, as well as search through existing ones. As with Gnome Transcript, we thought looking at this application would help expand your own ideas for GTK+-based database applications.

Installing Gaby

Those of you have relied on using RPMs for installation are finally going to get your hands dirty. We were unsuccessful in finding any relevant RPMs for use with Gaby, so let's just plunge into installing from source code. Let's assume for simplicity's sake that you have the correct Linux libraries already installed (check your distribution for details). Before you can install Gaby, you will need to install the following:

- GTK+ Version 1.2.5 or better

- Imlib Version 1.9.3 or better

- EsounD Version 0.2.8

You might find that some or all of these modules are already installed on your system, as they were with our own RedHat 6.0 distribution. Once the libraries are installed, you can install Gaby itself, as follows:

1. Download the source code from *http://gaby.netpedia.net*.

2. Unpack the Gaby file.

3. Run the automatic configuration process as follows:

   ```
   $ cd gaby-1.9.23
   $ ./configure
   ```

4. Compile:

   ```
   $ make
   ```

5. Carry out the installation as the *root* user:

   ```
   $ make install
   ```

In a nutshell, that's it. There are a lot of little things that can go wrong, of course, so watch out for any errors Gaby reports; they're usually reasonably self-explanatory. You may also be missing a library, or you may not have a new enough version of a particular library. But we're confident that you'll be able to jump over these character-building hurdles and quickly finish the installation process.

Using Gaby

Gaby is pretty easy to understand, so we won't try to provide a detailed description of each of its menus and features. Just fire it up and enter some new records. Use the *Previous* and *Next* buttons to jump through your records, and use the *Sort* button to modify the sorting.

In Figure 10-15, we're editing John Doe's contact information.

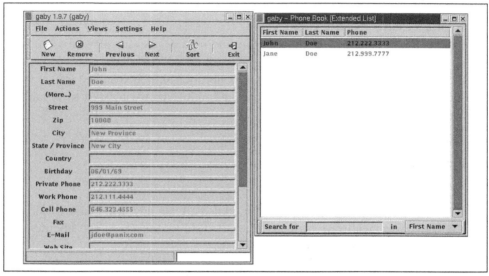

Figure 10-15. Gaby creating and editing a simple address book

Oracle8i And Linux

By now, you surely know how pleased we are that Oracle has been ported to Linux. This appendix describes how you can obtain the Oracle8*i* database on Linux and install the product on your Linux platform.

Downloading Oracle8i for Linux

If you're not already familiar with the Oracle Technology Network (OTN) web site (which we introduced in the preface), point your browser to *http://technet.oracle. com* and browse through it. You'll need to register and become a member (which is free) to be able to use the web site for downloading software and viewing documentation. The Oracle8*i* port for Linux is available through OTN.

Alternately, if you want to go straight to the source, FTP on over to *ftp.oracle.com* and check the directory */pub/www/otn/linux*. Here you'll find a small but lucrative gold mine of Linux goodies for Oracle. You should also note the location of various patches and bug fixes for the Oracle port to Linux; you might not need them now, but you probably will in the future. You'll find them at *external-ftp.us.oracle. com* in the directory */server/patchsets/unix/LINUX*.

Because things are moving so quickly in the world of Oracle on Linux, we won't be more specific here about directory and file names and specific instructions. You should be able to find everything you need on these sites to get Oracle going on your Linux system.

Installing Oracle8i on Linux

If you've never installed Oracle before, the Linux installation will be only one of the many things you need to learn about. The OTN provides a wide variety of documentation on installing and using the Oracle database and its many associated tools. Spend the necessary time getting up to speed before you begin with the Linux installation. On the other hand, if you have previous experience installing Oracle on other versions of Unix, you'll find that a Linux-based installation is pretty much the same.

Before getting started with this installation process, make sure to read the release notes and *README* files. This may seem rather obvious advice, but take it seriously. On some other systems, you might be able to get away with skipping this step, but don't overlook it here: some parts of the Linux installation are not at all obvious. With some versions of Linux, for example, a *glibc* patch is needed, because new releases of Linux (containing an updated and changed *glibc* library) often come out faster than the corresponding Oracle releases.* Essentially, a set of compatibility libraries is installed to provide the old interface and include files, and then Oracle's patch merely relinks its various executables through that library compatibility layer. This description might sound somewhat cryptic, but if you read through the release notes and check your version of *glibc* to see if it applies to your versions of Oracle and Linux, all should become clear.

Once you've read through the release notes, simply follow the installation guide just as you would on any version of Unix. We won't try to itemize the detailed instructions here, but simply give you a broad-brush introduction to the installation. These are the basic steps you will need to follow before you begin the detailed Linux installation:

1. Set up your environment variables. These are the most important:

   ORACLE_BASE
   ORACLE_HOME
   ORACLE_SID
   LD_LIBRARY_PATH
   DISPLAY

2. Get Java installed and working. Try the following URL for all your Java/Linux needs:

   http://www.blackdown.org

3. Fire up the installer.

   Oracle Corporation has put quite a bit of work into getting this installer working better than it did in the past. Nevertheless, if you have any experience with Oracle installations, you'll probably find it as infuriating as we did that the old text-based installer now seems to be missing! Remote installations are now nothing but trouble. There is now a non-interactive installer that requires

---

* Remember the famous Torvaldian phrase, "Release early, release often."

a configuration file to be edited. Once you've done this, supposedly you can then get Oracle installed without using the Java GUI. However, our experience fiddling with the configuration file didn't leave us with a good experience. Come back, *orainst*, all is forgiven!

For detailed installation information, check out these fine online documents:

http://jordan.fortwayne.com/oracle/
  "Oracle on Linux Installation Guide"

http://www.intrex.net/miket/SetupConfig.txt
  "Novice Linux/Oracle8 Installation Guide"

Both of these sites are excellent. The first, in particular, is updated regularly with the latest information for each new release. Good luck and may the Source be with you.

Q & A for Oracle on Linux

In this brief, hardcopy appendix, we can't teach you everything about installing Oracle on Linux. However, we do want to share some of our experiences by answering the five most pressing questions people have when they try to run the installation procedures:

I'm getting core dumps when I run server manager. What's the problem?

  With Red Hat versions after 5.x, a new version of *glibc* was introduced. Unfortunately, Oracle isn't released as often or as quickly as Linux, so it currently uses this older *glibc*. What Red Hat provides is a backward compatibility library for programs that use the older *glibc*. This is a set of interfaces that translate to the new calls.

  Go to your Red Hat install disk and, in the directory */RedHat/RPMS,* search for the RPMs with the *compat* prefix. Go ahead and install those RPMs.

  Next, download Oracle's *glibcpatch.tgz* patch file, untar and unzip it, and read through the installation instructions. As long as you have all your environment variables set, and the compatibility libraries mentioned above are already installed, the patch procedure should go forward without a hitch.

I've installed the glibc patch, but I'm still getting core dumps. Why?

  It's possible that the relink phase of the reinstall failed. Check in the *$ORACLE_HOME/bin* directory; there you should find various *.pre-glibcpatch* files. Each should be associated with a binary without that extension. For example, the program *orapwd* is the newly linked version, and *orapwd.pre-glibcpatch* is the old version. You can also check dates on the files. The dates in the newer files should correspond to the dates when you relinked these executables during the patch install. Finally, you can use the Unix *ldd* program to show all library dependencies:

```
$ echo $ORACLE_HOME
/home/oracle/product/8.0.5
$ ldd orapwd
    /lib/libNoVersion.so.1 => /lib/libNoVersion.so.1 (0x40014000)
    libclntsh.so.1.0 => \
    /home/oracle/product/8.0.5/lib/libclntsh.so.1.0 (0x40016000)
    libnsl.so.1 => /lib/libnsl.so.1 (0x4039d000)
    libm.so.6 => /lib/libm.so.6 (0x403b3000)
    libdl.so.2 => /lib/libdl.so.2 (0x403cf000)
       libc.so.6 => /lib/libc.so.6 (0x403d2000)
       /lib/ld-linux.so.2 => /lib/ld-linux.so.2 (0x40000000)
```

This last step may reveal a hidden clue to the problem that needs resolution.

Whenever I start up svrmgrl, I get the following message: "Message 4505 not found; No message file for product=SVRMGR, facility=MGR Error while trying to retrieve text for error ORA-12545." What's going on?

Be sure the ORACLE_HOME environment variable is set. This variable enables Oracle programs to find associated files—in this case, error message files. It's a good idea to set up these environment variables all in one file and call it from your *.bashrc* file, or whatever your login *rc* file is for your favorite shell. You should set ORACLE_HOME, ORACLE_BASE, ORACLE_SID, and your PATH to include the Oracle executables in *$ORACLE_HOME/bin*. You might also need to set LD_LIBRARY_PATH to include *$ORACLE_HOME/lib*, and possibly *$TNS_ADMIN* as well.

Why am I asked for a password when I try to connect to Oracle to start up my database?

This problem tends to present itself in the following way:

```
SVRMGR> connect internal
Password:
Password:
ORA-01031: insufficient privileges
```

Be sure that you are logged in as the *oracle* owner. Check the permissions on the Oracle binaries as follows:

```
$ ls -l $ORACLE_HOME/bin
```

Also be sure that you're logged in as the user who owns these files. If the files are not owned by the *oracle* user (that's the user you should be logging in as), you can change them all at once with:

```
$ chown -R oracle $ORACLE_HOME
```

This recursively iterates down the directory tree and resets the ownership on all your files.

Can I run Oracle with Red Hat 7?

No, at least not at the time we were writing this book. The reason is that with the latest release of Linux, the *glibc* library had been changed again (one day, there will be a perfect world!). Once a backward compatibility library is available for this and other future Red Hat Linux versions, Oracle will likely release another patch that will fix some of its libraries and then relink them against the new backward compatibility library. At least, that's the regular update plan, as we understand it.

For many more answers to many more questions, check out the two installation sites listed above, as well as the following lifesaving question-and-answer site:

http://www.doag.de/mirror/frank/faqunix.htm

Improving Performance on Linux

Let's assume that you've been able to install Oracle on Linux, but you're not satisfied with its performance. In addition to all the usual tuning tricks you can try on any Oracle database, check out the following specific suggestions for Linux ports. These suggestions should really make your Oracle/Linux system fly:

Use raw I/O as of the Linux 2.4 kernel

As of the 2.4 release, Linux includes raw I/O support. Adopted from the commercial Unix world, the raw I/O feature enables data to be written directly to disk without being buffered by the filesystem. With the raw I/O device, you can create a datafile that does not exist in the filesystem; nevertheless, Oracle can easily and efficiently write to this datafile.

Use the ext3fs filesystem

Linux 2.4 includes a new filesystem that provides journaling and various speed optimizations. Journaling provides crash recovery protection by writing changes to a change log. In the event of a crash, cached changes can be used to restore data by rolling forward or backward. Of course, Oracle already provides this type of recovery via mirrored redo logs, control files, and datafiles, so most Oracle users will find the speed improvements available in the Linux 2.4 release to be the most useful new features.

Use RAIDed disks

Linux supports various RAID controllers that can be used to bundle disks together, interacting with them as a unit. RAID provides features such as these:

— Hot swapping, which allows a new drive to replace a broken one without interruption of access

— Hot standby, which keeps such a drive online at all times

— Striping, which speeds up reads and writes to disk

— Mirroring, which provides redundancy

We think this is a pretty impressive list of features for an operating system that was once so easily dismissed by its proprietary rivals. We can't wait for Linux 3.0 to come out!

For additional tuning hints, check out the following sites for RAID solutions and information from Tom's Hardware Guide:

http://linas.org/linux/raid.html
http://www.tomshardware.com

B

PL/SQL and Open Source

In this book we've concentrated on open source applications for end users (particularly GUI and web-based applications) and on open source server software (such as Apache). However, we're also starting to see some interesting middleware developments linking open source programs to commercial systems. One of the most fertile areas is that of Oracle PL/SQL. PL/SQL is Oracle's procedural language based on SQL. It's a very popular and powerful language used by Oracle Corporation and developers everywhere. This short appendix can't do justice to all the activity going on today, but we will try to give you the flavor of a few of the most interesting open source developments we've seen.

PLNet.org

PLNet is a project inspired by the Perl CPAN (Comprehensive Perl Archive Network) project (described briefly in Chapter 2, *Connecting to Oracle*). The goal is to develop and maintain a repository containing a large collection of reusable PL/SQL software and documentation written by and for the global PL/SQL development community. PLNet is the brainchild of Bill Pribyl, coauthor (with Steven Feuerstein) of *Oracle PL/SQL Programming*, considered by many to be the bible of PL/SQL development.

PLNet is still in a very early stage, but you can watch its development at this site:

http://plnet.org

If you are interested in being part of this exciting project, check out:

http://plnet.sourceforge.net

As Bill points out, if you assume that there are one million PL/SQL programmers in the world, then even if only one hundredth of one percent contribute to the repository, that's 100 contributors right there. We hope that many more developers jump on board.

Quite a bit of useful material has already been committed to the effort. Here is a sampling of things slated for access through PLNet.org:

- Chapters and scripts from various PL/SQL books (and since, between them, Steven and Bill have written what we consider to be the best books around, this should give the rest of us plenty to work with)

- The MD5 message digest algorithm for security; you can find more on cryptography and other PL/SQL resources at the PL/SQL Cellar at:

  http://www.gt.ed.net/keith/plsql/

- Source code for PL/Vision Lite, a code library developed by Steven Feuerstein that consists of more than 60 packages (containing 1,000-plus procedures and functions) that perform a myriad of useful tasks in PL/SQL applications

- Steven Feuerstein's PL/SQL training materials

- Relevant content from Steven Feuerstein's older PL/SQL articles

- Bill Pribyl's Oracle8*i* PL/SQL training materials

Initially, PLNet.org contains just high-level summary information and links to the contributed software modules. The eventual goal is to provide a rich catalog of information to aid in searching and to keep the reusable PL/SQL modules—and possibly even the metadata—physically distributed across the Internet. One way this might be achieved is by creating an XML-based description of each module, relying on the same principles that have made Netscape's RSS (Rich Site Summary) a wildly successful standard for distributing news, discussions, and product announcements as information "channels." (For an example, see *http://www.oreillynet.com/meerkat/*).

Other future goals for the PLNet project include the following:

- Ensuring maximum ease for the repository submission procedures

- Developing a one-step extraction and installation process for PL/SQL modules that automatically handles code dependencies

- Influencing Oracle to provide language features to better support sharing of PL/SQL

We're hoping the PLNet project will ramp up into something massive. If you'd like to help with this effort, get on over to Bill's place.

utPLSQL

The utPLSQL project is an open source unit-testing framework for PL/SQL developers, created by PL/SQL author Steven Feuerstein. He has modeled utPLSQL on Junit, which is part of a lightweight methodology known as XP (Extreme Programming). Extreme Programming is characterized by clean, simple design and rigorous planning, coding, and testing. You can check out the unfolding utPLSQL project at this site:

> *http://oracle.oreilly.com/utplsql/*

For more about Extreme Programming, see:

> *http://www.extremeprogramming.org*

utPLSQL is based on six XP design axioms:

Work with human nature

Testing is painful. There are always a hundred and one better things to do than test—but testing is essential if you're going to write good software. So utPLSQL attempts to help coders overcome this natural aversion by creating a lightweight test framework that is easy to install, use, and run.

Write tests first

Any graduate of the corporate IT quality initiatives of the early 1990s will probably remember having this principle drilled into them by serious people in large suits. It's a bit like English teachers throughout the world force-feeding their pupils Shakespeare: this sort of thing can turn people off for life. The utPLSQL project attempts to square the circle here by making test planning an essential and desired time-saving process, as opposed to something you'll do when you have a little spare time.

Code a little, test thoroughly

This is an axiom of most open source developers; it's a truism to say that the best coders are usually the best coders because they are the best testers. utPLSQL tries to encourage this approach, too.

Isolated, automated testing

In a bid to find the bugs and ease the workload, the utPLSQL methodology attempts to make testing as fine-grained and automatic as possible.

Red light, green light

utPLSQL tries not to waste precious time studying complex test output. It tries to make things simple so you can know at a glance whether a test has passed or failed.

Transform bug reports into test cases

Don't just fix code in a panic and on the fly. Build the alleged bug into the automated test suite. Provide yourself with both reliable evidence that the bug actually exists and reliable pointers to how it can be removed most effectively.

utPLSQL certainly sounds like an interesting and thorough project, and one that will be particularly helpful for developers working on large PL/SQL systems. If it sounds like your cup of tea, you may also want to add yourself to the discussion group here:

> *http://www.egroups.com/group/utPLSQL/*

More PL/SQL Links

For further access to all things PL/SQL, check out the following additional sites. These are some of the best PL/SQL sites we've found; note that most of them contain other types of Oracle and open source information as well:

http://dmoz.org/Computers/Programming/Languages/PL-SQL/
http://dmoz.org/Computers/Programming/Languages/PL-SQL/Developer_Tools/

An edited list of sites with good PL/SQL content; this is a good place to start your search. There is also a page for developer tools, which is perhaps the most comprehensive list of PL/SQL-specific developer environments and editors you will find anywhere. (While you're there, check out the rest of DMOZ, which is a project to create the "largest human-edited catalog of the Web.")

http://otnxchange.oracle.com

The OTN Xchange is an embryonic Oracle Technology Network site where developers will eventually be able to freely download software and obtain information on jobs and other Oracle-related resources. Search on "PL/SQL".

http://www.revealnet.com/Pipelines/PLSQL/index.htm

The Revealnet PL/SQL Pipeline is a great community resource for Oracle PL/SQL developers who can use the site to ask questions, share code, and obtain useful software and advice. See the main RevealNet site (*http://www.revealnet. com*) for information on PL/SQL and access to Oracle products.

http://www.stevenfeuerstein.com

Steven Feuerstein's personal page containing all sorts of personal and technical information of interest to him, with links to various other helpful Oracle sites.

http://www.lonyx.com

Lonyx is a helpful set of Oracle resources, including technical, career, and financial information. Search on "Oracle" and "PL/SQL" to find useful programs and advice.

http://members.nbci.com/uwagner/kora/

Kora Oracle Sql Communicator is an Open Source Qt/KDE Linux client for compiling and debugging PL/SQL.

http:/www.datacraft.com

Bill Pribyl's web site, providing links to the latest headlines on news about Oracle and Linux, among other things.

C

For Further Reading

We have covered an enormous number of technologies in this book. If you are interested in exploring any of these topics in greater depth, we encourage you to read the books referenced in this appendix. All of the books listed here are in our own personal collections, and we used them, along with the many web references found throughout this book, in our research for *Oracle & Open Source*.

Chapter 1, Oracle Meets Open Source

Open Sources: Voices from the Open Source Revolution, edited by Chris DiBona, Sam Ockman and Mark Stone (O'Reilly & Associates)*

Open Source Development with CVS, by Karl Fogel (Coriolis)

Capitalism and Freedom, by Milton Friedman (University of Chicago Press)

A Brief History of the Future: From Radio Days to Internet Years in a Lifetime, by John Naughton (Overlook Press)

CVS Pocket Reference, by Gregor N. Purdy (O'Reilly & Associates)

The Cathedral & The Bazaar, by Eric S. Raymond (O'Reilly & Associates)†

Chapter 2, Connecting to Oracle

Oracle8i Internal Services for Waits, Latches, Locks and Memory, by Steve Adams (O'Reilly & Associates)

Programming the Perl DBI, by Alligator Descartes and Tim Bunce (O'Reilly & Associates)

---

* You can read the book online at *http://www.oreilly.com/catalog/opensources/book/toc.html.*

† For more on this book, see *http://www.oreilly.com/catalog/cb/*, and for most of the essays in their original form, visit *http://www.tuxedo.org/~esr/writings/cathedral-bazaar/index.html.*

Essential System Administration, by Æleen Frisch (O'Reilly & Associates)

C Programming Language, by Brian W. Kernighan and Dennis M. Ritchie (Prentice Hall)

The Art of Computer Programming, by Donald Knuth (Addison-Wesley)

Learning Perl, by Randal L. Schwartz and Tom Christiansen (O'Reilly & Associates)

Learning Perl on Win32 Systems, by Randal L. Schwartz, Erik Olson, and Tom Christiansen (O'Reilly & Associates)

Perl in a Nutshell, by Ellen Siever, Stephen Spainhour, and Nathan Patwardhan (O'Reilly & Associates)

Programming Perl, by Larry Wall, Tom Christiansen, and Jon Orwant (O'Reilly & Associates)

Chapter 3, Tcl, Perl, and Python

Oracle Built-in Packages, by Steven Feuerstein, Charles Dye, and John Beresniewicz (O'Reilly & Associates)

Mastering Regular Expressions, by Jeffrey Friedl (O'Reilly & Associates)

Effective Perl Programming, by Joseph N. Hall (Addison-Wesley)

Python Programming on Win32, by Mark Hammond and Andy Robinson (O'Reilly & Associates)

Programming Python, by Mark Lutz (O'Reilly & Associates)

Learning Python, by Mark Lutz and David Ascher (O'Reilly & Associates)

Tcl and the Tk Toolkit, by John Ousterhout (Addison-Wesley)

Advanced Perl Programming, by Sriram Srinivasan (O'Reilly & Associates)

Learning Perl/Tk, by Nancy Walsh (O'Reilly & Associates)

Chapter 4, Building Oracle Applications with Perl/Tk and Tcl/Tk

Oracle SQL High-Performance Tuning, by Guy Harrison (Prentice Hall)

Tcl/Tk Tools, by Mark Harrison et al (O'Reilly & Associates)

Perl/Tk Pocket Reference, by Stephen Lidie (O'Reilly & Associates)

Oracle Scripts, by Brian Lomasky and David C. Kreines (O'Reilly & Associates)

Tcl/Tk in a Nutshell, by Paul Raines and Jeff Tranter (O'Reilly & Associates)

Chapter 5, Web Technologies

The Data Webhouse Toolkit, by Ralph Kimball and Richard Merz (Wiley)

Apache: The Definitive Guide, by Ben Laurie and Peter Laurie (O'Reilly & Associates)

Official Guide to Programming With Cgi.Pm, by Lincoln Stein (John Wiley & Sons)

Web Client Programming with Perl, by Clinton Wong (O'Reilly & Associates)

Chapter 6, Building Web-Based Oracle Applications

Professional PHP Programming, by Jesus Castagnetto et al (Wrox Press)

PHP Pocket Reference, by Rasmus Lerdorf (O'Reilly & Associates)

Writing Apache Modules with Perl and C, by Lincoln Stein and Doug MacEachern (O'Reilly & Associates)

MySQL & mSQL, by Randy Jay Yarger, George Reese, and Tim King (O'Reilly & Associates)

Chapter 7, Java

Java Swing, by Robert Eckstein, Marc Loy, and Dave Wood (O'Reilly & Associates)

Java in a Nutshell, by David Flanagan (O'Reilly & Associates)

Beginning Java 2, by Ivor Horton (Wrox Press)

Java Servlet Programming, by Jason Hunter with William Crawford (O'Reilly & Associates)

Learning Java, by Pat Niemeyer and Jonathan Knudsen (O'Reilly & Associates)

Database Programming with JDBC and Java, by George Reese (O'Reilly & Associates)

Chapter 8, Building Oracle Applications with Java

Core Servlets and JavaServer Pages (JSP), by Marty Hall (Prentice Hall and Sun Microsystems Press)

Building Oracle XML Applications, by Steve Muench (O'Reilly & Associates)

Professional Java Server Programming: with Servlets, JavaServer Pages (JSP), XML, Enterprise JavaBeans (EJB), JNDI, CORBA, Jini and Javaspaces, by Andrew Patzer et al (Wrox Press)

Professional XML Databases, by Kevin Williams (Wrox Press)

Chapter 9, GNOME and GTK+

Grokking the GIMP, by Carey Bunks (New Riders)

GTK+/GNOME Application Development, by Havoc Pennington (New Riders)

Programming Web Graphics with Perl & GNU Software, by Shawn P. Wallace (O'Reilly & Associates)

Chapter 10, Building Oracle Applications with GNOME and GTK+

Beginning GTK+ and GNOME, by Peter Wright (Wrox Press)

DBA's Guide to Databases Under Linux, by Paul C. Zikopoulos (Syngress Media)

Appendix A, Oracle8i And Linux

Red Hat Linux 7 Unleashed, by Bill Ball, David Pitts, et al (Sams)

Oracle 8i for Linux Starter Kit, by Steve Bobrowski (Oracle Press)

Running Linux, by Matt Welsh and Lar Kaufman (O'Reilly & Associates)

Appendix B, PL/SQL and Open Source

Oracle PL/SQL Programming, by Steven Feuerstein and Bill Pribyl (O'Reilly & Associates)

Index

A

Aas, Gisle, 227
abiword (word-processing program), 321
Abstract Windowing Toolkit (AWT), 27,
    245, 258
    java.awt.event.* packages, 266
ACS (Ars Digita Community System), 23,
    190
actionPerformed( ) function, Java, 267
Active Server Pages, 189
ActivePerl, 23
    DBD::Oracle module, downloading for
        use with OraExplain, 101
    downloading and installing, 48
    Perl DBI (web site), 52
ActiveState
    ActivePerl (see ActivePerl)
    ActivePython, installing, 110
    package installation process, Perl
        DBI, 55
    Win32 Perl portal site, 95
Ada programming language, 331
Adams, Steve, 368
adapter classes (Java), linking DB Prism
    and Oracle, 306
address book application (see Gaby
    application)

addresses (process), finding with Orac User
    menu, 139
administration, database
    functions for (Oratcl module), 83
    Karma application, 202–210
    Oracletool, 211
        DB Admin menu, 216
    Orasoft kit for, 333
    PhpMyAdmin application, 31, 201,
        223–225
    PhpOracleAdmin application, 31, 201
    @?/rdbms/admin scripts, adding to Server
        Manager, 137
    web applications for, 3, 172
Advanced Networking Option (ANO),
        Oracle encryption technology, 252
Advanced Research Projects Agency
        (ARPA), 11
Advantio web site, supporting Orasoft, 335
AIX (Unix freeware packages), 23
Albrecht, Bruce, xv, 125, 146
alert email messages (Karma), 206
Allen, Woody, 310
All-Objects menu, Oddis, 158–160
Amoeba distributed operating system, 20
Analyze submenu (Oddis, Options
        menu), 161
Ant tool, 23

We'd like to hear your suggestions for improving our indexes. Send email to *index@oreilly.com*.

373

About the Author

Andy Duncan is a psychology graduate and inveterate software dabbler who lives in Oxfordshire, England. He was the initial author of the Orac open source tool for Oracle database administration, development, and tuning. After a spell with Sun Microsystems in the late 1990s, working on Java-based software delivery systems, Andy began a period with Oracle Corporation in 1998 as an Oracle DBA contractor, at their central EMEA Data Centre in the U.K. He remained there as a senior DBA through the January 2000 hurdle; he then returned to Sun as a Perl and Java web consultant, moving away from database administration and back into full-time software development. He now combines various Internet projects for different clients with leading commercial Perl training courses for Learning Tree. He can be reached at *andy_j_duncan@yahoo.com.*

Sean Hull is an Oracle DBA and web developer plying his trade as an independent consultant with his own firm, iHeavy Inc., in New York City. He focuses on integrating open source technologies with commercial technologies such as Oracle, and has serviced many successful Silicon Alley companies. His practice is growing steadily with an expanding network of associates offering a wide range of database, web, and Internet-related services. He is the author of Karma, a web-based open source Oracle monitoring tool, and a major contributor to the Orac DBA tool. He also contributes to the telelists Oracle email list and the dbi-users email list. On his days off, you might find him practicing Capoeira, a Brazilian martial art. He resides in Manhattan, where he enjoys the fast pace, great restaurants, culture, and art. He can be reached at *shull@iheavy.com.*

Colophon

Our look is the result of reader comments, our own experimentation, and feedback from distribution channels. Distinctive covers complement our distinctive approach to technical topics, breathing personality and life into potentially dry subjects.

The animals on the cover of *Oracle & Open Source* are garden spiders. Garden spiders (*Areneus diadematus*) are orb-spinning garden dwellers. They're about one to one and three-quarter inches long, generally brownish in color, with a white cross pattern on their abdomen, formed by the guanine crystals they excrete as a waste product.

All spiders are members of the class Arachnida. In mythology, Arachne was a master weaver who, bold and supremely confident of her abilities, challenged the goddess Minerva to a weaving contest. Both wove beautiful, perfect tapestries, but even Minerva had to admit that Arachne's was superior. In a fit of jealous rage, Minerva destroyed Arachne's tapestry, and Arachne, humiliated and despondent, tried to hang herself. Minerva turned the rope from which Arachne hung into a web, and Arachne herself into a spider.

The orb web that a garden spider weaves is the quintessential spiderweb, several spokes radiating from a central point, joined by a widening spiral of silk. The silk comes from six spinnerets on the underside of the spider's body. Each spinneret has hundreds of tiny spigots, each of which in turn is connected to a silk gland that can produce five different types of silk. The output of the spigots is joined together into a thread, and the spider uses one thread or several joined together to perform different tasks. The spiral lines of the web, for instance, are made up of two threads of one type of silk plus a third thread of sticky silk; the spider "twangs" each stretch of line to distribute the sticky glue into many tiny globules along the length of the line.

Once the garden spider has finished weaving her web (and it's only the female garden spiders who weave webs), she builds herself a small nest a short distance from the web; she keeps in contact with the web through a telegraph line of silk, which alerts her when an insect blunders into the web. If it's a small bug that she can overpower, she takes it directly to the nest to kill and eat. Larger bugs she traps in a cocoon of silk and often stores to eat later.

Leanne Soylemez was the production editor and copyeditor for *Oracle & Open Source*. Colleen Gorman was the proofreader, and Emily Quill and Sarah Jane Shangraw provided quality control. Ellen Troutman Zaig wrote the index.

Ellie Volckhausen designed the cover of this book, based on a series design by Edie Freedman. The cover image is a 19th-century engraving from the Dover Pictorial Archive. Emma Colby produced the cover layout with QuarkXPress 4.1 using Adobe's ITC Garamond font.

Melanie Wang and David Futato designed the interior layout based on a series design by Nancy Priest. Anne-Marie Vaduva converted the files from Microsoft Word to FrameMaker 5.5.6 using tools created by Mike Sierra. The text and heading fonts are ITC Garamond Light and Garamond Book; the code font is Constant Willison. The illustrations that appear in the book were produced by Robert Romano and Jessamyn Read using Macromedia FreeHand 9 and Adobe Photoshop 6. This colophon was written by Leanne Soylemez.

Whenever possible, our books use a durable and flexible lay-flat binding. If the page count exceeds this binding's limit, perfect binding is used.

Lightning Source UK Ltd.
Milton Keynes UK
UKOW06f0051121014

239931UK00001B/30/P